Women Poets of *the* World

Edited by Joanna Bankier
Deirdre Lashgari

Associate Editor Doris Earnshaw

Macmillan Publishing Co., Inc. • *NEW YORK*
Collier Macmillan Publishers • *LONDON*

Macmillan Publishing Co., Inc.
866 Third Avenue, New York, New York 10022

Collier Macmillan Canada, Inc.

Library of Congress Cataloging in Publication Data
Main entry under title:

Women poets of the world.

Includes index.
1. Poetry—Women authors. I. Bankier, Joanna.
II. Lashgari, Deirdre. III. Earnshaw, Doris.
PN6109.9.W66   808.81   82-7794
ISBN 0-02-305720-3   AACR2

Printing: 1 2 3 4 5 6 7 8   Year: 6 3 4 5 6 7 8 9 0

ISBN 0-02-305720-3

*PN
6109.9
W66
1983*

Acknowledgments

Helen Adam. HELEN ADAM, "I Love My Love," used by permission of the poet.

Etel Adnan. ETEL ADNAN, "Beirut-Hell Express" from *Women of the Fertile Crescent. Modern Poetry by Arab Women*. Reprinted by permission of the poet.

Africana Publishing Company, a division of Holmes & Meier Publishers, Inc. ANNA GRÉKI, "The Future Is for Tomorrow" translated by Mildred P. Mortimer, from "Algerian Poetry of French Expression" by Mildred P. Mortimer, in Volume 6 of *African Literature Today*, edited by Eldred Durosini Jones (New York: Africana Publishing Company). Reprinted by permission of Africana Publishing Company, a division of Homes & Meier Publishers, Inc. MWANA KUPONA MSHAM, "Poem to Her Daughter" adapted by permission of Africana Publishing Company from "Mwana Kupona's Poem" in *Tendi* by Mwana Kupona Msham, translated by J. W. T. Allen. Copyright © 1971 by Africana Publishing Company, a division of Holmes & Meier Publishers, Inc., New York.

Maureen Ahern. ROSARIO CASTELLANOS, "Useless Day," from *Poésia no eres tú* (Mexico City: Fondo de Cultura Economica, 1972), translated by Maureen Ahern. Reprinted by permission of the translator. This translation first appeared in *Colorado State Review*, Spring 1979.

Jaakko Ahokas. EEVA-LIISA MANNER, "Lunar Games," translated by Jaakko Ahokas. Translation copyright © Jaakko Ahokas 1979. Original Finnish text copyright © Eeva-Liisa Manner and her agents, Kustannus Oy Tammi, Publishers, Helsinki, Finland.

Ahsahta Press and Marnie Walsh. MARNIE WALSH, "Thomas Iron-Eyes. Born *circa* 1840. Died 1919, Rosebud Agency, S.D." from *A Taste of the Knife*. Reprinted by permission of Ahsahta Press (Boise State University, Boise, Idaho) and Marnie Walsh.

Akwesasne Notes. DOLLY BIRD, "Can I Say," from *Akwesasne Notes*, Spring 1972. Reprinted by permission of Akwesasne Notes.

Margaret Walker Alexander. MARGARET WALKER, "Childhood," from *For My People*. Reprinted by permission of the poet.

Paula Gunn Allen. PAULA GUNN ALLEN, "Catching One Clear Thought Alive." Reprinted by permission of the poet.

Lynne Alvarez. BLANCA VARELA, "The Captain". Translated by Lynn Alvarez. Reprinted by permission of Lynn Alvarez.

House of Anansi Press. MARGARET ATWOOD, "At first I was given centuries." Copyright © Margaret Atwood 1971, from *Power Politics* (Toronto: House of Anansi Press). Reprinted by permission of House of Anansi Press.

J. & F. Anderson, W.S. MECHTHILD VON MAGDEBURG, "Love Flows From God" and "Here too the Spirit shafts" from *The Revelations of Mechthild of Magdeburg* by Lucy Menzies, published by Longman, Harlow, Essex, England. "Love Flows From God" and "Here too the Spirit shafts" reprinted by permission of J. & F. Anderson, W.S., Edinburgh, Scotland, solicitors for the estate of Lucy Menzies.

Ariel, The Israeli Review of Arts and Letters. RACHEL, "His Wife," translated by Sholom J. Kahn, from *Ariel* (No. 38), p. 23. Reprinted by permission of *Ariel*. ZELDA, "The Wicked Neighbor," translated by Hannah Hoffman, from *Ariel* (No. 33–34), pp. 75–77. Reprinted by permission of *Ariel*.

Marylin B. Arthur. Erinna, from "The Distaff", translated by Marylyn B. Arthur. Reprinted by permission of Marylyn Bentley Arthur.

Artisjus. JUDIT TOTH, "To the Newborn" and Dead Embryos" translated by Laura Schiff, from *Modern Hungarian Poetry* edited by Miklos Vajda. Copyright Judit Toth. Reprinted by permission of Artisjus, Budapest, as agents for Judit Toth.

ASALH—The Association for the Study of Afro-American Life and History, Inc.

ALICE DUNBAR NELSON, "I Sit and Sew" from *Negro Poets and Their Poems* edited by Robert T. Kerlin (Washington, D.C., 1923). Reprinted by permission of ASALH, publishers.

Astra Books. ANNE HÉBERT, "The Wooden Chamber," from *An Anthology of Modern French Poetry*, edited and translated by Birgit Swenson (New York: Astra Books, 1973). Reprinted by permission of Astra Books.

Martin Banham. MINJI KARIBO, "Supersition," from *Nigerian Student Verse*, 1959, edited by Martin Banham, published at Ibadan, Nigeria, 1960. Reprinted by permission of Martin Banham as editor.

Joanna Bankier. CHRISTINE DE PISAN, "Marriage is a lovely thing" and "Fountain of tears, river of grief" SONJA ÅKESSON "Evening Walk" and "Ears," and KARIN BOYE "The Sword" translated by Joanna Bankier. Reprinted by permission of Joanna Bankier. Used by permission of the author.

Wendy Barker. WENDY BARKER. Introduction to section on "North America: Cultural Influences: Euro-American." By permission of the author.

Mary Barnard. Sappho, "Although they are", translated by Mary Barnard. Reprinted by permission of Mary Barnard.

Anita Barrows. LEILA DJABALI, "For My Torturer, Lieutenant D——," translated by Anita Barrows. Reprinted by permission of Anita Barrows. ANNA GRÉKI, "Before Your Waking," translated by Anita Barrows. Reprinted by permission of Anita Barrows.

Beacon Press. JUNE JORDAN, "Unemployment/Monologue" from *Passion: New Poems 1977–1978* by June Jordan. Copyright © 1980 by June Jordan. Reprinted by permission of Beacon Press.

Emilie Bergmann. EMILIE BERGMANN, Introduction to Section on "Europe: Sixteenth and Seventeenth Centuries." By permission of the author.

Mei-Mei Berssenbrugge. MEI-MEI BERSSENBRUGGE, "Spring Street Bar" from *Random Possession* by Mei-Mei Berssenbrugge (New York: I. Reed Books, 1979). Reprinted by permission of the poet.

Chana Bloch. DAHLIA RAVIKOVITCH, "Hills of Salt" and "On the Road at Night There Stands the Man" translated by Chana Bloch. Reprinted by permission of Chana Bloch.

Meg Bogin. BEATRICE DE DIE, "Handsome friend, charming and kind" translated by Meg Bogin, from *The Women Troubadours* edited by Meg Bogin (New York: Paddington Press). Copyright © by Meg Bogin. Reprinted by permission of Meg Bogin.

Kamal Boullata. NAZIK AL MALA'IKA, "Jamila" translated by Kamal Boullata. Reprinted by permission of Kamal Boullata.

Gordon Brotherston and Gisela Brotherston. SARAH KIRSCH, "Dandelions for Chains" translated by Gordon and Gisela Brotherston, From *East German Poetry* edited by Michael Hamburger (New York: E.P. Dutton, out of print). Translation of "Dandelions for Chains" Copyright © Gordon and Gisela Brotherston. Reprinted by permission of Gordon and Gisela Brotheston.

Cambridge University Press. RABI'A AL-ADAWIYYA, "Two Prayers" translated by Margaret Smith, adapted from p. 55 (3 11.) and p. 57 (4 11.) of *Rabi'a the Mystic and Her Fellow Saints in Islam* by Margaret Smith (Cambridge, England: Cambridge University Press, 1928). Reprinted by permission of Cambridge University Press.

Janine Canon. RICARDA HUCH, "Young Girl" translated by Janine Canon. Reprinted by permission of Janine Canon.

Jonathan Cape Ltd. INGRID JONKER, "I Drift in the Wind" from *Selected Poems* by Ingrid Jonker, translated from the Afrikaans by Jack Cope and William Plomer

(London: Jonathan Cape Ltd.). Copyright © the estate of Ingrid Jonker. Reprinted by permission of Jonathan Cape Ltd.

Lorna Dee Cervantes. LORNA DEE CERVANTES, "The Woman in My Notebook" from *Canto al Pueblo: An Anthology of Experience*. Reprinted by permission of the poet.

Chicago Review Press. TOMIOKA TAEKO, "Please say something" and "Living together" translated by Sato Hiroaki, from *See You Soon* (Chicago: Chicago Review Press). Reprinted by permission of Chicago Review Press.

Barbara Christian. BARBARA CHRISTIAN, Introduction to section on "North America: Cultural Influences: Afro-American." Used by permission of the author.

Eilean ni Chuilleanain. EILEAN NI CHUILLEANAIN, "Swineherd" and "Wash" from *The Macmillan Book of Irish Verse*. "Swineherd" and "Wash" reprinted by permission of the poet.

Ling Chung. LING CHUNG, Introduction to section on "China." Used by permission of the author.

Columbia Univeristy Press. SILABHATTARIKA, "He who stole my virginity"; VIJJIKA, "Hiding in the / cucumber garden"; both from *Sanskrit Love Poetry* edited by W. S. Merwin and J. Moussaieff-Masson (New York: Columbia University Press, 1977). Reprinted by permission of Columbia University Press.

Confrontation (A Literary Journal of Long Island University). DIANA CHANG, "Cannibalism," from *Confrontation* No. 8 (Spring 1974). Reprinted by permission of *Confrontation*.

Bridget Connelly. HIND BINT UTBA, "Fury Against the Moslems at Uhud'" and "Tambourine Song for Soldiers Going into Battle"; HIND BINT UTHATHA, "To a Hero Dead at Al-Safra" SAFIYA BINT MUSAFIR, "At the Badr Trench" all translated by Bridget Connelly. Used by permission of Bridget Connelly and Deirdre Lashgari. TUMADIR AL-KHANSA, "Elegy for Her Brother, Sakhr" translated by Bridget Connelly. Used by permission of Bridget Connelly. CARENZA and ISELDA, "Tenson" translated by Bridget Connelly and Deirdre Lashgari. Used by permission of Bridget Connelly and Doris Earnshaw. Introduction to section on The Arab World, by permission of the author, Bridget Connelly.

Jonathan Crewe. BERTHA JACOBS, "A Ditty"; translated by Jonathan Crewe. HENRIETTE ROLAND-HOLST, "I Looked for a Sounding Board," "Concerning the Awakening of My Soul" and "Small Paths". HELENE SWARTH, "Candles" and "Ecstasy" all translated by Jonathan Crewe. Used by permission of Jonathan Crewe.

Mary Crow. MARY CROW, Introduction to section on "Latin America." By permission of the author. DELMIRA AUGUSTINI, 13 lines beginning "Blue pupil of my park." JUANA DE IBARBOUROU, five lines beginning "I grew." GABRIELA MISTRAL, "Old Woman" and "Interrogations" all translated by Mary Crow. These four poems are quoted in Mary Crow's Introduction to section on "Latin America" with the permission of Mary Crow.

Curbstone Press. TERESA DE JESÚS, "All of a Sudden" and "They Go By, Love, Go By, Love, The Days and the Hours," translated by Maria A. Proser, Arlene Scully, and James Scully, published by Curbstone Press. Reprinted by permission of Curbstone Press.

Kamala Das. KAMALA DAS, "An Introduction." Used by permission of the poet.

André Deutsch. SHIRAISHI KAZUKO, "Phallic Root" translated by Thomas Fitzsimmons, from *Japanese Poetry Now* published by André Deutsch. Reprinted by permission of André Deutsch.

Patrick Diehl. HILDEGARD VON BINGEN, "O crimson blood" and "Like the honeycomb dropping honey" from *Carmina*, translated by Patrick Diehl. By permission of Patrick Diehl. KASSIA, "Selected Epigrams" and "Sticheron for Matins, Wednesday of Holy Week" translated by Patrick Diehl. Reprinted by permission of Patrick Diehl as translator. HROSWITHA VON GANDERSHEIM, "From the play *Paphnutius*," translated by Patrick Diehl. Reprinted by permission of Patrick Diehl as translator.

Patricia Dienstfrey and Marina La Palma. MARGHERITA GUIDACCI, "At Night" translated by Marina La Palma, from *Poems from Neurosuite* by Margherita Guidacci, translated by Marina La Palma (Kelsey Street Press, Berkeley, Ca.). Reprinted by permission of Patricia Dienstfrey for Kelsey Street Press and Marina La Palma as translator.

Doubleday & Company, Inc. ANONYMOUS, "Women Transport Corps," from *Twentieth Century Chinese Poetry* by Kai-yu Hsu. Copyright © 1963 by Kai-yu Hsu. Reprinted by permission of Doubleday & Company, Inc. URSULA KOZIOL, "Alarum" from *Postwar Polish Poetry* selected and translated by Czesław Miłosz. Copyright © 1965 by Czesław Miłosz. Reprinted by permission of Doubleday & Company, Inc. MARGE PIERCY, "The Total Influence or Outcome of the Matter: The Sun" from *To Be of Use* by Marge Piercy. Copyright © 1969, 1971, 1973 by Marge Piercy. Reprinted by permission of Doubleday & Company, Inc.

Gerald Duckworth & Co., Ltd. CHARLOTTE MEW, "The trees are down" and "Smile, Death" from *Collected Poems* by Charlotte Mew. Reprinted by permission of Gerald Duckworth & Co., Ltd.

Doris Earnshaw. CARENZA AND ISELDA, "Tenson," ROSALIA DE CASTRO, "Plants don't talk," and BEATRICE DE DIE, "My true love makes me happy," all translated by Doris Earnshaw. Reprinted by permission of Doris Earnshaw. DORIS EARNSHAW, Introduction to the section on "Medieval Europe." Used by permission of the author.

Norma Millay Ellis. EDNA ST. VINCENT MILLAY, "Conscientious Objector" from *Collected Poems* by Edna St. Vincent Millay, published by Harper & Row. Copyright © 1934, 1962 by Edna St. Vincent Millay and Norma Millay Ellis. Reprinted by permission of Norma Millay Ellis.

Faber and Faber Limited. MARIANNE MOORE, "the mind is an enchanting thing" from *The Complete Poems of Marianne Moore* published by Faber and Faber Limited. Reprinted by permission of Faber and Faber Limited.

Farrar, Straus & Giroux, Inc. LOUISE BOGAN, "Roman Fountain" from *The Blue Estuaries* by Louise Bogan. Copyright © 1952, 1954, 1957, 1958, 1962, 1963, 1964, 1965, 1966, 1967, 1968 by Louise Bogan. Reprinted by permission of Farrar, Straus & Giroux, Inc. NELLY SACHS, "Chorus of the Rescued" from *O The Chimneys* by Nelly Sachs, translated from the German by Michael Roloff. Copyright © 1967 by Farrar, Straus & Giroux, Inc. Reprinted by permission of Farrar, Straus & Giroux, Inc.

Angel Flores. ANNETTE VON DROSTE-HÜLSHOFF, "On the Tower" translated by J. E. Tobin, from *An Anthology of German Poetry from Hölderlin to Rilke* (New York: Gordian Press). Reprinted by permission of Angel Flores.

Allan Francovich. MANUELA MARGARIDO, "You Who Occupy Our Land" translated by Allan Francovich. Used by permission of Allan Francovich.

Anne Freeman. TOVE DITLEVSEN, "Self Portrait 4" translated by Anne Freeman. Copyright © 1976 by Anne Freeman. Reprinted by permission of Anne Freeman.

Mirène Ghossein and Samuel Hazo. ANDRÉE CHEDID, "The Future and the Ancestor" from *Women of the Fertile Crescent:* Modern Poetry by Arab Women. Reprinted by permission of Mirène Ghossein and Samuel Hazo.

Eloah F. Giacomelli. CECILIA MEIRELES, "Song" translated by Eloah F. Giacomelli, from *Contemporary Literature in Translation*. Reprinted by permission of Eloah F. Giacomelli.

Linda Gregg. LINDA GREGG, "Lilith". By permission of the author.

Susan Griffin. SUSAN GRIFFIN, "Song My," first published in *Dear Sky* by Susan Griffin (Berkeley, CA: Shameless Hussy Press). Copyright © by Susan Griffin. Reprinted by permission of Susan Griffin.

Grove Press, Inc. LADY ISE, "Not even in dreams" and "If I consider" from *Japanese Literature: An Introduction for Western Readers* translated and edited by Donald Keene (New York: Grove Press, Inc., 1958). Reprinted by permission of Grove Press, Inc.

Michael Hamburger. INGEBORG BACHMANN, "The Respite"; MARIE-LUISE KASCH-NITZ, "Humility" and "Resurrection"; GERTRUD KOLMAR, "Out of the Darkness"; ELSE LASKER-SCHÜLER, "My People"; CHRISTINE LAVANT, "Buy Us a Little Grain" and "Do Not Ask"; and FRIEDERICKE MAYRÖCKER, "Patron of Flawless Serpent Beauty"; all from *German Poetry 1910–1975* (New York: Urizen Books, Inc.) translated and edited by Michael Hamburger, copyright © Michael Hamburger 1979. These eight poems from *German Poetry 1910–1975* reprinted by permission of Michael Hamburger.

Harcourt Brace Jovanovich, Inc. ALICE WALKER, "Women" copyright © 1970 by Alice Walker. Reprinted from her volume *Revolutionary Petunias and Other Poems* by permission of Harcourt Brace Jovanovich, Inc.

Harper & Row, Publishers, Inc. GWENDOLYN BROOKS, "When You Have Forgotten Sunday: The Love Story" copyright © 1945 by Gwendolyn Brooks Blakely. Reprinted by permission of Harper & Row, Publishers, Inc. SYLVIA PLATH, "The Moon and the Yew Tree" from *Ariel* by Sylvia Plath, copyright © 1963 by Ted Hughes. Reprinted by permission of Harper & Row Publishers, Inc. Fourteen lines from *The Bell Jar* by Sylvia Plath, pp. 62–63, quoted in the Introduction to the section "North America Cultural Influences: Euro-American" reprinted by permission of Harper & Row, Publishers, Inc.

George Hart. AUVAIYAR, "You stand and hold the post of my small house" translated by George Hart. Used by permission of George Hart.

Harvard University Press. EMILY DICKINSON, "I'm ceded–I've stopped being Theirs" and "The Spider holds a Silver Ball." Reprinted by permission of the publishers and the Trustees of Amherst College from *The Poems of Emily Dickinson*, edited by Thomas H. Johnson, Cambridge, Mass.: The Belknap Press of Harvard University Press, Copyright © 1951, 1955 by the President and Fellows of Harvard College. VIJJIKA, "I praise the disk of the rising sun" and "You are fortunate, dear friends." Reprinted by permission of the publishers, The Belknap Press of Harvard University Press, from *Sanskrit Poetry* edited by Daniel Ingalls, Copyright © 1955, 1968 by the President and Fellows of Harvard College.

Heinemann Educational Books Ltd. STELLA NGATHO, "Footpath" from *Poems of East Africa* edited by Cook and Rubadiri (London: Heinemann Educational Books). Reprinted by permission of Heinemann Educational Books, Ltd.

Albert Herzing. JOYCE MANSOUR, "Yesterday evening I saw your corpse" from *Birds of Prey* translated by Albert Herzing (Van Nuys, CA: Perivale Press). Reprinted by permission of Albert Herzing.

Holt, Rinehart and Winston. KADIA MOLODOWSKY, "God of Mercy" translated by Irving Howe and "Song of the Sabbath" translated by Jean Valentine, both from *A Treasury of Yiddish Poetry* edited by Irving Howe and Eliezer Greenberg. Copyright © 1969 by Irving Howe and Eliezer Greenberg. Reprinted by permission of Holt, Rinehart and Winston, Publishers.

Hatem Hosseini. FADWA TUQĀN, "From Behind the Bars: 3: From the Diary of
———" translated by Hatem Hosseini, from *Enemy of the Sun* edited by Naseer
Aruri and Edmund Ghareeb. Reprinted by permission of Hatem Hosseini.
Houghton Mifflin Company. ANNE SEXTON, "Her Kind" from *To Bedlam and Part
Way Back* by Anne Sexton (Boston: Houghton Mifflin Company). Reprinted by
permission of Houghton Mifflin Company.
Daniel Huws. INGEBORG BACHMANN, "from *Songs in Flight* VI and VII, translated by
Daniel Huws, from *Modern Poetry in Translation* (No. 3). Reprinted by permis-
sion of Daniel Huws.
Indiana University Press. JUANA DE ASBAJE, "Green enravishment of human life"
translated by Samuel Becket and Octavio Paz, from *Anthology of Mexican Poetry*
edited by Samuel Becket and Octavio Paz (Bloomington, IN: Indiana University Press). Reprinted by permission of Indiana University Press. ATIMANTIYAR,
"Nowhere, Not Among the Warriors at Their Festival"; AUVAIYAR, "Shall I
Charge Like a Bull?"; and KACCIPETTU NANNAKAIYAR, "My Lover Capable of
Terrible Lies" translated by A. K. Ramanujan, both from *The Interior Landscape*
edited by A. K. Ramanujan (Bloomington, IN: Indiana University Press). Reprinted by permission of Indiana University Press. KIRTI CHAUDHARI, "Inertia"
translated by L. E. Nathan, from *Modern Hindi Poetry* edited by Vidya Niwas
Misra (Bloomington, IN: Indiana University Press, 1965). Reprinted by permission of Indiana University Press.
International Publishers. LINDIWE MABUZA, "Summer 1970 (a thought to Barbara
Masekela)" from *Speak Easy/Speak Free* edited by Cosmo Pieterse and Antar
Sudan Katara Mberi (New York: International Publishers, 1977). Reprinted by
permission of International Publishers.
Elizabeth Jones. INGRID JONKER, "Don't Sleep" and "When You Laugh" translated
by Elizabeth Jones, from *Contemporary Literature in Translation*, No. 13. Re-
printed by permission of Elizabeth Jones.
Stina Katchadourian. EDITH SÖDERGRAN, "Violet Twilights" translated by Stina
Katchadourian. Used by permission of Stina Katchadourian.
Jascha Kessler and Amin Banani. FORUGH FARROKHZAD, "O Realm Bejeweled"
translated by Jascha Kessler and Amin Banani, from *Modern Poetry in Transla-
tion* (No. 25), Summer 1975. Reprinted by permission of Jascha Kessler and
Amin Banani.
Anne D. Kilmer. ANNE D. KILMER, Introduction to section on "Sumero-Babylonia."
Used by permission of the author. ENHEDUANNA, passage from *Inanna Exalted*,
translated by Anne D. Kilmer. Used by permission of Anne D. Kilmer.
Alfred A. Knopf, Inc. SYLVIA PLATH, "Mushrooms" from *The Colossus and Other
Poems* by Sylvia Plath. Reprinted by permission of Alfred A. Knopf, Inc.
Elene Margot Kolb. 'AISHA BINT AHMAD AL-QURTUBIYYA, "I am a lioness" trans-
lated by Elene Margot Kolb. Used by permission of Elene Margot Kolb.
MARYAM BINT ABI YA'QUB AL-ANSARI, "What can you expect" translated by
Elene Margot Kolb, from *Grove* (Autumn 1980). Reprinted by permission of
Elene Margot Kolb.
Deirdre Lashgari. MARCELINE DESBORDES-VALMORE, "The Roses of Saadi"; PARVIN
E'TESAMI, "To his father on praising the honest life of the peasant"; FORUGH
FARROKHZAD, "Someone Like No One Else"; MAHSATI, "Quatrains"; MEHRI
(MIHRU'N-NISA OF HERAT, "Each subtlety hard for the pedant" and (quoted in
introduction to section on "Iran") a quatrain written in prison; PADESHAH
KHATUN, "Sovereign Queen"; QORRATU'L-AYN, from "He the Beloved"; RABIA
OF BALKH, "My wish for You"; RABIA BINT ISMAIL OF SYRIA, "Sufi Quatrain";
TAHEREH SAFFARZADEH, "Birthplace". All translated by Deirdre Lashgari and

used by permission of Deirdre Lashgari. HIND BINT UTBA, "Fury Against the Moslems at Uhud" and "Tambourine Song"; HIND BINT UTHATHA, "To a Hero Dead at al-Safra"; SAFIYA BINT MUSAFIR, "At the Badr Trench." Translated with Bridget Connelly and used by permission of Deirdre Lashgari and Bridget Connelly. WALLADA, "To Ibn Zaidun." Translated with James Monroe and used by permission of Deirdre Lashgari and James Monroe.

Philip Levine. GLORIA FUERTES, "I Write Poems," "Love Which Frees," and "We're OK" translated by Philip Levine. Translations used by permission of Philip Levine.

Alexis Levitin. SOPHIA DE MELLO BREYNER ANDRESEN, "The Young Girl and the Beach" translated by Alexis Levitin, first published in *The Literary Review*; and "The Small Square" translated by Alexis Levitin, first published in *Poetry Now*. Both translations reprinted by permission of Alexis Levitin.

Dianne Levitin. ANNA AKHMATOVA, "There is in human closeness" translated by Dianne Levitin. Used by permission of Dianne Levitin. ZINAIDA GIPPIUS, "She" translated by Dianne Levitin. Used by permission of Dianne Levitin.

Little, Brown and Company. ANNA AKHMATOVA, "Everything Is Plundered" and "July 1914" from *Anna Akhmatova: The Poems* translated and edited by Stanley Kunitz and Max Hayward. Copyright © 1967, 1968, 1972, 1973 by Stanley Kunitz and Max Hayward. Reprinted by permission of Little, Brown and Company in association with the Atlantic Monthly Press. EMILY DICKINSON, "My life had stood–a loaded Gun," "The first Day's Night had come," and "The Spider holds a Silver Ball" from *The Complete Poems of Emily Dickinson* edited by Thomas H. Johnson. "My life had stood–a loaded Gun," Copyright © 1929 by Martha Dickinson Bianchi. Copyright © 1957 by Mary L. Hamson. "The first Day's Night had come," Copyright 1935 by Martha Dickinson Bianchi. Copyright © 1963 by Mary L. Hampson. Two poems by Emily Dickinson reprinted by permission of Little, Brown and Company.

Macmillan Publishing Co., Inc. MARIANNE MOORE, "The Mind Is an Enchanting Thing," copyright © 1944 by Marianne Moore, renewed 1972 by Marianne Moore. Reprinted by permission of Macmillan Publishing Co., Inc. NTOZAKE SHANGE, "Somebody almost walked off wid alla my stuff," copyright © 1975, 1976, 1977 by Ntozake Shange. Reprinted by permission of Macmillan Publishing Co., Inc.

Marjorie Oludhe Macgoye. MARJORIE OLUDHE MACGOYE, "For Miriam" from *Song of Nyarloka* (Dar es Salaam: Oxford University Press, Eastern Africa, 1977). Reprinted by permission of the poet.

Malki Museum Press. WENDY ROSE, "I Expected My Skin and My Blood to Ripen" from *Lost Copper* (Malki Museum Press, October 1980). Reprinted by permission of Malki Museum Press and the poet, Wendy Rose. "I Expected My Skin and My Blood to Ripen" was also previously published in *Academic Squaw: Reports to the World from the Ivory Tower* (Marvin, SD: Blue Cloud Press, 1977) and in *The Third Woman* (Boston: Houghton Mifflin Company, 1978).

Joyce Mansour. JOYCE MANSOUR, "North Express" from *Flying Piranha*. Reprinted by permission of the poet.

Laureen Mar. LAUREEN MAR, "My Mother, Who Came from China" from *The Third Woman* edited by Dexter Fisher. Reprinted by permission of the poet.

Vasa D. Mihailovich and Ronald Moran. VESNA PARUN, "A Return to the Tree of Time" translated by Vasa D. Mihailovich and Ronald Moran, from *Modern Poetry in Translation* 19–20 (Spring 1974), p. 26. Reprinted by permission of Vasa D. Mihailovich and Ronald Moran.

Janice Mirikitani. JANICE MIRIKITANI, "Sing with Your Body" from *Awake in the River* by Janice Mirikitani (San Francisco: Isthmus, 1978). Reprinted by permission of the poet.

Stephen Mitchell. LEAH GOLDBERG, "Observation of a Bee" translated by Stephen Mitchell. Used by permission of Stephen Mitchell.

Momo's Press. JESSICA TARAHATA HAGEDORN, "Listen" from *Dangerous Music* by Jessica Tarahata Hagedorn (San Francisco: Momo's Press, 1975), copyright © 1975 by Jessica Tarahata Hagedorn. "Listen" reprinted by permission of Momo's Press.

James T. Monroe. WALLADA: "Wait till the darkness is deep" and "To Ibn Zaidun" translated by James T. Moore. Reprinted by permission of James T. Monroe as translator.

Mosaic Press. MARYA FIAMENGO, "In Praise of Old Women" from *In Praise of Old Women* by Marya Fiamengo. Reprinted by permission of Mosaic Press, Oakville, Ontario.

William Morrow & Company, Inc. NIKKI GIOVANNI, "They Clapped" from *My House* by Nikki Giovanni (New York: William Morrow & Company, Inc., 1972), copyright © 1972 by Nikki Giovanni. Reprinted by permission of William Morrow & Company, Inc.

Mundus Artium. VESNA KRMPOTIC, "A December Forest" translated by Vasa D. Mihailovich, from *Mundus Artium* (Vol. IV, No. 2, 1971). EVELYN ARCAD ZERBE, "In Memory of My Arab Grandmother" translated by Reiner Schulte, from *Mundus Artium* (Vol. IX, No. 2, 1976). Reprinted by permission of *Mundus Artium.*

John Murray (Publishers) Ltd. ZIBU'NISA, "I will not lift my veil" translated by Magan Lal and Jessie Duncan Westbrook, from *The Diwan of Zeb-un-Nissa*, edited and translated by Magan Lal and Jessie Duncan Westbrook. Reprinted by permission of John Murray (Publishers) Ltd.

William M. Murray. ANA BLANDIANA, "The Couple" translated by William M. Murray, from *Modern Poetry in Translation.* Reprinted by permission of William M. Murray and the poet, Ana Blandiana.

National Museum of Natural History—Smithsonian Institution. JANE GREEN, "Songs of Divorce" from *Music of the Indians of British Columbia*, Bureau of American Ethnology Bulletin No. 136 (1943), pp. 84–85. Publications of the Bureau of American Ethnology lie in the public domain.

Virgil Nemoianu and Laura Schiff. NINA CASSIAN, "Lady of Miracles" and "The Blood" translated by Virgil Nemoianu and Laura Schiff. Reprinted by permission of Virgil Nemoianu and Laura Schiff as translators.

New Directions Publishing Corporation. MARIE-FRANÇOISE-CATHERINE DE BEAU-VEAU, MARQUISE DE BOUFFLERS, "Air: Sentir avec ardeur" translated by Ezra Pound, and SAINT TERESA OF AVILA, "Bookmark," translated by Henry Wadsworth Longfellow, from *Confucius to Cummings* edited by Ezra Pound and Marcella Spann, Copyright © 1964 by New Directions Publishing Corporation. Reprinted by permission of New Directions. (The translation of "Bookmark" by Longfellow lies in the public domain.) H.D. (HILDA DOOLITTLE), "The Mysteries Remain" from *Selected Poems* by H.D. Copyright © 1957 by Norman Holmes Pearson. Reprinted by permission of New Directions. EMPRESS EIFUKU, "We dressed each other"; LADY IZUMI SHIKIBU, "In the dusk" and "It is the time of rain and snow"; LADY KASA YAKAMOCHI, "To love somebody"; these four poems translated by Kenneth Rexroth, from *100 More Poems from the Japanese*, copyright © 1974, 1976 by Kenneth Rexroth. Reprinted by permission of New Directions. LADY IZUMI SHIKIBU, "I go out of the darkness"; LADY KASA YAKAMOCHI, "I dreamed I held"; these two poems translated by Kenneth Rexroth, from *100 Poems from the Japanese*. All rights reserved. Reprinted by permission of New Directions. DENISE LEVERTOV, "Woman Alone" from *Life in the Forest* by Denise Levertov. Copyright © 1978 by Denise Levertov. Reprinted by permission of New Directions.

Nicaraguan Ministry of Culture and Nina Serrano. MAGDALENA DE RODRIGUEZ R., "June 10" translated by Nina Serrano. Used by permission of the Nicaraguan Ministry of Culture and Nina Serrano.

Northwestern University Press. GASPARA STAMPA, "I am now . . . " and "Deeply repentant" from *Renaissance and Baroque Lyrics* edited by H. M. Priest. Reprinted by permission of Northwestern University Press.

W. W. Norton & Company, Inc. AURE LORDE, "Between Ourselves" reprinted from *The Black Unicorn*, poems by Audre Lorde, by permission of W. W. Norton & Company, Inc. Copyright © 1978 by Audre Lorde. ADRIENNE RICH, "Translations" reprinted from *Diving into the Wreck*, Poems 1971–1972, by Adrienne Rich, by permission of W. W. Norton & Company, Inc. Copyright © 1973 by W. W. Norton & Company, Inc.

Oasis Books. ELENI VAKALO, "But there was once a time" translated by John Stathatos, from *Six Modern Greek Poets*. Reprinted by permission of Oasis Books, London.

Dorothy S. Obi. DOROTHY S. OBI, "Winds of Africa" from *Black Orpheus* (Vol. 1, No. 10), p. 10. Reprinted by permission of the poet.

Raymond Oliver. GABRIELLE DE COIGNARD, "Prayer," PERNETTE DE GUILLET, "Non que je veuille ôter la liberté", and LOUISE LABÉ, "Elegy XXIII" and "Sonnet XVIII" all translated by Raymond Oliver. Used by permission of Raymond Oliver.

The Oriental Institute. KUBATUM, "Love Song to King Shu-Suen" translated by Thorkild Jacobsen, from *Most Ancient Verse*, translated and selected by Thorkild Jacobsen and John A. Wilson. Reprinted by permission of the Oriental Institute of the University of Chicago.

Oxford University Press. BRENDA CHAMBERLAIN, "Lament" from *The Green Heart: Poems* by Brenda Chamberlain (Oxford: Oxford University Press, 1958). Reprinted by permission of Oxford University Press. ANNA MARIA LENNGREN, "The Portraits" from *Anthology of Swedish Lyrics from 1750–1915* translated by C. W. Stork (Oxford: Oxford University Press, 1917). Reprinted by permission of Oxford University Press.

Oyez. EDITH SÖDERGRAN, "Pain" and "We women" translated by Samuel Charters, from *We Women* by Edith Södergran. Reprinted by permission of Oyez Press, Berkeley.

Renata Pallottini. RENATA PALLOTTINI, "Message" translated by Monique and Carlos Altshul. Reprinted by permission of the poet.

Edgar Pauk. GINA LABRIOLA, "Orgy (that is, vegetable market, at Sarno)" translated by Edgar Pauk, from *Modern Poetry in Translation* (No. 26). Reprinted by permission of Edgar Pauk.

Penguin Books. ROSARIO CASTELLANOS, "Foreign Woman" in English translation, from *Latin American Writing Today*, translated by J. M. Cohen (Penguin Books, 1967). Copyright © Penguin Books Ltd., 1967. Reprinted by permission of Penguin books. MAHADEVIYAKKA, "Like/treasure hidden in the ground" and "O brothers, why do you talk" from *Speaking of Siva* translated by A. K. Ramanujan (Penguin Classics, 1973). Copyright © A. K. Ramanujan, 1973. Reprinted by permission of Penguin Books. OTOMO NO SAKANOE NO IRATSUME, "Sent from the capital to her elder daughter" from *The Penguin Book of Japanese Verse*, translated by Geoffrey Bownas and Anthony Thwaite (Penguin Poets, 1964). Copyright © Geoffrey Bownas and Anthony Thwaite, 1964. Reprinted by permission of Penguin Books. WYSŁAWA SZYMBORSKA, "The Women of Rubens" translated by Celina Wieniewska, copyright © Celina Wieniewska, 1967; "Starvation Camp Near Jasło" translated by Jan Darowski, copyright © Jan Darowksi, 1967; both poems from *Polish Writing Today* edited by Celina Wieniewska (Penguin Books, 1967). Reprinted by permission of Penguin Books. Tomioko Taeko, "Life Story" from *Post-War Japanese Poetry*, edited and translated by Harry and Lynn Guest and Kajima Shozo (Penguin Poets, 1972). Copyright © Harry Guest, Lynn Guest, and Kajima Shozo, 1972. Reprinted by permission of Penguin Books.

Perivale Press. Delmira Augustini, "Vision"; Amanda Berenguer, "Housework"; Juana de Ibarbourou, Life-Hook"; Olga Orozco, "Sphinxes inclined to be"; and Alfonsina Storni, "Ancestral Weight" and "They've Come"; all from *Open to the Sun* translated and edited by Nora Jacquez Weiser (Van Nuys, CA: Perivale Press). These six poems reprinted by permission of Perivale Press.

A. D. Peters & Co Ltd, Writers' Agents. Liadain, "Gain without gladness" translated by Frank O'Connor, from *The Penguin Book of Irish Verse* edited by Brendan Kennelly. Reprinted by permission of A. D. Peters & Co Ltd.

Jonny Sullivan Price. Jonny Kyoko Sullivan, "Sagimusume: The White Heron Maiden" from *Hawaii Review* (Spring 1976). Reprinted by permission of Jonny Kyoko Sullivan (Jonny Sullivan Price).

Amrita Pritam and Khushwant Singh. Amrita Pritam, "The Annunciation" translated by Khushwant Singh and Krishna Corowara, from *Contemporary Literature in Translation* (No. 26, Spring 1977). Reprinted by permission of Amrita Pritam and Khushwant Singh.

Revista Chicano-Riqueña. Ana Castillo, "Napa, California" from *Revista Chicano-Riqueña* (4, No. 4, Autumn 1976). Reprinted by permission of *Revista Chicano-Riqueña*.

Catherine Rodriguez-Nieto. Maria Beneyto, "Nocturne in the Women's Prison" translated by Catherine Rodriguez-Nieto, from *Poesiá Femenina Española* (1939–1950) edited by Carmen Conde. Reprinted by permission of Catherine Rodriguez-Nieto. Gertrudis Gómez De Avellaneda, "On Leaving Cuba, Her Native Land" translated by Catherine Rodriguez-Nieto. Used by permission of Catherine Rodriguez-Nieto. Macuilxochitl, "I lift my songs" translated by Catherine Rodriguez-Nieto. Printed by permission of Catherine Rodriguez-Nieto.

Catherine Rodriguez-Nieto and Lucha Corpi. Lucha Corpi, "Dark Romance," translation copyright © Catherine Rodriguez-Nieto 1978. This translation of "Dark Romance" was first published in *San Jose Studies* (Vol. 4, No. 2, May 1978) published by San Jose State University, San Jose, California and appeared in "Palabras de mediodía/Noon Words" published by *Fuego de Aztlan*, Berkeley, California, 1980. Reprinted here by permission of Catherine Rodriguez-Nieto as translator and Lucha Corpi as author.

Ross-Erikson Publishers. Maria Sabina, "Shaman" excerpted by permission of Ross-Erikson publishers.

Alan F. C. Ryder. Alda Do Espirito Santo, "Where are the men seized in this wind of madness" and Noémia Da Sousa, "Appeal", both translated by Alan F. C. Ryder, both from *Modern Poetry from Africa* (Penguin Poets, 1963). Reprinted by permission of Alan F. C. Ryder.

Sahitya Akademi and Usha Priyamvada Nilsson. Mira Bai, "O king, I know you gave me poison" and "Wake up, dear boy that holds the flute" translated by Usha Priyamvada Nilsson in her monograph on Mira Bai published by Sahitya Akademi (National Academy of Arts and Letters), New Delhi. Reprinted by permission of Sahitya Akademi and Usha Priyamvada Nilsson.

St. Martin's Press, Inc. and Judy Grahn. Judy Grahn, "Carol, in the park, chewing on straws" from *The Work of a Common Woman* by Judy Grahn. Reprinted by permission of St. Martin's Press, Inc., and the poet, Judy Grahn.

Stella Sandahl. STELLA SANDAHL, Introduction to the section on "India." Used by permission of the author.

Sonia Sanchez. SONIA SANCHEZ, "Present" from *I've Been a Woman (A Blues Book for Blue Black Magical Women)* by Sonia Sanchez. Reprinted by permission of the poet.

John Schaffner Associates, Inc. MARIE DE FRANCE, "Song from Chartivel" translated by Arthur O'Shaughnessy from *Lyrics of the Middle Ages* edited by Hubert Creekmore. Reprinted by permission of John Schaffner Associates, Inc. as agents for the estate of Hubert Creekmore.

Laura Schiff. KATA SZIDÓNIA PETRÖCZI, "Swift Floods" translated by Laura Schiff. Used by permission of Laura Schiff.

Betty L. Schwimmer. ANNA DE NOAILLES, "Poem on azure" translated by Betty L. Schwimmer. Used by permission of Betty L. Schwimmer.

Michael Scott. HAFSA BINT AL-HAJJ, "Shall I come to you there, or you here?" translated by Michael Scott. Used by permission of Michael Scott.

Seabury Press. AKAZOME EMON, "I, Who Cut Off My Sorrows" and "In my Heart's Depth"; LADY HORIKAWA, "How long will it last"; LADY ISE, "Since 'the pillow knows all'"; ISE TAYU, "The Farmer's Clothes Are Soaked Through"; KAWAI CHIGETSU-NI, "Grasshoppers"; LADY KII, "I know the reputation"; MURASAKI SHIKIBU, "From *The Tale of the Genji*"; ONO NO KOMACHI, "Doesn't He Realize?"; UKIHASHI, "Whether I sit or lie"; YOSANO AKIKO, "A Bird Comes" and "I Can Give Myself to Her"; all from *The Burning Heart: Women Poets of Japan*, edited by Kenneth Rexroth and Ikuko Atsumi. Reprinted by permission of Seabury Press. HUANG O, "To the Tune: Soaring Clouds," "To the Tune: Red Embroidered Shoes," and "To the Tune: The Fall of a Little Wild Goose"; SUN YÜN-FÊNG, "On the Road Through Chang-Te"; TAN YING, "Drinking the wind"; T'ANG WAN, "To the Tune: The Phoenix Hairpin"; TS'AI YEN, "From 'Eighteen Verses Sung to a Tatar Reed Whistle'"; TZU YEH, "It Is Night Again," "I had not fastened my sash over my gown," and "The bare branches tremble"; WANG WEI, "Seeking a Mooring"; WU TSAO, "For the Courtesan Ch'ing Lin" and "In the house of the scholar Wu Su-Chiang"; all from *The Orchid Boat, Women Poets of China*, edited by Kenneth Rexroth and Ling Chung (Seabury Press, 1972). Reprinted by permission of Seabury Press.

Anthony Shiel Associates Ltd. MARIA KONOPNICKA, "A Vision", from *Five Centuries of Polish Poetry* edited by Jerzy Peterkiewicz and Burns Singer. Reprinted by permission of Anthony Shiel & Associates Ltd.

Sidgwick & Jackson, Ltd., Publishers. AMBAPALI, "Black and glossy as a bee" from *The Wonder That Was India* edited by A. L. Basham. Reprinted by permission of Sidgwick & Jackson, Ltd.

Leslie M. Silko. LESLIE MARMON SILKO, "Where Mountain Lion Lay Down with Deer" from *Laguna Woman* by Leslie Marmon Silko. Reprinted by permission of Leslie Marmon Silko.

Stanford University Press. Four lines beginning "I chisel" quoted in Introduction to section on "Native America," quoted in *Daily Life of the Aztecs on the Eve of the Spanish Conquest* by Jacques Soustelle (Stanford University Press, 1961). Reprinted by permission of Stanford University Press.

Laura Stortoni. COMPIUTA DONZELLA, "To leave the world" translated by Laura Stortoni.

Rob Swigart. PAN CHAO, "Needle and Thread," translated by Rob Swigart. Used by permission of Rob Swigart. ONO NO KOMACHI, "No moon, no chance to meet," "If it were real," and "Since I've felt this pain" translated by Rob Swigart. Used by permission of Rob Swigart. ROB SWIGART, Introduction to section on "Japan." Used by permission of Rob Swigart.

Three Continents Press. FAWZIEH ABOU KHALED, "Mother's Inheritance"; MONA SAUDI: "When the loneliness of the tomb," "How do I enter the silence of stones," and "Why don't I write in the language of air?"; all from *Women of the Fertile Crescent* edited by Kamal Boullata, published by Three Continents Press, Washington, D.C. Reprinted by permission of Three Continents Press.

Times Change Press. NANCY MOREJÓN, "The Reason for Poetry" translated by Anita Whitney, from *Somos/We Are: five contemporary cuban poets* edited by Anita Whitney. Reprinted by permission of Times Change Press.

Frederick Ungar Publishing Co., Inc. CATHARINA REGINA VON GREIFFENBERG, "Spring-joy praising God," translated by George C. Schoolfield, from *Anthology of German Poetry* edited by Alexander Gode and Frederick Ungar. Reprinted by permission of Frederick Ungar Publishing Co., Inc.

Unicorn Press. MRIRIDA N'AIT ATTIK, "Mririda" and "Azouou" from *Songs of Mririda* by Mririda n'Ait Attik, translated by Daniel Halpern and Paula Paley. Copyright © 1974 by Daniel Halpern and Paula Paley. Reprinted by permission of Unicorn Press, P.O. Box 3307, Greensboro, NC 27402.

University of California Press. QUEEN HATSHEPSUT, "From the Obelisk Inscriptions," 45 lines, from *Ancient Egyptian Literature*, Vol. II, edited and translated by Miriam Lichtheim. Reprinted by permission of University of California Press, Berkeley, CA.

University of Chicago Press. CORINNA, "I disapprove even of eloquent/Myrtis" and "To the white-mantled maidens"; PRAXILLA, "Loveliest of what I leave behind" and "Girl of the lovely glance"; SAPPHO, "Like the very gods," "Some there are who say" and "Come to me from Crete"; all from *Greek Lyrics* translated by Richmond Lattimore. Reprinted by permission of University of Chicago Press.

University of Iowa Press. BELLA AKHMADULINA, "Fifteen Boys, or Perhaps Even More" and NOVELLA MATVEYEVA, "The eggplants have pins and needles," both translated by Daniel Weissbort. Reprinted by permission of University of Iowa Press. DESANKA MAKSIMOVIC, "For All Mary Magdalenes" from *Contemporary Yugoslav Poetry* edited by Vasa D. Michailovich. Reprinted by permission of University of Iowa Press. ISHIGAKI RIN, "Cocoon," from *The Poetry of Postwar Japan* edited by Kijima Hajime. Reprinted by permission of University of Iowa Press.

University of Pennsylvania Press. JUANA DE ASBAJE, "Sonnet" ("Stay, shade of my shy treasure! Oh remain") translated by Alice Stone Blackwell, from *Some Spanish-American Poets* translated by Alice Stone Blackwell. Reprinted by permission of University of Pennsylvania Press.

University of Pittsburgh Press. LORNA DEE CERVANTES, "Poem for the Young White Man Who Asked How I, an Intelligent, Well-Read Person, Could Believe in War Between the Races" from *Emplumada* by Lorna Dee Cervantes. Copyright © 1981 by Lorna Dee Cervantes. Reprinted by permission of the University of Pittsburgh Press. AKJARTOQ, "An Old Woman's Song"; KIBKARJUK, "Song of the Rejected Woman"; KILIMÉ, "The Abduction"; ORPINGALIK, prose quotation in Introduction to section on "Native American"; QERNERTOQ, "The Widow's Song"; TUTLIK, "Dancing Song"; and UVAVNUK, "Moved"; all reprinted from *Eskimo Poems of Canada and Greenland*, edited and translated by Knud Rasmussen, English edition & translation by Tom Lowenstein. Published in 1973 by the University of Pittsburgh Press. Copyright © by Tom Lowenstein. Used by permission.

University of Southern California Press. TERESA PALMA ACOSTA, "My Mother Pieced Quilts" from *Festival de Flor y Canto*. Reprinted by permission of the University of Southern California Press.

University of Washington Press. YOSANO AKIKO, "A wave of coldness" and "As I am unhappy" translated by Glenn Hughes and Yozan I. Iwasaki, from *Three Women Poets of Japan*, edited by Glenn Hughes. Reprinted by permission of University of Washington Press.

Viking Penguin, Inc. ANNA LEE WALTERS, "I have bowed before the sun" from *The Man to Send Rain Clouds*, edited by Kenneth Rosen. Copyright © 1974 by Kenneth Rosen. Reprinted by permission of Viking Penguin, Inc.

Alma Villanueva. ALMA VILLANUEVA, "I was always fascinated" from *Mother, May I?* (Pittsburgh: Motheroot Publications, 1978). Copyright © 1978 by Alma Villanueva. Reprinted by permission of the poet.

Marsha L. Wagner. LICH'ING-CHAO, "Poem to the Tune of 'Yi chien mei'" and "Poem to the Tune of 'Tsui hua yin'" translated by Marsha L. Wagner. Used by permission of Marsha L. Wagner.

Jan W. Walls. YÜ HSÜAN-CHI, "Willows by the Riverside" translated by Jan W. Walls, from *Sunflower Splendor* edited by Wu-chi Liu and Irving Yucheng Lo (Doubleday). Reprinted by permission of Jan W. Walls.

Kathleen Weaver and Allan Francovich. GABRIELA MISTRAL, "Bread" translated by Kathleen Weaver and Allan Francovich. Used by permission of Kathleen Weaver and Allan Francovich.

Kathleen Weaver and Magda Portal. MAGDA PORTAL, "Woman" translated by Kathleen Weaver, with the permission of Magda Portal. Translation used by permission of Kathleen Weaver and Magda Portal.

Brenda Webster. VITTORIA COLONNA, "When the Orient is lit" and "As a hungry fledgling" translated by Brenda Webster. Used by permission of Brenda Webster. GASPARA STAMPA, "Hunger" translated by Brenda Webster. Used by permission of Brenda Webster.

Daniel Weissbort. NATALYA GORBANEVSKAYA, "Love, love, what nonsense it is . . ." translated by Daniel Weissbort, from *Post-War Russian Poetry*. Reprinted by permission of Daniel Weissbort.

Westview Press. ELISE BOULDING, *The Underside of History: A View of Women Through Time* (Boulder, CO: Westview Press, 1976). Quoted in Introduction to section on "Medieval Europe" by permission of Westview Press.

Roberta Hill Whiteman. ROBERTA HILL, "Leap in the dark" from *The Third Woman* edited by Dexter Fisher. Reprinted by permission of Roberta Hill Whiteman.

Miller Williams. LUCIENNE DESNOUES, "First Things" translated by Miller Williams. Copyright © 1979 by Miller Williams. Used by permission of Miller Williams.

Wire Press. KATERINA ANGHELAKI-ROOKE, "The Body is the Victory and the Defeat of Dreams" translated by Philip Ramp, from *The Body Is the Victory and the Defeat of Dreams* by Katerina Anghelaki-Rooke. Reprinted by permission of Wire Press.

Manfred Wolf. JUDITH HERZBERG, "Vocation" and "On the Death of Sylvia Plath" translated by Manfred Wolf. Used by permission of Manfred Wolf.

Nellie Wong. NELLIE WONG, "How a Girl Got Her Chinese Name" from *Dreams in Harrison Railroad Park*. Reprinted by permission of Nellie Wong.

Mitsuye Yamada. MITSUYE YAMADA, "On the bus" and "In the outhouse" from *Camp Notes*. Reprinted by permission of Mitsuye Yamada. Introduction to section on "North America Cultural Influences: Asian/Pacific American." Used by permission of Mitsuye Yamada.

Yvonne Yarbro-Bejarano. YVONNE YARBRO-BEJARANO, Introduction to the section on "North America Cultural Influences: Chicana." Used by permission of Yvonne Yarbro-Bejarano.

Preface

TEN YEARS AGO, much poetry by women was inaccessible. Since then excellent collections of the work of women poets have appeared—first, poetry written in English, then translations from other languages. Now that enough work is available to constitute a field, we can go a step further and place the poems—and the poets—in the context of the cultures that shaped them.

This anthology reaches back in time from our own century to 2300 BC, and embraces over 70 cultures. It affirms the connections among women poets not by ignoring their cultural distinctions, but by defining them more attentively, more clearly. The kinds of poetry women wrote reflect the historical conditions—social, economic, literary—that shaped their lives. We emphasize this larger context first by grouping the poems by culture or cultural area, and then by introducing each section with an overview of the conditions under which women wrote.

Especially in the older poems, but in much contemporary work as well, this context is crucial to understanding. There is much in the experience of women throughout time and across cultures that is universal, that speaks to us as readers in this country shaped by late twentieth-century perceptions. But we lose much if we stop there—if we read everything through the blinders of our own generalized cultural assumptions.

The introductory essays let us see these poets as the exceptions they usually were. They help us to remember, as Tillie Olsen insists, how much of an almost miraculous combination of courage and chance made it possible for each of these women to write. Again and again there are entire periods, centuries at a time, so uncongenial to women that almost no poetry by women appears. It's important that we not lose sight of the numbers of women in each age, each culture, who had poetry in them and were silenced.

Difference, distinctiveness—that is also a key to the way we chose the poems in this book. People often ask "What type of poetry were you looking for?" Our answer—as wide a variety of themes, of voices, of perspectives, from as many different periods and cultures as possible. We made our final selection above all on the basis of quality—the poetic strength of the poem and of the translation. Again and again we had to omit poems that were clearly powerful in the original because the English translation just did not work, or poems that moved us but were in some way flawed aesthetically. Certain poetic genres like narrative poetry were excluded almost completely because space was so limited.

We wanted a range of voices in the translations. Stylistic sameness, homogeneity, was not what we were after. Rather, whatever seemed to work for a particular poet or poem. Not even the best translation, of course, can convey the fullness of the original poem. Often what comes through most closely is image; what gets lost is the intricate interplay of metrical systems, rhyme and other echoings of sound, and especially the rich suggestiveness of multiple meanings in a single word, only fragments of which the translator will be able to save.

We have kept the traditional selections from the United States to a minimum, a touchstone. They are what we are closest to, have widest access to, yet we have been concerned not to set our own poetic tradition at center, as implicit norm. Our structuring of the anthology reflects this concern.

The book starts with China, and proceeds by culture (or cultural area) geographically from East to West. Within each section, the poets appear chronologically. Thus the Sumerian poet Enheduanna—who preceeds the earliest included Chinese poet by more than two thousand years—comes later in the book, after "Iran" and "The Arab World." We need this orientation in space as well as in time as we come face to face with poets of unfamiliar cultures.

The Native American section, and the four cultural subsections within "North America," again have the effect of shifting us away from the Euro-American center from which most poetry published in this country is presented and read. It should be fairly clear why "Native American" is a section in its own right. Culture in the Americas didn't start with the arrival of the Europeans. Moreover, there was no way we could subsume under either "Latin America" or "North America" alone an Aztec poet of the 15th century, an early 20th century Canadian Eskimo oral poet, and a university-trained Oneida Indian from the United States. Yet each is rooted, at least in part, in a cultural history which antedates the European. "Native American" as a distinct section calls attention to a historical reality too often obscured or ignored. The solution, of course, has its own limitations, since "Native American" encompasses widely diverse languages and traditions, and the cultural roots of an individual poet may involve a complex interweaving of Native and European influences. Because the section spans a longer history than either the Latin American or North American, and because it represents a synthesis, an integration and renewal, it seems appropriate to give it the powerful concluding position in the book, closing with the words of shaman/artist Anna Lee Walters

"My name is 'I Am Living.' I am here."

A word on "Anonymous," who—alas—is not represented in this anthology (except for one fairly recent poem from the People's Republic of China, composed at a time when personal attribution was considered bad form). Our concern has been to include only poems we were sure beyond any shade of doubt were by women. Although many anonymous songs and poetry are almost certainly by women—lullabies and women's work songs especially—that "almost" leaves just enough doubt to make it inappropriate to include them here. In many cultures and periods there has been a tradition of male poets adopting a woman's voice, often borrowing expressions, modes of speech, whole lines from the "anonymous" poetry and songs of the women around them. The old Gaelic poem by the "Hag of Beare" seems to be a sophisticated instance of this type. (See Doris Earnshaw's valuable study of this "poetry in a woman's voice.")

We have also omitted poems traditionally attributed to specific women whenever historical evidence seemed to place that attribution in question. For instance, since the Biblical "Song of Hannah" contains words which only appear in Hebrew several hundred years after Hannah lived, the poem in the form we now have is probably the work not of Hannah, but of several scribes living much later. On the other hand we have included the "song of Deborah" because its language, contemporaneous with Deborah's life, validates her authorship of this work.

This book owes its existence to many friends and colleagues, too numerous to mention, whose support has kept us going through these past ten years. We trust they know how deeply their help has mattered. A few deserve special acknowledgment— Above all, Doris Earnshaw, whose vision and faith in the impossible plunged us in, and whose tough perseverance kept us afloat. All those who took part in our early translation workshops, where collectively we worked through snags and shared our discoveries. Bridget Connelly and Catherine Rodriguez, who were with us from the very start, and gave generous hours of inspiration and hard work. All the writers of introductory essays for difficult work in unexplored territory, for the dedication and love of the work that kept them going with no other reward: Ling Chung, Rob Swigart, Stella Sandahl, Bridget Connelly, Anne Kilmer, Doris Earnshaw, Emilie Bergmann, Mary Crow, Wendy Barker, Barbara Christian, Mitsuye Yamada, Yvonne Yarbro-Bejarano. Tillie Olsen and Adrienne Rich, who gave encouragement, invaluable advice, and the unending inspiration of their work and lives. Sandra Gilbert and Susan Gubar for their helpful responses to the manuscript. Dexter Fisher, Odette Meyer, Jonathan Crewe, Tom D'Evelyn, and VèVè Clark for all they contributed in ideas, in criticism, in vision. Nancy Zak, whose long distance phone calls brought new energy just when we most needed it. Kemal Baullata for all he has done to see to it that silenced voices be heard. Miller Williams and Robert Hass, who gave us support when it really counted. Andreas Schroeder and Daniel Weissbort for all they have given to those who care about poetry in translation, and specifically for the generous assistance they gave us as co-conspirators in this task. Tony English and Pat Cabeza, our editors at Macmillan, whose skill, sense of humor, and professional acumen have meant so much in the realization of our vision. All the poets and translators and publishers who were willing to give us poems for reduced fees or free, without which an anthology of this scope would have remained impractical. And last but by no means least, the employees of Cody's and Woman's Place Bookstore, and the reference librarians at the University of California and the Berkeley Public Library, whose patience and perseverance and unfailing kindness helped us find the unfindable and track down what would otherwise have been lost.

J.B.
D.L.

. . . Although they are

only breath, words
which I command
are immortal . . .

—Sappho

Contents

GENERAL INTRODUCTION 1

China 9

Introduction 9
Pan Chao (48–117?), *Needle and Thread* 15
Ts'ai Yen (c. 200), from *Eighteen Verses Sung to a
    Tatar Reed Whistle* 15
Tzu Yeh (3rd–4th centuries), *It is night again* 18/ *I
    had not fastened my sash over my gown* 18/ *The bare
    branches tremble* 19
Yü Hsüan-chi (c. 843–868), *Composed on the Theme
    "Willows by the Riverside"* 19
Li Ch'ing-chao (1084–1151), *Poem to the tune of "Yi
    chian mei"* 20/ *Poem to the tune of "Tsui hua
    yin"* 20
T'ang Wan (12th century), *To the tune "The Phoenix
    Hairpin"* 21
Huang O (1498–1569), *To the tune "Soaring
    Clouds"* 21/ *To the tune "Red Embroidered
    Shoes"* 22/ *To the tune "The Fall of a Little Wild
    Goose"* 22
Wang Wei (17th century), *Seeking a Mooring* 23
Sun Yün-fêng (1764–1814), *On the Road Through
    Chang-Te* 24
Wu Tsao (19th century), *For the Courtesan Ch'ing
    Lin* 24/ *In the Home of the Scholar Wu Su-
    chiang* 25
Ping Hsin (1902), from *The Stars* 26/ from *The
    Spring Waters* 26
Tan Ying (1943), *Drinking the Wind* 27
Anonymous (c. 1958), *Women Transport Corps* 28

Japan 29

Introduction 29

Otomo no Sakanoe (8th century), *Sent from the
capital* 35

Lady Kii (8th century), *I know the reputation* 35

Lady Kasa (8th century), *I dreamed I held* 36/ *To love
somebody* 36

Ono no Komachi (9th century), *Doesn't he realize* 36/
No moon, no chance to meet 37/ *If it were real* 37/
Since I've felt this pain 37

Lady Ise (9th–10th centuries), *Since "the pillow knows
all"* 37/ *Not even in dreams* 37/ *If I consider* 38

Murasaki Shikibu (974–1031), from *The Tale of the
Genji* 38

Izumi Shikibu (10th–11th centuries), *I go out of
darkness* 38/ *In the dusk the path* 39/ *It is the time
of rain and snow* 39

Akazome Emon (11th century), *In my heart's
depth* 39/ *I, who cut off my sorrows* 39

Ise Tayu (11th century), *The farmer's clothes are soaked
through* 40

Lady Horikawa (12th century), *How long will it
last?* 40

Empress Eifuku (1271–1342), *We dressed each
other* 40

Ukihashi (late 17th century), *Whether I sit or lie* 41

Kawai Chigetsu-Ni (1632–1736), *Grasshoppers* 41

Yosano Aikiko (1878–1942), *A wave of coldness* 41/
As I am unhappy 41/ *I can give myself to her* 41/ *A
bird comes* 42

Ishigaki Rin (1920), *Cocoon* 42

Shiraishi Kazuko (1931), *Phallic Root* 43

Tomioka Taeko (1935), *Please say something* 45/ *Life
Story* 46/ *Living Together* 48

India 49

Introduction, 49

Ambapali (4th century B.C.(?),
Pali), *Black and glossy as a bee* 53

Kaccipettu Nannakaiyar (3rd century(?),
Tamil), *My lover capable of terrible lies* 54

Atimantiyar (3rd century(?), Tamil), *Nowhere, not among the warriors at their festival* 54

Auvaiyar (between 1st and 3rd century(?), Tamil), *Shall I charge like a bull* 54/ *You stand and hold the post of my small house* 55

Vidya (Vijjika) (between 700 and 1050, Sanskrit), *I praise the disk of the rising sun* 55/ *You are fortunate, dear friends* 55/ *Hiding in the / cucumber garden* 55

Śilabhattarika (between 700 and 1050, Sanskrit), *He who stole my virginity* 56

Mahadeviyakka (12th century, Kannada), *Like / treasure hidden in the ground* 57/ *O brothers, why do you talk* 57

Lalleswari (Lal Ded) (late 14th century, Kashmiri), *I set forth hopeful* 58/ *With my breath I cut my way* 58/ *Good repute is water carried in a sieve* 58

Mira Bai (1498–1547, Hindi), *O King, I know you gave me poison.* 58/ *Wake up, dear boy that holds the flute!* 59

Makhfi (Zibu'n-Nisa) (1639–1703, Farsi), *The beauty of the Friend it was that taught me* 59

Kirti Chaudhari (1935, Hindi), *Inertia* 60

Kamala Das (1934, English), *An Introduction* 61

Amrita Pritam (1919, Punjabi), *The Annunciation* 62

Iran   66

Introduction 66

Rabi'a of Balkh (10th century), *My wish for you* 73

Mahsati (12th century), *Selected Quatrains* 73

Padeshah Khatun (14th century), *Sovereign Queen* 74

Mehri (c. 1404–1447), *Coming Across* 75

Qorratu'l-Ayn (1814–1852), from *He the Beloved* 75

Parvin E'tesami (1910–1941), *To his father on praising the honest life of the peasant* 77

Forugh Farrokhzad (1935–1967), *O Realm Bejewelled* 77/ *Someone Like No One Else* 77

Tahereh Saffarzadeh (1939), *Birthplace* 84

Akhtar Amiri (contemporary), from *I Am a Woman* 85

The Arab World 88

Introduction 88

ARABIA

Tumadir al-Khansa' (late 6th century),   *Elegy for her brother, Sakhr* 93

Safiya bint Musafir (early 7th century),   *At the Badr Trench* 94

Hind bint Utba (early 7th century),   *Fury Against the Moslems at Uhud* 94/ *Tambourine Song for Soldiers Going into Battle* 95

Hind bint Uthatha (early 7th century),   *To a Hero Dead at al-Safra* 95

Rabi'a bint Isma'il (d. 755),   *Sufi Quatrain* 96

Rabi'a al-Adawiyya (712–801),   *Two Prayers* 97

ANDALUSIAN SPAIN

Aisha bint Ahmad al-Qurtubiyya (late 10th century),   *I am a lioness* 97

Wallada (early 11th century),   *To Ibn Zaidun* 98/ *Wait till the darkness is deep* 98

Maryam bint Abi Ya'qub al-Ansari (early 11th century),   *What can you expect* 99

Hafsa bint al-Hajj (d. 1184),   *Shall I come there, or you here?* 99

EGYPT

Andrée Chedid (1921),   *The Future and the Ancestor* 99

PALESTINE

Fadwa Tuqan (1917),   *From Behind the Bars* 100

IRAQ

Nazik al-Mala'ika (1923),   *Jamila* 101

LEBANON

Etel Adnan (1925),   from *The Beirut—Hell Express* 102

Evelyn Arcad Zerbe (contemporary),   *In Memory of My Arab Grandmother* 106

SAUDI ARABIA

Fawziyya Abu Khalid (1955),   *Mother's Inheritance* 107

JORDAN
Mona Sa'udi (1945), *When the loneliness of the
tomb* 109/ *How do I enter the silence of stones* 109/
Why don't I write in the language of air? 109

Sumero-Babylonia 111

Introduction 111
Enheduanna (c. 2300 B.C.), from *Inanna
Exalted* 114
Kubatum (c. 2038 B.C.), *Love Song to King Shu-
Suen* 118

Israel 119

Introduction 119
Deborah (11th century, B.C.), from the *Song of
Deborah* 128
Leah Goldberg (1911–1970), *Observation of a
Bee* 129
Rachel (Blaustein) (1890–1931), *His Wife* 130
Hannah Senesh (1921–1944), *One-two-three . . .* 131
Zelda Shneurson (contemporary), *The Wicked
Neighbor* 131
Dahlia Ravikovitch (1936), *On the Road at Night
There Stands the Man* 134/ *Hills of Salt* 134

Greece of Antiquity 136

Introduction 136
Sappho (6th century, B.C.), *Like the very gods in my
sight* 142/ *Come to me from Crete* 142/ *Some there
are who say* 143
Corinna (late 6th-early 5th centuries, B.C.), *I disapprove even of eloquent / Myrtis* 143/ *To the white-
mantled maidens* 143
Praxilla (mid-5th century, B.C.), *Loveliest of what I
leave behind* 144/ *Girl of the lovely glance* 144
Erinna (3rd century, B.C.), *The Distaff* 144

Medieval Europe   146

Introduction   146

IRELAND
Liadain (7th century),   *Gain without gladness*   151

BYZANTINE GREECE
Kassia (9th century),   *Selected Epigrams*   152/ *Sticheron for Matins, Wednesday of Holy Week*   152

GERMANY
Hroswitha von Gandersheim (935–after 973, Latin),   from the play *Paphnutius*   153
Hildegard von Bingen (1098–1197),   *O crimson blood*   153/ *Like the honeycomb dropping honey*   154
Mechthild von Magdeburg (1210–1294, Low German),   *Love Flows From God*   154/ *Here too the Spirit shafts*   154

PROVENCE
Carenza and Iselda (12th century?),   *Tenson*   155
Beatrice de Die (late 12th century),   *My true love makes me happy*   156/ *Handsome friend*   157

ITALY
Compiuta Donzella (13th century),   *To leave the world*   157

FRANCE
Marie de France (1155–1190),   Song from *Chartivel*   158
Christine de Pisan (1363–1430),   *Marriage is a lovely thing*   160/ *Fountain of tears, river of grief*   160

HOLLAND
Bertha Jacobs (1427–1514),   *A Ditty*   161

Europe: Sixteenth and Seventeenth Centuries   163

Introduction   163

SPAIN
Saint Teresa of Ávila (1515–1588),   *Bookmark*   171/ *En las internas entrañas*   171

ITALY
Vittoria Colonna (1490–1547),   *When the Orient is lit
    by the great light* 172/ *As a hungry fledgling, who
    sees and hears* 172
Gaspara Stampa (1523–1554),   *Hunger* 173/ *I am
    now so weary with waiting* 173/ *Deeply repentant of
    my sinful ways* 174

FRANCE
Pernette de Guillet (1520–1545),   *Non que je veuille
    ôter la liberté* 174
Louise Labé (c. 1524–1566),   *Sonnet XVIII* 175/ *Elegy
    XXIII* 175
Gabrielle de Coignard (d. 1594),   *Prayer* 176

GERMANY
Catharina Regina von Greiffenberg (1633–
    1694),   *Spring-Joy Praising God.* 176

HUNGARY
Kata Szidónia Petröczi (1662–1708),   *Swift
    Floods* 177

ENGLAND
Katherine Philips (1631–1664),   *To My Excellent
    Lucasia* 178
Aphra Behn (1640–1689),   Song from *The Lucky
    Chance* 179/ from the "Epilogue" to *Sir Patient
    Fancy* 180
Mary Lee, Lady Chudleigh (1656–1710),   *To the
    Ladies* 180
Anne Finch, Countess of Winchilsea (1661–
    1720),   *The Introduction* 181

Europe: Eighteenth and Nineteenth Centuries   183

Introduction   183

FRANCE
Marie-Françoise-Catherine de Beauveau, Marquise
    de Boufflers (1711–1786),   *Air: Sentir avec Ar-
    deur* 192

SWEDEN
Anna Maria Lenngren (1755–1817),   *The Portraits* 193

ENGLAND
Charlotte Smith (1749–1806),   *Thirty-Eight* 195
Elizabeth Barrett Browning (1806–1861),   from
    Aurora Leigh 197/ *A Curse for a Nation* 197
Christina Rossetti (1830–1894),   *A Soul* 201

FRANCE
Marceline Desbordes-Valmore (1786–1859),   *The
    Roses of Saadi* 202

GERMANY
Annette von Droste-Hülshoff (1797–1848),   *On the
    Tower* 202
Ricarda Huch (1864–1947),   *Young Girl* 203

FRANCE
Anna de Noailles (1876–1933),   *Poem on azure* 204

HOLLAND
Hélène Swarth (1859–1941),   *Candles* 205/
    Ecstasy 206
Henriette Roland-Holst (1869–1952),   *I Looked for a
    Sounding-Board* 206/ *Concerning the Awakening of
    My Soul* 207/ *Small Paths* 207

POLAND
Maria Konopnicka (1842–1910),   *A Vision* 208

SPAIN
Rosalia de Castro (1837–1885),   *plants don't talk,
    people say* 208

ENGLAND
Charlotte Mew (1870–1928),   *Smile, Death* 209/ *The
    Trees Are Down* 210

RUSSIA
Zinaida Gippius (1869–1945),   *She* 211

Europe: 1914 and After   213

Introduction   213

SOVIET UNION
Anna Akhmatova (1889–1966), *July 1914* 219/
Everything is Plundered 219/ *There is in human
closeness a sacred boundary* 220
Marina Tsvetaeva (1892–1941), *An Attempt at
Jealousy* 220
Natalya Gorbanevskaya (1936), *Love! love! what non-
sense it is* 222
Novella Matveyeva (1934), *The Eggplants Have Pins
and Needles* 222
Bella Akhmadulina (1937), *Fifteen Boys, or Perhaps
Even More* 223

POLAND
Wisława Szymborska (1923), *The Women of
Rubens* 224/ *Starvation Camp Near Jasło* 225
Urszula Kozioł (1935), *Alarum* 227

ROMANIA
Ana Blandiana (1942), *The Couple* 228
Nina Cassian (1924), *Lady of Miracles* 228/ *The
Blood* 230

YUGOSLAVIA
Vesna Krmpotic (1932), *A December Forest* 230
Vesna Parun (1922), *A Return to the Tree of
Time* 231
Desanka Maksimovic (1898), *For All Mary Mag-
dalenes* 232

HUNGARY
Judit Tóth (1936), *To the Newborn* 232/ *Dead Embryos* 234

GERMANY
Else Lasker-Schüler (1876–1945), *My People* 235
Nelly Sachs (1891–1969), *Chorus of the Rescued* 236
Gertrud Kolmar (1899), *Out of the Darkness* 237
Marie Luise Kaschnitz (1901), *Humility* 238/ *Resur-
rection* 239
Christine Lavant (1915), *Buy Us a Little Grain* 240/
Do Not Ask 240
Friederike Mayröcker (1924), *Patron of Flawless Ser-
pent Beauty* 241
Sarah Kirsch (1935), *Dandelions for Chains* 241

AUSTRIA
Ingeborg Bachmann (1926–1973),   *The Respite* 242/
    from *Songs in Flight* 243

HOLLAND
Judith Herzberg (contemporary),   *Vocation* 244/ *On
    the Death of Sylvia Plath* 245

DENMARK
Tove Ditlevsen (1918–1976),   *Self Portrait 4* 246

FINLAND
Eeva-Liisa Manner (1921),   *The Lunar Games* 247
Edith Södergran (1892–1923, Swedish),   *We
    Women* 248/ *Violet Twilights* 248/ *Pain* 249

SWEDEN
Karin Boye (1900–1941),   *A Sword* 250
Sonja Åkesson (1926–1977),   *Evening Walk* 251/
    Ears 252

GREECE
Eleni Vakalo (1921),   *But there was/once/a time* 254
Katerina Anghelaki-Rooke (1939),   *The Body Is the
    Victory and the Defeat of Dreams* 255

ITALY
Margherita Guidacci (1921),   *At Night* 256
Gina Labriola (contemporary),   *Orgy (that is, vegetable
    market, at Sarno)* 257

PORTUGAL
Sophia de Mello Breyner Andresen (1919),   *The
    Small Square* 258/ *The Young Girl and the
    Beach* 259

SPAIN
Gloria Fuertes (1920),   *I Write Poems* 259/ *We're
    OK* 260/ *Love Which Frees* 260
Maria Beneyto (1925),   *Nocturne in the Women's
    Prison* 261

FRANCE
Joyce Mansour (1928),   *Yesterday evening I saw your
    corpse* 262/ *North Express* 263
Lucienne Desnoues (1921),   *First Things* 263

IRELAND
Eilean ni Chuilleanain (1942), *Swineherd* 265/
    Wash 265

SCOTLAND
Helen Adam (1909), *I Love My Love* 266

WALES
Brenda Chamberlain (1912), *Lament* 269

ENGLAND
Ruth Pitter (1897), *The Lost Tribe* 270

Africa   271

Introduction 271

ANCIENT EGYPT
Hatshepsut (fl. 1503–1482 B.C.), from the *Obelisk In-
    scriptions* 277

EAST AFRICA
Mwana Kupona Msham (c. 1810–1860), from *Poem
    to Her Daughter* 278

MOROCCO
Mririda n'Ait Attik (fl. 1940–1945), *Azouou* 279/
    Mririda 280

ALGERIA
Anna Gréki (1931–1967), *Before Your Waking* 281/
    The future is for tomorrow 282
Leila Djabali (1933), *For My Torturer, Lieutenant D—*
    283

SÃO TOMÉ
Manuela Margarido (1926), *You Who Occupy Our
    Land* 284
Alda do Espírito Santo (1926), *Where Are the Men
    Seized in This Wind of Madness?* 284

MOZAMBIQUE
Noémia da Sousa (1927), *Appeal* 286

NIGERIA
Dorothy S. Obi (contemporary), *Winds of Africa* 288
Minji Karibo (contemporary), *Superstition* 288

KENYA
Stella Ngatho (1953),   *Footpath* 289

LESOTHO
Lindiwe Mabuza (contemporary),   *Summer 1970* 290

SOUTH AFRICA
Ingrid Jonker (1933–1965),   *When You Laugh* 292/
    Don't Sleep 292/ *I Drift in the Wind* 292

KENYA
Marjorie Oludhe Macgoye (contemporary),   *For
    Miriam* 293

GHANA
Ama Ata Aidoo (1942),   *Cornfields in
    Accra* 295

Latin America   299

Introduction 299

MEXICO
Juana de Asbaje (1651–1695),   *Stay, shade of my shy
    treasure* 304/ *Green enravishment of human
    life* 304

CUBA
Gertrudis Gómez de Avellaneda (1814–1873),   *On
    Leaving Cuba, Her Native Land* 305

URUGUAY
Delmira Augustini (1886–1914),   *Vision* 305
Juana de Ibarbourou (1897–1979),   *Life-Hook* 307
Amanda Berenguer (contemporary),   *Housework* 308

ARGENTINA
Alfonsina Storni (1892–1938),   *Ancestral Weight* 308/
    They've Come 309/ *Pain* 309
Olga Orozco (contemporary),   *Sphinxes inclined
    to be* 310

BRAZIL
Cecilia Meireles (1901–1964),   *Song* 312
Renata Pallottini (contemporary),   *Message* 313

CHILE
Gabriela Mistral (1889–1957),   *Bread* 314

Teresa de Jesús (contemporary), *All of a Sud-den* 316/ *"They go by, go by, love, the days and the hours"* 317

PERU
Magda Portal (contemporary), *Woman* 318
Blanca Varela (contemporary), *The Captain* 319

NICARAGUA
Magdalena de Rodriguez (contemporary), *June 10* 320

MEXICO
Rosario Castellanos (1925), *Useless Day* 321/ *Foreign Woman* 321
Lucha Corpi (1945), *Dark Romance* 324

CUBA
Nancy Morejón (1944), *The Reason for Poetry* 325

North America   327

Introduction

CULTURAL INFLUENCES: EURO-AMERICAN 327
CULTURAL INFLUENCES: AFRO-AMERICAN 334
CULTURAL INFLUENCES: ASIAN/PACIFIC
    AMERICAN 338
CULTURAL INFLUENCES: CHICANA 342

EURO-AMERICAN: CANADA 347
Anne Hébert (1916, French), *The Wooden Chamber* 347
Marya Fiamengo (contemporary, English), *In Praise of Old Women* 348
Margaret Atwood (1939, English), *At first I was given centuries* 350

EURO-AMERICAN: UNITED STATES
Anne Bradstreet (1612–1672), *Before the Birth of One of Her Children* 352/ from *Contemplations* 352
Emily Dickinson (1830–1886), *I'm ceded—I've stopped being Theirs* 353 *My life had stood—a Loaded Gun—* 354 *The first Day's Night had come* 355/ *The Spider holds a Silver Ball* 355
H. D. (1886–1961), *The Mysteries Remain* 356

Marianne Moore (1887–1972), *The Mind is an Enchanting Thing* 356

Edna St. Vincent Millay (1892–1950), *Conscientious Objector* 358

Kadia Molodowsky (1894), *Song of the Sabbath* 358/ *God of Mercy* 359

Louise Bogan (1897–1970), *Roman Fountain* 361

Muriel Rukeyser (1913–1980), *The Question* 361

Denise Levertov (1923), *Woman Alone* 362

Anne Sexton (1928–1974), *Her Kind* 363

Adrienne Rich (1929), *Translations* 364

Sylvia Plath (1932–1963), *The Moon and the Yew Tree* 365/ *Mushrooms* 366

Marge Piercy (1936), *The Total Influence or Outcome of the Matter: THE SUN* 367

Judy Grahn (1940), from *The Common Woman: Carol, in the park, chewing on straws* 369

Susan Griffin (1943), *Song My* 370

Linda Gregg (contemporary), *Lilith* 371

AFRO AMERICAN

Phillis Wheatley (c. 1753–1784), *To the Right Honourable William, Earl of Dartmouth* 373

Frances Harper (1825–1911), *Deliverance* 373

Alice Dunbar Nelson (1875–1935), *I Sit and Sew* 374

Margaret Walker (1915), *Childhood* 375

Alice Walker (1944), *Women* 376

June Jordan (1936), *Unemployment/Monologue* 376

Gwendolyn Brooks (1915), *When You Have Forgotten Sunday: The Love Story* 377

Sonia Sanchez (1935), *Present* 379

Nikki Giovanni (1943), *They Clapped* 380

Audre Lorde (1934), *Between Ourselves* 382

Ntozake Shange (1948), *somebody almost walked off wid alla my stuff* 383

ASIAN/PACIFIC AMERICAN

Laureen Mar (1953), *My Mother, Who Came from China, Where She Never Saw Snow* 385

Nellie Wong (1934), *How a Girl Got Her Chinese Name* 386

Jessica Hagedorn (1949), *Listen* 388

Mitsuye Yamada (1923), from *Camp Notes: On the bus* 389/ *In the outhouse* 389

Jonny Kyoko Sullivan (contemporary), *Sagimusume:*
   The White Heron Maiden 390
Janice Mirikitani (contemporary), *Sing with Your*
   Body 391
Mei-Mei Berssenbrugge (1947), *Spring Street*
   Bar 392
Diana Chang (contemporary), *Cannibalism* 393

CHICANA
Teresa Palma Acosta (contemporary), *My Mother*
   Pieced Quilts 393
Ana Castillo (1953), *Napa, California* 395
Alma Villanueva (1944), *I was always fascinated* 396
Lorna Dee Cervantes (1954), *Poem for the Young*
   White Man Who Asked Me How I, an Intelligent,
   Well-Read Person, Could Believe in the War Between
   Races 397/ *The Woman in My Notebook* 399

Native American   401

Introduction 401

Tekahionwake (1869–1913, Mohawk), *The Cattle*
   Thief 401
Macuilxochitl (1435–late 15th century, Aztec), *Battle*
   Song 414
Maria Sabina (1894, Mazatec), *Shaman* 415
Kibkarjuk (fl. c. 1920, Caribou Eskimo), *Song of the*
   Rejected Woman 416
Akjartoq (fl. c. 1920, Caribou Eskimo), *An Old Wo-*
   man's Song 417
Uvavnuk (fl. c. 1920, Iglulik Eskimo), *A Woman*
   Shaman's Song 418
Jane Green (fl. c. 1940, Ojibwe), *Songs of Di-*
   vorce 418
Roberta Hill (1947, Oneida), *Leap in the Dark* 419
Leslie Marmon Silko (1948, Laguna Pueblo), *Where*
   Mountain Lion Lay Down with Deer 422
Wendy Rose (1948, Hopi), *I Expected My Skin and*
   My Blood to Ripen 423
Marnie Walsh (contemporary, Lakota
   Sioux), *Thomas Iron-Eyes* 424
Dolly Bird (1950), *Can I Say* 426
Paula Gunn Allen (1939, Laguna Pueblo), *Catching*
   One Clear Thought Alive 428

Anna Lee Walters (1946, Pawnee-Otoe), *I Have Bowed Before the Sun* 429

A NOTE ON NAMES 430

INDEX OF AUTHORS 431

INDEX OF TRANSLATORS 436

INDEX OF TITLES AND FIRST LINES 438

General Introduction

WHEN WE TALK WITH COLLEAGUES about what we have been doing for the last few years, collecting poetry by women for an anthology, they say, "How interesting. But why an anthology of women poets? Do you feel there's a need for that? After all, truly great poets always become recognized in time. Look at Sappho, Emily Dickinson, Anna Akhmatova. They're in all the anthologies."

The assumption here is that if there had been other great women poets, they of course would have been recognized as well. This attitude rests on the further assumption that the literary community is exempt from the codes and social roles that govern behavior and limit opportunity in any normal human society. "In the literary community, the best always rise to the top, regardless of circumstances, like cream on fresh milk." But we all know better. We all know that literature does not exist in a social vacuum, that throughout history few but the well-to-do, the elite, mostly male, ever set pen to paper. Slaves have left no written testimonies of their experience. Women in Classical Greece were illiterate. It's no surprise that the "cradle of Western Civilization" did not include a single woman writer.

The fact is that there can be no written literature without literacy and a minimum of leisure and wealth. And women have only rarely and exceptionally been able to read and write or been economically independent. Our book is a record of these exceptions: those few women who had a father rich enough to hire a tutor and enlightened enough to encourage his daughter to study—the princesses and aristocrats; those who entered convents and—if they were lucky—were allowed to pursue a literary activity; those who happpened to live in one of those rare moments in history when it was acceptable for women to write poetry; those who had the supreme good fortune to possess—besides education, economic security, and leisure—access to a literary community and the stimulating company of the best minds of the time.

When have women created poetry? Generally speaking, in oral cultures, when poetry is communal and confers no special prestige on the individual, there are many women poets as well as men. Although in some cultures—American Indian, Eskimo—the women poet may be named, this poetry is most often anonymous; and women's poetry tends to remain anonymous long after men have taken to putting their names to their compositions. In pre-literate Finland, according to Jaakko Ahokas, epic poetry was re-cited and probably composed by men, while lyric poetry was com-posed and sung by women. The recital would begin with a formulaic statement that differed according to whether the per-former was a man or woman: a man would say he was going to "harness the horse of song to the carriage or sleigh of words"; a woman would say she was about to "spin the thread of verse, to weave the fabric of poems."

Much of the anonymous poetry from the European Middle Ages is women's poetry. Women used to sing while they worked—while they were washing, spinning, weaving—but most of the songs they composed and sang are lost; so are the lullabies and nursery rhymes they created for their children. They were seldom re-corded but passed on from mother to daughter, from one genera-tion to the next. There is a rich body of pre-Islamic Arab poetry extant only because seventh-century religious scholars, who had little or no interest in poetry but a strong concern that the Qoran be read accurately, went around the tribes recording any evidence they could find of the language of the generation of Mohammad. Indeed, what oral poetry has survived is the result of accident and chance encounters: Frances Densmore meeting the Chippewa poet Jane Green; Knud Rasmussen's transcriptions of the poetry of the Canadian and Greenland Eskimos; Mririda's songs preserved by the French officer of the Foreign Legion René Euloge. Much oral poetry, moreover, is secret and sacred, hidden even from other members of the society, like the songs from the initiation rites of young girls in some African tribes.

In some oral cultures women performed a function that was prestigious and central. In early Hebrew and pre-Islamic Arab societies, there were women leaders who were at the same time prophets, singers, seers. Deborah, one of the judges of Israel, is said to have sung her song in the midst of a battle to raise the courage and spirit of her people.

There were other cultures in which women composed poetry for religious festivals or other communal celebrations, especially mar-riages and funerals. Such poetry, linked to a particular social ac-tivity, appears within carefully circumscribed limits and provides only marginal roles for women poets. Yet the existence of such roles may create a framework for training in writing poetry and an intense poetic activity. This seems to have happened on Lesbos, since much of Sappho's poetry, though by no means all, was originally composed to order for local marriage ceremonies.

There are other instances in which the marginality of women and of the literary forms in which they worked had a significant effect. In Japan in the Heian period (700–1200) the established literature was written in Chinese. At the beginning of this period the development of a syllabary made writing in Japanese possible. It was used largely by court women in diaries and love letters in poetic form. So while men were writing poetry that was considered "serious" in Chinese, women used Japanese, the vernacular, for subjects thought trivial and non-literary. Nevertheless, this "marginal" activity developed new forms such as the *haiku* and the *tanka*, as well as the novel (Lady Murasaki's *Tale of the Genji*). Japanese literature for the first five hundred years was thus shaped by women, who created the themes, forms, and moods which were later to define the Japanese literary tradition. Around 1200, when this Japanese literature had replaced Chinese as the established culture, women writers had all but disappeared from the major anthologies. Indeed, a literary tradition invented by women was perpetuated by men.

There existed a parallel situation in the Jewish tradition. While men retained a monopoly on Hebrew, the official and sacred language, there existed another, secular language spoken by all: Yiddish. It was to the Jewish women that the early printed works in Yiddish were directed, and Jewish women participated in the literature in Yiddish from its inception at the end of the nineteenth century. Women never became as prominent in Yiddish literature as they had been in the Japanese literature, but there have been some outstanding Yiddish women poets, particularly here in the United States.

A more obvious example of marginality can be found in the emergence of the novel in late eighteenth- and early nineteenth-century England. The prestigious genre of the time was poetry, an almost totally male domain. Novels were a popular form, not regarded as serious literature; novel writing was something a woman could do if she needed to make a living or occupy her time. It was precisely when novel writing was looked upon as insignificant and nobody was paying much attention to it that women had a shaping influence on the genre and produced some of its greatest classics.

As to the poetry of the time, prejudice and fixed notions as to what constituted "true womanhood" determined what women wrote and how their work was received. To be published in serious journals one had to write like a man, which invariably laid one open to the charge of being "unwomanly." Many women wrote and published poetry in ladies' magazines, work that was full of conventional sentiment and reflected a cliché image of the "true woman"—all the many poems about "babies and roses." This poetry, modeled on the lives women were expected to live, is interesting only as an example of thoroughgoing alienation. If the term "poetess" has fallen into disrepute, it is because of these poems; these women played their role so well that their work was seen as proof of women's inability to write serious literature.

The strong independent poetry in that period was written in isolation. The situation of Emily Dickinson is instructive. Her life was a series of strategies intended to keep the world at bay: spinsterhood, social life reduced to a minimum, contacts with the literary community narrowed to a thread. She knew she had to protect her genius from the contamination of alienation, from what others thought a woman poet could say and the proper way for her to say it.

That isolation was necessary to the development of a woman poet is also borne out by the life of the Swedish poet Edith Södergran. She lived with her mother in a remote part of Finland and communicated with only two literary friends through letters. The poetry she published in her lifetime was ridiculed. She responded to the storm of protest and indignation with which one of her publications was received by writing, "It does not befit me to make myself appear less than what I am." Once she had died, barely thirty years old, she was discovered to have been the most innovative poet of her generation.

The fact that Dickinson and Södergran, the two major poets in their respective cultures, emerged out of such extreme isolation points to a correlation between the significant participation of a woman poet in a culture and her marginal place in the society. This is not all that surprising if we consider that official poetry of the kind that confers prestige, membership in honorary societies, royal patronage and—when the poet dies—a state funeral, has always been the province of men. A female national poet crowned with laurels is unimaginable. Indeed, the concept of the national poet, which arose in Europe in the seventeenth century as the monarchies were consolidating their power, was exclusively associated with men. When the function of the poet was to lend prestige to newly established institutions, to strengthen the royal power, or give dignity and validity to an emerging sense of nationhood, poetry became prestigious. By the same token women vanished from the Parnassus in every capacity but that of mistress or Muse.

One could argue that women were always free to write poetry for posterity without approval or fame. But what was possible for one or two exceptional women was not possible for the whole sex: the suffering, the isolation involved could be endured only by a truly exceptional individual. Moreover, much talent would be wasted in the struggle to overcome formidable obstacles. For in denying women access to schools and universities, to the intellectual and literary community—so crucial in the shaping of literary talent— and to journals and publications, men were in fact protecting their privilege, not only in the present but for the future as well. It is obvious that as long as men controlled the institutions that determine preservation and transmission of literature—criticism, anthologies, literary histories—there was little chance that the work of women would ever reach posterity. This was especially so since these restrictions were accompanied by a value system that rationalized personal interest into dogma; women were assigned qualities the culture considered inferior and the area of female experience was looked upon as trivial and unworthy of literary expression. "Women's lives bore men," Louise Bernikow tells us, and they do indeed.

Even today, when women go to college in great numbers, what passes for literature most of the time is written from the exclusive unchallenged male perspective, in which woman is the quintessential "other," defined not in relation to her subjective experience of herself, but in relation to a man. How is a woman to read, for example "To His Coy Mistress"? Should she identify with the man? Or with the objectified woman? The problem, however, is not the existence of such poems, but the image of woman they perpetuate and the frequency and insistence with which the image appears uncontested in literature. Women are, Elaine Showalter notes, "estranged from their own experience and unable to perceive its shape and authenticity, in part because they do not see it mirrored and given resonance in literature. They are expected to identify with masculine experience, which is presented as the human one, and have no faith in the validity of their own perceptions and experience." If the woman wants to become a writer this lack of self-confidence is a major liability. Tillie Olsen asks us to consider "how much it takes to become a writer . . . how much conviction as to the importance of what one has to say, one's right to say it. And the will, the measureless store of belief in oneself to be able to come to, cleave to, find the form for one's own life comprehension. Difficult for any male not born into a class that breeds such confidence. Almost impossible for a girl, a woman."

The image of woman as "other" also informs much of the literary criticism of the well-known women poets. It underlies the *cherchez l'homme* school of inquiry, in which serious attention to the woman poet's work is replaced by speculations about the man in her life. The formidable courage and strength of Emily Dickinson, who in order to write chose to live as a recluse, is transformed in the hands of her critics into lack and failure; volumes have been written searching for the man who might have enabled her to "fulfill her female destiny."

It is this trivialization of women's experience, this systematic muffling of the female voice, that makes the need for a rewriting of literary history from a feminist perspective so urgent. There is a pressing need for models, for examples of visions of the world seen through the eyes of women. This is important, as Showalter says, because experience must be mirrored in literature in order to be perceived. We may appreciate poetry of all kinds, but women's poetry sometimes stirs a unique response, for it confirms and validates our experience. It happens that we say, "This is my life. This is an experience or a perception I did not dare trust, since no one else had seen it this way." The poems by women often give us this sense of recognition, of coming home, of coming back to ourselves.

This poetry has of course always been with us, but it has been tucked away in obscure corners of the library, absent from the academic canon, and for the most part unknown to the present generation of women poets. The time has come for a fresh look at women's poetry as a global, historical phenomenon. For what has happened in the late 1960s and the 1970s is quite unique: not only have women emerged as a major shaping force in contemporary poetry, but feminism has prompted a keen interest in women's history and the feminist past. That for most of us the discovery of this past came as a surprise, that we had been ignorant of so much of the feminism of the 1930s, of the interaction of feminism with liberal, utopian, and socialist ideas throughout the nineteenth century, of how feminism and socialism combined to create a groundswell of poetic activity in Russia at the time of the Russian Revolution, is living proof of how easily a social group can become estranged from its own history. To keep records of the past and to disseminate these records is one of the most important tasks of feminists. For if we women are unable to remember our past and unwilling to pass on what we know, nobody else will do it for us and new generations of women will have to begin from the beginning. What other women scholars have done in the field of English literature with the publication of many outstanding anthologies (*The Women Poets in English, The World Split Open, Salt and Bitter and Good*), in literary scholarship (*Shakespeare's Sisters, Signs*) and in history (*Becoming Visible, The Underside of History*) we have attempted to do here for poetry from a comparative perspective. Reading the work of women from cultures other than our own is a natural way of broadening our understanding of poetry and of our own situation.

And the interaction goes both ways. Consider how in many cultures, in the past fifty years, contact with the literature of Europe has broken the stranglehold of a long and rigidly enforced poetic tradition. In Japan, at the turn of the century, Yosano Akiko expanded the poetic forms of her culture through her awareness of modern poetry in the West. She is acknowledged as one of the creators of modern Japanese poetry. Similarly Nazik al-Mala'ika is recognized as having led the way in creating the Arab "free verse" movement—the first real challenge in centuries to the forms of Arab classical poetry. Forugh Farrokhzad played a comparable role in Iran, opening poetry up to the language and rhythms and experience of daily life. Influence from the outside coincided with the emergence of women in central positions on the literary scene in Japan, in Iran, in the Arab world, places where the female voice had been silent for centuries.

Among women in the U.S., an enormous amount of talent and creativity has gone into the field of poetry. There is a much more receptive audience now than, say, twenty years ago. But even now, nothing has been definitively achieved, every position must be reconquered again and again. For the pressures of internalized values and role models from within and social pressures from without, particularly in the 1980s, still make it extremely difficult for a woman to write in her own voice, unhampered, to have confidence in the validity of her own experience.

This is all the more so for the poets in the final sections of the book. For Black, Native American, Chicana, Asian American women, the difficulties are compounded: they are invisible both as women and as members of a minority culture. There is a double bind operating. These poets want and deserve to be recognized simply as "poets." But there are serious obstacles to their breaking into the mainstream one by one by virtue of individual talent alone. For one thing, as long as editors of literary magazines and teachers of writing workshops operate on the assumption that a certain poetry is the norm, any poet speaking from an experience and in a voice outside this norm will have a hard time being heard at all. There is a strong pressure on the poet to self-censure, to modify her voice in order to gain access to the established literary community. In order for the individual's true voice to be heard, she needs to be read, at least initially, within the context of her distinctive culture.

Similarly, women poets on the whole need to be placed in the context of a large body of poetry by women—at least until their work has become established in the literary community and readers have developed an ear for the specificity and diversity of the voices of women in poetry. Diversity is especially important here, for as Ellen Moers once wrote, "literary women have worked in every available form and style, have exhibited every mood and character, have been radical and conservative, narrow and wide-ranging, tragic and comic in their writings. There is no point saying what women cannot do in literature, for history shows they have done it all."

It is a commonplace that no work arises out of itself, out of the author's solitary genius and imagination. The first work of a poet is often an imitation of some predecessor's, and throughout their active lives poets hold an unending dialogue with their tradition. Women poets are often unaware of other women poets, especially those outside their own culture and their own time. In order for contemporary women poets to be able to respond to other women—both to react against and to identify with them—a strong, multivocal, multiform body of poetry must be made available. There is a pressing need for a sense of ancestors that could lay the groundwork for an authentic female poetic tradition. Our book attempts to answer this need. The poems here are of couse only an intimation of the wealth to be explored, as much as could be encompassed within a single volume, yet enough to establish beyond doubt the intensity, originality and diversity of poetry by women.

China

WRITING POETRY WAS AN ESSENTIAL PART of the education and social life of any educated man in ancient China, but it was not so for a woman. Most of the poems of those women who did write were not handed down to posterity. Poetry by women, especially love poetry, was often shown only to their intimates and never published, because it could lead to gossip that the author was an unfaithful wife. Not until the Ch'ing Dynasty (1644–1911) with the promotion of several leading gentlemen scholars did writing poetry become fashionable for ladies of the scholar gentry class. Also, the comparative importance of upper-class women under the Ch'ing Dynasty derived in part from influence of the Manchus, among whom women were more free than under the Confucian system.

According to the *Li Chi*[1] (The Book of Rites), supposedly edited by Confucius, a girl of seven was to be separated from men except her closest relatives, and at ten years confined to the women's quarters. The daughters of farmers, artisans, and merchants had more freedom of movement than upper-class women and helped their parents or husbands in the fields and shops. The daughters of imperial bureaucrats could travel only in closely-curtained sedan-chairs or carts on visits to relatives or temples, and their experience of nature was limited to the gardens of the women's quarters, the interior section in a huge compound where the members of a clan lived together.

Since marriages were prearranged, the couple seldom saw each other until their wedding. If the bridegroom did not like his bride, he could later take concubines. But the bride was permanently and exclusively tied to the caprice of her husband. Romantic love between husband and wife occurred rarely. Many husbands sought romantic relations with professional courtesans while their wives lived in loneliness and depression. As a result the woman gave most of her affection to her sons. Sometimes she turned into a fiercely jealous wife.[2] A couple like Li Ch'ing-chao and Chao Ming-ch'eng, who had mutual respect and understanding for each other's talents and who collaborated in scholarly work, was very uncommon. Women were not only intellectually and emotionally deprived, but often physically isolated as well, and might not see their husbands for long periods—often years. A husband might leave his wife behind at home to join the army, to take examinations at the capital, go on business trips, travel with friends to scenic spots, or take up a post in another province, accompanied by a concubine. Songs of farewell and loneliness occupy a great part of women's poetry. This theme became so popular that famous male poets, including Li Po and Su Tung-p'o, wrote poems impersonating the role of the disconsolate wife.

In the Imperial Chinese social system only male descendants could perform the ceremony of ancestor worship. Although they bore heirs, women were secondary in the continuity of the family. A woman belonged to the family of her husband, not to her parents. A daughter had to be provided with food, clothing, a dowry, and a husband. In poor families female infanticide was practiced at least as early as the Han Dynasty (206 B.C.–219 A.D.).[3] The laws of the T'ang Dynasty (618–907) reflect the inferior status of wives and concubines:

> If a husband assaults and injures his wife, his punishment will be two grades lighter than the normal punishment meted out for such a crime. . . . If a husband assaults and badly injures his concubine, his punishment will be two grades lighter than the punishment for injuring his wife. . . . If a wife assaults her husband she will perform slave labor for one year. . . . If the husband is seriously injured, her sentence will be three grades heavier than the punishment for heavy assault and injury.[4]

With few exceptions over two thousand years, women held no official posts, other than appointed attendants in the palace, nor were they allowed to take the examinations for entrance into the imperial bureaucracy. Other than wife, concubine, or maid, a woman could be a Buddhist nun, a Taoist priestess, a courtesan, prostitute, matchmaker, herbalist or midwife. Literacy was restricted to ladies of the elite circle, nuns, priestesses, and courtesans.

Women rarely inherited family property. According to the laws of the Ch'ing Dynasty:

The family property . . . shall be equally divided among the sons, whether they were born to wives, concubines, or maids. The illegitimate son shall have half as much as a legitimate son . . . If the family has no sons, and no adopted son selected from its clan, to inherit the property, daughters may inherit . . . [5]

The eldest son's wife who had borne a male child became matriarch after her mother-in-law's death, and held absolute authority in domestic affairs. In the imperial family, if the Empress was an ambitious woman, she might become *de facto* ruler. But Wu Tse-t'ien (seventh century) was the only empress in Chinese history to rule in her own right, after she had seized power from her husband and sons. As for the concubine, her lot was very insecure, unless she gained her master's lifelong attention, or her own son established himself firmly in the society. Often she was persecuted harshly by the jealous chief wife or mother-in-law.

Young girls in the families of wealthier officials were sometimes allowed to study with boys in the school of their clan, or under private tutors. Daughters of great scholars or historians often became renowned scholars themselves, as did Ts'ai Yen and Li Ch'ing-chao; but usually they were only educated so that they could study books on women's conduct. Books like *Lieh Nü Chuan (Biographies of Women)*, first century A.D., and *Kui Fan (Standards in the Women's Quarters)*, sixteenth century A.D., taught women to be passive and yielding toward their husbands and parents-in-law, and modest, moderate, and plain in thought, speech, and appearance. For example, in *Precepts for Women*, written by Pan Chao, a woman historian in the Han Dynasty, the model woman she created is in fact insipid, submissive, and uninteresting:

> The virtues of women are not brilliant talent, nor distinction and elegance. The virtues of women are reserve, quiet, chastity, orderliness, governing herself to maintain a sense of shame, and conducting herself according to the rules of Confucian etiquette. . . . The appearance of woman does not depend on fairness of face. The principles for a woman's appearance are to wash away dirt, wear clean and new clothing and ornaments, bathe often, and keep her body clean.[6]

The imperial palaces throughout the centuries included lower-ranking women, usually numbered in the thousands, who came from families of commoners, or were forfeited female relatives of officials convicted of crimes. Some of these women, and those selected from noble families as candidates to become imperial consorts, were well educated; they sometimes were appointed by the emperors as tutors to other palace women, or as monitors of the harem. The poetry of the Palace generally had two subjects— praise of the Emperor and of palace life, and loneliness. According to the *Chou Li (the Rites of the Kingdom of Chou)*, an emperor should have one empress and 126 concubines.[7] In reality the number of his formal consorts varied from several to more than one hundred, and the remaining palace attendants, musicians and dancers were also at his disposal. As long as they lived in the palace, many for their entire lives, the only man they were allowed to see except the eunuchs and little boys was the Emperor. Since one man cannot satisfy several hundred women, these women express their sexual deprivation in poems of forlorn hope.

Because of these conditions, which prevailed through two thousand years, women poets are very few and their surviving poems even fewer. However, those that have survived stand out in the history of Chinese literature as great works of refinement and exquisite beauty. In the anthology *Three Hundred Poems* of the T'ang Dynasty,[8] there is only one poem written by a woman. In *Ch'uan T'ang Shih (A Complete Collection of Shih Poetry of the T'ang Dynasty)* among the 2,200 authors, there are only around 190 women poets.

A class of cultivated courtesans—girls sold for reasons of poverty, or who came from disgraced official households, or who had been kidnapped—had flourished at least since the Six Dynasties (299–588). They were owned by a brothel, and were freer than housewives and concubines. They could write love lyrics without being condemned for spoiling the family reputation. The more talented they were as poets, the more successful they were with their customers. In the Six Dynasties, China came to have something resembling an aristocracy, and the wealthier members kept in their mansions bands of literate women musicians and dancers called *chia chi*, "house courtesans," who entertained at banquets.

In the T'ang Dynasty another class of cultivated courtesans flourished, called *kuan chi*, "official courtesans," because they were registered with the government and were often summoned to entertain at official banquets. They came from the most expensive brothels in major cities. In the capital prosperous courtesans' houses were built near to the hall for imperial examinations, and when the winners were announced, the courtesans traditionally held a celebration. Leading courtiers and officials frequented these houses. When the court held great banquets, the most accomplished among these women would be summoned. Familiar with the art of poetry, the most talented would be treated as equals and join in the poetry discussions and contests that were the highlights of the banquet. Many were ransomed by wealthy, powerful men and became their concubines, among them the poetess K'uan P'an-p'an. Many men wrote of the beauty and talent of these courtesan poets, and of their love for them.

In the T'ang Dynasty, Taoist priestesses also became a special social class and enjoyed even more freedom than courtesans, for the priestess was no one's property. She could move, travel, and associate freely. Unlike a Buddhist nun, she was not prohibited from having intimate relations with men. During this period many princesses and wealthy women became priestesses and their temples became the centers of social gatherings for the scholar gentry, and they took lovers at will. The poets Yü Hsüan-chi and Li Yeh were among the most influential priestesses of their time.

In the Ch'ing (Manchu) Dynasty the ability of upper-class women to write poetry was esteemed enough to be accepted as part of a lady's dowry. A scholar-poet-official often preferred to marry an educated woman with whom he could have poetry contests, discuss the Confucian classics and the great poets. But in the same period the romantic notion that talented women were always ill-fated was a common one.[9] Fortunately, women poets flourished in the Ch'ing Dynasty, although none among them can be compared to the great poets of the Sung Dynasty (960–1279), Li Ch'ing-chao and Chu She-chen.

Not until the turn of the twentieth century did Chinese women start to move away from the strict moral code of the Confucian system. They began to enjoy more education, social freedom, and financial status, and also were no longer forced to bind their feet in order to be married into decent families. The long period of nightmare for Chinese women had finally passed into history, but the achievements of those few women poets glow like pearls in the depths of the dark sea.

LING CHUNG

Notes and References

[1] *Li Chi* (Taipei: 1965), *chüan* 8, chapter 12, *"nei tse,"* "regulations of the interior."

[2] According to another ancient book of rites, *I Li* (Taipei: 1965), in chapter

"*sang fu,*" a wife's jealousy was one of the seven reasons for divorce. Many stories later tell how famous officials suffered from jealous wives because their wives refused to let them take concubines.

[3]Ch'en Tung-yüan, *Chung Kuo Fu Nü Sheng Huo Shih* (a history of the lives of Chinese women) (Taipei, 1965), p. 61.

[4]*T'ang Lü Shu I* (the laws of T'ang with commentaries) annotated by Ch'ang-sun Wu-chi, (Taipei: 1956), volume III, p. 98, chüan 22, items 9 and 10. According to this book the normal punishment for injuring another person with objects other than hands and feet and causing bleeding, is sixty lashes by whip or stick. Therefore if a husband injures his wife this way, he will receive from the court a sentence of forty lashes instead of sixty, and if he inflicts bleeding wounds upon a concubine, he will receive only twenty lashes.

[5]*Ta ch'ing Lü Li Hui T'ung Hsin Tsuan* compiled by Yao Yü-chiang (a new comprehensive edition of the laws and cases of the Ch'ing Dynasty) (Taipei: Hsien, 1964), volume II, p. 44, *chüan* 7, "*hu lü,*" "*hu i,*" item 14. In most cases if a family did not have male children, a boy would be selected from the members of the clan as the adopted son of the family. Daughters rarely had any chance to inherit family property, except jewelry and private savings given by their mothers.

[6]Translated from the text quoted in Ch'en Tung-yüan, *Chung Kuo Fu Nü Sheng Huo Shih,* pp. 52–53. For an abreviated English translation of *Nü Chieh* (Precepts for women) by Pan Chao, see Florence Ayscough's *Chinese Women: Yesterday and Today* (Boston: Houghton Mifflin 1936).

[7]Ch'en Tung-yüan, pp. 35–56.

[8]The version translated into English by Witter Bynner is entitled *The Jade Mountain,* (New York: Knopf, 1929).

[9]Ch'en Tung-yüan, pp. 191 and 270.

Pan Chao

Needle and Thread

Tempered, annealed, the hard essence of autumn
   metals
finely forged, subtle, yet perdurable and straight,

By nature penetrating deep yet advancing by inches
to span all things yet stitch them up together,

Only needle-and-thread's delicate footsteps
are truly broad-ranging yet without beginning!

"Withdrawing elegantly" to mend a loose thread,
and restore to white silk a lamb's-down purity . . .

How can those who count pennies calculate their worth?
They may carve monuments yet lack all understanding.

Translated from the Chinese by Richard Mather and Rob Swigart

Ts'ai Yen

from Eighteen Verses Sung to
a Tatar Reed Whistle

I

I was born in a time of peace,
But later the mandate of Heaven
Was withdrawn from the Han Dynasty.

Heaven was pitiless.
It sent down confusion and separation.
Earth was pitiless.
It brought me to birth in such a time.
War was everywhere. Every road was dangerous.
Soldiers and civilians everywhere

Fleeing death and suffering.
Smoke and dust clouds obscured the land
Overrun by the ruthless Tatar[1] bands.
Our people lost their will power and integrity.
I can never learn the ways of the barbarians.
I am daily subject to violence and insult.
I sing one stanza to my lute and a Tatar horn.
But no one knows my agony and grief.

II

A Tatar chief forced me to become his wife,
And took me far away to Heaven's edge.
Ten thousand clouds and mountains
Bar my road home,
And whirlwinds of dust and sand
Blow for a thousand miles.
Men here are as savage as giant vipers,
And strut about in armor, snapping their bows.
As I sing the second stanza I almost break the
    lutestrings.
Will broken, heart broken, I sing to myself.

VII

The sun sets. The wind moans.
The noise of the Tatar camp rises all around me.
The sorrow of my heart is beyond expression,
But who could I tell it to anyway?
Far across the desert plains
The beacon fires of the Tatar garrisons
Gleam for ten thousand miles.
It is the custom here to kill the old and weak
And adore the young and vigorous.
They wander seeking new pasture,
And camp for a while behind earth walls.
Cattle and sheep cover the prairies,
Swarming like bees or ants.
When the grass and water are used up,
They mount their horses and drive on their cattle.

---

[1]The Tatars (or Tartars) were a tribe that raided China from the north and west.
Their descendants still live in Mongolia.

The seventh stanza sings of my wandering
How I hate to live this way!

XI

I have no desire to live, but I am afraid of death.
I cannot kill my body, for my heart still has hope
That I can live long enough
To obtain one and only one desire—
That someday I can see again
The mulberry and catalpa trees of home.
If I had consented to death,
My bones would have been buried long ago.
Days and months pile up in the Tatar camp.
My Tatar husband loved me. I bore him two sons.
I reared and nurtured them unashamed,
Sorry only that they grew up in a desert outpost.
The eleventh stanza—sorrow for my sons
At the first notes pierces my heart's core.

XIII

I never believed that in my broken life
The day would come when
Suddenly I could return home.
I embrace and caress my Tatar sons.
Tears wet our clothes.
An envoy from the Han Court
Has come to bring me back,
With four stallions that can run without stopping.
Who can measure the grief of my sons?
They thought I would live and die with them.
Now it is I who must depart.
Sorrow for my boys dims the sun for me.
If we had wings we could fly away together.
I cannot move my feet,
For each step is a step away from them.
My soul is overwhelmed.
As their figures vanish in the distance
Only my love remains.
The thirteenth stanza—
I pick the strings rapidly
But the melody is sad.

No one can know
The sorrow which tears my bowels.

XVII

The seventeenth stanza. My heart aches, my tears fall.
Mountain passes rise before us, the way is hard.
Before I missed my homeland
So much my heart was disordered.
Now I think again and again, over and over,
Of the sons I have lost.
The yellow sagebrush of the border,
The bare branches and dry leaves,
Desert battlefields, white bones
Scarred with swords and arrows,
Wind, frost, piercing cold,
Cold springs and summers
Men and horses hungry and exhausted, worn out—
I will never know them again
Once I have entered Chang An.[2]
I try to strangle my sobs
But my tears stream down my face.

Translated from the Chinese by Kenneth Rexroth and Ling Chung

[2]Chang An was a city in China, capital of the Han Dynasty.

Tzu Yeh

China   3rd–4th centuries

It is night again
I let down my silken hair
Over my shoulders
And open my thighs
Over my lover.
"Tell me, is there any part of me
That is not lovable?"

❖

I had not fastened my sash over my gown,
When you asked me to look out the window.
If my skirt fluttered open,
Blame the Spring wind.

❖

The bare branches tremble
In the sudden breeze.
The twilight deepens.
My lover loves me,
And I am proud of my young beauty.

Translated from the Chinese by Kenneth Rexroth and Ling Chung

Yü Hsüan-chi
China   c. 843–868

Composed on the Theme "Willows by the Riverside"

Kingfisher green lines the deserted shore,
the misty vision stretches to a distant tower.
Their shadows overspread the autumn-clear water
and catkins fall on the angler's head.
Old roots form hollows where fish hide;
limbs reach down to moor the travelers's boat.
Soughing, soughing in the wind and rain of night
they startle dreams and compound the gloom.

Translated from the Chinese by Jan W. Walls

Li Ch'ing-chao
China   1084–1151

Poem to the tune of "Yi chian mei"

The fragrance of the red lotus fades,
    and the bamboo mat is touched by autumn chill.

I loosen my thin robe
and board the orchid boat alone.
Who sends this elegant letter through the clouds?
As the wild geese return in formation,
moonlight fills the western chamber.

Petals are falling, waters flow.
One image of love,
two places of separate sorrow.
There is no way to banish this feeling.
As it leaves the eyebrows,
it enters the heart.

Poem to the tune of "Tsui hua yin"

At dusk heavy clouds grieve the long day;
Bright agate incense fades in the animal-censer.
The festival comes again, ninth day of the ninth
    month.[1]
At midnight the cold seeps through a gauze screen,
Chills my jade pillow.

At the eastern hedge I take wine after twilight;
An obscure fragrance fills my sleeves.
Do not say my heart is unbroken;
As the window screen rolls up in the west wind,
I have grown more frail than a thin yellow
    chrysanthemum.

Translated from the Chinese by Marsha Wagner

[1]On this day it was customary to go to a mountain or high place to look for
travellers coming from afar.

T'ang Wan
China   12th century

To the tune "The Phoenix Hairpin"

The world's love runs thin.
Human love turns evil.
Rain strips, in the yellow twilight,
The flowers from the branches.
The dawn wind will dry my tear stains.
I try to write down the trouble of my heart.
I can only speak obliquely, exhausted.
It is hard, hard.
We are each of us alone.
Today is not yesterday.
My troubled mind sways
Like the rope of a swing.
A horn sounds in the cold depth of the night.
Afraid of people's questions,
I will swallow my tears
And pretend to be happy.
Deceit. Deceit. Deceit.

Translated from the Chinese by Kenneth Rexroth and Ling Chung

Huang O
China.   1498–1569

To the tune "Soaring Clouds"

You held my lotus blossom
In your lips and played with the
Pistil. We took one piece of
Magic rhinoceros horn
And could not sleep all night long.
All night the cock's gorgeous crest
Stood erect. All night the bee
Clung trembling to the flower
Stamens. Oh my sweet perfumed
Jewel! I will allow only

My lord to possess my sacred
Lotus pond, and every night
You can make blossom in me
Flowers of fire.

To the tune "Red Embroidered Shoes"

If you don't know, why pretend?
Maybe you can fool some girls,
But you can't fool Heaven.
I dreamed you'd play with the
Lotus blossom under my green jacket,
Like a eunuch with a courtesan.
But lo and behold
All you can do is mumble.
You've made me all wet and slippery,
But no matter how hard you try
Nothing happens. So stop.
Go and make somebody else
Unsatisfied.

To the tune "The Fall of a Little Wild Goose"

Once upon a time I was
Beautiful and seductive,
Wavering to and fro in
Our orchid scented bedroom.
You and me together tangled
In our incense filled gauze
Bed curtains. I trembled,
Held in your hands. You carried
Me in your heart wherever
You went. Suddenly
A bullet struck down the female
Mandarin duck. The music
Of the jade zither was forgotten.
The phoenixes were driven apart.

I sit alone in a room
Filled with Spring, and you are off,
Making love with someone else,
Happy as two fish in the water.

That insufferable little bitch
With her coy tricks!
She'd better not forget—
This old witch can still
Make a furious scene!

Translated from the Chinese by Kenneth Rexroth and Ling Chung

Wang Wei
China   17th century

Seeking a Mooring

A leaf floats in endless space.
A cold wind tears the clouds.
The water flows westward.
The tide pushes upstream.
Beyond the moonlit reeds,
In village after village, I hear
The sound of fullers' mallets
Beating the wet clothing
In preparation for winter.
Everywhere crickets cry
In the autumn frost.
A traveller's thoughts in the night
Wander in a thousand miles of dreams.
The sound of a bell cannot disperse
The sorrows that come
In the fifth hour of night.
What place will I remember
From all this journey?
Only still bands of desolate mist
And a single fishing boat.

Translated from the Chinese by Kenneth Rexroth and Ling Chung

Sun Yün-fêng
China   1764–1814

On the Road through Chang-Te

On the last year's trip I enjoyed this place.
I am glad to come back here today.
The fish market is deep in blue shadows.
I can see the smoke for tea rising
From the thatched inn.
The sands of the river beaches
Merge with the white moon.
Along the shore the willows
Wait for their Spring green.
Lines of a poem run through my mind.
I order the carriage to stop for a while.

Translated from the Chinese by Kenneth Rexroth and Ling Chung

Wu Tsao
China   19th century

For the Courtesan Ch'ing Lin
To the tune "The Love of the Immortals"

On your slender body
Your jade and coral girdle ornaments chime
Like those of a celestial companion
Come from the Green Jade City of Heaven.
One smile from you when we meet,
And I become speechless and forget every word.
For too long you have gathered flowers,
And leaned against the bamboos,
Your green sleeves growing cold,
In your deserted valley:
I can visualize you all alone,
A girl harboring her cryptic thoughts.

You glow like a perfumed lamp
In the gathering shadows.

We play wine games
And recite each other's poems.
Then you sing "Remembering South of the River"
With its heart breaking verses. Then
We paint each other's beautiful eyebrows.
I want to possess you completely—
Your jade body
And your promised heart.
It is Spring.
Vast mists cover the Five Lakes.
My dear, let me buy a red painted boat
And carry you away.

Translated from the Chinese by Kenneth Rexroth and Ling Chung

In the Home of the Scholar Wu Su-chiang from Hsin-An, I Saw Two Psalteries[1] of the Late Sung General Hsieh Fang-tê[2]

Half of our borders, rivers and mountains were gone,
With their Spring orioles and blossoms.
Your former career was only a painful memory.
You watched the melancholy moon
Over an abandoned temple in the wilderness.
You could no longer see the beacon fires of Sung,
So you lived disguised as a fortune teller,
In a kiosk on a bridge, and no one knew you.
You who had a will of iron,
And held back the billowing flood of the world,
All by yourself in a besieged city.
You chanted Tu Fu's songs of homesickness,[3]
You chose death to preserve your integrity.
At the end of the years of hiding
On these slopes amongst the tea bushes
Haunted by the cuckoos crying as if in pain,
You left behind two psalteries
Of tung wood and these ancient songs,
And went to death, a handful of yellow dust,

[1]Stringed instrument.
[2]Hsieh Fang-tê (thirteenth century) was a general of the Sung Dynasty.
[3]In Tu Fu's poem "Wu Chia Pieh" (Alone without a Home), a man returns to his village after the long war and discovers it has become a ghost town.

But deserving a royal grave.
Now as I play them I can imagine
Dragons dancing in the depths
And the moss on the shore burning red.

Translated from the Chinese by Kenneth Rexroth and Ling Chung

Ping Hsin (Hsieh Wan-ying)
China   1902

from The Stars

34

The builder of continents
Is not the surging billow
But the tiny grains of sand down beneath.

48

Fragile blades of grass,
Be proud!
Only you so impartially adorn the entire world.

from The Spring Waters

25
In shaping the snow into blossoms—
The north wind is tender after all.

105

O, Lord—
If in life eternal
Is allowed only one happiness extreme,
This would be my earnest plea:
"Let me be in my mother's lap,
Let mother be in a tiny boat,
And that boat float on a moonlit sea."

Translated from the Chinese by Kai-yu Hsu

Tan Ying
China 1943

Drinking the Wind

She is a black crow being driven out of sight.
Her furious cry cannot awaken the flowers.
So she holds under her wings the cold currents
Wandering

                      on the edge of waters,
And searching beyond the borders—
There is not a tree, nor a song.
That year,
When Autumn perched on her left shoulder,
Snow and homesickness had already
Fallen on her right shoulder.
She is exiled to this icy horizon,
Searching far ahead and behind,
There is no trace of man.
Only her own wandering footprints on the snow
Stretching away to the deep winding corridor of

                      her mother's eyes.
That year
According to the legend, her footprints were carried by

                    the West Wind
                    to the remote River of
                    Oblivion
And her voice melted away with the deep snow.
Not even one among the sixty-four diagrams of the
    I Ching could

                    burn and show a definite
                    oracle.
For she is a black crow cast away beyond memory.
After pecking and breaking a full glass
Of the wine of reunion,
She flies into the night, and with one draught drinks
All the sighs of a thousand miles.

Translated from the Chinese by Kenneth Rexroth and Ling Chung

Anonymous

People's Republic of China   *c. 1958*

Women Transport Corps

The stars have not yet retired, and the sky is still dark.
From down the road comes the woman transport corps,
Pushing small carts and pulling large carts.
They have a load of laughter for every load of coal.

She pushes her cart, fast as flying,
Crushing the pearly dewdrops on the grass.
That big sister, she has picked a twig of flower,
Wonder to whom she wants to give it.

"Speaking of yesterday's labor hero meeting,
The hero of steel production is named Wang K'uei.
If you, big sister, have him in mind,
I'd be glad to deliver the message, without charge."

She wets her hand with dewdrops and wipes it on her
    friend,
Scolding her: "You and your nasty mouth.
Wait until our steel output has risen,
If you want to marry him, I can be your go-between."

They push their carts, fast as flying,.
With a load of laughter for every load of coal.
With stars on their shoulders and the moon above they
    keep busy running.
One more drop of their sweat, one more drop of molten
    steel.

Translated from the Chinese by Kai-yu Hsu

Japan

POETRY BEGINS IN LIFE AND ITS NECESSITIES, but in order to flourish as a written art it requires leisure, the time to pursue and to perfect. The Heian Period (794–1185 A.D) in Japan provided an abundance of that leisure and the desire to perfect a tradition which is unique in the histories of world literature.

The word *Heian* itself means "peace," "tranquillity." Culture—visual arts, literature, philosophy, music—was concentrated in Kyoto, where an elegant court gathered around the Emperor and his family. Outside of the capital there was little of interest to these perhaps two thousand people; enormous energy was concentrated in just a few square miles, an energy which could be devoted entirely to clothing, poetry, food, incense and intrigue. There were no wars, no invasions from outside this insulated and insular country, no popular uprisings to distract attention from the refinement of the senses.

Intrigue was as much erotic as it was political. Women in this society came in from the provinces to act as ladies-in-waiting to the Empress. These positions required expertise in the arts of refinement, among them poetry, for this was a culture in which much of courtship was carried on through words put down on paper; a spontaneous and elegant poem written in lovely cursive calligraphy, folded inside a beautiful fragment of hand-made paper and delivered with impeccable timing, could make all the difference in the evolution of a love affair. There was in these productions an air of the transitory, the occasional, the spontaneous; but because these poems were such an important part of the communications of courtship and seduction, men and women alike could write many thousands during a lifetime. Like a knowledge of French or a facility on the piano in nineteenth-century England, poetry was one of the accomplishments a woman was expected to have.

At this time the glittering T'ang court in China was viewed as the center of world culture, and Chinese was the established literary language. "Serious poetry," philosophical poetry befitting high rank and high literary aspirations, was written in Chinese. For a long time writing in Chinese was obligatory for the Japanese poet. No Japanese script existed until near the beginning of the Heian era, when Chinese ideographs were adopted for the Japanese language. It provided a peculiar kind of literacy, though, an alien monosyllabic ideography grafted on to the polysyllabic and highly inflected Japanese. Yet once it was adapted into a simplified cursive syllabary to carry the inflections, with the more complex Chinese ideographs for root meanings when desired, Japanese had a flexible and lovely script.

Nevertheless Japanese was, during the entire Heian era, considered unsuited to the lofty thoughts of serious poetry, for which the Chinese language was reserved. Japanese would be used for occasional poems, love verses, the literature of seduction and lament. It was left to women to write in Japanese, in the vernacular, while men reserved the supposedly more difficult Chinese for themselves, unaware that what they were writing was imitation Chinese literature, inferior to the original, and, above all, inferior to what contemporary women were writing in their native tongue. There were other reasons, too, of course. Men were busy with official affairs (not to mention the unofficial ones), which occupied much time; but that is not a unique factor, for early in many cultures the strong distinction between public and private duties is created along sexual lines. Greece, China, even England come to mind. But in time it became apparent that all that once appeared trivial and marginal was in fact the outsanding achievement in Japanese literature, and one of the greatest achievements in all of world literature. Women produced the best, the greatest classics in Japanese: not simply *The Tale of Genji*, Murasaki's *Diary*, the *Pillow Book of Sei Shonagon*, but the poetry of Ono no Komachi, Ise, Otomo no Sakanoe and others. So important were women to the native literature that when men set their hands to writing poetic diaries, as Ki no Tsurayuki did in the *Tosa Diary*, they often wrote under the persona of a woman.

It is clear then that women occupied a strong position in Japan during the first centuries following the development of literacy, so long as the vernacular remained outside the realm of power and prestige. During these first five hundred years they created the themes, forms and moods which shaped subsequent Japanes literary tradition: the *tanka*, with its elegaic tone and characteristic imagery; the diary; and the novel.

Deeply embedded in the poems of this section are feelings of regret about the shortness of life, the fickleness of love, and the ravages of age, which imbue them with a brooding melancholy. They rapidly became conventionalized and traditional, a sorrowful lament, perhaps, for the passing of desire as much as for the torment of it. These elegaic feelings, and a dark mysteriousness, are an essential part of the tradition, with special literary terms and meanings; they are no longer confined to women.

At the end of the Heian era, when political and military upheaval destroyed the leisurely culture in Kyoto, men, and martial virtues, took over the vernacular as well as official culture. Then poetry became something to occupy the rare moments of rest in a soldier's life, or in the lives of hermits, priests, or courtiers confined to the distant court far from important events.

The imitation of Chinese poetry became a secondary occupation even for men; women surrendered their pre-eminence in the vernacular literature, and finally, as in so many other cultures, nearly vanished from the anthologies. The tradition they had done so much to shape was carried on by men.

Not until the beginning of the twentieth century did women reappear as an important force in Japanese literature, despite the existence of one or two significant *haiku* poets, for example Chiyo, in the Tokugawa period. Some modern women poets, like Yosano Akiko,[1] returned to traditional forms, *haiku* and *tanka* (which had fallen into disuse), and made use of traditional imagery, but expanded the range of feeling and experience to include more psychological and emotional complexity. Others, like Shiraishi Kazuko, have absorbed various manifestations of Western culture, from T. S. Eliot, Ezra Pound and other modern poets to jazz rhythms and cabaret songs. The swift industrialization of post-World War II Japan has produced changes in lifestyle and in the conditions of women; these changes have had a profound effect on their poetry.

Women dominated the early years of the literary tradition in Japan not only in numbers, but in formal, aesthetic terms as well—in originality of subject and perception. But this pre-eminence was not confined to Japan. A comparison between Ono no Komachi, who wrote within 150 years of the beginnings of literacy in her country, and the poet Sappho, who lived near the beginnings of written language in Greece, might be illuminating.

Komachi, considered by her peers of both sexes to be one of the greatest poets the country had ever produced, listed as one of the "Six Poetic Geniuses," was an innovator, a poet who discovered new material and new ways to express it. She made the most subtle discoveries in the content of mind and poem, and altered irrevocably the border between the two.

Sappho as well redefined the interface between mind, experience and poem, between inner and outer. Her *phainetai moi kenos isos theoisin,* "Like the very gods in my sight is he . . ." and Komachi's *hito ni awamu,* "No moon, no chance to meet," demonstrate this new awareness of consciousness and technique.

Both poems deal with interiorized erotic feeling, what is most physical and "real" about longing, desire: fever, pain, blood thundering in the ears, shortness of breath. These things are acknowledged to come from inside the body, feeling made manifest. Perhaps the traditional province of women has been what is domestic, interior, private, but in both the cultures before us here these poems reflect a revolution in the perception of emotion and desire.

In Sappho's time emotions were still felt as they were in Homer, as something external and unwilled, a voice, as Julian Jaynes speculates in *The Origin of Consciousness in the Breakdown of the Bicameral Mind,*[2] from the right hemisphere of the brain, an auditory hallucination. In the *Iliad,* for example, when Achilles is angered and prepares to draw his sword against Agamemnon, Athena appears, visible only to him, and counsels restraint and caution—a feeling to counteract the adrenalin of anger and to divert the direction of emotion. And Homer in his formulae and epithets, his regular dactylic hexameter, is sonorous, public, declamatory, narrative, external, hence unselfconscious. His listeners are the crowd, caught in the events of the story, which are the events of the poem.

With Sappho and some of the other lyricists of the seventh and sixth centuries B.C., the personal poem found fertile ground, evident in a rhythmic alteration, more introverted, private, involved, difficult, as in the Alcaic and Sapphic strophe. In this way the poem itself becomes an event rather than a narrative of other events. This is a significant change, this internalization in the intent of poetry.

The alternations of short and long syllables of the Sapphic strophe are more complex than the simple long-short-short of the dactyl. At the same time the feeling goes inward to its source. The lyric is a personal voice. We listen closely to these new quantities, this interplay of sounds, the way in which the /ai/ of *phainetai,* for example, modulates from its repetition into the /oi/ of *moi,* and from there into the long /e/ of *kenos,* the repetitions of the /s/ sound, the /oi/ once more in *theoisin,* and so on; and how all these transmutations of sound are played through the changing long and short syllables of the strophe. These are not merely private effects, this attention to sound and rhythm, they are distinctly intimate;

only a small group gathered close could catch the subtleties, hear the complex patterns, the open and closed vowels, follow the changes in imagery from the visual *phainetai* ("he appears"), to the kinesthetic sensations of "tenuous flame," the experience of "paler I turn than grass is." Even Alcaeus, Sappho's contemporary and fellow poet from Mytilene in Lesbos, whose strophe is as complex as hers, did not understand this inner nature of desire, for to him its suffering is a sickness from the gods, still external though his voice is lyric. Phrases like "underneath my breast all the heart is shaken," "under my skin the tenuous flame suffuses," "my ears are muted in thunder," "paler I turn than grass is," all show a new awareness of the inner torment that is related not to disease or the will of the gods but to the emotions of desire.

It is the same with Komachi. "I wake on fire with longing,/ a running fire in my breast/ that turns my heart to ashes." And we might expect to find, with this inward shift in imagery, the same intensification of rhythmic complexity we see in Sappho, one of the tools needed to deal with this new complexity of feeling.

It is there. In her poems the available rhythmic technique is extended. The nature of the Japanese language precludes rhythms based on quantity, as in Sappho's Greek, or stress, as in English. It is not stressed, but intonated, and all syllables are essentially the same length, a consonant and a vowel, or, the one exception, a syllable-length /n/ or /m/ sound. So the rhythmic unit becomes, of necessity, the syllable itself, carefully counted out in (usually) asymmetrical lines. The *tanka*, which Komachi wrote, had the five-seven-five alternation of the later *haiku* plus a final couplet of seven-syllable lines. On top of this carefully imbalanced line would be placed such devices as the pillow-word, a kind of traditional epithet, and the pivot-word, or *kakekotoba*, which we would call a pun, though the effect in Japanese is far from humorous.

Take this poem, *hito ni awamu*. The first word of the second line is *tsuki*, which contains a number of meanings, among them a strike or jab, an impression, moon, luck or chance. These last two are the primary meanings, the ones on which the poem pivots in this line. The line reads: *tsuki no naki ni wa*, literally "as for there not being any moon," or, "as for there not being any luck/chance," i.e., bad luck. On a night when there is no moon, Komachi says, then there is no chance to for us to meet: her lover cannot find his way to her house in the dark. Further, bad luck has intervened. All this meaning in the first twelve syllables.

The next line is similar, one word, really, a compound containing three: *Omohiokite* or *omoikite*. This central line is the pivot of the poem. *Omo*, or *omoi*: thought or feeling or longing; *hi*, both the conventional way of writing the single /i/ sound and a word in itself, meaning both "day" (contrasting with the darkness of the moonless night) and "fire." Komachi avoids using the Chinese ideograph for "fire," which is different from that for "day," although in Japanese the sound is the same, for the ideograph would emphasize one meaning over the other. Finally, in this line, we have *okite*, to wake up—six syllables (and we note here the carefully symmetrical variation on the standard five-syllable line) with a wealth of meanings: "I wake up in the morning afire with longing, my thoughts only of you." All this in six syllables.

So Komachi and Sappho living at the time when literature seemed to be dominated by men, forged their newly discovered written languages into a powerful instrument for the expression of a new understanding and perception of emotions. It could be said, then, that in Japan as well as in the West poetry as we have come to know it originated with a woman.

ROB SWIGART

Notes and References

[1]This text observes Japanese usage, in which the surname or family name precedes the personal name.
[2]Boston: Houghton Mifflin, 1976.

Otomo no Sakanoe
Japan   8th century

Sent from the capital to her elder daughter

More than the gems
Locked away and treasured
In his comb-box
By the God of the Sea,
I prize you, my daughter.
But we are of this world
And such is its way!
Summoned by your man,
Obedient, you journeyed
To the far-off land of Koshi.
Since we parted,
Like a spreading vine
Your eyebrows, pencil-arched,
Like waves about to break,
Have flitted before my eyes,
Bobbing like tiny boats.
Such is my yearning for you
That this body, time-riddled,
May well not bear the strain.

Had I only known
My longing would be so great,
Like a clear mirror
I'd have looked on you—
Not missing a day,
Not even an hour.

Translated from the Japanese by Geoffrey Bownas and Anthony Thwaite

Lady Kii
Japan   8th century

I know the reputation
of the idle ways
of the beach of Takashi.

I will not go near them,
for I would surely wet my sleeves.

Translated from the Japanese by Kenneth Rexroth and Ikuko Atsumi

Lady Kasa
Japan   8th century

I dreamed I held
A sword against my flesh.
What does it mean?
It means I shall see you soon.

To love somebody
Who doesn't love you
Is like going to a temple
And worshipping the behind
Of a wooden statue
Of a hungry devil.

Translated from the Japanese by Kenneth Rexroth

Ono no Komachi
Japan   9th century

Doesn't he realize
that I am not
like the swaying kelp
in the surf,
where the seaweed gatherer
can come as often as he wants.

Translated from the Japanese by Kenneth Rexroth and Ikuko Atsumi

No moon, no chance to meet;
He does not come and I wake
On fire with longing,
A running fire in my breast
That turns my heart to ashes.

✤

If it were real
Perhaps I'd understand it;
But when in my dreams
I see people stare at me
I shrink into misery.

✤

Since I've felt this pain
I think I could not refuse
To cut loose my roots,
and like the drifting duckweed
Give in to the water's will.

Translated from the Japanese by Rob Swigart

Lady Ise
Japan   *9th–10th centuries*

Since "the pillow knows all"
we slept without a pillow.
Still my reputation
reaches to the skies
like a dust storm.

Translated from the Japanese by Kenneth Rexroth and Ikuko Atsumi

Not even in dreams
Can I meet him anymore—
My glass each morning
Reveals a face so wasted
I turn away in shame.

If I consider
My body like the fields
Withered by winter,
Can I hope, though I am burnt,
That spring will come again?

Translated from the Japanese by Donald Keene

Murasaki Shikibu
Japan   974–1031

from The Tale of the Genji

Lady Murasaki says:

The troubled waters
are frozen fast.
Under clear heaven
moonlight and shadow
ebb and flow.

Answered by Prince Genji:

The memories of long love
gather like drifting snow,
poignant as the mandarin ducks
who float side by side in sleep.

Translated from the Japanese by Kenneth Rexroth and Ikuko Atsumi

Izumi Shikibu
Japan   10th–11th centuries

I go out of darkness
Onto a road of darkness
Lit only by the far off
Moon on the edge of the mountains.

❖

In the dusk the path
You used to come to me
Is overgrown and indistinguishable
Except for the spider webs
That hang across it
Like threads of sorrow.

❖

It is the time of rain and snow.
I spend sleepless nights
And watch the frost
Frail as your love
Gather in the dawn.

Translated from the Japanese by Kenneth Rexroth

Akazome Emon
Japan   11th century

In my heart's depth
I keep our secret smothered
although this morning I suffer
like a snipe scratching its feathers.

❖

I, who cut off my sorrows
like a woodcutter,
should spend my life in the mountains.
Why do I still long
for the floating world?

Translated from the Japanese by Kenneth Rexroth and Ikuko Atsumi

Ise Tayu
Japan   11th century

The farmer's clothes are soaked through and never
   dried,
in the long May rains
that fall without cease,
from a sky with never a rift in the clouds.

Translated from the Japanese by Kenneth Rexroth and Ikuko Atsumi

Lady Horikawa
Japan   12th century

How long will it last?
I do not know
his heart.
This morning my thoughts are as tangled
as my black hair.

Translated from the Japanese by Kenneth Rexroth and Ikuko Atsumi

Empress Eifuku
Japan   1271–1342

We dressed each other
Hurrying to say farewell
In the depth of night.
Our drowsy thighs touched and we
Were caught in bed by the dawn.

Translated from the Japanese by Kenneth Rexroth

Ukihashi
Japan   late 17th century

Whether I sit or lie
My empty mosquito net
Is too large.

Translated from the Japanese by Kenneth Rexroth and Ikuko Atsumi

Kawai Chigetsu-Ni
Japan   1632–1736

Grasshoppers
Chirping in the sleeves
Of a scarecrow.

Translated from the Japanese by Kenneth Rexroth and Ikuko Atsumi

Yosano Akiko
Japan   1878–1942

A wave of coldness
Passes between us,
And the distance of a foot
Becomes a thousand miles.

As I am unhappy
And feel myself becoming a coward,
I may marry you
After all.

Translated from the Japanese by Glenn Hughes and Yozan T. Iwasaki

I can give myself to her
In her dreams
Whispering her own poems
In her ear as she sleeps beside me.

A bird comes
delicately as a little girl
to bathe
in the shade of my tree
in an autumn puddle.

Translated from the Japanese by Kenneth Rexroth and Ikuko Atsumi

Ishigaki Rin
Japan   *1920*

Cocoon

It isn't that the threat of the bomb is great
but that the earth is small.

The silkworm eats
the mulberry leaves,
someone feeds on the world.
Who is gaining weight—a country or an ism?
(Anyway, not one of us.)

Look
something like thread
goes up in the air
something like smoke from a volcano
solidly surrounds the earth
and by the time it becomes a perfect cocoon
the chrysalis inside is killed.
What's left is an inch of silk.

Translated from the Japanese by Ayusawa Takako

Shiraishi Kazuko
Japan *1931*

Phallic Root
(for Sumiko, on her birthday)

God if he isn't is
and laughs a lot
like people some
people.

Today a picnic
out where my dream
touches the sky
horizon I come to carrying
the phallus
the long white root.

Sumiko's birthday
and I gave her nothing
could have given her at least
the seeds of this God given root
seeded that faint small pretty
voice I can hear on the phone
would like to.

May I Sumiko
but forgive me
this phallus has grown with the days
and now is so solidly rooted
among flowers of sun and moon
that it will no more move
than a broken down bus
so if you should want to see
night sometimes seeded with stars
or some man roaring
down the road with a hot bellied woman
you would have to lean
far out of the bus and peer
very carefully.

When the root is rooted
phallic among stars among flowers

it is good to see
Sumiko
and the glow of the seeded sky
the strange chill of noon
pulls at our bowels and
what can be seen must be seen
quite clearly
and all must go mad
root without name or suchness
ageless root
known in itself only when carried
high on the shoulders
of men in procession sacred
and you can only tell where it is
by the noise
vague disturbance
commotion and curses and the beginnings
of riot signs of the primitive seed
still ungoverned by god
who often absent
leaves behind him void and the root.

Look
the root abandoned of God
walks this way
young gay and innocently
cocky yet smiling the smile
of experience.

Now it is many
a whole crowd of cocks
walking around
but really it is one
and comes alone
faceless wordless
from every horizon.

That
is the gift
I would give you Sumiko
to honour your birth
wrap you all up in it
that you might disappear
into the very will of the root

become yes itself
wandering endlessly
then I would vastly hold
and embrace you.

Tomioka Taeko
Japan   1935

Please say something

To a man eating a pear
you pose a question
like why the hell
he's turning on
and off the light
only when
you're sitting like an insect
on a chair
in the dark of
an autumn house
when revenge and such shit
doesn't count.
Which reminds us   doesn't it
how a nine-year-old girl
took off her kimono
yesterday
better than her mom does.
Then   remember
the insect like a golden green
grass ball creeping up
the outstretched arm.
Oh I know   all of
these stories sound too good
to believe   right.
Have a pancake
or something
for a night snack
and give it good thought
OK?

Translated from the Japanese by Sato Hiroaki

Life Story

Daddy and Mummy
also the midwife
all the fortune-tellers
bet it'd be a boy and so
inevitably
it decided to be a girl
and burst the placenta

And because everyone was disappointed
I agreed to turn into a boy
And then because everyone praised me
I turned into a girl
And then because everyone persecuted me
I turned into a boy

When I got older
I fell in love with a boy
So there was nothing for it
but to turn into a girl
And then everyone except my boyfriend
commented on the fact I'd become a girl
So for everyone except my boyfriend
I turned into a boy
But I was sorry for my boyfriend
because he felt left out
But he said if I were a boy
we couldn't sleep together
so I became a girl

Meanwhile how many centuries passed by
This time
the poor fomented a bloody revolution
and were controlled by a single piece of bread
And so then
the Church in the Middle Ages came along
saying 'There is love there is love'
I walked down alleys distributing
second-hand clothes and rice-balls

Meanwhile how many centuries passed by
This time
when God's Kingdom came

rich and poor were becoming enormously intimate
and so inflammatory leaflets were scattered
from a private helicopter

Meanwhile how many centuries passed by
This time
a clique of bloody revolutionaries
were genuflecting
to the rusty Cross of Christ
The fire of order
was visible in the midst of disorder
And so in underground bars
drinking and playing cards with Byron
and Musset and Villon and Baudelaire
and Hemingway[1] and girls in black slacks
I argued
about the unique quality
of what we call bohemianism in Japan
and we all kidded each other about
the equivalence everywhere of love

Because Daddy and Mummy
also the midwife
said I was a born genius
I tried to be an imbecile child
Because they said I was a fool
I became an intellectual
and built a house behind my parents' one

I was finding my strength unwieldy

When living there behind my parents' house
I started getting famous
So I stepped out in front
and walked by myself
on the pavement that formerly
belonged to Daddy and Mummy

I've always been rather perverse
I've suffered for the honour of perverseness

---

[1]George Gordon, Lord Byron (1788–1824), English poet; Alfred de Musset (1810–1857), François Villon (1431–1463), Charles Baudelaire (1821–1867), French poets; Ernest Hemingway (1899–1961), American novelist.

But I've become a splendid girl
I've turned into a boy for my lover
and won't let him talk back to me

Translated from the Japanese by Harry and Lynn Guest and Kajima Shozo

Living Together

You'll make tea
I'll make toast
While we do things like this
Maybe early in the evening
A friend may notice the rising moon dyed scarlet
And maybe feel like visiting us
But that will be the last time he comes
We'll shut all the doors   lock them
Make tea   make toast
Talk as usual about how
Sooner or later
There will be a time you bury me
I bury you in the garden
And go out as usual to hunt for food
There will be a time you bury me
Or I bury you in the garden
The one left sipping tea
Then for the first time one will refuse fiction
Your freedom too
Was no better than a fool's story

Translated from the Japanese by Sato Hiroaki

India

IN THE ANTHOLOGIES OF POETRY in ancient India names occur that are unmistakenly feminine. The information stops there: who these women were, where and under what circumstances they lived remain unknown. And it is meant to be so. It was not because they were women that they remained unknown: the whole Indian classical poetic tradition was to a large extent impersonal. A poet's life seldom was recorded unless he happened to be a king, and if he was, his biography was a eulogy rather than an actual account of his life. Only in medieval India did poets' lives start to inspire a sometimes wild vegetation of legends. This happened not because they were poets, but because they were at the same time saints and their poetry was religious. Such was the case of Mira Bai, a Rajasthani princess who was so devout that the legend says she finally merged into a statue of the god, and of Lalla, a Kashmiri saint who naked and half mad sang her songs of the Absolute in the bazaars, to the glee of the village lads and the outrage of decent society.

Classical Indian poems, however, were never spontaneous folksongs—if such a thing exists; they were the polished gems of a very sophisticated tradition in which the rules of the game were implacable. In the case of Sanskrit, the language itself was not a common, spoken one, but had to be learnt through studious efforts. It follows that poetry was written by an educated elite and also enjoyed by the same kind of people.

Who were these educated men and women with the leisure to indulge in the arts? Education as such was dispensed by the Brahmins, the priestly caste, to perpetuate their own learning and to serve the economically and politically influential castes, usually the kings and the rich merchants. Few men were educated, even fewer women. However, education was never denied to a woman, provided she was born into one of the upper classes. Of course, her

primary duty was to get married to a suitable man chosen by her
family and to give him sons. But apart from that she had servants
to take care of the daily chores. If she wanted to be a scholar,
nothing much prevented her from becoming one. One restriction,
however, was imposed upon her. A respectable lady did not mingle
freely with men, although women in classical India never wore the
veil. Medieval India was a different matter. Turks, Persians and
Afghans, all Muslim peoples, penetrated northern India from the
tenth century onward and established a Muslim rule that was to last
until the coming of the British in the seventeenth century. Muslim
rule changed the condition of women, particularly in the North. In
the South, where Islam never really influenced the cultural life,
women continued to enjoy the greater liberty and tolerance of
Hinduism. Although Hindu women, in the South as well as in the
North, never had to wear the *burga,* the cloak that covered up
Muslim women from head to toe, Muslim puritanism and low
opinion of women did make its imprint on them as well.

Women's freedom was, and still is, linked to economics. Even if a
Hindu wife in classical India was not subject to the total dependence of a medieval Muslim wife, there were restrictions. She could
not possess more than a certain amount of wealth in jewelry and
clothing, and this was usually her dowry. She could not dispose of
her own earnings without her husband's consent and she could not
possess "immovable property," i.e., real estate.

Classical India, like any other civilization, knew one category of
women who did indeed mingle with men and disposed of their own
earnings, namely the prostitutes. But there are prostitutes and
prostitutes. Those we encounter in classical Indian literature were
widely respected, envied, and admired. The reason for this was
that courtesans were educated, often even highly educated. They
were supposed to know the 64 arts, a somewhat bizarre list of skills
found in the *Kamasutra,* the famous handbook in erotics from the
third century A.D. Besides knowledge of cooking, arranging flower-
beds, mineralogy, and strategy (*sic!*), the list contains several items
that suppose a high degree of education, such as knowledge of
languages and vernacular dialects, reasoning and inferring, arith-
metical recreation (number games), knowledge of dictionaries and
vocabularies, and composing poems. The list also mentions literary
games such as completing stanzas or verses on hearing part of them
and similar forms of witty entertainment. Vatsyayana, the supposed author of the *Kamasutra,* concludes: "A public woman . . . versed in the above arts . . . receives a seat of honor in an
assemblage of men. She is, moreover, always respected by the king,
and praised by learned men, and her favor being sought for by all,

she becomes an object of universal regard." It is noteworthy that Vatsyayana also says that "the daughter of a king, too, as well as the daughter of a minister, being learned in the above arts, can make her husband favorable to her, even though he may have thousands of other wives." Even more interesting is the remark that "if a wife becomes separated from her husband and falls into distress, she can support herself easily, even in a foreign country, by means of knowledge of these arts." It must be made clear here that nowhere in the list of the 64 arts is lovemaking as such mentioned, and one should not conclude that a wife in distress had to become a prostitute. A courtesan usually did offer her skills in erotics as well, but she didn't have to, since her company was sought after also because of her learning and wit. A well-known courtesan could amass great wealth, since there were no laws restricting her possessions as was the case with legally wedded wives. She could possess houses and gardens as well as jewelry and gold. She was in every respect an independent woman, master over her own life.

Poetry in ancient India was not read, it was recited. The kings were the patrons of the arts. Poets, musicians, dancers, actors and learned men gathered at their courts. Evenings in the palaces were devoted to singing and dancing—performed by professionals—witty conversations, philosophical discussions and reciting of poetry. To this illustrious company the courtesans also brought their *esprit* and beauty. It is tempting to draw the conclusion that the short poems by women found in the anthologies were written by courtesans and once recited in the assembly of *pandits* (scholar-teachers) and *rajas* (rulers). This temptation becomes even greater when one considers that most of the poems written by women deal with love and erotics.

There was, however, another category of educated women in classical India: the Buddhist nuns and other religious women. It is significant that in a Sanskrit drama, only courtesans and Buddhist nuns speak Sanskrit. Other women, including the Queen, speak vernacular dialects, not being instructed in the language of the kings and the gods and the Brahmins. This convention must have been based on some factual ground, although it seems likely that not all courtesans or nuns were literate, and not all wives illiterate. The collection in Pali called the "Songs of the Sisters" (the *Therigatha*), included in the Buddhist canon, also presents a short biography of the sisters, since, once enlightened, they remembered their previous lives in many incarnations and this was considered edifying. Most of these nuns came from royal or priestly families, some of them were public women and a few of them came from the lower classes, Buddhism being an anti-caste religion. Still, by a strange coincidence, one of the most famous among the songs of the sisters is a poem by Ambapali, in her youth an illustrious courtesan, beautiful and rich, in her old age a Buddhist nun, wrinkled and destitute. The circle closes, the sacred and the profane are inseparable. There never was any distinction between the sacred and the profane in ancient India: this sharp division belongs to Islam and Christianity. Classical India, a glorious civilization, was blissfully spared both of them.

STELLA SANDAHL

Ambapali

Black and glossy as a bee and curled was my hair;
now in old age it is just like hemp or bark-cloth.
Not otherwise is the word of the truthful. . . .

My hair clustered with flowers was like a box of sweet
   perfume;
now in old age it stinks like a rabbit's pelt.
Not otherwise is the word of the truthful. . . .

Once my eyebrows were lovely, as though drawn by an
   artist;
now in old age they are overhung with wrinkles.
Not otherwise is the word of the truthful. . . .

Dark and long-lidded, my eyes were bright and flashing
   as jewels;
now in old age they are dulled and dim.
Not otherwise is the word of the truthful. . . .

My voice was as sweet as the cuckoo's, who flies in the
   woodland thickets;
now in old age it is broken and stammering.
Not otherwise is the word of the truthful. . . .

Once my hands were smooth and soft, and bright with
   jewels and gold;
now in old age they twist like roots.
Not otherwise is the word of the truthful. . . .

Once my body was lovely as polished gold;
now in old age it is covered all over with tiny wrinkles.
Not otherwise is the word of the truthful. . . .

Once my two feet were soft, as though filled with down;
now in old age they are cracked and wizened.
Not otherwise is the word of the truthful. . . .

Such was my body once. Now it is weary and tottering,
the home of many ills, an old house with flaking plaster.
Not otherwise is the word of the truthful.

Translated from the Pali by A. L. Basham

Kaccipettu Nannakaiyar

India: Tamil   3rd century(?)

My lover capable of terrible lies
at night lay close to me
in a dream
that lied like truth.

I woke up, still deceived,
and caressed the bed
thinking it my lover.

It's terrible. I grow lean
in loneliness,
like a water lily
gnawed by a beetle.

Translated from the Tamil by A. K. Ramanujan

Atimantiyar

India: Tamil   3rd century(?)

Nowhere, not among the warriors at their festival,
nor with the girls dancing close in pairs,
nowhere did I see my lover.

I am a dancer;
my pride, my lover,
            —for love of him
                these conch-shell bangles slip
                from my wasting hands—
he's a dancer too.

Translated from the Tamil by A. K. Ramanujan

Auvaiyar

India: Tamil   3rd century (?)

Shall I charge like a bull
against this sleepy town,
or try beating it with sticks,

or cry wolf
till it is filled with cries
of Ah's and Oh's?

It knows nothing, and sleeps
through all my agony, my sleeplessness,
and the swirls of this swaying south wind.

O what shall I do
to this dump of a town!

Translated from the Tamil by A. K. Ramanujan

You stand and hold the post of my small house,
and you ask, "Where is your son?"
Wherever my son is, I do not know.
This is the womb that carried him,
like a stone cave
lived in by a tiger and now abandoned.
It is on the battlefield that you will find him.

Translated from the Tamil by George Hart

Vidya (Vijjika)

India: Sanskrit   *between 700 and 1050*

I praise the disk of the rising sun,
red as a parrot's beak, sharp-rayed,
friend of the lotus grove,
an earring for the goddess of the east.

❖

You are fortunate, dear friends, that you can tell
what happened with your lovers:
the jests and laughter, all the words and joys.
After my sweetheart
put his hand to the knot of my dress,
I swear that I remember nothing.

Translated from the Sanskrit by Daniel Ingalls

Hiding in the
cucumber garden
simple country girl shivers
with desire
her lover on a low cot
lies tired with love
she melts into his body
with joy
his neck tight in her arms
one of her feet
flicking a necklace of
sea shells hanging
on a vine
on the fence
rattles them to scare off
foxes there in the dark.

Translated from the Sanskrit by W. S. Merwin and J. Moussaieff Masson

Śilabhattarika

India: Sanskrit   *between 700 and 1050*

He who stole my virginity
is the same man
I am married to
and these are the same
spring nights and
this is the same moment of
the jasmine's opening
with winds just coming of age carrying
the scent of its flowers mingled
with pollen from Kadamba trees
to wake desire
in its nakedness
I am no different yet I
long with my heart
for the delicate
love-making back there under
the dense cane-trees
by the bank of the river
Narmada in
the Vindhya mountains

Translated from the Sanskrit by W. S. Merwin and J. Moussaieff Masson

Mahadeviyakka

India: Kannada   *12th century*

Like
> treasure hidden in the ground
> taste in the fruit
> gold in the rock
> oil in the seed

> the Absolute hidden away
> in the heart

> no one can know
> the ways of our lord

> white as jasmine.

✤

O brothers, why do you talk
> to this woman,
> hair loose,
> face withered,
> body shrunk?

O fathers, why do you bother
> with this woman?
> She has no strength of limb,
> has lost the world,
> lost power of will,
> turned devotee,

she has lain down
with the lord, white as jasmine,
and has lost caste.

Translated from the Kannada by A. K. Ramanujan

Lalleswari (Lalla)
India: Kashmiri   *late 14th century*

I set forth hopeful—cotton-blossom Lal.
Dealt many kicks by cleaner, carder, then
lifted finespun from the spinner's wheel—
hung in the weaver's room, kicked again—
flung to the washer's stone, tumbled about,
rubbed and scrubbed with soap and fuller's clay—
scissored to pieces by the tailor's hand—
all that once done, Lal won the highest way.

With my breath I cut my way through the six forests
till the moon awoke, the material world dried up.
With the fire of love, I parched my heart like seeds.
At that very instant, Śiva was there with me.

Good repute is water carried in a sieve.
Only if you can grasp the wind in your fist
or hold an elephant chained secure with a hair
will you maybe succeed in keeping your good name
      clear.

Prose translation from the Kashmiri by George Grierson; adapted by Deirdre
Lashgari

Mira Bai
India: Hindi   *1498–1547*

O King, I know you gave me poison.
But I emerged
as gold burned in fire
comes out bright as a dozen suns.
Family pride, fear of the world's opinion
I threw away as water.
You should hide yourself, O King.
I am a woman, powerless and mad.
Krishna's arrow pierced my heart,

took away my reason.
Body and soul I give to the holy men,
I cling to their lotus feet.
Mira's Lord acknowledges
her as his servant.

Wake up, dear boy that holds the flute!
wake up my dear, wake up my child.
The night has passed, the dawn has come,
each house has opened up its doors.
We hear, as milkmaids churn the curd,
their bracelets' jingle-jangle sound.
Get up, dear child, the dawn has come,
outside the door wait gods and men.
The cowherd lads all raise a noise,
they shout the greeting, "Jai! Jai!"[1]
The men who watch the cattle hold
their bread and butter in their hands.
The comely Girdhar,[2] Mira's Lord,
saves those who for salvation come.

Translated from the Hindi by Usha Nilsson

[1]"Hail! Hail!" Also implies "Victory."
[2]Girdhar is a name of the Hindu deity.

Makhfi (Zibu'n-Nisa)
Moghul India: Farsi   1639–1703

The beauty of the Friend it was that taught me
    The ways of love, the paths of grief and care,
And I am dazed and giddy since He caught me
    In the bright eddies of His whirling hair.

My tears break forth, my will is overridden,
    Reason retreats and resolutions wane;
The stormy bursts of weeping come unbidden,
    Wayward and fitful as the April rain.

Yet I stand firm, with all around me reeling;

The waves of trouble, breaking round my head,
Move me—no more than storms and thunder pealing
Disturb the still memorials of the dead.

Not like a falcon do I spread my pinions,
    Mounting to tumble downwards on my prey;
Upwards and onwards through the sun's dominions
    I soar, a Huma,[1] to the source of day.

Translated from the Farsi[2] by Paul Whalley

[1]Huma is a mythological bird.
[2]Farsi is the language of Iran and of the Mogul civilization of India (1526–1857).

Kirti Chaudhari
India: Hindi   1935

Inertia

The sunlight that pulls itself over the roof-tops looks
    vacant,
And the vagrant shades of its radiance
Fall weakly on grasses,
On flowers, on grottoes, all looking vacant.

Noon, then, grows tidal and its idiot brightness
Boils over, but still it looks vacant;
Then, shadow by shadow, lightness collapses—
Yet comes back to do
The selfsame labor again, compulsion of one whose look
    is vacant.

I swear as usual to start
Making use of my days
Tomorrow—
And tomorrow,
O tomorrow, what change will amaze,
But
The day is always now and is vacant.

Translated from the Hindi by Leonard Nathan

Kamala Das
India: English 1934

An Introduction

I don't know politics but I know the names
Of those in power, and can repeat them like
Days of the week, or names of months, beginning with
Nehru. I am Indian, very brown, born in
Malabar, I speak three languages, write in
Two, dream in one. Don't write in English, they said,
English is not your mother-tongue. Why not leave
Me alone, critics, friends, visiting cousins,
Every one of you? Why not let me speak in
Any language I like? The language I speak
Becomes mine, its distortions, its queernesses
All mine, mine alone. It is half English, half
Indian, funny perhaps, but it is honest,
It is as human as I am human, don't
You see? It voices my joys, my longings, my
Hopes, and it is useful to me as cawing
Is to crows or roaring to the lions, it
Is human speech, the speech of the mind that is
Here and not there, a mind that sees and hears and
Is aware. Not the deaf, blind speech
Of trees in storm or of monsoon clouds or of rain or the
Incoherent mutterings of the blazing
Funeral pyre. I was child, and later they
Told me I grew, for I became tall, my limbs
Swelled and one or two places sprouted hair. When
I asked for love, not knowing what else to ask
For, he drew a youth of sixteen into the
Bedroom and closed the door. He did not beat me
But my sad woman-body felt so beaten.
The weight of my breasts and womb crushed me. I
    shrank
Pitifully. Then . . . I wore a shirt and my
Brother's trousers, cut my hair short and ignored
My womanliness. Dress in saris, be girl,
Be wife, they said. Be embroiderer, be cook,
Be a quarreller with servants. Fit in. Oh,
Belong, cried the categorizers. Don't sit
On walls or peep in through our lace-draped windows.

Be Amy, or be Kamala. Or, better
Still, be Madhavikutty. It is time to
Choose a name, a role. Don't play pretending games.
Don't play at schizophrenia or be a
Nympho. Don't cry embarrassingly loud when
Jilted in love . . . I met a man, loved him. Call
Him not by any name, he is every man
Who wants a woman, just as I am every
Woman who seeks love. In him . . . the hungry haste
Of rivers, in me . . . the ocean's tireless
Waiting. Who are you, I ask each and everyone,
The answer is, it is I. Anywhere and
Everywhere, I see the one who calls himself
I; in this world, he is tightly packed like the
Sword in its sheath. It is I who drink lonely
Drinks at twelve, midnight, in hotels of strange towns,
It is I who laugh, it is I who make love
And then feel shame, it is I who lie dying
With a rattle in my throat. I am sinner,
I am saint. I am the beloved and the
Betrayed. I have no joys which are not yours, no
Aches which are not yours. I too call myself I.

Amrita Pritam
India: Punjabi   *1919*

The Annunciation

All a-tremble she awoke
Smoothed the creased coverlet with her hands
Blushed, covered her bare shoulders with her crimson
    veil
And glanced at the man lying beside her.
Timidly she stroked the white bedsheet
And began to tell him her dream:
"Remember the January night I slipped my foot into the
    stream?
Freezing cold it was but the water was warm.
What could not be, came to pass.
I touched the water, it turned to milk.
It was a miracle. I bathed in milk.

Near Talwandi, is there such a stream?
Or is it all my fancy, all a dream?
The moon floated on the bosom of the water;
I cupped my hands, scooped it up and drank it down.
Waters of the stream coursed in my veins
The moon quickened within my womb.

In February's bowl I mixed the seven colours of the
    rainbow
Not a word escaping my lips
(But in my mind I muse)
This thing within me will one day be warm with life
Within me a bird has made its nest.
What prayers should I say?
What penances perform?
Might a mother-to-be have a vision of God within her?

The cravings of early pregnancy,
Restless palpitation of the heart;
 I force myself to work, to sit before the churn
And imagine that the milk is churned into butter.
I dip my hand into the pitcher
And shape the butter into a piece of sun-gold.
What has united us, two into one?
What destiny has brought us together?
Such were my dreams in the month of March.

From me to the womb within me
Yawns a dream-distance,
My soul falters,
My heart trembles,
April is harvest time.
What kind of wheat did I harvest?
I put it in a sieve, separated grain from chaff
My platter glittered with stars.

One evening in the month of May
In the gloom of twilight
I heard a strange sound. What was it?
A surge of melody over land and sea
Was it Maya's fancy, self's delusion?
Was it the Lord's hymn of creation?
An aroma of incense filled the air.
Was it the fragrance of musk rising from my navel?

I was seized with terror
I followed the ethereal sounds into the woods
Did the music have a meaning?
Did the dream have a meaning?
This music and this dream.
How much of them are for me?
How much for someone else?
I was like a wounded doe;
I put my ears against my belly
to catch the sound."

It was the month of June
When her eyes opened,
Softly as the flower opens its petals,
Gently as the dawning of the day.
"My life's streams are fed by bewitched water
I dreamt I saw a swan alight upon them
And when I woke I felt the flutter of its wings
Within my womb."

I see no man near me
Nor any tree above
Wherefrom came this coconut in my lap?
I split the shell;
People came for the kernel
And the sweet juice of the unripe fruit.
I poured some into drinking bowls,
I performed no ritual,
Chanted no magic abracadabra,
No mantra said, no evil warded off,
Yet the multitudes flocked to my door.
I gave a sliced nut to each, and was left with more;
What species of coconut was this?

How bizarre a dream was this
With strings stretching into eternity?
Rain-soaked July!
I press my bosom,
Milk like coconut juice oozes out of my breast
What new miracles has the month of August in store for
    me?

All that passed was passing strange;
Who will stitch the clothes

For this child within me?
Spool in basket I spun all hours of the night
Strings that shone like rays of light.

Came the month of September
The awakening painful and yet joyous.
My dear soul! for whom do you spin
This yarn so lovingly?
From the sky its gossamer warp
From the sun its gilded woof
This thing called truth
How is it woven into a garment?
I made obeisance to my belly
And knew what my dreams had meant.

"The child is not yours nor anyone else's
It is a timeless Yogi
Spurred by its own mood to turn this way
For a moment tarried to warm his hands
Before the sacred fire in my womb."

October brings my faith to its fullness
Fulfils the dreams of a life-time
The burning embers within me burst into flame
My body becomes a fire-lit torch.
Ho someone! Send for the mid-wife, old Mother Earth
Is come upon me. I am ready to give birth.

Translated from the Punjabi by Khushwant Singh and Krishna Gorowara

Iran

IRAN—OR PERSIA, as it has been known in the West[1]—
has a written literature dating from the sixth century B.C. It was the
Zoroastrian priests, or magi, who were largely responsible for
preserving and transmitting the literature; consequently, little of a
secular nature remains, and almost no writers are known by name.
After the Iranian empire of the Sassanians was overthrown by the
Moslem Arab invasion of 641 A.D., nearly two centuries passed
before the resurrection of the Iranian language and literature were
made possible by the rise of local Islamic rulers. This new literature, in a modernized Iranian dialect using Arabic script, sprang
from collections and translations of the "old stories" of Iran, along
with influences from the rich traditon of pre-Islamic Arab poetry.[2]

One of the earliest poets of this renaissance was a woman of the
tenth century, Rabi'a of Balkh. How typical was she of the women
of her time, and of the considerable number of women who have
written poetry in Iran during the past ten centuries[3]? For one
thing, like most poets regardless of their sex she was economically
privileged and of the ruling class. Her father, Ka'b, was king in
Balkh, and his court was an important cultural center. During this
period, and for centuries to come, local courts were meeting places
for writers, artists, and scholars, and an often generous source of
economic support and political protection. Royal patronage had
certain disadvantages. Although some courts provided relative artistic freedom, the poet often risked exile, imprisonment, or death
for stepping out of line.

For a woman the situation was even more precarious. In addition
to wealth and rank, male protection and support were crucial.
Rabi'a's father seems to have given her superior education and
encouraged her abilities, and while he was alive she played an
active part in the literary life of the court. Her brother Haris,
however, was not pleased, complaining that it was unbecoming for
her, as a woman and a princess, to be writing and reciting poetry.[4]

After her father's death, her brother overheard public reference to a poem which Rabi'a had purportedly addressed to his slave Bektash, and feeling his honor at stake, ordered her bled to death.[5]

The situation of women in the Islamic world at this time was contradictory. Initially, Islam had improved the condition of women considerably, especially in legal status. It had also, however, codified the assumed superiority of men over women which was a premise of the previous society; and it defined men as being "in charge" of women. The actual condition of women in any given place or period was determined not only by the religious code, but by the interaction between this code and older tribal and family custom.[6] As Islam spread beyond the Arab world, encompassing other cultures such as the Iranian and Turkish, its rules were modified in practice by the traditions of these cultures. The customs of veiling and seclusion, for instance, were not a part of Islamic law; they only became prevalent several centuries after Islam, when Persian administrators brought with them the pre-Islamic Iranian ruling class's habit of keeping its women hidden.[7]

Paradoxically, as women in the upper classes were under more constraint in some ways, they also had more freedom. All girls except the poorest received a minimal education, enough to learn the Qoran and prayers. In the upper classes, however, girls received considerable instruction, usually from private tutors, sometimes in schools and colleges. Some became scholars and teachers themselves. Elise Boulding speaks of "women professors and doctors in many of the major schools in the Moslem world [during the 11th, 12th, and 13th centuries], in Baghdad, Cairo . . . , and Toledo, as well as in Constantinople."[8] In Anatolia, Princess Gevher Nesibe built a famous medical school and hospital in 1206; and Müneccime Hatun is mentioned by historians as a great astronomer.[9]

Iranian women, like women elsewhere, were in a double bind. The greater their access to education and to the literary community, the more vulnerable they were to the uncertainty of male protection. Rabi'a's literary fame was no defense against her brother's displeasure. Although the thirteenth-century poet Mahsati was in a slightly more secure position, married to a man who was himself an important poet at court, her outspoken poetry earned them both a dubious reputation. Mehri, in the fifteenth-century court of Tamerlane's[10] son Shahrokh, was imprisoned for indiscreet verses and suspicion of "undue intimacy" with the queen's nephew.[11] Some of her quatrains are in fact off-color and biting in their wit. That she saw her role as satirist and poetic gadfly is suggested in these lines written from prison:

> The king has bound the silver-limbed tree
> and women and men cry loud for me.
> Alas that this hand should waste to a grave
> which was pillory once to both knight and knave.[12]

There are aspects of Iranian classical poetry (continuing into the twentieth century) that may need to be explained for the poetry to be accessible to a Western reader. One is the pervasive influence of Sufi imagery and thinking, even in poetry which is not itself mystic. Another is the largely untranslatable formal quality of the poetry.

Classical Iranian poetry not only adheres to strict patterns in rhyme and meter, it is crafted in a highly self-conscious way, with internal sound play, puns, symmetries within the line, and especially complex echoes and allusions to previous poets and poems, as well as elaborations of conventional imagery. It is also distinctive in its internal structure. Connections from one line to the next are often implicit, even extremely subtle—so that the reader must contribute half the art by creating the connections in the reading, leaping the unstated, the logical gaps left for poetic intuition.

Sufi tradition developed in Iran and elsewhere in the Islamic world within a few centuries after Mohammad and became a powerful cultural influence. An elaborate body of symbolism grew up around the analogy between mystic union with the Divine on the one hand, and passionate love and intoxication on the other. Since alcohol and physical love outside marriage were both condemned by orthodox Islam, the use of these symbols became a way of questioning and criticizing institutional religion and conventional values. For the Sufi, the formally religious person is actually furthest from God, and the apparent rake may in fact be drunk with Divine Love, able to see with the inner eye, not the outer and physical eye alone.

Similarly the imagery of love, while contrary to literal morality, affirms the deeper and paradoxical meanings of faith. Only by throwing oneself into the sea of Love can one find life; holding back means the inability to receive the grace of the Beloved. Physical life is transitory, lasts only a flicker of the eyelid; by clinging to it, to the form of things, we lose all that really matters.

The symbolism and underlying attitudes of Sufi poetry entered into the secular poetry as well, often making it difficult to distinguish the two. Rabi'a was known in her own time and since primarily as a mystic poet, and her poems addressed to the slave Bektash were read as expressions of love for God. Did her mysticism perhaps provide a vehicle for the expression of human love as well? Where is the line drawn? For her, and for other women poets, it was a delicate and dangerous line to walk.

From the late fifteenth century to the nineteenth, except for the "Indian school" there was little development in Iranian poetry: primarily repetition of classical forms and conceits. During the same period, after several centuries in which some women had received education and a few held political power,[13] possibilities open to women suffered a similar constriction under the theocratic rule of the Safavids.[14]

Since the nineteenth century, the condition of women and the place of poetry in the society have grown increasingly intertwined with politics, influenced by progressive movements on the one hand and by repressive established governments on the other. Reform movements begun in the 1800s, inspired by both Islamic and Western democratic ideals, culminated in the Revolution of 1906, which sought to limit the shah to figure-head status under a constitutional government. During the next two decades, poetry was influenced both by revolutionary ideas and by formal and linguistic experimentation. Parvin E'tesami has remained one of the most beloved and widely quoted poets from this period. Though traditional in form, in subject matter and tone her poetry was part of the new movement—didactic, rhetorical, speaking passionately for the dispossessed.

Literary expression became increasingly difficult after 1925, when an army officer named Reza Khan established himself as first shah of a new dynasty, the Pahlavi, which he named after the ancient language of the Iranians. In the name of nationalism and modernism, he broke the old feudal political and economic structure to consolidate power into his own hands, and imposed an increasingly brutal system of censorship. Those poets who continued to speak openly were imprisoned, often tortured or executed. For several years after 1941, when Reza Shah was forced by the British to abdicate in favor of his son Mohammad Reza, Iran experienced a vital outpouring of ideas; the political excitement embodied in the wide range of journals and newspapers permeated poetry and fiction as well. This period ended in 1953, when the nationalist parliamentary government of Mohammad Mosaddeq was overthrown and the Shah reinstated with U.S. support. Once again, strict control of expression was imposed, and writers and poets were forced to speak with veiled indirection. At this time, Forugh Farrokhzad broke new ground in poetry with her use of everyday language and imagery, and the care and affection with which she gave voice to the lives of ordinary people. She also expressed for the first time the sexual and emotional experience of women, a subject that had been taboo. Her more outspoken political poetry, written in opposition to the shah's regime, was not published until after her death at thirty-two.

For the most part, improvements in conditions for women during this period affected a very few, or existed more on paper than in fact. A concerted policy of Westernization brought benefits mainly to the urban well-to-do. The majority, especially in the countryside, still lacked safe housing and minimal health care, and labored long hours for barely enough to live on. Most village women managed farm labor, child care, and housekeeping without either electricity or running water.

Some changes did take place. Women were given the vote in 1963, a right undercut by the fact that elections were controlled and there was in effect only one party. Family Protection Laws gave official support to women's rights in marriage; literacy increased significantly, although higher education remained the privilege of a few; and urban women had access to a wider range of jobs. As more women received education and experience beyond the home, more of them began to write and publish, though much of this work was cautious and abstract. The stifling effect of censorship and widespread imprisonment for dissent influenced not only what was published, but the consciousness out of which that writing came. Only with the increasingly open popular resistance that led to the overthrow of the Shah in 1979 did strong poetry by women—direct and concrete—again emerge.

DEIRDRE LASHGARI

Notes and References

[1]The ancient Greeks misnamed Iran "Persia" after the empire's politically most important province Pars, and this name has stuck in Western references to the country. After coming to power in 1925, Reza Shah proclaimed that the country should henceforth be spoken of in the West as Iran; although this change has been accepted in political contexts, the old terms "Persia" and "Persian" are still commonly used when speaking of the culture or literature. It seems most appropriate as far as possible to speak of both as the Iranians themselves always have: "Iran" for the country, "Iranian" for the people and culture, and "Farsi" for the language. I also prefer transcription

rather than transliteration of names, to give some indication of their actual pronunciation in Farsi.

[2] Women seem to have played a role as both singers and musicians in pre-Islamic and early Islamic Iran, judging from the evidence of Rudaki's poetry, which embodies very early sources. The ninth-century Arab poet Abu Tammam at-Ta'i mentions hearing a slave girl sing in Farsi at the court of the Tahirids (one of the earliest Iranian ruling families after the Islamic invasions). Cf. C. E. Bosworth, "The Tahirids and Persian Literature," in *The Medieval History of Iran, Afghanistan and Central Asia* (London, 1977), reprinted from *Iran* VII (1969), 103–106.

[3] For collections of poetry by Iranian women, see Mohammad Ishaque, *Four Eminent Poetesses of Iran, with a Brief Survey of Iranian and Indian Poetesses of Neo-Persian* (Calcutta, 1950); Keshavarz Sadr, *Az Rabi'a ta Parvin: Zanani ke be Farsi she'r gofte-and: qarne 3 ta qarne 14* (Tehran: Kavyan, 1955); Ali Akbar Salimi, *Daftare zanane sukhanvar as yek hezar sal pish ta emruz ke be zabane parsi sukhan gofte-and* (Tehran: Elmi, 1956–7, 3 volumes).

[4] G. H. Nawabi, *Rabia-i Balkhi*, p. vii, as quoted in Mohammad H. Razi, "Rabiah Balkhi," *Middle Eastern Muslim Women Speak*, Elizabeth Warnock Fernea and Bassima Qattan Bezirgan, eds. (Austin: University of Texas, 1977).

[5] Mohammad H. Zhobal, *Tarikh-i Adabiyat-i Dari dar Afghanistan*, pp. 82–83, as quoted in Razi, ibid.

[6] See Fernea and Bezirgan for a full presentation of this valuable way of viewing the place of women in the Moslem world.

[7] As Elise Boulding points out, historians characteristically blame cultures other than their own for the seclusion of women. "So the Christians blame the Moslems, and the Moslems the Persians. But Persian women . . . came into the empire politics of the Mediterranean world with strong tribal traditions of women's participation. When the Persians conquered the Greeks [545–479 B.C.], Persian women had nothing but contempt for *gynaeceum*-bound Athenian women." (Elise Boulding, *The Underside of History: A View of Women through Time*, (Boulder, Colorado: Westview Press, 1976), p. 344. In fact, seclusion of upper class women goes at least as far back as the Babylonians. The whole issue of seclusion is complex, however. As Boulding shows, there was often a powerful "underlife" within the women's quarters, which has not been given sufficient attention.

[8] Boulding, *The Underside of History*, p. 472.

[9] A. Afetinan, *The Emancipation of the Turkish Woman* (Paris: UNESCO, 1962), 23–24. In Anatolia at this time, the mother-tongue spoken at home was Turkish; Farsi was the official language; and Arabic was ordinarily used for literature, although Farsi was occasionally used for poetry (cf. the woman writer Erguvan Hatun).

[10] Tamerlane, actually Teymur Lang, or Timur the Lame (1336?–1405), Tatar (Mongol) conqueror of the Near East.

[11] Mohammad Ishaque, *op. cit.*

[12]Translated by Deirdre Lashgari

[13]E.g., Malaka Qarakhta; Malaka Torkan; Malaka Saljuqi (daughter of Toghril Saljuqi). See *Tarikh-i Habibu's-Seyr* (pp. 566, 568, 633–634, 661), as mentioned in Sadr, *op. cit.*

[14]Molla Ahmad Naraqi forbade women to participate in religious ceremonies; and the great Shi'ite theologian Molla Mohammad Baqer Majlesi (d. 1700) argued that young girls should be taught only carefully censored portions of the Qoran. See Hassan Javadi, "Women and Satire," in *Satire in Persian Literature* [forthcoming].

Rabi'a of Balkh
Iran   10th century

My wish for you
        that God should make your love
fall on a heart as cold and stony as your own
till you too know love's ache
                separation's sting
                        long-dragging sorrow—
then when loneliness wrings you in its coils
        think of me, and know the worth you've lost

Translated from the Farsi by Deirdre Lashgari

Mahsati
Iran   12th century

Selected Quatrains

Better to live as a rogue and a bum,
    a lover all treat as a joke,
to hang out with a crowd of comfortable drunks,
    than crouch in a hypocrite's cloak.

✤

Unless you can dance through a common bar
    with a vagabond's step, you're not going to make it.
This is the road of the reckless who gamble
    their lives; risk yours, or you're not going to make
      it.

✤

I knew like a song your vows weren't strong,
    I knew they'd soon be broken.
This cruelty you've shown me, my friend, this wrong,
    I knew before it was spoken.

✤

Gone are the games we played all night,
    gone the pearls my lashes strung.

You were my comfort and my friend.
 You've left, with all the songs I'd sung.

✤

Good-looking, I'll never stoop for you
 nor for any man several heads your better,
nor curl so much as a lock of my hair—
 I can sleep in the sea and be none the wetter.

Translated from the Farsi by Deirdre Lashgari

Padeshah Khatun
Iran   14th century

Sovereign Queen

I am that woman whose works are good
 Under my veil is kingly power
The curtain of chastity is my strength
 where idle westwind travellers cannot pass
I withhold the beauty of my shadow
 from the sun that gads about in the marketplace
I hold lordship over all the world
 yet before the Lord my business is to serve
Two yards of veil won't make any woman a lady
 nor a hat make any head worthy of command
For whom should I remove my veil
 when in its place would be a priceless crown?
I am a ruler from the dynasty of Ologh Soltan
 If there is sovereignty in this world, it takes after
 us

Translated from the Farsi by Deirdre Lashgari

Mehri (Mihru'n-Nisa of Herat)
Iran   c.1404–1447

Coming Across

Each subtlety hard for the pedant to solve
    I found a drop of wine would dissolve.
I went to the schools to unravel this fable;
    when I knocked, all the scholars were under the
        table.
I thought the candle might soothe my unrest;
    its flame but gave tongue to the fire in my breast.
I walked in despair in the garden at dawn;
    tulips burned with my grief and sank down on
        the lawn.
The naughty tale of the angel's fall—
    your mischievous eyes unveil it all.
            What fortune to gaze on Mihri's face!
            Too bad it's all for so brief a space.

Translated from the Farsi by Deirdre Lashgari

Qorratu'l-Ayn (Umm-i Salma)
Iran   1814–1852

from He the Beloved

Cupbearer, O victorious Falcon, come!
    Pour full my cup with Spirit's reddest wine.
Pour free, and freely I'll a cup consume
    Till it consume me, burn me all entire.

Come Saqi, come, and fill my cup with wine
    To wash my heart of yesterday's dark pain.
Breathe the breath of life on those who've died,
    For the despondent, fill their cups again.

I'm like a salamander couched in fire,
    So freely fill my cup with flaming wine.
Now! throw the veil from off Your radiant face.
    Enter through this door, come give me wine.

Fill me to brimming from the crystal cup,
    Transfigure, with the radiant Friend, my soul.
Like Moses, strike me dumb with bolt of light.
    Like Sinai, bring my body's mountain low.

Burn all I am to ashes—body, mind
    Till I lose all consciousness of either world.
I sit with sorrow. Saqi, bring me wine.
    My heart's disheveled, like a lover's curls.

Still half drunk from wine of night before,
    Remove, with one cup more, what mind is left
    me.
I bound my heart to Your curls of flowing hair
    And now from the bonds of both worlds I'm set
    free.

Religion to me has always seemed dusty, old
    Only the light of Love has marked my path.
With this eternal covenant I hold
    To love You— chosen freely and in faith.

Since I have opened myself to Love and You
    Come give me wine, don't leave me in despair.
Be gracious—every moment pour anew,
    I'm drowning in a sea of bitter care.

With every cup I drink, still more I crave.
    O Saqi, teach me now His sea to find
So I can dive deep within its waves
    Dissolve my soul, and leave my self behind.

Within my own heart's sea I'll find the shell
Break it, and hold at last my soul's clear pearl.

Translated from the Farsi by Deirdre Lashgari

Parvin E'tesami
Iran   1910–1941

To his father on praising the honest life of the peasant

The son replied, "For all your good advice,
      wealth's cruelty thunders round our heads.
The rich man's work is unremitting ease;
      bitter pain our constant bread.
If all their easy power and wealth and rank
      are rights, then what became of ours?
Hardship seasons the only food we eat,
      bread snatched from a dragon's mouth.
Harvest past, and granaries unfilled;
      winter, and not a stick of wood.
We produce, and others take the yield;
      we cannot claim our labor's fruit.
Still young, the peasant's back is doubled low
      with fear of rain and snow and flood.
Empty stomachs in our town are hurting;
      the table's bare of drink or food.
We often have no oil—no lamp at night,
how can darkness look to our house for light?"

Translated from the Persian by Deirdre Lashgari

Forugh Farrokhzad
Iran   1935–1967

O Realm Bejewelled

I came out a winner
Got myself registered
Dressed up in an ID Card with a name
I'm numbered, therefore I am
Long live 678 stamped at Precinct 5 Tehran resident

Now all my worries are over
At the loving breast of my motherland
Glorious history trickling warmly down

Crooning culture and civilization
Rattlerattle goes its law
Oooo
My worries are all over now

Ecstatic with joy
I stride to my window and fervidly, six hundred
    seventyeight
        times, gulp lungfuls of air, shitdusted
and treated with essence of piss and garbage
And at the bottom of six hundred seventyeight IOU's
and on the heads of six hundred seventyeight jobforms
    I sign

                    Forugh Farrokhzad

What bliss to live
in this land of poetry, roses and bulbul birds
especially since they've taken note, after so many years,
        that one actually exists

What do I see here
with my first registered glimpse through the blinds
        but six hundred seventyeight poets
every one of them with the mug of some exotic bum
scrounging in the dump for rhymes and meters, the
    phonies

And at the noise of my first registered steps
six hundred seventyeight mystical bulbuls flit
        from their slimy swamp
transmogrifying themselves into six hundred
    seventyeight
        old crows flapping lazily
off the edge of the day

And my first registered inhalation
comes soaked with the scent of six hundred seventyeight
        neoprene roses
distilled at the giant PLASCO factory

Yes what bliss living
in the town Sheik Abou Ben Boffo the junkie fiddler
        was born in

and Sheik Heartthrob Tambourine, that son of a son of
   a drum
My city of superstar legs and hips and boobs and slick
   pix
     on the covers of *ART*
incubator of that school of thought whose founders
   declare
    What the hell you want me to do about it
nursery of intellectual Olympics *Ye-Ye*
where Media Central is broadcasting turned on
   prodigies
blowing their own kazoos on our portable TV's

And as for our Persian intelligentsia
whenever they put in an appearance at senior citizen
   classes
their chests are bedecked with six hundred seventyeight
    electric kebab griddles
left wrists and right wrists braceleted with six hundred
    seventyeight Timex watches, and they know
in their hearts the empty pocket makes you weak,
    and not the empty head
  '
I came out a winner   oh my yes   came out a
                                winner
Now by way of celebrating
I place six hundred seventyeight votive candles at my
   dressing
    table mirror and proudly light them (charge it to
    my account)

And hop on my windowsill to offer for your
   consideration
    some words concerning
pardon the expression, please, the authorized goals of
   life

And to thunderous applause I raise my pick
to break ground for the lofty tower of my life
just where the hair parts on top of my head

I live   oh my yes   like the abandoned Zend River,
                            which lived once too

snatching my share of whatever we the living have
sole rights to
Beginning tomorrow I'll stroll
through our towns alleys where national blessings
abound,
among shady groves of carefree telephone poles
I will scrawl six hundred seventyeight times, yes
proudly,
on the walls of the public johns
THIS SONG I SANG FOR JACKASS HEEHAWS

Beginning tomorrow, like a bold patriot
I'll cherish in heart and mind
some of the noble ideal we pursue
each Wednesday afternoon
so avidly so anxiously
one share in that hundred-dollar lottery of whims
good for furniture, curtains and a fridge
or redeemable for six hundred seventyeight naturalized
votes
which I can donate tomorrow night to six hundred
seventyeight sons of the fatherland

Beginning tomorrow, after a few snorts
at a bag of pure firstrate shit
in the back room of Xachik's shop
and three glasses of ersatz Pepsi
and intoning some Hallelujahs and woofwoofs and
miaows
I'll be ready to enroll in the ranks of academe among the
surplus ordures of the intellectual elite
and disciples of the Oompah Oompahpah School
and the manuscript of my Great Persian Novel
will go to the bankrupt press
some time in the Tabriz Solar Year One Thousand
Six Hundred Seventy & Eight
its plot outline on both sides of six hundred
seventyeight packets of
Genuine Special OSHNU cigarettes

Beginning tomorrow, with utter confidence
I can invite myself to six hundred seventyeight sessions
of a certified velvet-upholstered association

at the Congress for Collecting and Guaranteeing the
    Future
or the Senate of Grateful Praise
because I've read *every* issue of the JOURNAL OF ART
    & SCIENCE and all the numbers of
     ETIQUETTE & SUCKING
and learned 'How to Write'

So, here I am front and center with the chorus of
      constructive citizens
advanced through our awe-inspiring science skills
to the breakthrough point for synthesizing clouds
thanks to our discovery of the neon billboard
where else but in the R&D Institutes of our
     fried chicken stands
Here am I front and center with the chorus of
      constructive clients
who, lacking bread, have substituted for it
an empty horizon
bordered on the North by the refreshing greenery of
     Arrow Piazza
on the South by our venerable Execution Square
and reaching, via the overpopulated wards,
     all the way to Artillery Plaza,
and, safe beneath its bright Canopy of Security
all the livelong day six hundred seventyeight
     plum plaster swans
accompanied by six hundred seventyeight amoretti—
cherubs concocted of mud and sand, by the way—are
    busily
     propagandizing our projects for stability,
     and silence

Translated from the Farsi by Jascha Kessler and Amin Banani

Someone Like No One Else

I dreamed that someone's coming
I dreamed of a red star
My eyelids flutter
my shoes line up side by side
and may I die
if I lie
I was wide awake when I dreamed
of that red star
Someone's coming
someone's coming
someone new
someone better
someone like no one else —not like Father, not like
                              Onsi
                              not like Yahya, not like
                              Mother
like just who he should be—
tall as the trees in the neighbors' yard
his face shining like the Lord of Ages[1]
And Sed Javad's brother, who's gone
and put on a police uniform
doesn't scare him
He's not even scared of Sed Javad himself,
   who owns our whole house
And his name is what Mother calls out
at the beginning and end of her prayers
Judge of Judges
Provider of Needs
And he can read all the hard words in the third grade
   reader
with his eyes closed
And he can even subtract a thousand
from twenty million without coming out wrong
And he can get anything he needs from Sed Javad's
   shop on credit
And he can do something to make the neon sign
   "Allah"

[1]The Twelfth Imam, "the Hidden," is expected to return at the millenium to establish justice in the world.

[2]The "Thousand Families" were the traditional ruling elite in Iran; the total population of the country at the time the poet wrote was about twenty million.

that was blue-green, like the sky at dawn
turn on again over the Moftahyan mosque

Oh
how nice light is
how nice light is
And how I wish Yahya
had a cart of his own
with a Coleman lantern
And oh how I wish
I could sit on the cart with the melons and
    cantaloupes
and ride all around the square
Oh what fun to ride around the square!
What fun to sleep out on the roof
and going to play in the park
I love drinking Pepsi
and seeing Fardin movies
Oh I love everything that's fun
And how I'd love to pull Sed Javad's daughter's hair!

Why do I have to be so little
that I get lost in the streets?
Why can't Father
who's not little, and doesn't get lost
do something
to make the someone I've seen in my dreams
come sooner?

The people who live near the slaughterhouse
with blood soaking their gardens
and blood seeping into their ponds
and blood staining their shoes—
why don't they do something?
why don't they do something?

How lazy it is, this winter sun

I've swept the steps to the roof
I've washed all the windows
Why does Father
have to be asleep to dream?
I've swept the steps to the roof
and washed every one of the windows

Someone's coming
someone's coming
Someone who's with us in his heart, in his breath, in
    his voice
Someone whose coming
can't be stopped
and handcuffed, or thrown in jail
Someone who created a child under Yahya's old trees
who every day
gets bigger and bigger
Someone of rain, of the swishing sound of rain, of the
    rustle of petunias whispering
someone who will come from the sky full of fireworks
    over Cannonhouse Square—
And he'll spread out a cloth
and give everyone bread
and give everyone Pepsi
and a share of the park
and free syrup for coughs
and a chance to sign up for school
and a place in line at the hospital
and new rubber boots
and a Fardin movie
and he'll give away all of Sed Javad's daughter's trees
and everything left over in the stores
And he'll give us all a share
I dreamed—

Translated from the Farsi by Deirdre Lashgari

Tahereh Saffarzadeh
Iran   contemporary

Birthplace

I have never seen the place where I was born

the place my mother
laid down beneath a ceiling
her womb's cumbrous load—

The first tick-tockings of my small heart
still live in the chimney fittings
and in the crannies of the old bricks
and there still visible on the door and walls
is that look of shame,
my mother's look
at my father
and my grandfather

A choked voice murmured
"It's a girl"
The midwife trembled
unsure of her birthing fee
—and goodbye to the circumcision feast

The first visit I make to my birthplace
I'll peel from the walls
that shamed look of my mother
and there where the bold rhythm of my pulse began
I'll make confession:
my clear hands
bear no urge to clench and strike
Brawling drunk isn't my language
I take no pride in killing
Male supremacy
never fattened me at its table

Translated from the Farsi by Deirdre Lashgari

Akhtar Amiri
Iran   contemporary

from I Am a Woman

My home is the mountain.
My neighbors are the goat, the cat, the dog, the cow.
My natural enemies—the coyote, hyena, wolf, and
    eagle.
Every spring I rebuild the four stone walls of my house.[1]

[1]house used only in summer when the herds are pastured in the mountain.

My ceiling in spring is the cloud,
in summer, the broken branches of trees and stalks of
    plants
through which the warm sun peers, outlining
flowers and branches on the small bare floor of my hut.
From what I've said, do not imagine I am poor.
I am not poor.
I have all I need.
A husband whose hands make our fields and garden
    bloom.
My young sons who lead the flock across the
    mountainside
and bring in the evening souvenirs of their passage—
zul[2] and *kangar*[3] for the livestock
gum and birds eggs from the thornbush for me.
In spring wild fragrance of flowers,
in autumn manna[4], *katira*[5], and tamarisk.
We have all we need—
wide turquoise sky,
river of crystal singing through the lonely valley.
During the day the river carries my thoughts,
and at night it twines around my dreams.
My home is the mountain.
My house, a few stones piled by my hands.
Before me, my mother lived here.
And before her, perhaps her mother.
When I was born my mother was alone.
My father had gone to a neighboring village
to buy matches, tobacco, tea, sugar, and oil for our
    lamp.
As he approached,
the lantern of the moon hung low in the sky
illuminating our hut.
Along the river
crickets and frogs were singing their nightly melody
celebrating my birth.
My father's keen ears caught the sound of my crying.
He knew he had become father to a girl,

[2]thornbush with large flowers which are crushed and fed to livestock.
[3]prickly artichoke.
[4]*gaz:* a thornbush the sap of which is used in candy.
[5]gum tragicinth, used medicinally.

and he named her Zahra—
and this is me.

Translated from the Farsi by Fereshte Mahamadi

The Arab World

THREE EVENTS WERE CELEBRATED in the desert nomad's encampment in the Arabian peninsula where Arabic poetry begins: the birth of a son, the foaling of a mare, and the appearance of a poet. Poetry was an everyday event. A birth, a death, a fleet horse, a sturdy camel, a cup of wine, a marriage, a journey, a hunter's chase, a desert storm, a lover's encounter in camel *howda,* an enemy reviled, a dead brother lamented, the patron praised, or the guest greeted—all were the occasion for extempore oral verse.

Entire families had the gift of poetry. Father, mother, sister, brother could declaim lines before an audience, boasting or cursing as the occasion demanded, praising the tribe's pride or blaming an enemy on the battlefield, evoking familiar subjects in concrete pictorial images. The spoken word had power, and the word was the deed. The poet was the feeler, the kenner, whose perceptions were more intense than the ordinary person's, whose words and feelings the *jinn* inspired, and who could express the emotions of the whole tribe in verse. The test of a poem was its truth, that the listener should murmur, "Ah, yes, I, too, have seen that!" The poet was the oracle of the tribe. Verse, as remembered and recited by apprentice poets, was the record of the collective memory of the past.

Poetic tournaments took place frequently at markets, fairs, and pilgrimage sites. Men and women competed equally in these contests before enthusiastic and demanding audiences and judges. The lines recited at Ukaz one day were known all over Arabia the next. Al-Khansa'[1] a well-known woman poet of the tribe of Sulaim in West Central Arabia in the early seventh century, participated in tournaments at Ukaz in the company of other famous poets. Tradition has it that at one such contest, as al-Khansa' finished reciting some particularly beautiful lines, a jealous opponent announced: "We've never seen a better woman poet than you." Al-Khansa' is said to have retorted: "Don't you mean to say that there is no poet better than me, man or woman?"[2]

One of the outstanding poets of her day and of Arabic literature as a whole, al-Khansa' represents the several women whose poetry survives from the oral tradition of pre- and early Islamic Arabia. Dirges lamenting the death of her brothers make up most of the large corpus of poetry that comes down to us under her name. Indeed, the bulk of early Arab women's poetry is lamentation for the death of a brother, and uncle, a father, or a son. In a world where women had no rights of inheritance, where they gave up procreative rights to their husbands' tribe, where tribal patriarchs controlled marriages as political alliances with outside groups, the woman's bond with her brother, and with all her male kin, provided her permanent protection and personal safeguard, for husbands answered to brothers.

The woman's voice in the poetry of this period is heroic. Almost exclusively, it praises the virtues of manliness, valor in battle, and the stoic pride of the desert chieftains. Sorrow is the major sentiment, and it is often assumed to be the only sentiment. Looking closely at the corpus of women's poetry from the earliest days of Arabic literature, however, one finds a variety of voices, tones, moods. These few selections, for example, include not only lamentations but also a flirtatious tambourine song for soldiers going into battle and a furious, boasting invective.

Several of the poems presented here were composed during the battles of Badr and Uhud, two major conflicts in the wars that were to establish Muhammad as the leader of the Arabs and to transform Arabia by uniting the tribes in the name of the new religion, Islam. With the spread of Islam and the military expansion of the new Arab nation beyond the Arabian peninsula in the years following Muhammad's death, the character of poetry changed along with the transformation of society. Poetry continued to have a political-social function, as it did in the early days, but increasingly in service to the Court, the State, and the Religion. Poets were almost exclusively male. Few instances of the female voice have been recorded.

The frankly erotic encounters that characterized the relationship of men and women in pre-Islamic poetry, the scenes of women and men side by side in an integrated Bedouin society, of women on the battlefront lamenting their dead warriors, urging the troops on to battle, change in the poetry of the Umayyad dynasty of the late seventh century. Men and women yearn hopelessly for each other; they languish as they are kept apart by cruel fate in the form of family pressures, satisfied by a mere glimpse of the beloved. Explicitly sexual expression is reserved for homosexual love. Women are veiled, the poetry is courtly and urban. No longer directly experiential, by the Abbassid period (eighth century), court poetry recalls past experiences in nostalgic terms.

Even the fact that the work of women poets from pre-Islamic times has come down to us at all is the result of a curious and paradoxical twist in literary history. For, although critical prejudice in favor of the high literary tradition of court poetry written in classical Arabic pushed the continuing tradition of orally composed poetry in the various tribal dialects out of the realm of "literature," the early oral poetry, including that of women poets, was held in high esteem. Since the Bedouin poetic dialect of the Qoran in the course of a few centuries had become obscure, theologians turned philologist and went to the reciters and poets of the Bedouin tribes to collect poetry whose language might explain the Qoran. So great was the esteem of the early philologists and collectors for the dialect of the Qoran and the tribal poetry that it was to become the classical idiom of all Arabic literature. The themes, the sixteen metres, the dialect of pre-Islamic poetry became the canon of all future poetry.

In Arabic poetry of the high tradition written in the Islamic era, two women's names emerge: Rabi'a al-Adawiyya, the great Sufi mystic of the eighth century; and Wallada, of eleventh-century Spain. Wallada was a princess and Rabi'a a saint. Surely, neither is typical of the women of her time. Legends about Wallada abound. The daughter of a dissolute ruler of Cordoba and an Ethiopian Christian slave, the Princess Wallada never married. She inherited a large fortune at the death of her father when she was about thirty. Ibn Bassam, who anthologized much Andalusian poetry of the eleventh century, tells us that Wallada defied the social conventions of her time, not only casting off her veil but opening her house to poets, artists, and musicians. Men and women mixed freely at her salon. The notorious princess is said to have embroidered verses of her own poetry on the sleeves of her gown, flaunting her lofty pride and sexual liberation.

Although Wallada is constantly mentioned as a foremost poet in an era of rich poetic production, we have only twenty lines of her poetry, while we have entire volumes of poems penned by her lover, the court poet Ibn Zaidun. The reason for this may well be stated by the twelfth-century anthologer who excused himself from quoting some of Wallada's verse along with some written by her handmaiden and purported lover, Muhja, on the grounds that it was too obscene to print.

Whether or not Wallada, unveiled, unmarried, unsegregated from male society, and unshackled by male economic authority, was typical of a group of poets and artists of her time, we have no way of knowing. References to her are scandalous and fascinating, the fragments of her poetry that come down to us disappointingly innocuous.[3]

Rabi'a, on the other hand, is representative of one way of life open to a Muslim woman. One socially permissible outlet has from the first days of Islam been the religious vocation. Saints' shrines throughout the Middle East commemorate holy women, and Muslim women flock to saints' sanctuaries for solace in times of distress. Rabi'a's life[4] follows the biographical pattern seen by Moroccan sociologist Fatima Mernissi[5] as standard for female Muslim saints. Through her ecstatic vision and devotion to God, Rabi'a escaped a life of domestic serfdom to pass fourteen years in the desert as a celibate hermit praising God. Subsequently, she returned to Basra to devote her life to good works and performing miracles. The few lines of verse attributed to Rabi'a, though beautifully simple and eloquent expression of mystical devotion to God, are but mere fragments of poetry, obscured by a legendary haze, as compared to the many volumes of male mystic verse.

Both Rabi'a and Wallada are typical examples of the fate of Arab women poets and their poetry. Very few lines of their poetry remain today. It was never recorded in the anthologies that preserve Arabic letters for us. Women no doubt continued to compose poetry, to celebrate or lament the occasions of life in song and verse after the time of al-Khansa', but we have few written records of this poetry. The continuing oral, vernacular tradition of poetry was disdained by critics and anthologists in favor of political poetry of the high court tradition. Nor did writing in the classical mode guarantee that a woman's compositions would be passed on to posterity—as witness the case of Wallada. Sheikh Abdul Badi Saqr, in the 1967 introduction to his anthology entitled *Arab Women Poets,* summarized the situation aptly in saying that his collection, of course, omits the poetry of the dancing girls, the courtesans, and other such people whose poetry treated unsuitable subjects.

BRIDGET CONNELLY

Notes and References

[1] Al-Khansa' was the name by which the woman poet Tumadir was known. Until the adoption of surnames in some Arab nations in recent times, people were known by their personal name, plus name of father,

and/or name of tribe or place they lived, etc. "Bint" means "daughter of"; "Umm" means "mother of."

[2]See E. Fernia *Middle Eastern Muslim Women Speak* (Austin: Univ. of Texas Press, 1977), pp. 3–6.

[3]For an account of the life of Wallada, see Fernia, *Middle Eastern Muslim Women Speak,* pp. 67–75.

[4]See Fernia, pp. 37 ff., and also Margaret Smith, *Rabiya the Mystic and her Fellow Saints in Islam* (London: Cambridge University Press, 1928).

[5] Fatima Mernissi, in "Women, Saints, and Sanctuaries", *Signs* 3, No. 1 (Fall 1977), p. 109.

Tumadir al-Khansa
Arabia   *late 6th century*

Elegy for Her Brother, Sakhr

Stream sorrow, eyes:
   wailing-weary
   coursing streamlets.

Cry your brother:
   courageous
   without weakness
Cry your brother:
   his orphans
   his widow.
Cry your brother:
   honorer of neighbor
   and of guest.

His favors a flood
   flowing from fingertips

A full moon shining
   for night travellers.

Faithful debtor
Captive woman's bail.

     Gallant lion
     Crushing all rivals

Valley-wanderer
Standard-bearer

     Open-handed
     Unniggardly

Camel-slaughterer

     rebel's refuge

      healer of broken bones.

Translated from the Arabic by Bridget Connelly

Safiya bint Musafir
Arabia   early 7th century

At the Badr Trench[1]

Emptied with weeping
my eyes are
two buckets of the waterman
as he walks among orchard trees

No jungle lion
father of cubs
leaping on his prey with claw and tooth
mighty in wrath and fury
can equal my love when he died
confronting men whose faces were changed in anger
in his hand a sharp sword of finest steel

Your spear-thrust left great wounds
gushing hot blood

Translated from the Arabic by Bridget Connelly and Deirdre Lashgari
[1]Burial place for the fourteen Muslim martyrs killed at the Battle of Badr.

Hind bint Utba
Arabia   early 7th century

Fury Against the Moslems at Uhud

Rrrrrrraaarghr
We have paid you back
Battle feeds battle
and war that follows war is always violent
I could not bear the loss of Utba
nor my brother and his uncle
nor my first-born

Wahshi, savage
take the gory necklace
calm the fire in me

I shall thank you till my life fails
till my bones rot in the grave

Vengeance was thirst
and I slaked it on Hamza at Uhud
I ripped open his belly
I ripped out his life source
his liver
I soothed the grief that burned in me
the pain that tore me

War will hit you hard
coming at you like lions raging.

Tambourine Song for Soldiers Going into Battle

Forward, sons of the tribe!
protect us
strike with spear thrust

Advance
and our embraces
and softest rugs
        await you

Retreat
and all our loving
we'll take
        and leave you

Translated from the Arabic by Bridget Connelly and Deirdre Lashgari

Hind bint Uthatha
Arabia   early 7th century

To a Hero Dead at al-Safra

Midway between Mecca and Medina
Al-Safra holds glory and authority
deep-rooted culture, ample intelligence

Weep for 'Ubayda
mountain of strength to strange guests
and to the widow nursing a dishevelled child;
to the people in winter
under skies red with famine;
to orphans when the wind raged

He heated the kettle till it seethed
foaming with milk.
When the fire burned low and its flame died
he brought brush and sticks
and revived it.

Mourn him for the night traveller,
for one who hungers,
the wayfarer lost
whom he made to feel at ease

Translated from the Arabic by Bridget Connelly and Deirdre Lashgari

Rabi'a bint Isma'il of Syria
Arabia   d. 755

Sufi Quatrain

My traveling provisions are short, and won't see me
      through—
            Is it want of supplies I lament? or the length of
                                               the way?
But if You consume me in fire, goal of my longing,
            where then lies my hope of You, and where my
                                               fear?

Translated from the Arabic by Deirdre Lashgari

Rabi'a al-Adawiyya
Arabia   712–801

Two Prayers

Stars are shining
the eyes of men are closed
kings have shut their doors
and every lover is alone with his beloved

and here am
I
my Lord
alone with Thee

❖

My Lord
if I worship Thee from fear of Hell
burn me in Hell

and if I worship Thee from hope of Paradise
exclude me thence

but if I worship Thee
for Thine own sake alone
do not withhold from me Thine Eternal Beauty

Translated from the Arabic by Margaret Smith; adapted by Deirdre Lashgari

'Aisha bint Ahmad al-Qurtubiyya
Spain: Arabic   late 10th century

I am a lioness
and will never allow my body
to be anyone's resting place.
But if I did,
I wouldn't yield to a dog—
and O! the lions I've turned away!

Translated from the Arabic by Elene Margot Kolb

Wallada

Spain: Arabic   *early 11th century*

To Ibn Zaidun

Can't we find some way
to meet again
and speak our love?

In winter with you near
no need for coals—
our passion blazed.

Now—cut off, alone
day darkens deep
the fate I feared

Nights pass. You're still away
Longing chains me
and Patience brings no release

Where morning finds you
may God stream down upon your land
refreshing, fertile rain

Wait till the darkness is deep;
　　be then my guest.
Night knows how to keep
　　love's secret best.

The sun if it loved as I do
　　would hide its light,
full moon not come into view
　　stars not journey by night.

Translated from the Arabic by James Monroe and Deirdre Lashgari

Maryam bint Abi Ya'qub al-Ansari
Spain: Arabic   early 11th century

What can you expect
from a woman with seventy-seven years,
frail as the web of a spider?
Crawling like a baby,
bent over a cane,
she walks like a captive
in fetters.

Translated from the Arabic by Elene Margot Kolb

Hafsa bint al-Hajj
Spain: Arabic   d. 1184

Shall I come there, or you here?
My heart bends to your desire
My mouth is cool spring water
My flowing hair gives shade and shelter
So if siesta time should bring me to you,
you'd have no fear of sun or thirst
Now hurry—send me an answer
It doesn't become you
to refuse Buthayna, O Jamil[1]

Translated from the Arabic by Michael Scott

[1]Jamil was a famous Umayyad poet (seventh–eighth centuries) whose verse celebrated his hopeless love for Buthayna.

Andrée Chedid
Egypt   1921

The Future and the Ancestor

The dead's right grain
is woven in our flesh
within the channels of the blood
Sometimes we bend
beneath the fullness of ancestors.

But the present that shatters walls,
banishes boundaries
and invents the road to come,
rings on.

Right in the center of our lives
liberty shines,
begets our race
and sows the salt of words.

Let the memory of blood
be vigilant but never void the day.
Let us precede ourselves
across new thresholds.

Translated from the French by Samuel Hazo and Miréne Ghossein

Fadwa Tuqan
Palestine   1917

From Behind the Bars
3. From the Diary of "———"

From the ravine pours silent angry darkness
and night spreads its large sails here
the light of the stars and the dawn
cannot sneak in
A night without light
where our voices are lost
and the echo dies
and time cannot move

Time has lost its shoes here
it stood still
turning around the axis of stillness and boredom
confusing days and seasons
Is it the season for planting?
Is it the season for harvest?
Is it—who can say? No news
and the jailor stands, his face a stone

his eye a stone
robbing from us the sun, robbing the moon

Translated from the Arabic by Hatem Hossaini

Nazik al-Mala'ika
Iraq   1923

Jamila[1]

Yonder you weep
Your hair is loose, your hands are weak
Jamila
But men sang extravagant songs
for you they offered their best
Aren't you drowned in their praise?
Why weep?
    We melted with her smile
    her face and the dimple,
    her braids;
    Our passions were kindled
    with her beauty
    in chains.
We sighed: they made her quench her thirst
    with human blood
    and flames
We were convinced they nailed a heroine to the cross
    and we sang to the glories of martyrdom.
      We will save her, we gasped
    and then drowned amidst our drunken words
    we shouted: Long live Jamila.

They have wounded her with knives
we with words

[1] Jamila Buhaired is an Algerian woman who was a fighter with the Front for the National Liberation of Algeria (FLN). She was twenty-two when she was wounded in a military confrontation with the French and later arrested. In prison she was subjected to torture several times and on July 15, 1957, condemned to death. Georges Arnaud and Jacques Verges, two Communist supporters of the Algerian Revolution, defended her before world opinion. Jamila's name became the symbol of Algeria's determination to be free. In the mid-1950s every major Arab poet wrote on Jamila. Al-Malaika's poem is a reaction.

and the wounds afflicted by one's kin
are deeper than those afflicted by the French
Shame on us
for the doubled wounds of
Jamila.

Translated from the Arabic by Kamal Boullata

Etel Adnan
Lebanon   1925

from The Beirut—Hell Express

> ... but there are different treatises
> always taken again as a heritage in
> which like tired continents great figures
> closed into their insanity have sunk ...
>
> —MALEK ALLOULA
> *"Villes," Algiers '68.*

The human race is going to the cemetery
in great upheavals

two horses reciting MAO

my uneasiness
to be heroic

                              bread and roses
                              flowers and flames

Gamal Abdel Nasser's[1] death is
lived in the universe of
JAZZ Mingus's[2] bass
shocks with no return
what to do with wonder if not
some pain in the head   one California
night   the road   and black
trees against which are rubbing
their faces   two men in waiting? ...

[1]Gamal Abdel Nasser (1918–1970), first president of modern Egypt.
[2]Charles Mingus, American jazz bassist (1922–1979).

taxi drivers urinate standing
on the Damascus-Beirut-Damascus
          road
          inglorious itinerary
          I inhabit the tiniest country
          in an expanding universe

          I love the women who are veiled
          like my aunt used to be
          and those who go naked
          at the American crossroads where
          drugs are growing: they are
          crabs lying on the back of
          star-fish in the sea

          I love the men who cover their
          head and show but one eye
          not the blind one but the one
          which looks inside.
          From two thousand years of History I
          keep but JAZZ
          because it is Black. I banished
          colors and dried up the sea
          here you only eat sand . . .

                              *   *   *   *

My father was Ouranos[3]
and my mother Queen Zenobia[4]
I am the initial Fish
rejected on the beach
but determined to live.

Do you know   imbeciles   that Rimbaud
was among us a century ago
from Beirut to Aden-Arabia
and that Fouad Gabriel Naffah the poet
I repeat Fouad Gabriel Naffah
is among us

[3]Ouranos or Uranus; in Greek mythology, personification of the sky; son and mate of Gaia, the earth.

[4]Zenobia, queen of Palmyra, an ancient city of the northern edge of the Syrian desert.

crucified by your thickness
burned with nitrogen
yes people of Beirut go on
snoring let nitrate burn
these pine-tree forests where
you throw your garbage   your paper towels
the country is the dumpsite
for the foreign merchandise
that everyone refuses

Tammouz's[5] country is an
open sore
his degenerate descendants
have their shoes shined
by the hands of a herd of beggars
                    you borrowed your masks
                    from the pigs and the cows
there have been three earthquakes
in the Third century
destroying three times Beirut
and a fourth one is coming!

the world is being born
the people are coming
the people are coming
          the eagle has carried the message
                    to the tribe
          the camel has carried the message
                    to the tribe
          the shark has carried the message
                    to the tribe

from everywhere in the world they are
          coming.
The Revolution is coming . . .

In New York I say the hell with America
In Moscow I say the hell with Stalin
In Rabat[6] I say the hell with Hassan II[7]

---

[5]Babylonian and Assyrian god whose annual death and resurrection, symbolizing the winter and spring cycle, was seen as restoring life to the earth.
[6]The capital of Morocco.
[7]The present King of Morocco.

hello the beggar
hello to the fedai
hello to Mohammad the visionary
hello to the prisoner

In the evening when darkness moves
as slow as mud
I watch the prostitutes
it is forbidden that women
think
I watch our servants
it is forbidden that women go
to sleep
I watch our brides
going to bed alone
it is forbidden that women
lie as gazelles
on the infinite fields of the Arabian plains

On the fields
on the Arabian plains
on the face of the desert
on the streets of our
bitch-in-heat cities
there are only
the maimed
and governments with no end
crime barks higher than
hyenas
BABYLON BABYLON
I announce your resurrections
and your death.

Written in English by the author (San Francisco 1970)

Evelyn Arcad Zerbe
Lebanon   contemporary

In Memory of My Arab Grandmother

Barely twelve years old
Conscripted into a marriage bed
Sacrifice of a lamb
Sucking still the milk of innocence
Games in the sun, childhood crucified
Silence of a frozen morning

He was there, a man
a father
knife of sacrifice
Whiteness, marauding hand
He lifted your trembling veil
Your timid gestures, hiding
Yet imploring
Those greedy eyes, chin gritty with stubble
hoarse breathing
The sword awakens

He paralyzed you in the silence
Morning of blood
The detonation of rape
Dusty torsion of a frantic escape
Shredding of the dawn
setting beneath stone

In silence your abdomen was swollen
Staggering tumor
on rickety legs
Rending of silken skin
Gutted fruit
Millenial kneeling
of the woman
Mary keeping everything in her heart
Mary receiving the shepherds and magi
Mary cradling the child
A child was born to us
To us a son was given

You named him Fuad
Heart
Your heart offered in sacrifice

Written in English by the author

Fawziyya Abu Khalid
Saudi Arabia   *1955*

Mother's Inheritance

Mother,
You did not leave me an inheritance of
         necklaces for a wedding
but a neck
      that towers above the guillotine
Not an embroidered veil for my face
but the eyes of a falcon
      that glitter like the daggers
      in the belts of our men.
Not a piece of land large enough
      to plant a single date palm
but the primal fruit of The Fertile Crescent:
My Womb.

You let me sleep with all the children
      of our neighborhood
that my agony may give birth
      to new rebels

In the bundle of your will
I thought I could find
      a seed from The Garden of Eden
      that I may plant in my heart
      forsaken by the seasons
Instead
You left me with a sheathless sword
      the name of an obscure child carved on its blade
Every pore in me
      every crack

opened up:
A sheath.

I plunged the sword into my heart
    but the wall could not contain it
I thrust it into my lungs
    but the window could not box it
I dipped it into my waist
    but the house was too small for it
It lengthened into the streets
    defoliating the decorations
    of official holidays
Tilling asphalt
Announcing the season of
The Coming Feast.

Mother,
Today, they came to confiscate the inheritance
    you left me.
They could not decipher the children's fingerprints
They could not walk the road that stretches
    between the arteries of my heart
    and the cord that feeds the babe
    in every mother's womb.
They seized the children of the neighborhood
    for interrogation
They could not convict the innocence in their eyes.
They searched my pockets
    took off my clothes
    peeled my skin
But they failed to reach
    the glistening silk that nestles
    the twin doves
    in my breast.

Translated from the Arabic by Kamal Boullata

Mona Sa'udi
Jordan 1945

When the loneliness of the tomb went down into the
　　marketplace
dropped into nameless objects
and ascended as funeral sounds
I grew harder than tears
tears turned to stone
and stone was a passing friend I could not place

I shatter in all my dimensions
I multiply
I take on shapes like water.

❖

How do I enter the silence of stones
　　as evening enters the city,
crush my being into forms of chaos,
to a god-like shape?
My essence is a crystal procession in
　　the weddings of death and despair
I fashion a wedding for death
and I am the bride.

❖

Why don't I write in the language of air? master a new
　　tongue with a different taste, a language that dances,
that goes drunk through the streets, embraces trees,
　　walks on water . . . that cries? a language
that burns the world, and gathers autumn leaves?
If I tell the sea to become a word—will the sea consent?
If I tell the word to die, if I pile up the words of the ages
past, present, and future, and say to the sun:
　　Burn heaps of words
and say to the earth: Bury the ashes of words
and say to the ashes: Word-ashes
bring forth a sorcerer's tongue
　　to tell fire: Be word

and word: Be a poem
without words,
which can neither be read, nor seen, nor heard.

Translated from the Arabic by Kamal Boullata

Sumero-Babylonia

THE FIRST RECORDED WOMAN POET—in fact, the first named poet of either sex—is the priestess/politician/poet Enheduanna, whose work was instrumental in unifying the Near Eastern city-states of Akkad and Sumer in the 24th century B.C. The influence of her work seems to have continued for hundreds of years after her death. Several Old Babylonian literary catalogues mention it; and the poem excerpted here, "Inanna Exalted," was copied extensively—nearly fifty copies written in cuneiform on clay tablets have been discovered. Now, over 4,000 years after her death, several great hymn cycles and other compositions by her are still in existence.

The later Sumerian love poem "Love Song to King Shu-Suen" was likewise popular, still being copied by scribes 300 years after it was composed. Although the poet is not directly named, there is good reason to believe it was the work of Kubatum, concubine of Shu-Suen, next to the last king of the Third Dynasty of Ur (c. 2038–2030 B.C.).

Some scholars believe that in early Sumerian times women had greater rights and higher status than they did later; this argument is based largely on the roles played by goddesses in the myths. Others see a growth in the importance of women, since feminine names appear in Royal Lists increasingly as the dynastic age progresses. Hallo says that "the election of charismatic leaders gave way to an institutionalized accession by right of birth—hence women formed an important link in legitimating the succession."[1] The earliest ruling queen known is Queen Kubau (c. 2400 B.C.), who apparently reigned independently and not because of descent or marriage.

In early Sumer, princesses were often elevated to the influential

111

position of High Priestess, while some functioned as prophetesses. Many women had professions in the performing arts as dancers, singers, musicians. Women from royal or wealthy families were often educated. Women retained some rights to property, could buy and sell, inherit and bequeath in their own names, and sometimes ran businesses of their own. They could initiate divorce, and were permitted to take their dowries and any property acquired during marriage upon returning to their parents' home. In the Old Babylonian period in particular (c. 1850–1550 B.C.), the large group of cloistered women known as the *naditu* played an important role in the economy as independent money lenders. They commonly were unmarried and, if married, childbearing was to be avoided; the reason for this may have been the desire of the *naditu*'s family not to disburse the family wealth and property through inheritance to children. It is of interest that in the city of Sippar, where there was a large *naditu* institution at this time, many more women worked as scribes than did elsewhere.[2]

In Sumerian literary texts, women speak a dialect unique to them; this speech is known as *eme-sal*, literally "thin" or "fine" speech. Evidence for a general spoken dialect among women is inconclusive, however. And although Enheduanna's hymn to Inanna conveys the often-personal voice of the poet, there are no direct quotations of a woman's words in the poem, and no use of *eme-sal*.

It is interesting to note that Enheduanna was engaged in creative writing only a few hundred years after the introduction of writing in Sumer, and very shortly after the first uses of writing for literary purposes. She was influential throughout the reign of her father and well into the time of his successors. Her father, Sargon the Great, was in the process of uniting his own city-state, Akkad, with Sumer to the south (the two principal cities of which were Ur and Uruk). Enheduanna seems to have played an important role in this unification through her appointed position as priestess and "wife" of the god An in Uruk and the god Nanna in Ur. Moreover, in her poetry[3] she redefined the theology of Sumer in accordance with that of Akkad—raising the goddess Inanna from a diminished position as minor deity to a rank equal to that of An, god of Heaven.[4] In this poem she describes in present tense a particular instance of rebellion against Sargon, and its futility, as Inanna, goddess of Love and War,[5] restores Enheduanna from banishment to her rightful position as High Priestess.

ANNE DRAFFKORN KILMER

Notes and References

[1]W. W. Hallo, "Women of Sumer," in *The Legacy of Sumer,* ed. by Denise Schmandt-Besserat. *Bibliotheca Mesopotamica* 4, (Undena Publicàtions, Malibu, CA, 1976), pp. 23–40.

[2]Rivkah Harris, *Ancient Sippar. A Demographic Study of an Old Babylonian City (1894–1595 B.C.).* Publications dell'Institut Historique et Archéologique Néerlandais de Stamboul, Vol. 36, viii–360, (Leiden: Nederlands Instituut voor het Nabije Oosten, 1975).

[3]The 152-line hymn from which these excerpts are taken is in the form called *shirkuga*. For a recording of ancient Mesopotamian music, see Kilmer, Crocker and Brown, *Sounds from Silence* (Bit Enki Publications, P. O. Box 9068, Berkeley CA 94705,1976).

[4]W. W. Hallo, *The Exaltation of Inanna* (New Haven: Yale University Press).

[5]The combination of sexual love and violence in Inanna has close parallels in the goddesses of many mythologies, e.g., the Ugaritic Anath and the Hindu Kali.

Enheduanna
Sumero-Babylonia: Sumerian   *c. 2300* B.C.

from Inanna Exalted

> *Hymn in praise of Inanna, goddess of*
> *Love and the planet Venus, daughter of*
> *Nanna, the Moon god. She is portrayed*
> *by the poet as endowed by An, god of*
> *Heaven, with the Eternal Truths—the*
> *me's—which she wears as adornment.*
> *The hymn seems to have been chanted*
> *in four beats to the line to the*
> *accompaniment of the balang, a round*
> *or boat-shaped harp.*

O lady of all truths   bright light going forth
Righteous woman clothed in halos   loved of
                                                    Heaven and
                                                           Earth

Heaven's[1] goddess of Love   of great adornment
Of the truths, those seven   your hand has attained
The true crown loving   worthy of priesthood
My Lady of great truths   you are their keeper
You picked the truths   hung them on your hand
You gathered the truths   clasped them to your
                                          breast

Like a dragon—on the land   venom you spewed
Like a storm—roaring at earth   even trees fall
                                                  before you
Like   a   flood—from   the   mountain   you   can
                                                            descend
Of heaven and earth, Supreme One   you are that
                                                      Inanna

*   *   *   *

Destroyer of lands   on storm-lent wings
Beloved of Enlil[2]   you fly through the nation
The decrees of Heaven   you are ready to serve

---

[1]Heaven is equivalent to An, the Sky god.
[2]Enlil is one of the supreme deities, god of earth's atmosphere.

O my Lady, the lands	bow low at your sound
At your stormy radiance	when mortals approach
They all tremble	filled with fear
What they deserve	from you they receive
In songs of lamenting	they weep before you
By the house of sighs	they walk toward you
In the forefront of battle	you strike all down
As a winged creature	you tear at (the land)
Like a charging storm	——you charge
Like a roaring storm	——you roar
With thunder unceasing	——you thunder
With all evil winds	——you snort
Your feet are filled	with restlessness
To the harp of sighs	your dirge pours forth

O my Lady, the Anunna[3]	the great of the gods
They flee you like bat-birds	to crannies and clefts
In your fearful glance	they dare not walk
Past your awesome face	they cannot proceed
For your raging heart	who can control it?
Your furious heart	is past controlling

*   *   *   *

Against any city	that has denied homage
That has not declared	it is yours and your father's
You spoke your command	drove it off from your fold
From out of its byre	you have taken your foot
Thus there the women	speak no love to their men
Thus there at nighttime	no longer make love
Their innermost selves	no longer reveal

*   *   *   *

You of the eternal truths	O great queen of queens
Born of the holy womb	now greater than your mother
You the all-wise one	Lady of the lands
Faithful provider	of your truths I have sung

*   *   *   *

[3]*Anunna* is the collective term for a group of great gods.

Into the chamber[4]   you beckoned me enter
I, the High Priestess   I, Enheduanna
I bore the cult basket   intoned the praises
Yet I have been banished   not allowed to be with
                            you
They move toward the light   light is kept from me
Shadows move toward the light   the sandstorm
                                    obscures it
My honeyed tongue   is tied with confusion
My loveliest features   are turned to dust

*   *   *   *

In the place of sustenance   what am I, even I?
This rebellious place   defies your Nanna
Malevolent city[5]   be it riven by An!
By the great Enlil   may it be cursed!
May its weeping child   not be soothed by its
                                mother!
Your harp of mourning   is laid on the ground
Your sad ship is beached   on a hostile shore
At the sound of my song   they are ready to die

As for me, my Nanna   pays me no need
Gives me over to ruin   in murderous times
The Shining Moon   spoke not my judgment
If he had, what care I?   had he not, what care I?
Me, once triumphant   he drove from the temple
Made me fly from the window   like a swallow—life
                                    is going
In mountain bramble   he forced me to walk
He stripped me of the crown   due the high
                                    priesthood
Gave me dagger and sword—   "It suits you" he
                                    told me

*   *   *   *

But I am the shining   High Priestess of Nanna
O Inanna loved of An   take pity on me!

---

[4]"Into the *chamber* you beckoned me enter": a special temple chamber, called the
gipar, where the sacred marriage took place, probably to be associated with the
birthing hut whose reed post is Inanna's symbol. [A.D.K.]
[5]The "malevolent city" is Uruk.

*   *   *   *

Not for Nanna, but Inanna	these praises I sing
Your highness, like Heaven's	let it be known!
Your breadth, like Earth's	let it be known!
Your suppression of rebels	let it be known!
Your roaring at the lands	let it be known!
Your smiting of heads	let it be known!
Your devouring of corpses	let it be known!
Your terrifying glance	let it be known! . . .
O my Lady, loved of An	I have told of your fury

They heaped up the coals	prepared the lustrations
The bride-bed awaits you	your heart, be it calmed
With cries of labor	I gave birth to this hymn
This song, late at night	I recited for you
May the cantor, at noon	repeat it for you

*   *   *   *

The Lady Supreme	pride of the throne
Her holy offerings	took in her hands
The heart of Inanna	was restored to its place
The day was auspicious	she was clothed in delight
In sensuous beauty	in femininity draped
When the Moon god came forth	appeared in full view
Blessings they gave	to Ningalla, her mother[6]
The threshold of heaven	"All Hail!" proclaimed

For the goddess of Love	the poet's words were exalted
O land-destroyer	endowed with all truths
My Lady wrapped in beauty	Inanna be praised!

English verse rendered from the Sumerian by Anne Draffkorn Kilmer, based on the text edition of W. W. Hallo and J. J. A. van Dijk

[6]"Ningalla her mother" is wife of the moon god Nanna.

Kubatum

Sumero-Babylonian:Sumerian   *c. 2032 B.C.*

Love Song to King Shu-Suen

Youth of my heart, my beloved one,
   O that to sweeten still more
   your charms, which are sweetness,
   are honey—

Lad of my heart, my beloved one,
   O that to sweeten still more
   your charms, which are sweetness,
   are honey

You, my own warrior, might march against me—
   I would flee before you, youth,
   into the bed.

O that you, my own warrior, might march against me—
   I would flee before you, lad,
   into the bed.

O that you might treat me, youth, with all sweetness,
   my sweet and darling one,
   with whom I would speak (words of) honey,
   on the quilt of the bed
   we would rejoice in your charm
   and all your sweetness.

O that you might treat me, lad, with all sweetness,
   my sweet and darling one,
   with whom I would speak (words of) honey—
   youth, I am in love with you!

Translated from the Sumerian by Thorkild Jacobsen

Israel

IN ANCIENT ISRAEL as well as in orthodox Judaism the ideal Jewish woman is the wife, not the virgin. Herein lies maybe the most fundamental difference between Christian and Jewish attitudes to women. The dichotomy between the pure woman, the venerated, unapproachable ideal on the one hand, and the sinful, evil temptress on the other hand, is more characteristic of the Christian tradition; the division of purity and impurity in relation to women in Judaism runs along different lines. Chastity is not emphasized as a virtue per se. Judaism did not foster cloisters or encourage celibacy. The virgin is seen as an uncomplete, unfinished creature, "a lump of unformed clay," as one rabbinical text has it, until she marries and finds fulfillment in her relation to her husband and her children. Although a woman is considered unclean during and after menstruation and during and after childbirth, this is a temporal, not an absolute injunction. One of the most often quoted examples of the respected position of the married woman is the closing section of the Book of Proverbs. Read in the Jewish home on Saturday nights, this is a paean to the Jewish female ideal.

> A perfect wife—who can find her?
>   She is far beyond the price of pearls.
>
> Her husband's heart has confidence in her,
>   from her he will derive no little profit.
>
> Advantage and not hurt she brings him
>   all the days of her life.
>
> She is always busy with wool and with flax,
>   she does her work with eager hands.

She is like a merchant vessel
   bringing her food from far away.

She gets up while it is still dark
   giving her household their food
   giving orders to her serving girls.

She sets her mind on a field, then she buys it;
   with what her hands have earned she plants a vineyard.

She puts her back into her work
   and shows how strong her arms can be.

She finds her labor well worth while;
   her lamp does not go out at night.

She sets her hand to the distaff,
   her fingers grasp the spindle.

        *   *   *   *

Snow may come, she has no fears for her household,
   with all her servants warmly clothed.

She makes her own quilts,
   she is dressed in fine linen and purple.

Her husband is respected at the city gates,
   taking his seat among the elders of the land

        *   *   *   *

Her sons stand up and proclaim her blessed,
   her husband, too sings her praises:

Many women have done admirable things,
   but you surpass them all!"[1]

    The Jewish wife is seen as a person of importance with a remarkably wide field of action. Beyond the ordinary wifely duties she buys property, plants vineyards, and conducts business. She is the pivotal member of the family: her husband owes his sons, the continuation of the family line, to her; he owes his wealth and his reputation to her industry and her competence. In return she receives his gratitude and respect and an honored place in the community.

    This cultural ideal was shaped over many centuries. It is present in the most ancient biblical texts but becomes more pronounced during the formative years of Judaism, from the second century

B.C.E. to the fifth century C.E. Women in the ancient texts of the Bible have strong personalities and independent minds. Sarah, Rebecca, and Rachel are women to be reckoned with, but it is as wives and mothers, as members of the family and the tribe that they excel. Judith is a proper widow before becoming a national hero, and it is made clear that her independence would have been less appreciated had she not conformed to the female ideal.

There are only a handful of women in the Bible whose fame rests on their individual accomplishments. Deborah rose to a unique position of authority and power in the period after the Exodus and the conquest of Canaan (around 1200 B.C.E.). She was a prophet and a judge who rallied the tribes to resistance and goaded their military leader into action. Through her initiative and determination a decisive battle was won. Deborah is sometimes associated with the *kahina*, who among Arab tribes was a judge in a sanctified place, a prophet and a poet who aroused the warriors to battle with a song. The song of Deborah, one of the oldest Hebrew heroic poems, is the only text in the Bible that seems with some certainty to have been composed by a woman: it contains female images, and internal linguistic evidence places its composition as contemporaneous with Deborah's life.

Huldah, another exceptional woman, ranks among the great prophets of Israel: her prophecy even had precedence over that of Jeremiah. But the most intriguing and unexpected figure is Beruriah. She is the only Jewish woman who studied the Bible and produced learned commentaries. She lived at the time of the destruction of the Jewish homeland by the Romans in 135 C.E. Despite growing misogyny in the rabbinical community, she was highly respected as a scholar and interpreter of biblical law and her opinion was heeded by the rabbis and incorporated into the canon. In her story stereotypical sex roles are reversed. She is shown as more intelligent, capable of greater moral and intellectual subtlety than the men around her. One source reveals her wisdom:

> There were once some highwaymen in the neighborhood of Rebbe Meir who caused him a great deal of trouble. Rebbe Meir accordingly prayed that they should die. His wife, Beruriah, said to him: How do you make out (that such a prayer should be permitted)? Because it is written "Let <u>hattaim</u> (sins) cease? Is it written <u>hottim</u> (sinners)? It is written <u>hattaim</u> (sins)! Further, look to the end of the verse "and let the wicked men be no more." Since the sins will cease, there will be no more wicked men! Rather pray for them that they should repent, and there will be no more wicked. He did pray for them and they repented.[2]

Anne Goldfield comments on how the passage shows Beruriah in a favorable light and also how it indicates a great deal of mutual respect between husband and wife. Nevertheless, she is the exception that proves the rule and medieval commentators eagerly argue her death by suicide as proof of the temerity of her position.

Although these female figures are few and far between, they indicate the existence, within carefully circumscribed limits in a fundamentally patriarchal culture, of a tradition of strong and independent womanhood. The *Song of Songs* suggests that the relation between the sexes could be one of full equality. In the sections written in the female voice, the woman boldly asserts her sexuality, states her desire and invites her beloved to join her for a night of love.

> As an apple tree among the trees of the orchard,
> so is my Beloved among the young men.
> In his longed-for shade I am seated
> and his fruit is sweet to my taste.
> He has taken me to his banquet hall,
> and the banner he raises over me is love.
> Feed me with raisin cakes,
> restore me with apples,
> for I am sick with love.
>
> His left arm is under my head,
> his right embraces me.
>
> I charge you,
> daughters of Jerusalem,
> by the gazelles, by the hinds of the field,
> not to stir my love, nor rouse it,
> until it pleases to awake.[3]

It is a unique document in the Bible but a central one and its emphasis on mutuality and equality constitutes a strain that runs through the Jewish tradition.

The dominant ideal, however, is the one in conformity to which generations of women married early, gave birth to sons (daughters did not count) and patiently fulfilled their wifely duties. The persistence of the cultural ideal owes much to historical circumstances. Under Greek and later Roman rule, during the seven hundred years of formative Judaism (200 B.C.E. to 500 C.E.), the Jewish people were no longer an independent nation and had lost their political and military institutions. In order to withstand the pressure of foreign rule, and after repeated revolts had ended in bloodbath and political disaster, the people closed upon itself, so to speak, and began to rely for the survival of a sense of identity on two factors: the teachings of the Bible, the holy Word, which confirmed the covenant between God and His people; and the family, the smallest social unit capable of preserving customs and values and passing them on to later generations. Duties were divided along sexual lines: everything related to the family became incumbent upon women, while the elaboration and transmission of the Law drawn from the Bible became the responsibility of men. The emphasis placed on the family was the response of the Jewish people to the loss of independent nationhood, to being, as it were, dropped from the historical calendar for two thousand years. The family as transmitter of cultural values and cultural identity is an ideal institution: self-perpetuating and small enough to be geographically transplanted without losing its innate qualities. The solidarity among its members is capable of withstanding much economic hardship and political repression. The system has proved resilient and has contributed greatly to the survival of the Jewish people. Within this framework, the role of the Jewish wife and mother has been paramount.

At the same time, the division of roles has tended to confine women exclusively to the home and to keep them out of active participation in study, worship and communal affairs. Women are not admitted into the centers of learning. Rabbi Eliezer said: "If any man teach his daughter Torah (the Bible) it is as though he taught her lechery." In the house of prayers the sexes are segregated during worship, and women have a passive role and are not under obligation to participate in the daily services. A woman cannot be counted as a person in order to complete the congregation of ten required for public worship. A man earns a respected position in the community if he obeys God's command and devotes his life to study and prayer. No such demands are made on women. "Women were praised in their place—if they looked well to the ways of their households, provided their husbands with sons, and set their sons on the way of learning if the husband would not or could not."[4]

As the community of scholars was an all-male society it not unexpectedly developed a strong misogynist bent. During the years of formative Judaism, the rabbis produced a mountain of disparaging comments on the female sex. Above all, independence in women was feared: "Keep a headstrong daughter under firm control, or she will abuse any indulgence she receives. Keep a strict watch on her shameless eye, do not be surprised if she disgraces you. Like a thirsty traveller she will open her mouth and drink any water she comes across; she will sit in front of every peg, and open her quiver to every arrow."[5] The sexual imagery is a vehicle for hostility and contempt. Still, the Jewish male world of scholarship, of obedience to the Law and the holy word, has to be understood within its historical context: its function, just like that of the family, was to unite the people in times of exile.

Strength and resilience were badly needed, for the history of the Jewish people after the Roman conquest, and especially from the twelfth century on, is an unending series of persecutions, expulsions, bans, pogroms, and mass suicides. By the end of the fifteenth century, the few cities in which Jews were permitted to live prohibited settlement elsewhere than in small walled-in areas, called ghettos, the gates of which were closed at night. The stifling physical and spiritual closeness of these tiny enclaves gradually were wearing down the spirit of the people. Opportunities were scarce for Jewish men and for women they were nonexistent.

Change came suddenly and as an immediate consequence of the French Revolution, which sought to realize the liberal ideals of the Enlightenment. The "Rights of Man" were to be extended to Jews. The spirit of freedom spread abroad with Napoleon's armies as they moved victorious over Europe. "In Italy," Cecil Roth writes, "as the French forces entered one sundrenched city after the other, the gates of the Ghetto were broken down, and the Jews summoned forth to the pure air of the outer world, to enjoy all the privileges of other human beings. In Venice, the gates of the Ghetto were removed and burned, amid great popular jubilation on July 10, 1799."[6]

Slowly, the next fifty years brought Jews progressive emancipation, access to civil status, public and higher education and a variety of occupations including civil service—in Western Europe that is. The change in the situation of women did not immediately follow suit. For Jewish women, emancipation was a slow process that did not become a reality for a significant number of women until the first three decades of this century. There were several paths: one could remain within the tradition, break away from it completely, or try to fuse the old and the new into an ideal in keeping with the times.

The successive waves of the European process of liberalization— from Liberalism to Utopianism and Marxism—opened avenues of political commitment and activism. Many Jewish men and women threw themselves with passion into the radical political activities of their time. Many abandoned traditional Jewish ways and formed the vanguard of movements working for political and social change. The best known, in addition to Karl Marx and Leon Trotsky, was probably Rosa Luxemburg, the leader of the radical left-wing German party Spartakusbund, who was murdered in Berlin in 1919. What characterized her above all else was a natural propensity to treat others as equals. According to the philosopher Hannah Arendt, "It was within the circle of the Jewish family that her unique ethical code evolved: The hidden equalizer was . . . the essentially simple experience of a childhood world in which mutual respect and unconditional trust, a universal humanity and a genuine, almost naive contempt for social and ethnic distinctions were taken for granted. What the members of the peer group had in common was what can only be called moral taste, which is so different from 'moral principles'; the authenticity of their morality they owed to having grown up in a world that was not out of joint (i.e., their family)."[7] This was the legacy of the Jewish family, with woman at its center, to the generation of emancipated Jewish women in the European revolutionary movements.

As to the women who remained attached to the traditional Jewish way of life, they experienced explosive changes, especially in the area of education. By the third decade of this century, in response to a growing feminist movement, it was no longer socially acceptable that a woman remain uneducated. Since, in the orthodox family, the woman often was the provider, it was not economically feasible either in an increasingly complex technological society. When Sarah Schenirer, a simple seamstress from Poland with an irrepressible desire for books and learning, opened her first school for orthodox girls in 1918, 25 students enrolled. In 1937, her small seminar had grown into an international network of 250 schools offering general and vocational training to more than 38,000 students.

A third alternative existed for women who wanted to assert their Jewishness, yet had been influenced by the secular socialist ideas of the time. The various Zionist organizations offered a new ethic that was secular, nationalist, and socialist. The young men and women who emerged from the many East European schools, sports clubs, youth organizations, or model farms preparing for agricultural work in Palestine combined a strong sense of Jewish identity with a passionate commitment to egalitarian values, socialist as well as feminist.

It was as if a New Jewish Woman was being fashioned from scratch: her archetype is best observed in the pioneer woman of the successive waves of immigration to what was then still Palestine, before the partition in 1948 and the creation of the state of Israel. Part myth and part reality, she lives on as a cultural ideal. Intellectually and physically well trained, at ease behind the tractor and in the political meeting, liberated from the burden of childrearing by communal institutions, she is the very embodiment of the liberated woman. Among these pioneer women, the life of Hannah Senesh is especially exemplary. The daughter of an assimilated and distinguished Hungarian Jewish family, her road led from the model farm to a kibbutz in Israel to her death at 23 at the hands of the Nazis, after she had been parachuted behind German lines in 1944. Her poetry, written in Hungarian and Hebrew, is imbued with intense idealism and yearning for self-sacrifice in the name of Zionism and Socialism.

However, the myth was not easy to maintain as the ideal changed into reality, and it seems as if the long wave of liberation, which had carried Jewish women from their confinement in the ghetto to independence as equal members in Israeli kibbutzim and labor organizations had exhausted itself by the middle of the century. We are now witnessing a return to more traditional ways of life; and women in the Israeli army, in the kibbutzim, in the professions have fallen back on old female roles. In the kibbutz today, women almost exclusively work in the service fields: kitchen, laundry, and children's house. Women in the military hold desk jobs and rarely participate in active combat, although they still are required to do military service. Life in Israel is hard, with constant wars and a taxing climate. For the time being, innovation and idealism seem to have receded in favor of a more self-protective attitude.

Nevertheless, in the field of literature women have suffered no setbacks. In the past, the male monopoly of study and writing in Hebrew had excluded women from literary activity. We possess only a few anonymous women's songs from the high period of Jewish philosophy and letters in Spain before the Inquisition (1492), and a single woman writer and biblical scholar from the Italian Hebraic renaissance (1400–1900), Rachel Morpurgo. But from the end of the nineteenth century on there has been a strong female presence in Jewish literature.

There had been no barriers to women's participation in the literature of Yiddish, the language spoken by Jews in Eastern Europe. Tales, homilies, ballads, and a simplified version of the Bible, addressed to "women, children, and other uneducated people," as the expression went, had long circulated before the emergence of a full literature. When a literature developed in Yiddish, during the second half of the nineteenth century, women were involved in it from the very beginning. There are numerous women poets writing in Yiddish in all parts of the world. In the United States, Kadia Molodowsky is probably the most outstanding. Today, however, Hebrew has been revived as a secular language and established as the official language in Israel, and the poets presented here—with the exception of Kadia Molodowsky—all wrote or are writing in Hebrew. The poetry that is being written in Israel now is in Hebrew, not in Yiddish, as fewer and fewer young people are able to speak it.

But what happened to the women who took the third path, choosing neither Jewish nationalism nor Jewish tradition, but strove to assimilate into the culture in which they lived? The assimilation must have been successful, for there are many women of Jewish origin who have become prominent poets in many countries of the world. But, although Jewish themes and concerns are often present in their work, they do not quite belong in this story, for they have long since become incorporated into the national traditions with which they chose to identify. Still, when we read a Nelly Sachs or an Else Lasker-Schüler we are reminded almost on every page of their Jewish origin. Even among the most assimilated among the poets some faint trace of Jewish thinking and Jewish tradition remains, revealing that the Jewish roots have not been entirely severed.

JOANNA BANKIER

Notes and References

[1] Proverbs 31:10–31. The Jerusalem Bible (New York: Doubleday, 1966).
[2] Elizabeth Koltun, ed., *The Jewish Woman: New Perspectives* (New York: Schocken Books, 1976), p. 265.
[3] The Song of Songs 2:3–7. The Jerusalem Bible (New York: Doubleday, 1966).
[4] Leonard Swidler, *Women in Judaism: The Status of Women in Formative Judaism* (New York: Scarecrow Press, 1976), p. 93.
[5] Swidler, p. 94.
[6] Cecil Roth, *A History of the Jews* (New York: Schocken Books, 1970), p. 320.
[7] Hannah Arendt, *Men in Dark Times* (New York: Harcourt Brace, 1955), p. 41.

Deborah

Israel   *11th century* B.C.

Song of Deborah

Blessed above women
shall Jael the wife of Heber the Kenite be
blessed shall she be above women in the tent

He asked water
and she gave him milk
she brought forth butter
in a lordly dish

She put her hand to the nail
and her right hand to the workmen's hammer
and with the hammer she smote Sisera
she smote off his head
when she had pierced and stricken through his temples

At her feet he bowed
he fell, he lay down
at her feet he bowed, he fell
where he bowed, there he fell down dead

The mother of Sisera looked out at a window
and cried through the lattice
Why is his chariot so long in coming?
why tarry the wheels of his chariots?

Her wise ladies answered her
yea, she returned answer to herself

Have they not sped?
have they not divided the prey
to every man a damsel or two
to Sisera a prey of divers colours
a prey of divers colours of needlework
of divers colours of needlework on both sides
meet for the necks of them that take the spoil?

So let all thine enemies perish, O Lord

but let them that love him
be as the sun when he goeth forth in his might.

From the Bible, King James version (Judges 5:24–31)

Leah Goldberg
Israel   1911–1970

Observation of a Bee

1.

In the square of a lighted window—
on the pane, from outside,
the silhouette of a bee.
One can hardly see her wings.

Upside-down.
Narrow body.
Six thin legs.
With a naked exposure,
with an ugly threat,
crawls
the bee.

How shall we crown her with the words of a poem?
How shall we sing, and what?
A little boy will come and say:
the queen is naked.

2.

In the sun she was a falling leaf,
in the flower a speck of dark honey,
a dew-drop in a swarm of stars—
and here she is a shadow.

One word of a poem in the ringing swarm,
a fierce will in the languid garden,
a burst of light in the sunset's ash—
and here she is a shadow.

3.

Your honey? Who'll remember your honey?
It's there. Far away. In the hive.
Here on the lighted windowpane, your body, your head,
you're all sting, helpless blind miserable hatred.

Fear kills.

Watch out.

Translated from the Hebrew by Stephen Mitchell

Rachel (Blaustein)
Israel   1890–1931

His Wife

She turns and calls him by name,
as always;
but I cannot trust my voice:
speech betrays.

She walks in the street at his side,
in the day, in people's sight;
but I—in the secret dark
of the night.

Shining securely on her hand,
she wears a ring of gold;
but my fetters of iron are stronger—
sevenfold!

Translated from the Hebrew by Sholom J. Kahn

Hannah Senesh
Israel   1921–1944

One–Two–Three

One—two—three . . .
    eight feet long,
Two strides across, the rest is dark . . .
Life hangs over me like a question mark.

One—two—three . . .
    maybe another week,
Or next month may still find me here,
But death, I feel, is very near.

I could have been
    twenty-three next July;
I gambled on what mattered most,
The dice were cast. I lost.[1]

Translated from the Hungarian by Peter Hay

[1] Her last poem written in prison after having been parachuted into German-occupied Hungary in 1944.

Zelda (Shneurson)
Israel   contemporary

The Wicked Neighbor

My grandfather used to pray:
"Lead us not into temptation, nor into disgrace."
But those who died in martyrdom
sang in the sea:
Temptation is a crown of blood, a royal crown.
In innocent childhood, I listened to their song
with terrible longing,
savagely warding off
the cautious, homely prayers
that fled in trembling from lightning and storm.

And: "Deliver us this day and every day
from insolence and from the insolent,
from a wicked person and a wicked friend,
and from a wicked neighbour," grandfather used to
    pray.
Only when the black waters flooded my soul
and tore the petals from my hopes,
did I answer Amen
to my grandfather in Heaven.

In a different town, near different flowers,
on the eve of Passover,[1]
when they burnt the leaven
in every yard
and a flake of soot blew over
and soiled her dress,
she pounced at me
and accused me, quick as a bolt of lightning,
in tears:
"You, standing over there—"
she shouted,
"you do not care about me,
my dress is soiled and you say nothing!
Look at me—
I am sick, very sick and full of despair."

A curious complaint coming
from someone
who had moved in yesterday.
A strange and bold and fresh complaint.
Deep within me my soul kissed
her mad longing for gentleness,
her unbridled, lawless longing,
destructive as an earthquake.

Her mouth was hell—
when she opened the door, the children hid,
and neighbours slipped inside.
Her cold laughter haunted
our decent existence that shone
with the light of the seven days.

—Do not imagine that your goodness
is true goodness,

shrieked the savage laughter.
—Do not imagine
that your prayer is true prayer.
—Do not imagine that your courtesy
is true courtesy.
—Do not imagine that your joy
is true joy.
—And do not imagine that your happiness
  is true happiness.

When we heard
that she had gone to another town,
that the storm had passed and was no more,
we breathed a sigh, we opened windows.
Beat, beat the drums!
Blow the ram's horn!
Play the harp and psaltery!
Now we shall be left in peace.
Prepare the beds,
tonight we shall sleep.
When I saw golden flecks
in the eyes of the herd—
my heart was filled with loneliness.
I knew
we spoke of her soul, alive
and daily consumed by fire,
as if it were a stumbling block.
In vain had her curses spread
arms of smoke
to embrace our tepid souls
devoid of all imagination.
In vain had the wretched creature
waved her torn red flags at me
to draw me out of the enchanted circle of my being
and lead me to the hidden point of her existence.
I became one of the bowed women,
one of the mass of grey-haired women,
and not a trace was left in me
of that splendid courage.

Translated from the Hebrew by Hannah Hoffman

[1]The Jewish holiday commemorating the deliverance from bondage in Egypt.

Dahlia Ravikovitch
Israel   1936

On the Road at Night There Stands the Man

On the road at night there stands the man
Who once upon a time was my father.
And I must come to the place where he stands
Because I was his eldest daughter.

And night after night he stands alone in his place
And I must go down to his place and be there.
And I want to ask the man how long will I have to.
And I know, even as I ask, I will always have to.

In the place where he stands there is a fear of danger
Like the day he was walking along and a car ran him
     over.
And that's how I knew him and I found ways to
     remember
That this was the man who once was my father.

And he doesn't tell me one word of love
Though once upon a time he was my father.
And even though I was his eldest daughter
He cannot tell me one word of love.

Hills of Salt

Foam fluttered on the sea like birds' wings.
Two salt hills were left on the beach,
and the sea was a country of lakes,
with sailboats
gleaming
like soap bubbles.

The two of us sat, each by his pool,
two sand strips between us
and a wealth of seaweed.
The heavy leaves of fern swayed back and forth,
grasping at the teeth of the rocks in their lust.

A mass of seaweed broke loose and fell at my feet,
and my eyelids were heavy with sun.
And the sea rose up and spilled over
from pool to pool,
blue streams in a net of light.

Pools lapped at the palms of our hands,
the sand between us—the length of two arms.
We did not draw near all that day,
not by a hairsbreadth,
our bodies two salt hills and our feet seaweed.

Translated from the Hebrew by Chana Bloch

Greece of Antiquity

THE LITERATURE OF THE ARCHAIC PERIOD (800–500 B.C.) was dominated by the lyric, as that of the Classical, which followed, was by tragedy and philosophy. Many of the lyric poets were women—no less than nine women poets of this period are mentioned in ancient sources. But their poetry must not have seemed worth recording to later, more misogynist generations, for only a few fragments of the work of three of these poets—Corinna, Praxilla, and Sappho—remain today. The bulk of Sappho's work is said to have amounted to 9,000 lines; today we can read three or four poems at length. The rest are fragments, disconnected lines and words deciphered from papyrus sheets which had been torn to shreds and used as wrappings around objects stored in jars. Other fragments have survived in quotations by grammarians and rhetoreticians. But the work as a whole is lost.

We can infer from the quality of the writing that women during this period must have received a considerable amount of schooling and that female literacy was quite common. This stands in contrast to the later Classical period, when women were excluded from learning and from every aspect of the intellectual and artistic life of the community.

At the time of Corinna and Praxilla, women in Boeotia (a central region of mainland Greece) participated in poetry contests along with men, were skilled practitioners of the art of poetry, and lived surrounded by a circle of friends and poets whom they taught and influenced. Corinna, who flourished at the end of the sixth and beginning of the fifth century B.C., invented and perfected a metrical scheme later used by tragedians, in particular Sophocles. Many anecdotes are told about her, among others, that she successfully competed with Pindar, by many considered to be the greatest Greek poet. She is also said to have counseled him. Nevertheless, she was a very different kind of poet, writing in the vernacular on intimate and local themes, while Pindar, with his public tone and subject matter and his use of the Doric dialect, was addressing a wider audience.

Educated and accomplished, the women in the Archaic period were held in high esteem, which must have strengthened their self-confidence. As we might expect, the poetry of Praxilla has a fresh-ness of perception, a simplicity and directness of phrasing that indicates there is no doubt in her mind: a woman could be a strong poet and write on any subject she pleased. She has her Adonis express delight in the sensuous pleasures of simple things

> Loveliest of what I leave behind is the sunlight
> and loveliest after that the shining stars, and the moon's face
> but also cucumbers that are ripe, and pears, and apples

and is unaware of the scorn the lines were later to bring upon her. "Sillier than Praxilla's Adonis" became a proverb in Classical Greece. The poetry by women in earlier days gives us the happiest picture of women in Greek literature. They seem to love them-selves and each other. Indeed, as attachments of woman to woman were not discouraged, bonds were created that could last a lifetime and became the subject of female poetry.

The theme of intimacy, especially the poignancy of having to relinquish it when the friend marries, is the occasion and subject for a poem by Erinna. She was writing at a much later date, at a time when Greek culture had spread across the entire Mediterra-nean world, during the third century B.C., in the Hellenistic period. In the fragment of her poem "The Distaff," she writes with a directness which feels like friends talking—though the friend in this case is irrevocably lost to her. She speaks of present grief by evoking the everyday games and fears of childhood.

But it is Sappho who most often returns to the theme of one woman caring for another. It is clear from her poetry that women in her time found much happiness in the shared intimacies of everyday life and intense emotional excitement in participating in the rituals of the community. It is also clear that she lived sur-rounded by a circle of women, students or friends, whom she cherished and often wrote about.

Sappho was born about 630 B.C. on the island of Lesbos, one of the several cultural centers in Archaic Greece. She was married and had a daughter named Cleis and had to go into exile like other aristocrats from about 605 to 591 B.C. This is the extent of what is known of her biography, although there are many legends about her.

Sappho's fame rests on the qualities of her poetry. She wrote in a variety of meters, one of which, the sapphic stanza, bears her name. It consists of three lines of alternating long and short syllables followed by one shorter line. It was composed to be sung to the accompaniment of the lyre and has been widely used by later poets.

The name Sappho has also come to be associated with sharp observations of complex emotions. In fact, she is the first poet to make her inner life the subject of poetry. It requires a leap of the imagination to perceive how unique the choice of one's inner feelings for a poetic theme was in the sixth century B.C. As the German classicist, Bruno Snell, observes in *The Discovery of the Mind,* there was little consciousness of a self seen from within, whether rational or emotional, in Homeric epic, where events are always seen from the outside:

> In Homer, a man is unaware of the fact that he may think or act spontaneously, of his own volition and spirit. Whatever "strikes him," whatever thought comes to him is given from without, and if no visible external stimulus has affected him he thinks that a god has stood by his side and given him counsel.[1]

As Sappho turns her attention inward to observe her own perceptions and emotions and their physical manifestations, she is discovering consciousness, the distinction between the inner and the outer self.

Her tone is straightforward and devoid of irony or ambiguity. The unity of thought, feeling and utterance in her poetry has its origin in the strength of inner conviction: when Eros is passionate and serious, he not only engages emotion and physical desire, but also the highest moral qualities, the soul. We are reminded of Plato, whose ideas on love, however, differ from Sappho's on one significant point: in Plato's *Symposium* there are different forms of love constituting a ladder that the superior man is expected to ascend, from the lowest—physical love of women—toward disembodied spiritual and religious devotion. In Sappho's poetry love is not platonic: the soul thrives in the flesh, for what her entire being aspires to cannot but be morally good. Her devotion to Aphrodite lends divine authority to personal conviction.

Sappho contrasts her own values, her Eros, with the conventional preference for epic warfare:

> Some there are who say that the fairest thing seen
> on the black earth is an array of horsemen;
> some, men marching; some would say ships; but I say
>   she whom one loves best
>   is the loveliest . . .

In the same poem she goes on to compare herself to Helen, whom poets were expected to moralize: no manner of worldly satisfactions—wealth, fame, social rank—can outweigh the compelling force of inner conviction. Sappho is here asserting individuality: saying that the particularity of a human being lies in the choices s/he makes in the things s/he values and loves. She is "marking the distance between a traditonal public moral code and a self-consciously new and individualistic one."[2]

During the Classical period (400–300 B.C.) there were no women writers. The reason for this absence of women on the literary scene can be found in the specific social conditions that prevailed in Athens at this time: relegation of women to the private sphere, female illiteracy, and a pervasive misogyny.

The social structure of the Greek polis or city-state—based as it was on the *oikos*, the family, as the fundamental unit of the state— demanded the subordination of a woman to her father, and when she married, to the *oikos* of her husband. Since not only a man's right to citizenship, but also the right to vote, to participate in public life in any legal or governing capacity, depended on his place in a particular *oikos*, it was considered of paramount importance that the hereditary line be established beyond doubt. Women's childbearing capacity and fidelity to their husbands thus became a matter of public concern, and women were held in seclusion in the *gynaeceum,* the rooms reserved for women in the house. In order to avoid even the most fleeting contact with men outside the family, women were deprived of occasions for going out of doors that usually are not denied them even in segregated societies: slave girls were sent to fetch water and men did the shopping at the market.

Women in Athens received no schooling beyond what was considered necessary to run the household. They were often married quite young, in their teens, to husbands who only reluctantly abandoned their bachelor existence.

Athenian women occupied an intermediate position between their men and slaves, as society was segregated along sexual as well as national and class lines. The leisured class of Athenian male citizens had ample time to refine their taste and sensibility, to elaborate ideas, develop their minds and bodies, as their freedom from the pressing necessities of life was made possible by the work of their women and of numerous slaves. The public realm—the affairs of the city-state in peace and war—was their prerogative and responsibility. The wives and daughters of Athenian citizens enjoyed a certain measure of legal and communal protection—they could divorce their husbands and it was the task of the community to provide poor Athenian girls with a dowry—but they were denied citizenship and they worked, in a society which despised work.

Small wonder they were looked upon as inferior. They were in fact inferior, in experience, in intellectual training, and in actual political status. Men relied on each other for emotional and intellectual companionship. Male homosexuality was widespread and sanctioned by general opinion. There were exceptional women who moved freely among men and were treated as equals: the courtesans or haetaeras. These women, some of whom have become quite well known through their association with famous men, were usually foreigners, often quite educated, but they have left no written testimony in the form of poetry.

The low status of women in Athenian society is reflected in expressions of misogynist sentiment in Classical literature. At the root of the contemptuous attitude towards them lies the Greek notion of women as intrinsically inimical to civilized life. They were thought of as beings who live dangerously close to the natural world, whereas the Greek notion of civilization implied mastery over nature and the establishment of a rational order. Nature in its most disruptive aspects, as vegetative profusion, chaos, and boundless generative powers, tended to be associated with women. The whole generative cycle of growth and decay, of the appearance and disappearance of the crops and the change of seasons, as well as the generation of children was felt to be awesome, mysterious, and threatening. The irruption of the irrational, sexual, and other strong natural drives was seen as more potent and ungovernable in women than in men[3]; hence both female sexuality and other female activity were felt to be in need of male supervision and control.

The condition of women improved during the Hellenistic period (300–100 B.C.). Women acquired citizenship and were allowed to own property. Some women even held public office. At the same time, literary fashion shifted again from philosophy and tragedy to lyric poetry. The dominant mood was no longer metaphysical or sublime; everyday subjects were treated with intimate realism. Not surprisingly, we also see the emergence of several women poets in this period, of whom Erinna is the most important.

Nevertheless, Greek misogyny did not disappear when Athens ceased to be the political and cultural center. Inasmuch as we are indebted to Greece for our art and our ideas, we are also the inheritors of Greek misogyny. The periodic resurgence of this ill will can be traced throughout European history: it makes its presence felt in the writings of St. Paul and the Church Fathers who founded the Christian doctrine; it lends authority to the anti-woman outpourings of the scholastic writers; it provides arguments for the one-hundred-year-long literary hate campaign against women that goes under the name "la Querelle de la Rose"; it reappears in the Renaissance, when Classical Greek authors were read with renewed interest and veneration, and it provides the ideological underpinnings for Victorian paternalism.

JOANNA BANKIER, WITH THOMAS D'EVELYN

Notes and References

[1] Bruno Snell, *The Discovery of the Mind: The Greek Origins of European Thought* (Oxford: Basil Blackwell, 1958), p.21.

[2] Philip Damon, *Modes of Analogy in Ancient and Medieval Verse* (Berkeley, CA: University of California Press, 1961), p. 272.

[3] See Marylin Arthur, " 'Liberated' Women: The Classical Era" in Renate Bridenthal and Claudia Koonz, Eds., *Becoming Visible* (Boston: Houghton Mifflin Company, 1977) for an excellent discussion of this aspect of Greek misogyny.

[4] I am also indebted to Rob Swigart who provided essential information for this essay.

Sappho

Greece   6th century B.C.

Life the very gods in my sight is he who
sits where he can look in your eyes, who listens
close to you, to hear the soft voice, its sweetness
    murmur in love and

laughter, all for him. But it breaks my spirit;
underneath my breast all the heart is shaken.
Let me only glance where you are, the voice dies,
    I can say nothing,

but my lips are stricken to silence, underneath my skin the tenuous flame suffuses;
nothing shows in front of my eyes, my ears are
    muted in thunder.

And the sweat breaks running upon me, fever
shakes my body, paler I turn than grass is;
I can feel that I have been changed, I feel that
    death has come near to me.

❖

Come to me from Crete to this holy temple,
Aphrodite. Here is a grove of apple
trees for your delight, and the smoking altars
    fragrant with incense.

Here cold water rustles down through the apple
branches; all the lawn is beset and darkened
under roses, and, from the leaves that tremble,
    sleep of enchantment

comes descending. Here is a meadow pasture
where the horses graze and with flowers of springtime
now in blossom, here where the light winds passing
    blow in their freshness.

Here in this place, lady of Cyprus, lightly
lifting, lightly pour in the golden goblets
as for those who keep a festival, nectar:
    wine for our drinking.

❖

Some there are who say that the fairest thing seen
on the black earth is an array of horsemen;
some, men marching; some would say ships; but I say
    she whom one loves best

is the loveliest. Light were the work to make this
plain to all, since she, who surpassed in beauty
all mortality, Helen, once forsaking
    her lordly husband,

fled away to Troy-land across the water.
Not the thought of child nor beloved parents
was remembered, after the Queen of Cyprus
    won her at first sight.

Since young brides have hearts that can be persuaded
easily, light things, palpitant to passion
as am I, remembering Anaktoria
    who has gone from me

and whose lovely walk and the shining pallor
of her face I would rather see before my
eyes than Lydia's chariots in all their glory
    armored for battle.

Translated from the Greek by Richard Lattimore

Corinna

Greece   *late 6th–early 5th century* B.C.

I disapprove even of eloquent
Myrtis; I do, for she, a woman,
contended with Pindar.

❖

To the white-mantled maidens
of Tanagra I sing my sweet lays.
I am the pride of my city
for my conversational singing.

Translated from the Greek by Richard Lattimore

Praxilla of Sicyon
Greece   mid 5th century B.C.

Loveliest of what I leave behind is the sunlight,
and loveliest after that the shining stars, and the
   moon's face,
but also cucumbers that are ripe, and pears, and apples.

❖

Girl of the lovely glance, looking out through the
   window,
your face is virgin; lower down you are a married
   woman.

Translated from the Greek by Richard Lattimore

Erinna
Greece   3rd century B.C.

The Distaff

You leaped from the white horses
And raced madly into the deep wave—
But "I've got you, dear!" I shouted loudly.
And when you were the Tortoise
You ran skipping through the yard of the great court.
These are the things that I lament and
Sorrow over, my sad Baucis—these are
Little trails through my heart that are
Still warm—my remembrances of you.
For our former delights are ashes now.
When we were young girls we sat in our rooms
Without a care, holding our dolls and pretending
We were young brides. Remember—at dawn
the "mother," who distributed the wool
To the attendant servants, came and called
You to help with the salting of the meat.
And how afraid we were, when we were small,
Of Mormo—she had huge ears on her head,

Walked about on four feet,
And was always changing faces.
But when you mounted your husband's bed
You forgot all about those things,
All you heard from your mother
When you were still a little child.
Dear Baucis, Aphrodite set forgetfulness
In your heart.
And so I lament you and neglect my duties.
For I am not so irreverent as to set foot out-of-doors
Or to look upon a corpse with my eyes
Or let my hair loose in lamentation—
But a blush of grief tears my [cheeks].

Translated from the Greek by Marylin Arthur

Medieval Europe

MANUSCRIPTS AND EARLY PRINTED BOOKS preserve the lyrics of educated medieval women. The homely lullabies, nursery songs, and work songs that mothers taught and girls learned are lost to us, unless by happy accident a clerk copied some marginal scribblings into his text. Musical notation accompanies some lyrics; until the fourteenth century poetry was chanted or sung. In songbooks made for kings and nobles hundreds of lyrics are recorded, some of them created centuries earlier. While aristocratic society rescued secular poetry, the Christian Church guarded the lyrics composed by nuns for performance in Church ritual or as expressions of personal devotion.

The women whose names and works were thus recorded lived within the sheltering walls of courts and convents.[1] The wealth and rank of court brought noble ladies freedom from manual labor and a measure of independence from the governing hands of men—the fathers, husbands, brothers and sons whose wards they were. The convent was a refuge, too, where aristocratic women were educated in music, literature and science, free from the demands of marriage and childbearing. In a time when marriage was at best an economic alliance, and childbearing often fatal to both mother and child, those freedoms meant something more than they do today.

During the early Middle Ages (800–1100), women who were not participants in court and convent life led a laborious existence on large estates. Here several generations lived together in closely-bound units. Men were principally warriors, while women produced and managed the goods of the household. The chatelaine's ring of keys to cupboards and storehouses was an emblem of her power. The separate bakehouse, alehouse, and spinning rooms were under the care of women. Groups of women presided at rituals of birth, courting, marriage and death. Some beautiful anonymous ballads and dance songs are presumed to be remnants of the oral culture of these centuries.

From ancient times Europe had suffered from a chronic scarcity of women. This condition gave women some relative advantages in marriage customs and legal rights.[2] Dowries (the "morning gift") were paid to a bride by the groom's family. Women owned land and disposed of wealth in their own names under Visigothic[3] law. Divorce was permitted in Germanic law, wives gathering property from each successive husband. In time of war women held authority, even defending their castles if they were threatened or attacked. The Catholic church also allowed women to occupy positions of power. Frequently abbesses ruled communities of hundreds of monks and nuns in combined monasteries.

A watershed in the social and economic position of women in European life came with the late eleventh and early twelfth centuries. Wealth flowed northward as the Crusades opened the Mediterranean to trade. A "vital revolution" changed the face of Europe. Food became more plentiful as agriculture adopted a three-field crop rotation system, a more efficient plough, and power technology. The population increased; cities grew. The older, self-sufficient manorial economy began to be replaced by the earliest forms of capitalist enterprise centering in urban areas. Here women no longer held key positions of power. Male managers hired women to work, and goods were marketed at distant trade fairs. In the new exchange economy, the function of wealthy women became the display, not the exercise, of power. Wives of well-to-do merchants dressed in imported fabrics fashioned into fitted garments with elaborate trains, sleeves, and towering headdresses. These styles replaced the formerly loose clothing of a sexually neutral type.[4]

Greater wealth, the easier conditions of urban life, and better food increased the longevity of women by a few years; but as if in exchange, they lost their former advantages. The number of females increased relative to males, and after the year 1200 dowries had to be paid to a daughter by her father in order for her to obtain a husband. Dante notes this social change with sadness in the *Divine Comedy*. He pictures a father weeping over the misfortune of the birth of a daughter because the high cost of a husband will ruin him.[5] Large number of surplus women in towns meant that many would not be marriageable.

The concentration of single women in the cities, where there was a scarcity of jobs and places to live, led to the formation of sisterhoods, known as the Béguines, which provided autonomous work-

ing and living space on a communal basis. One historian describes
some aspects of this influential movement:

> The women who entered into these all-women households
> took no special vows. They were simply entering into a con-
> genial and practical living arrangement. Working women went
> on with their former trades; upper class women stirred by the
> Frauenbewegung[6] left their manor houses to join the working
> women in their workshops. They gave up fancy clothes, lived
> on the simplest food, and rose early for prayers before
> work. . . .
>
> Because Béguines were also oriented to the reconstruction of
> society they ran schools, hospitals, and workshops for the poor.
> The Béguine schools were so highly respected that many little
> girls were sent to them by ambitious parents with no religious
> interests.[7]

Although these were secular institutions, independent of the
church, many béguinages were deeply religious in character.
Mechthild von Magdeburg (1210–1294) was one of several great
mystics and poets who emerged from this movement. Her work
(the first mystic poetry written in the vernacular) takes its place
within a larger tradition of religious poetry by women, including
Kassia, (810–late 9th century?), whose work was influential in shaping early medieval church liturgy and hymns; Hroswitha von Gandersheim (*fl.* 935–973), whose long poetic dramas in Latin united
classical form and Christian vision; and Hildegard von Bingen
(1098–1197), who embodied extraordinary mystic visions in paint-
ing and poetry. All these held positions of considerable power and
influence within the institution of the church.

Later, as the Church grew into an increasingly powerful secular
institution, women were removed from positions of authority in
monasteries, and often in the popular religious movements as well.
In the cities, women tended to lose their actual power as producers,
managers, and administrators, as society was moving away from
the family as a basic unit of production and consumption.

Among the aristocracy, although the legal and economic status
of women did not improve, they acquired symbolic power. They
took on the role of civilizers and arbiters of manners, shaping and
embodying a new concern with the psychological intimacies of
human relationships. The poetry of the troubadours, in Provence
of the twelfth century, created a code of love that formulated the
rules for male and female interaction. In the poetic code, the lady is
noble, married and unattainable. In order to win her favor, the
lover has to prove his valor and his constancy. The courtship can

last for years; he sings her praises, adores her at a distance, and performs feats in her honor.

Through the prolongation of courtship and the withholding of sexual favors women at this time came to play an important role as active agents in the transformation of society. The fall of the Roman Empire had been followed by centuries of instability and chaos with innumerable local feuds and prolonged warfare. The code of courtly love taught men to abandon brute force and assume an attitude of greater civility and gentleness in manners, to restrain their appetites, and to respect those weaker than themselves. At least in theory, the chevalier was moved, out of love and admiration for his highborn lady, to acquire nobility of heart and manners. He was no longer allowed to jump in bed with his boots on.

Some of the troubadours were women, ladies of the Provençal nobility, such as Carenza and Beatrice de Die, but they give no hint of the courtly love code of prolonged service to the beloved. These women speak in their songs from a point of view that treats both lovers as subjects. They make use of the verbal wit for which Provençal literature was justly famous, and in clever conceits and twists of grammar tell us that love is not a heartbreak for them; even the gossips are a source of fun.

The influence of courtly love continued throughout the Middle Ages and beyond; its effects can still be discerned. As a poetic convention, it was widely used in the beginning of the fifteenth century. Christine de Pisan, who, along with Marie de France is the most important French woman poet of the Middle Ages, wrote numerous lyrics on the theme of courtly love. Unlike Marie de France, however, of whom we know nothing except that she lived in the twelfth century and was of the nobility, Christine de Pisan has left an instructive and fascinating life story. As a child, she came to France from Italy, where women were better educated than elsewhere in Europe. She was married at fifteen and enjoyed a few years of marital happiness. At the premature death of her husband, in order to support herself and her two children, she became the first woman to make a living from her writing. Her output was considerable. She wrote cycles of poems in the courtly style, learned treatises on philosophical and metaphysical questions, intimate lyrics expressing her affection for her husband and her sorrow at his death, and a defence of women, along with *La Cité des Dames,* the earliest feminist Utopia.

Her defence of women in *Épistre au Dieu d'Amours* is a response to the growing misogyny in France at this time,[8] which was to develop into a full-scale literary battle of the sexes, "Le Querelle de la

Rose," that lasted more than one hundred years. In the *Épistre*, Christine argues that clerics have propagated lies about women. If women were writing the books, she says, this would not have happened. Men hold up Adam, David, Samson, Solomon and others as examples, but no one mentions Dido, who died from sorrow, or Penelope, the noble and wise wife of Ulysses[9] in Homer's Odyssey. She is the first woman writer to make an extended public defense of women.

DORIS EARNSHAW

Notes and References

[1] Ireland is an exception here. Liadain was apparently a member of a guild of highly trained professional poets, which was open to women as well as men.

[2] David Herlihy, "Life Expectancies for Women in Medieval Society" in *The Role of Woman in the Middle Ages,* Rosmarie Thee Morewedge, ed. (Albany: State University of New York Press, 1975).

[3] Visigoths, division of the Goths, one of the most important groups of early German peoples.

[4] Eunice Goddard, *Women's Costume in French Texts of the Eleventh and Twelfth Centuries.* The Johns Hopkins Studies in Romance Literatures and Languages, v. VII, 1927.

[5] Dante, *Paradiso*, Canto XV, 103–105:
   Non faceva, nascendo, ancor paura
   la figlia al padre; che 'l tempo e la dote
   non fuggiem quinci e quindi la misura.
   Singleton's translation: Nor yet did the daughter at her birth cause fear to the father, for the time and the dowry did not outrun due measure on this side and that.

[6] *Frauenbewegung,* a contemporary women's movement.

[7] Elise Boulding, *The Underside of History: A View of Women Through Time,* (Boulder, Colorado: Westview Press, 1966).

[8] In the anti-woman texts in the fifteenth century, she is accused of being the instrument of the devil, the Great Prostitute, a sewer, a piece of dung, a bag of excrement, etc.

[9] Marguerite Favier, *Christine de Pisan: Muse des cours souveraines,* (Lausanne, Switzerland: Editions Rencontre, 1967).

Liadain

Gain without gladness
   Is in the bargain I have struck;
One that I loved I wrought to madness.

Mad beyond measure
   But for God's fear that numbed her heart
She that would not do his pleasure.

Was it so great
   My treason? Was I not always kind?
Why should it turn his love to hate?

Liadain,
   That is my name, and Curithir
The man I loved; you know my sin.

Alas too fleet!
   Too brief my pleasure at his side;
With him the passionate hours were sweet.

Woods woke
   About us for a lullaby,
And the blue waves in music spoke.

And now too late
   More than for all my sins I grieve
That I turned his love to hate.

Why should I hide
   That he is still my heart's desire
More than all the world beside?

A furnace blast
   Of love has melted down my heart,
Without his love it cannot last.

Translated from the Gaelic by Frank O'Connor

Kassia

Byzantine Greece   9th century

Selected Epigrams

A woman working hard and wisely
Has misfortune at her will;
A woman living soft and idly
Sees misfortune bring the bill.

❖

Poverty? wealth? seek neither—
One causes swollen hands.
The other swollen bellies.

❖

Wealth covers sin—the poor
Are naked as a pin.

Sticheron[1] for Matins,[2] Wednesday of Holy Week[3]

My Lord, fallen, sin-stained
   She[4] falls before You
Divinity, lowering her eyes
   Myrrh-bearer
Weeping, for your burial
   Presents the myrrh
'Alas, around me,' cries
   'Night falls
   Lightless desire
Darkness, moonless love
   Of evil-doing—
Hold my tears in Your heart
   Weaver of clouds
   With sea-water
     Bend down

---

[1]Sticheron is a complex metrical form used in Catholic liturgy.
[2]Matins: the first of the seven canonical hours in the Catholic breviary.
[3]Holy Week for Christians is the week preceding Easter.
[4]"She" refers to Mary Magdalene.

To gather my cries
In Whom is the unspeakable
Bending of Heaven to flesh—
My kisses fall on your glistening feet
My hair showers over them
Drying my tears—
Eve in Eden heard
The sound of their coming,
Heard with guilty ears
Hid in fear—
My multitude of sins
Or your unfathomed judgments
Who measures them,
Beloved, and my Savior?
Look down upon Your serving-maid
Lord of unmeasured mercies.

Translated from the Greek by Patrick Diehl

Hroswitha von Gandersheim
Germany: Latin   *935–after 973*

from the play Paphnutius

I bring you a goat
snatched half dead from the jaws of wolves—
Care for her, nurse her with tenderness
till she sheds her rough goatskin
and puts on the soft fleece of a lamb

Translated from the Latin by Patrick Diehl

Hildegard von Bingen
Germany: Latin   *1098–1197*

O crimson blood
Which fell from that high place
Divinity had touched,

You are the flower
The winter-storm the serpent breathes
Has never withered.

❖

Like the honeycomb dropping honey
Was Ursula[1] the virgin
Seeking the Lamb of God's embrace;
Honey and milk beneath her tongue;
A fruitful garden, flowers on flowers
In a flock of virgins
She spread about her.

Translated from the Latin by Patrick Diehl

[1]St. Ursula, virgin martyr; her virgin attendants were martyred with her.

Mechthild von Magdeburg
Germany   1210–1294

Love Flows From God

Love flows from God to man without effort
As a bird glides through the air
Without moving its wings—
Thus they go whithersoever they will
United in body and soul
Yet in their form separate—
    As the Godhead strikes the note
Humanity sings,
The Holy Spirit is the harpist
And all the strings must sound
Which are strung in love.

❖

Here too the Spirit shafts
Such heavenly floods of light
On all the Blest that they
Filled and enchanted, sing
For joy, and laugh and leap
In ordered dance. They flow

And swim and fly and climb
From tiered choir to choir
Still upward through the heights.
A mirror there they find,
Read there the will and work
Writ, of the Trinity,
Read how they have been wrought
Body and soul and so
Forever will remain,
See there within the flesh
Like a bright wick, englazed
The soul God's finger lit
To give her liberty,
And joy and power and love,
To make her crystal, like
As maybe, to Himself.
So where they will they fly
Like thought a thousand miles,
Yet never reach the bounds
Of Heaven, nor the corners
Of its bright streets, not gold
O finer far, not gems
But their eternal parts.

Translated from the Low German by Lucy Menzies

Carenza and Iselda
Provence   12th century(?)

Tenson[1]

Iselda: Pretty Lady Carenza
          Advise me as a sister
          Since you know what's best
          Tell me what you think
          Shall I take a husband
          Or stay a virgin? Here's what pleases me—
          To bear children seems no fine thing
          But to live without a husband is hard.

[1]or *tenzone,* Provençal poetic form from the twelfth century involving a dialogue.

Carenza: Lady Iselda, you are learned
Pretty, wise, youthful, fresh
And a better lady
Than anyone I know.
So I counsel you that to produce good
    offspring
Take for a husband the crown of knowledge
And you will give him a glorious son.

Iselda: Lady Carenza, I want to take a husband
But I think it's a great penance to have
    children
The breasts hang down
And the belly is loaded and cumbersome.

Carenza: Lady Iselda, remember me
In the light of salvation
When you are there
Beseech the glorious one
To keep me near you
At the Judgement.

Translated from the Provençal by Bridget Connelly and Doris Earnshaw

Beatrice de Die
Provence   late 12th century

My true love makes me happy
And I sing gaily
Feeling no remorse
Or heavy thoughts
And I don't even think of those tell-tale gossips
They just make me twice as jolly.

Those bad-talking gossips
No one who counts
Pays any attention to them
They are a fog that rises
Against the sunlight.

And you, loud-mouth, jealous husband

Don't think I'll be reluctant
To say I love youth and fun
No matter what pain that brings you.

Translated from the Provençal by Doris Earnshaw

Handsome friend, charming and kind,
when shall I have you in my power?
If only I could lie beside you for an hour
and embrace you lovingly—
know this, that I'd give almost anything
to see you in my husband's place,
but only under the condition
that you swear to do my bidding.

Translated from the Provençal by Meg Bogin

Compiuta Donzella
Italy   13th century

To leave the world   serve God
make my escape   from all pretension. . . .
That is my wish.

For what I see florish and ascend
the stalk   is only
insanity, low acts and lies of men.

And as I watch
all courtliness and grace wither and perish
I have no desire for husband or
lord and master,
nor for this world—if
I had my choice.

Aware that all men find evil
a proper ornament   I must
be haughty. My body
I turn over to God.

And yet my father has me in his power

makes me distraught . . .
turns me
from serving Christ   to give me
in marriage to
I-know-not-who.

Translated from the Italian by Laura Stortoni

Marie de France
France   1155–1190

Song from **Chartivel**

Hath any loved you well, down there,
      Summer or winter through?
Down there, have you found any fair
      Laid in the grave with you?
Is death's long kiss a richer kiss
      Than mine was wont to be—
Or have you gone to some far bliss
      And quite forgotten me?

What soft enamoring of sleep
      Hath you in some soft way?
What charmed death holdeth you with deep
      Strange lure by night and day?
A little space below the grass,
      Out of the sun and shade;
But worlds away from me, alas,
      Down there where you are laid.

My brightest waved and wasted gold,
      What is it now to thee—
Whether the rose-red life I hold
      Or white death holdeth me?
Down there you love the grave's own green,
      And evermore you rave
Of some sweet seraph you have seen
      Or dreamt of in the grave.

There you shall lie as you have lain,

Though in the world above,
Another live your life again,
Loving again your love:
Is it not sweet beneath the palm?
Is it not warm day rife
With some long mystic golden calm
Better than love and life?

The broad quaint odorous leaves like hands
Weaving the fair day through,
Weave sleep no burnished bird withstands,
While death weaves sleep for you;
And many a strange rich breathing sound
Ravishes morn and noon:
And in that place you must have found
Death a delicious swoon—

Hold me no longer for a word
I used to say or sing:
Ah, long ago you must have heard
So many a sweeter thing:
For rich earth must have reached your heart
And turned the faith to flowers;
And warm wind stolen, part by part,
Your soul through faithless hours.

And many a soft seed must have won
Soil of some yielding thought,
To bring a bloom up to the sun
That else had ne'er been brought;
And, doubtless, many a passionate hue
Hath made that place more fair,
Making some passionate part of you
Faithless to me down there.

Translated from the French by Arthur O'Shaughnessy

Christine de Pisan
France   *1363–1430*

Marriage is a lovely thing
—my own example proves it—
for her whose husband is as kind
as he whom God has found for me.
Since day by day he has sustained me,
praised be He who guards his life
and keeps him safe for me,
          and surely my gentle one loves me well.

On the night of our union,
the first time we slept together
I could see how kind he was.
Nothing did that could have hurt me
and before the rising sun
had kissed me, oh a hundred times
but never urged against my will,
          and surely my gentle one loves me well.

And how sweet the words he spoke:
'Dearest Friend, God led me to you
to serve you courteously and well
as if he wished to raise me up.'
Thus he mused all through the night
and his manner never faltered
but stayed the same, unwaveringly,
          and surely my gentle one loves me well.

O Prince, his love can drive me to distraction
when he assures me he's all mine
and of sweetness make me burst.

Fountain of tears, river of grief
torrent of pain, sea brimful with bitterness
I am submerged, I drown in deep misery
for my heart is too easily moved.

They press on and plunge me
into deep waters, wider than the Seine
fountain of tears, river of grief.

And their great streams keep flowing
as the wind of Fortune moves them
all about me; I'm fallen so low,
so sorely oppressed, I barely can right myself
fountain of tears, river of grief.

Translated from the French by Joanna Bankier

Bertha Jacobs (Suster Bertken)
Holland   1427–1514

A Ditty

I went into my garden to gather some herbs;
I found nothing there but thistles and burrs.

Those thistles and burrs I plucked from the earth;
I longed to grow plants of a far greater worth.

At last I have found one who will agree
To take proper care of my garden for me.

A tree had sprung up in no time at all;
I could not uproot it, my strength was so small.

He saw at once the harm in that tree,
And plucked it out of the earth speedily.

Now I must always submit to his will,
Or he will cease promptly my garden to till.

Although I must never cease hoeing the soil,
I still cannot clear it of weeds by my toil.

I must sow lilies by the light of the dawn,
And start my work early as the new day is born.

If he lets the dew fall, he who loves me,
The seeds will take root and grow speedily.

He loves to see lilies, he who loves me,
If they bloom as they should in sweet purity.

And if the red roses are blooming below,
Over their blossoms his sweet dew will flow.

If he shines down in his radiant sunshine,
He quickens the powers of this soul of mine.

Jesus I call him, he who loves me,
I will serve him and love him eternally.

His love has given me so great a worth,
That I care no more for things of this earth.

Translated from the Dutch by Jonathan Crewe

Europe: Sixteenth and Seventeenth Centuries

WHAT DID IT MEAN for women that the pan-European culture of the Latin Middle Ages became fragmented into discrete national identities by the fifteenth century? What does this mean for the diversity of women's voices in each of the countries of Western Europe? Education and social position of women had declined as a result of processes begun in the late Middle Ages: frontier situations and Crusades that had made it necessay for women to occupy positions of power had disappeared. The medieval shortage of female population that had made them a valuable resource was being filled. Towns became economic and cultural centers where specialization of work and concentration of wealth, as well as guild restrictions against women in many trades, were factors in the marginalization of women. This was a significant change for women's participation in processes of production that constituted everyday life for both sexes in the earlier period.[1] The institutionalization of law and medicine through the requisite of university training excluded women from those professions, as well as from positions in the growing court and urban bureaucracies for which a university degree functioned as a key. Although the new interest in pagan antiquity may have offset some of the misogynistic arguments drawn from Biblical and patristic sources, the Classical learning of the Renaissance was not accessible to women, except for the fortunate few whose fathers hired private tutors for them. In Catholic countries, the Inquisition strictly limited spiritual freedom for women, particularly in religious orders. Among the various Western European countries, cultural, political and economic factors were distinct enough to affect the condition of women in different ways, so that there were phases of leniency and repression that do not correspond from country to country. Religious history (Reformation, Counter-Reformation, persecution of heretics and witches) affected these varying phases, as did the attitudes of rulers.

The image of a strong female ruler like Elizabeth I in England had some impact on the image of women in general, though it did not affect the everyday lives of most of her female subjects. Elizabeth deliberately chose a literary and specifically Petrarchan image around which she structured the power relationships at court.[2] She created and played the role of Virgin Queen, unapproachable object of desire. Her courtiers occupied themselves in an elaborate social game which distracted them from forming alliances to challenge her authority. Like Petrarchist moths circling a flame, they were drawn into an innocuous courtly dance in homage of the Queen. Her humanist education was put to good political use.[3]

Among the numerous treatises on education, and defenses and attacks on educated women, the writings of Erasmus, Luis Vives and Thomas More assert that women are not merely capable of advanced learning but capable of making the moral choices that enable them to benefit, not be corrupted, by it.[4] More's own daughters were given a classical education at home. They were often cited as exemplary for their intellectual accomplishments and for their virtue which proved that learning in young women did not place them in moral jeopardy. Nonetheless, only a handful of women participated in the humanism of the Renaissance beginning in Italy and spreading throughout Europe. In Italy and France, these women lived almost exclusively in the sixteenth century. By the seventeenth, the new learning seems to have been thoroughly institutionalized in the universities, off limits to women. A liberal education was defined as one worthy of a free man. It qualified men for positions of power while even the education furnished by tutors to aristocratic women was tailored to the subservient function assigned to women in society.

The construction of the female in Renaissance ideology can be clearly observed in Castiglione's *Cortegiano,* a book that might lead the reader to believe that women in Renaissance Italy had great freedom of thought and movement since noble ladies participate in the imaginary dialogues on art, manners, language and love. Although noble women in Italy may have enjoyed greater freedom than in other countries at that time, the women who speak in *Il Cortegiano* are fictions of Castiglione's authorial imagination. He determines the statements they make, the context in which they are made, and the possibilities for protest which he gives them. The ladies present include Elisabetta Gonzaga, Duchess of Urbina in whose castle the learned conversations take place, and Emilia Pia, a widow whose wisdom and cleverness exemplify the accomplishments prescribed by Castiglione. The contributions of Emilia Pia to the discussion on love are made from the perspective of moderator, not as initiator or defendant. Other, male, participants in the discussion continue to ridicule women in the misogynistic style drawn from long Christian tradition while the main speaker on women and love, Giuliano de' Medici, deploys an array of positive images of women from Classical antiquity and contemporary Italian history.[5] We could expect greater freedom for intellectual women in Renaissance Italy, where the appreciation for pagan authors was reborn; yet women, no matter how well-educated, were seen through the prism of Petrarchist and Neoplatonic poetic imagery that distances them from their own physical bodies, and from the impulse to reciprocate love. When Giuliano de' Medici expounds upon the perfect lady in Book III, he is inventing a woman based upon models of legendary virtuous (i.e., chaste) women of antiquity. The most heroic women are those who prefer death to infidelity or marriage with a man they do not love; occasionally a woman is praised for defending her husband's property (his lands, his castle or herself). It is not insignificant that Giuliano praises women who insist upon marrying for love, but the ideal of the time was still a woman who lacked autonomy after marriage. Before that she was an unattainable object whose active role consisted in the denial of her lover's desires. The acknowledgement of her own still seems unthinkable.

How, then, could a woman write poetry in the Petrarchist mode? One illustration of the possibilities is Vittoria Colonna, eloquent in the construction of conceptually complex sonnets. The longing for death expressed in love poetry by her and other women poets of the period might seem on one hand simply an echo of the conventional antithesis of life as death, death as life. The female voice brings a different meaning to this shopworn conceit, making it new. Praising the strength and vitality of Renaissance women poets, Jacob Burckhardt calls the tone of their learned verse "manly." "The love sonnets like the religious poems are so precise and definite, and so far removed from the tender twilight of sentiment and all the dilettantism we commonly find in the poetry of women, that we should not hesitate to attribute them to male authors . . ."[6] Yet the equation of life with death, and the longing for death as an end to the sufferings of unrequited love, can be read as a cry of despair which has appropriated the language of male poets for its own purposes. For the courtier, the sufferings of love and the helplessness of the lover vis-a-vis the cold refusal of the woman were poses that in reality could be cast off; the woman poet's passive *persona* does not function as a mask. She is in fact helpless to demand anything and the face behind the mask of despair is identical in its desperation. A woman who sincerely begged to be loved in return could not expect her male audience to remain chastely aloof, as the courtly game of love required. She could not fail to notice how different the rules for women were from those for men. We know that Vittoria Colonna was renowned not only for her learned verse but for her piety and charity later in life. She was the friend of such humanists as the Erasmian Juan de Valdés, Peter Martyr and Michelangelo, and participated actively in the humanist reform of the Church. The note of despair in her poetry betrays a recognition that the position of women could not be escaped in the imagined world of neoplatonic exaltation of the divine nature of human relationships. For the Medieval Christine de Pisan widowhood was a catalyst for independent thought and writing; for Vittoria Colonna the disappointments of later life meant a withdrawal into the protection of the Church and finally of the convent.

Louise Labé's frank and passionate exposition of love earned her the derogatory title of "courtesan" although she was admired among the Lyonnaise group of poets of whom Maurice Scève was the stylistic guide. She owes more, perhaps, to Catullus' depiction of love than to Petrarch and his followers, but her imitation of Catullus' "Dame basia mille" ends with a curious turn: "For while my life is disciplined and lonely,/ My heart is ill, and can recover only/ When it escapes . . ." (Tousiours suis mal, vivant discrettement,/ Et ne me puis donner contentement,/ Si hors de moy ne fay quelque saillie.")[7] She finds no rest in conforming to strict moral "discretion" but must "get out of herself" to find peace. It is in imitating a passionate and playful male poet that she escapes the confines of the expectations imposed upon her as a woman: Catullus' *persona* is liberating as the Petrarchists' is not. The "sadness" noted in her poetry may also be attributed to her recognition of the impossibility of "getting outside herself" with impunity. She struggles against the poetic restraints of her milieu, and transforms the poetic elegy from a witty discourse on a point of amorous casuistry, to an intimate personal revelation.[8] She excuses her open discussions of love on the pretext that she's suffered for it, warning other women not to imitate her, as if to appease the voices of moral outrage. ("Ladies, do not reproach me for my love . . ." Son. XXIV).

The bourgeois town of Lyons may have been a more favorable milieu for the women who wrote in Scève's group because it lacked the rigid literary and aristocratic tradition of Paris. Its lack of a university could have been a positive element for the Lyonnaise group: Pontus de Tyard, Maurice Scève, Pernette de Guillet, and Louise Labé gave each other encouragement and intellectual stimulation, while the presence of a printer in the group furnished another circumstance favoring the development of one of the strongest female voices of the period. Not only was she educated, she had an audience in her immediate circle and a more distant one accessible in print.

The theme of death and suffering in women's poetry, and the recurring renunciation of the world in their lives, gives another view of the contradictions inherent in writing in the Petrarchist mode. The ironic apologies for boldness in Louise Labé are another form of recognition of contradictions faced by women poets.[9] This is why the Mexican nun Sor Juana Inés de la Cruz seems so innovative in her use of the familiar motif of *carpe diem* for devotional purposes. The *topos* was used by male writers as a mode of seduction: the young woman should yield to his demands because her youth and beauty will someday fade with age. Sor Juana turns the contemplation of time and change into a meditation on human mortality and the urgency of repentance, cleverly using phrases from her male models to leave no doubt as to her intention. She protests injustices against women directly, albeit with a subtle flavoring of conceptual wit. Of all the writers of the period, the speculative philosophical thought of this colonial Mexican woman is most daring, and she paid the price of her metaphysical and imaginative flights. Although she defended herself deftly against the accusations of worldliness and overweening pride made by her ecclesiastical superiors, she finally renounced her intellectual and artistic pursuits, signing away her creative life in her own blood. She proceeded to further defy authority by pursuing a life of extreme austerity and penitence, and died within a year. In spirit, she could not be dominated by the church hierarchy.

Comparable in her daring is the English writer Aphra Behn, who may owe some of her freedom from contemporary expectations of women's behavior and thought to her sojourn in the New World, in Surinam. While the Americas appear very rarely in the works of male writers, she used this exotic experience as background for a novel, *Oroonoko*. She is considered the first English woman to make her living by writing; she was also considered "among the rakes of her time."[10] Aphra Behn's life marks a new, though publicly disreputable, model for women writers. The note of protest clearly audible in the English poets Aphra Behn and Katherine Phillips, among others, is evidence of a greater freedom to perceive the injustices suffered by women. The despair of Italian and French women writers is a more hidden vein of protest that is poignant in its near-muteness. Conditions were not much better in England; but because the Renaissance was late in arriving there it may be supposed that there were fewer restrictions on thought, allowing enough leeway to perceive some major flaws in Renaissance thinking about women: that women were esteemed as objects of desire but were despised as the root of all corruption; that education ennobled men but led women astray; that so few opportunities were available to participate in life outside the home, yet women were regarded as being active in the corruption of men while they were exalted in purely spiritual terms.

Generally, women who wrote were more cloistered than Aphra Behn: they wrote as nuns or as wives and widows attending literary academies in Italy or holding salons in France. Whatever their situation in life, the poetry written by women takes on its peculiar voice at that point where it splits off from the conventions, however slight the angle of refraction might be. It is astonishingly great in Aphra Behn, and in the more ladylike Katherine Phillips' poem to a female friend, "Lucasia". She takes at face value the body-soul dichotomy offered by neoplatonic love poetry and presents the same imagery of the soul in a poem to a beloved friend. She opens up to question the coy evasions in love poetry by men insisting upon their spiritual intentions, and the fundamental meaning of neoplatonic conceits undergoes a radical renewal.

The fact that the few women poets we know of in Spain are members of religious orders is partly a result of the strict enclosure of women, the Islamic heritage of keeping women at home except to attend religious services. Education by male tutors would undermine the chastity of young women in the eyes of potential suitors, ever watchful for shades of doubt concerning their honor. Some but by no means all nuns were educated enough to read Castillian, and in rare cases Latin. Santa Teresa is one of several nuns who had visions, and who left documentation of their lives,[11] but she is exceptional in that she was able to write and she was prudent enough to evade the suspicious familiars of the Inquisition. Although visions and voices may have been a way for women with strong religious feelings to "get outside themselves", the church regarded zealous nuns and mystics in particular as potential heretics. Her superiors insisted at first that Teresa was possessed by demons. She, confirming her faith in God, said she had no fear of the Devil, but only of those who themselves feared him. She is better known for her lively and colloquial prose than for her poetry. Like many women writing of divine love, and her fellow Carmelite San Juan de la Cruz, she uses the metaphors of earthly love to express an ineffable mystical experience. While other women mystics followed what they experienced as irresistible messages and were discredited by the Holy Office, Santa Teresa waited until her fifties to write about her experiences of divine grace. As a founder of the reformed Discalced Carmelites and a reorganizer of convent life, she took on the role of a wise and powerful religious leader. She was, however, perceptive enough to see how her strength might be seen as a threat to the Church. Her prose was written at the request of her male superiors and she deliberately effaces herself as subject in the *Life* and in the *Interior Castle,* referring to herself as "someone I know". Her writing is directed toward her sisters in the Carmelite convents, and its style betrays a lively mind that had no time for revision. Hence the traces of an oral style: repetitions, grammatical vagueness and graphic imagery drawn from the kitchen, the garden and the adventurous books of chivalry that inspired her as a girl: the soul as a castle, sins as dragons. She compares four stages of mystical prayer with methods of watering a garden, each of increasing facility and decreasing effort on the gardener's part: drawing water in buckets from a well, using the device of a water-wheel, irrigating by diverting a river, and finally, simply letting the rain fall.[12] The deviation from the commonly-used imagery of devotional poetry and prose may be what has won her works a special place in the canon of mystical writings. In her verse, on the other hand, she does employ the familiar antitheses of life as death, death as life ("I die because I do not die"; "I am alive without living in myself.")

Whether it is through renunciation of the world, through putting on or criticizing available poetic masks, women poets of the Renaissance and the Baroque betray their discomfort in the new position imposed on them by humanist discourse in Renaissance society. The voices that are scarcely audible in the sixteenth century are effectively silenced by the seventeenth everywhere but in England. Exiled from the prestigious and venerable enclave of verse, women writers began to explore the uncharted territories of the novel.

EMILIE BERGMANN

Notes and References

[1]Kathleen Casey, "The Cheshire Cat: Reconstructing the Experience of Medieval Woman" in *Liberating Women's History,* Berenice A. Carroll, ed. (Urbana, Ill.: University of Illinois Press, 1976), pp. 225–227, and

Joan Kelly-Gadol, "Did Women Have a Renaissance?" in *Becoming Visible: Women in European History*, Renate Bridenthal and Claudia Koonz, eds. (Boston: Houghton Mifflin Co., 1977), pp. 139–164.

[2]Leonard Forster, *The Icy Fire: Five Studies in European Petrarchism* (Cambridge: Cambridge University Press, 1969), pp. 128–130.

[3]Susan Groag Bell, ed., *Women: From the Greeks to the French Revolution* (Stanford, California: Stanford University Press, 1973), pp. 214–216.

[4]Bell, p. 183, and Ruth Kelso, *Doctrine for the Lady of the Renaissance* (Urbana, Illinois: University of Illinois Press, 1956), pp. 58–78.

[5]Baldassare Castiglione, *The Book of the Courtier*, trans. Charles S. Singleton (Garden City, N.Y.: Doubleday, 1959), pp. 201–240. In the second half of Book III, on love, Emilia Pia does take a more active role in conversation, but the direction of the argument is nonetheless determined by the male participants.

[6]Bell, p. 201.

[7]Louise Labé, *Love Sonnets*, trans. Frederic Prokosch (New York: New Directions, 1947), Sonnet XVIII.

[8]*Poètes du XVIᵉ siècle*, ed. Albert-Marie Schmidt (Paris: Gallimard (Pléiade, v. 86, 1964), p. 272.

[9]Ann Rosalind Jones, "Assimilation with a Difference: Renaissance Women Poets and Literary Influence," *Yale French Studies* 62 (1981) 136–137.

[10]*The World Split Open: Four Centuries of Women Poets in England and America, 1552–1950*, ed. Louise Bernikow (New York: Vintage Books, 1974), p. 68.

[11]Electa Arenal and Amanda Powell, unpublished studies and translations of Sor Juana Inés de la Cruz and other Hispanic nuns; conversation with Electa Arenal, April 28, 1982.

[12]Saint Teresa of Avila, *The Life of Teresa of Jesus*, transl. E. Allison Peers (Garden City, N.Y.: Doubleday, 1960), pp. 127, 128, Chapter XI.

Saint Teresa of Ávila
Spain 1515–1588

Bookmark

Let nothing disturb thee,
Nothing affright thee;
All things are passing;
God never changeth;
Patient endurance
Attaineth to all things;
Who God possesseth
In nothing is wanting;
Alone God sufficeth.

Translated from the Spanish by Henry Wadsworth Longfellow

En las internas entrañas[1]

Within my heart a stab I felt—
A sudden stab, expecting naught;
Beneath God's standard was it dealt
For goodly were the deeds it wrought,
And though the lance hath wounded me,
And though the wound be unto death,
Surpassing far all other pain,
Yet doth new life therefrom draw breath!

How doth a mortal wound give life?
How, while life-giving, yet doth slay?
How heal while wounding, leaving thee
United to thy God alway?
Celestial was that hand, and though
With peril dire the fray was fraught,
I came forth victor o'er the lance
And goodly were the deeds it wrought.

Translated from the Spanish by Father Benedict Zimmerman

[1]In the inmost recesses

Vittoria Colonna
Italy   *1490–1547*

When the Orient is lit by the great light
that loosens night's black cloak,
dissolves earth's frost, and drives away
the cold shadow with its burning ray,

Then these first cares that sleep had gently
lessened, again grow heavy
and all my pleasures sink in shadows
just when the shadows vanish from every side.

Thus I'm forced by hostile fate
to seek the dusk, to flee the light
to hate life and desire death.

That which dims other eyes, brightens mine,
for, closing them, the door is opened
to sleep which brings me to my sun.

❖

As a hungry fledgling, who sees and hears
the beating of his mother's wings, when
she brings him nourishment, so that, loving
his mother and the food, he is consoled and joys,

and struggles, raging inside his nest
with desire to follow her, he too, flying,
and he thanks her with such singing,
that his tongue seems loosed beyond its power,

so I, when the hot and live ray
of the heavenly sun, whence I nourish my heart,
more clear than usual shines,

move my pen urged by love
within, and unaware
of what I say, write this praise.

Translated from the Italian by Brenda Webster

Gaspara Stampa
Italy   1523–1554

Hunger

As a man who soon must be without
the food which sustains his life
desires to take it more abundantly
while it remains to him;

Thus before the bitter parting,
my soul, invited to so cruel a fast,
craves better nourishment
to sustain such absence.

Therefore, gaze deep, my wandering eyes,
more than is your wont, taste the goodness
and the beauty of the cherished face.

And you, ears, fill yourselves more full
of the words whose harmonies are sweeter
than those of Paradise.

Translated from the Italian by Brenda Webster

I am now so weary with waiting,
so overcome with grief and with desire,
for the faithlessness and great forgetfulness
of him for whose return, alas, I long,
that her who with her scythe causes the world
to pale and brings the final penalty,—
her do I call upon for my relief,
so greatly wells the sorrow in my breast.

And she turns deaf to my pleading,
mocking my foolish, erring thoughts,
as he remains deaf to his returning.
So with plaints, whence my eyes are moist,
I make piteous these waves, this sea;
and he lives happily up in his hills.

Translated from the Italian by Harold M. Priest

Deeply repentant of my sinful ways
    And of my trivial, manifold desires,
    Of squandering, alas, these few brief days
    Of fugitive life in tending love's vain fires,
To Thee, Lord, Who dost move hard hearts again,
    And render warmth unto the frozen snow,
    And lighten every bitter load of pain
    For those who with Thy sacred ardours glow,
To Thee I turn, O stretch forth Thy right hand
    And from this whirlpool rescue me, for I
    Without Thine aid could never reach the land;
O willingly for us didst suffer loss,
    And to redeem mankind hung on the Cross,
    O gentle Saviour, leave me not to die.

Translated from the Italian by Lorna de'Lucchi

Pernette de Guillet
France   1520–1545

"Non que je veuille ôter la liberté"[1]

Not that I wish to take the liberty
Of someone born to be my overlord;
Not that I wish to act presumptuously,
For humble service is my sole reward;
Not that I wish to drive him left and right,
Command him like a workman in my hire;
But I would wish, to both our hearts' delight,
For his will to be joined with my desire.

Translated from the French by Raymond Oliver
[1]"Not that I wish to take the liberty"

Louise Labé
France   c. 1524–1566

Sonnet XVIII

Kiss me again, re-kiss and kiss me whole;
Give me one of your most delectable,
Give one of your most affectionate;
I'll give you back four more as hot as coal.

There, does it hurt? Come then, let me appease
Your pain by giving you, just as delicious,
Another ten. Thus mingling joyful kisses
Let us enjoy eath other at our ease;

So each will have two lives, a doubled state:
Each in himself will live, and in his mate. . . .
Permit me, Love, to be a little silly.

Apart from you, I always feel depressed
And cannot make myself content unless,
At times, out of myself I briefly sally.

Elegy XXIII

How does it help me if, with flawless art,
Some time ago you praised my golden hair
And likened my resplendent eyes to a pair
Of suns, from which the Love-god drew his dart,
Craftily, causing you a martyr's pain?
Where are you, tears that last so short a space?
And Death, which was supposed to seal, to grace
The deathless love you pledged again and again?

So this was the intention of your malice—
Make me a servant while pretending service.
Exasperation makes us all less shy,
So for these words, my Friend, please pardon me:
But I am sure, wherever you may be
You're suffering martyrdom as much as I.

Translated from the French by Raymond Oliver

Gabrielle de Coignard
France   *d. 1594*

Prayer

The fear of death disturbs me constantly;
For those in hell there can be no redemption;
Though I have sinned I cannot feel contrition;
The more I live, the worse my agony.

You will consume me like a brittle leaf
On the enormous day of tribulation:
Let me repent at last of my transgression,
For fastened to my soul is bitter grief.

You made me out of flesh, tendons, and veins,
Of blood and bones, of liver, lungs, and brains—
I'm dust and ashes, Lord; remember this.

You are the wind and I am straw, or less,
For you can sweep me into nothingness.
Ah, do not let me fall in the abyss!

Translated from the French by Raymond Oliver

Catharina Regina von Greiffenberg
Germany 1633–1694

Spring-Joy Praising God. Praise of the Sun

You empress of the stars, the heavens' worthy crown,
The world's great eye, and soul of all the spreading
    earth,
The middle-point of beams and joy's and beauty's birth,
The life of every thing and clarity's bright throne.

Folk's flame and treasure-house, from which all bliss is
    won,
God's mirror (for naught else can show His lustre's
    worth),

Eternal motion's show in your hot hastening girth,
You golden wonder-fount, incomparable sun!

A ship, which brings to us from God life's needed wares,
His wagon, which to us the heaven's crop relays,
You are the king of time, and rule the years and days.

Your noble presence well the continents repairs,
You lovely blessings-tree, set down by God's designs,
From out your bloom of light the Maker's beauty shines.

Translated from the German by George C. Schoolfield

Kata Szidónia Petröczi
Hungary   1662–1708

Swift Floods

I feel the stubborn humming
Of swift floods, cruel winds,
My heart's pains, hideous racks,
I can't stop the pouring
From my eyes,
Hourly I howl the change in my fate.

Growing daily, there's no cease
To my flooding sorrow.
The winds of sadness lay siege
To my forsaken mind, my wounded heart.
They shorten my life
These pains that destroy me.

I've already lost all hope
I don't wait for joyful hours
In fact, night and day grieving
I howl my agonies,
And as I suffer, I consume myself vilely
And ask for death.

There is no remedy, no happiness
For my sad pining heart,

Little to console it, little solace
For one so empty of hope,
And none even to appease, to aid
Me in my misery.

So with complete readiness, surfeit,
I wish to leave
This evil world, its impermanence
With great joy say farewell,
If God wishes, may the hour arrive,
I'm ready now to die.

For death can be my help
To forget my grief
And it will sooth, will dress my wounds
Heal my pains,
Draw them from my heart and from my eyes wipe
My constant flood of tears.

Translated from the Hungarian by Laura Schiff

Katherine Philips
England   1631–1664

To My Excellent Lucasia, on Our Friendship

I did not live until this time
      Crowned my felicity,
When I could say without a crime,
      I am not thine, but thee.

This carcass breathed, and walked and slept,
      So that the world believed
There was a soul the motions kept;
      But they were all deceived.

For as a watch by art is wound
      To motion, such was mine:
But never had Orinda found
      A soul till she found thine;

Which now inspires, cures, and supplies,
    And guides my darkened breast:
For thou art all that I can prize,
    My joy, my life, my rest.

No bridegroom's nor crown-conqueror's mirth
    To mine compared can be:
They have but pieces of this earth,
    I've all the world in thee.

Then let our flames still light and shine,
    And no false fear control,
As innocent as our design,
    Immortal as our soul.

Aphra Behn
England   1640–1689

Song from The Lucky Chance

Oh! Love, that stronger art than wine,
Pleasing delusion, witchery divine,
Want to be prized above all wealth,
Disease that has more joys than health,
Though we blaspheme thee in our pain,
And of thy tyranny complain,
We are all bettered by thy reign.

What reason never can bestow
We to this useful passion owe.

Love wakes the dull from sluggish ease,
And learns a clown the art to please,
Humbles the vain, kindles the cold,
Makes misers free, and cowards bold.
'Tis he reforms the sot from drink,
And teaches airy fops to think.

When full brute appetite is fed,
And choked the glutton lies, and dead:
Thou new spirits dost dispense,

And fine'st the gross delights of sense.
Virtue's unconquerable aid,
That against nature can persuade:
And makes a roving mind retire
Within the bounds of just desire.
Cheerer of age, youth's kind unrest,
And half the heaven of the blest.

from the "Epilogue" to Sir Patient Fancy

What has poor Woman done, that she must be
Debar'd from Sense, and sacred Poetry?
Why in this Age has Heaven allow'd you more,
And Women less of Wit than heretofore?
We once were fam'd in story, and could write
Equal to Men; cou'd govern, nay cou'd fight.
We still have passive Valour, and can show,
Wou'd Custom give us leave, the active too,
Since we no Provocation want[1] from you.

[1]*Want:* i.e., *lack.*

Mary Lee, Lady Chudleigh
England 1656-1710

To the Ladies

Wife and servant are the same,
But only differ in the name,
For when that fatal knot is tied,
Which nothing, nothing can divide,
When she the word "obey" has said,
And man by law supreme has made,
Then all that's kind is laid aside,
And nothing left but state and pride.
Fierce as an eastern prince he grows,
And all his innate rigour shows.
Then but to look, to laugh, or speak,
Will the nuptial contract break.

Like mutes, she signs alone must make,
And never any freedom take,
But still be governed by a nod,
And fear her husband as her God;
Him still must serve, him still obey,
And nothing act, and nothing say,
But her haughty Lord thinks fit,
Who with the power, has all the wit.
Then shun, oh! shun that wretched state,
And all the fawning flatterers hate;
     Value yourselves, and men despise,
     You must be proud, if you'll be wise.

Anne Finch, Countess of Winchilsea
England   1661–1720

The Introduction

Did I, my lines intend for publick view,
How many censures, wou'd their faults persue,
Some wou'd because such words they do affect,
Cry they're insipid, empty, uncorrect.
And many, have attain'd, dull and untaught
The name of Witt, only by finding fault.
True judges, might condemn their want of witt,
And all might say, they're by a Woman writt.
Alas! a woman that attempts the pen,
Such an intruder on the rights of men,
Such a presumptuous Creature, is esteem'd,
The fault, can by no vertue be redeem'd.
They tell us, we mistake our sex and way;
Good breeding, fassion, dancing, dressing, play
Are the accomplishments we shou'd desire;
To write, or read, or think, or to enquire
Wou'd cloud our beauty, and exaust our time,
And interrupt the Conquests of our prime;
Whilst the dull mannage, of a servile house
Is held by some, our outmost art, and use.
     Sure 'twas not ever thus, nor are we told
Fables, of Women that excell'd of old;

To whom, by the diffusive hand of Heaven
Some share of witt, and poetry was given.
On that glad day, on which the Ark return'd,
The holy pledge, for which the Land had mourn'd,
The joyfull Tribes, attend itt on the way,
The Levites do the sacred Charge convey,
Whilst various Instruments, before itt play;
Here, holy Virgins in the Concert joyn,
The louder notes, to soften, and refine,
And with alternate verse, compleat the Hymn Devine.
Loe! the yong Poet, after Gods own heart,
By Him inspired, and taught the Muses Art,
Return'd from Conquest, a bright Chorus meets.
That sing his slayn ten thousand in the streets.
In such loud numbers they his acts declare,
Proclaim the wonders, of his early war,
That Saul upon the vast applause does frown,
And feels, itts mighty thunder shake the Crown.
What, can the threat'n'd Judgment now prolong?
Half of the Kingdom is already gone;
The fairest half, whose influence guides the rest,
Have David's Empire, o're their hearts confess't.
    A Woman here, leads fainting Israel on,
She fights, she wins, she tryumphs with a song,
Devout, Majestick, for the subject fitt,
And far above her arms, exalts her witt,
Then, to the peacefull, shady Palm withdraws,
And rules the rescu'd Nation, with her Laws.
How are we fal'n, fal'n by mistaken rules?
And Education's, more than Nature's fools,
Debarr'd from all improve-ments of the mind,
And to be dull, expected and dessigned;
And if some one, wou'd Soar above the rest,
With warmer fancy, and ambition press't,
So strong, th' opposing faction still appears,
The hopes to thrive, can ne're outweigh the fears,
Be caution'd then my Muse, and still retir'd;
Nor be dispis'd, aiming to be admir'd;
Conscious of wants, still with contracted wing,
To some few friends, and to thy sorrows sing;
For groves of Lawrell, thou wert never meant;
Be dark enough thy shades, and be thou there content.

Europe: *18th and 19th Centuries*

WOMEN DID REMARKABLE WORK in prose during this time, particularly in England and France; the novel as a new genre owes much of its distinguishing shape to their influence. Only rarely, however, do we find women writing poetry of equal quality, and the few exceptions had virtually no impact on the tradition. There are no easy explanations. Still, there were general developments in the period that bear looking at, in which changing material conditions and ideology intersected to affect both what women wrote, and the likelihood of their writing at all. A central issue is the extent to which women had access to the world outside the home. Here there are contradictory tendencies at work—among them a growing concern throughout Europe for social and political equality, and the bourgeois ideology of "true womanhood."

The 17th century had been an age in which a small number of women, mostly aristocratic, had played a visible and influential role in several countries—at times as rulers, often as significant political forces behind the scenes, and preeminently, especially in France, as leaders of salons, those regular gatherings which served as arbiters of civilized manners and literary taste, and also as the unofficial embassies of the time, international meeting grounds for diplomats and political leaders, artists and intellectuals. In England at the same time, groups of women interested in science and literature, derided as "blue-stockings," organized assemblies in which the leading writers and thinkers of the day took part. In both cases it was the men primarily who did the talking, with one woman as central instigator and choreographer.[1]

These groups continued into the 18th century, even into the early part of the 19th, but with significant changes. In 18th century England with the rise of the middle class came a reaction against the relatively public and outspoken role of women during the Restoration (1660–1688), and an increasing insistence that it was not women's place to meddle in politics and literature. In France, as the rationalist ideas of the Enlightenment spread outward across Europe, the emphasis of the salons shifted from literary topics to politics and philosophy, centering more and more on equality, a logical ordering of human society, and the "rights of man." The democracy of classical Athens, in which women played no part, was held up as an ideal. Surprisingly, few of the thinkers of the time allowed their revolutionary thinking about rights to extend to women. Voltaire said little, and Diderot was inconsistent.

In Germany, at least among the influential group of writers and thinkers around the Schlegels and Schelling[2], the Enlightenment ideas of inherent rights and human perfectibility were very much assumed to extend to women. Although most women of the society were limited to the sphere of "Kinder, Kuche, Kirche"[3], and education for women was virtually unknown, Schlegel and others argued for the emancipation of women from conventional constraints. They called on women to live not simply as wives and mothers, but as human beings responsible for developing their whole personalities—emotional, intellectual, spiritual, sensual. Although women were expected to marry early, upper-class women in the Romantic *cénâcle*[4] were able to take advantage of a long tradition of lenient Germanic divorce laws. The daughters of university professors, like Dorothea Schlegel, were among the first to benefit from the new attitudes; given a broad though informal education by their fathers, they were idealized by the Romantics as epitomes of the "new woman." One of them, Caroline Michaelis, became the center of the circle of Romantics in Jena; and in the succeeding decades women such as Rachel Levin and Henriette Herz led influential salons.[5]

Each of these countries saw a few important works emerge that took seriously the extension of the "rights of man" to women. In France, Condorcet *(On the Admission of Women to the Rights of Citizenship,* 1787)[6] argued that women were being trivialized by their exclusion from effective action in the world, and that they and society as a whole would benefit by their participation in the political realm. And during the Revolution, Olympe de Gouges distributed her pamphlet *Declaration of the Rights of Woman and Citizen* (1791)[7], calling for equal rights to property and government employment, reform of the marriage laws, and freedom of thought. In 1792 in England, Mary Wollstonecraft *(Vindication of the Rights of Woman)*[8] called for education for women identical to that of men so that their contributions to the progress of human civilization could be realized. And the same year in Germany, Gottlieb von Hippel published anonymously his *On Improving the Status of Women*[9], in which he presents the historical background of the status of women, argues for their emancipation as a "human, legal, and natural right," and gives detailed suggestions for change.

These ideas had little immediate impact; but they reappear, in more radical form, in the work of early utopian socialists like Saint-Simon (1760–1825) and Fourier (1772–1837), who made women's issues central to their philosophy and practice[10]. Engels (1820–1895) in *Origin of the Family* provided an analysis of women's historically subordinate place in the social order; and women's equality was a theoretical given in the writings of Karl Marx (1818–1883). Women were involved in socialist thinking and organizing from the beginning. Flora Tristan (1803–1844), active in the utopian socialist movement, wrote theoretical works that also outlined practical plans to respond to the needs of women workers, including daycare and communal cooking facilities. She died during an exhausting trip through France speaking before workers' unions on issues affecting women[11]. The French woman writer George Sand—whose novels espousing the cause of women and workers had a committed following throughout Europe[12]—participated directly in the peoples' government of the February Revolution, sitting on committees, helping form policy, writing official *Bulletins de la République* which were posted in the communes.[13] In Russia numerous women of the 1860's modeled themselves after Vera, the autonomous "new woman" in Chernyevsky's widely read novel *What Is to Be Done?* (1863), written as a blueprint for the new society. A primary concern of the growing socialist movement there was the intellectual and economic emancipation of women through new schools, study groups, and communal workshops. By the end of the decade women were playing critical roles in revolutionary organization and actions.[14]

What was happening in general with women in this period? In the 18th century the rise of industry and the bourgeois ideology which supported it had a two-edged effect on the wives and daughters of the middle class. With the separation of shop and craft from the home, they were increasingly cut off from the world of productive work and action; yet as non-producing consumers they had the advantage of both financial security and leisure. Gradations of rank within the middle class became more important, and women became both embodiments and arbiters of those distinctions, both decoratively idle, and active managers of manners and social interactions.

In the course of the 18th century, middle-class women and domestic servants were becoming increasingly more educated, and were forming a significant part of the reading public. Circulating libraries gave these women access to popular novels; and their avid desire for reading material, plus the custom of subscribing by installment to works in progress, made it possible for a growing number of women to look on writing as a serious and paying profession.[15] These women writers had a profound influence on the direction the novel took in its formative stages. Early novels were frequently structured on the model of letter-writing, an art in which women were expected to excel.[16] Women also developed an important subgenre within the novel that grew out of popular pamphlets written to teach young girls the feminine and domestic virtues necessary to secure good husbands. Fanny Burney's *Evelina* (1778), for all the spunkiness of its heroine, reveals a great deal about contemporary assumptions concerning woman's "proper" character and role. Burney and many other women novelists who were confidently practicing the craft of writing—and laying the technical and psychological groundwork for the extraordinary achievement of women novelists such as Austen, the Brontës, and George Eliot in the 19th century—were themselves often creating novels that assumed a docile and subordinate role for women.

So we have already in the late 18th century the roots of the "cult of true womanhood," with its focus on marriage and domesticity as the goals of female existence. More and more the ideal woman was the pure and passive keeper of the hearth. The writings of Jean-Jacques Rousseau (1712–1778) on education were particularly influential: young girls were to be taught not to think deeply, but to "please." In schools for girls, academic subjects, especially the classics considered so essential to anyone presuming to write in the established tradition, were deemphasized; the focus was on the "accomplishments" and "duties" (religious, moral, and domestic) considered crucial if a girl was to succeed in the "marriage market." Young women were not prepared to earn their own living, except perhaps as teachers in boarding schools or as governesses in private homes. There was no respectable place in bourgeois society for the single woman without support.[17]

While middle-class women were suffering from enforced idleness, working women in the 18th century were saddled with a double load as the Industrial Revolution took them away from their harsh but familiar rural environment to a factory existence that was at the same time dehumanizing and too poorly paid to support a family. These women, no longer able to care for their children while they worked, were caught between the prevailing bourgeois ideology of the "good mother" and the physical and economic impossibility of living up to it. Children were left to fend for themselves in the streets, when they weren't forced to work in the factories themselves; and young unmarried women were frequently forced to augment their meager pay with prostitution. The growing numbers of workers crowded into city slums became increasingly difficult to ignore.[18]

As the 19th century progressed, middle-class women began to look beyond the walls of their own homes, to use their privileges to help alleviate the intolerable conditions of others. At first this was limited to the sort of "serving the poor" which had been part of the expected role of the lady—carrying baskets of food to the sick and hungry. Increasingly, it meant engaging in organized work toward social change. By midcentury, particularly in England, there were hundreds of thousands of women involved in charity and social reform work. They concerned themselves with inhumane working and living conditions of factory workers; became motive forces behind abolition; worked to restructure prisons, hospitals, and mental institutions; and organized for women's rights.[18] As women, who had in so many ways been rendered voiceless and powerless themselves, they felt a responsibility to speak for others who had even less voice, less power. Harriet Martineau included powerful narrations from experiences of workers in her *Illustrations of Political Economy;* and the novelist Mrs. Trollope, concerned about child labor, travelled to Manchester by train for first-hand observations in the factories.[19]

What sort of poetry was being written by women in this period? Virtually nothing, of course, by working-class or rural farm women, who were for the most part illiterate and lived on the margins of survival. Some songs of factory workers were written down and published in England in the 1830's.[20] Most poetry of the period came from the middle class, where—in contrast to the strong work women were doing in the novel—little poetry of real strength appeared. One wonders why. One reason may have been that in both centuries poetry was a prestigious, highly public genre; and whatever the literary "period" (defined always around male authors), the qualities most valued in the poetry tended to be the qualities women were not supposed to have. The dominant poetry of the 18th century was intellectual and authoritative, and dealt largely with the "male" domain of politics and philosophy. Some women—like Anne Finch—managed to create good poetry within the accepted constraints. She lived exiled in the provinces, and gained some of her strength from writing from the perspective of an outsider. In the late 18th century pre-Romantic period women such as Charlotte Smith wrote interesting nature poetry; but Romantic poetry, with its reaction against Reason and its emphasis on subjective experience, was still inappropriate to women because its lyric egoism was in conflict with the assumption that women should be unassertive. Later in the century we have the equally inaccessible model of the great laureates (Wordsworth, Tennyson) and national poets (Hugo, Arnold), speaking as conscience or cultural mentors for the whole society.

Meanwhile, the weight of social expectation pulled women in the direction not of the public world but the private. "Propriety" for women meant invisibility. Many professional women writers— from George Sand to George Eliot—chose male pseudonyms, as if defining themselves and their work outside the traditional female sphere. "Poetesses" writing in the popular magazines commonly signed their work with initials (e.g., AWOE—"A Woman of England").[21]

Other women hid their poetry behind an internalized "true womanhood." Numerous poems got published in the new women's journals which intoned the "true womanly" virtues of "purity, piety, submissiveness, and domesticity."[22] This saccharine verse, both sentimental and abstract, is at opposite poles from such poetry, for instance, as that of Anne Bradstreet, which draws its imagery from the domestic everydayness of her life, and makes the concrete things of sewing and cooking carry the weight and feel of human experience.[23] Still, this poetry played a critical role in a society shaken loose from most of its traditional sureties. It was seen as women's responsibility to keep home and hearth, morality and human values, safe from the ravages of the amoral world of industry and empire, to preserve a place to which men could return from their battles to have their humanity restored.[24] The very foundation of human society was seen as resting on a sharp demarcation between male and female spheres and "inborn" qualities. Women writers such as Mary Wollstonecraft, Harriet Martineau, and Margaret Fuller, who questioned this polarized and limited definition of woman, were considered dangerous "enemies of the social order."[25]

The weight of the ideology of "true womanhood" affected even the exceptional women poets of the period. Christina Rossetti tried to wear the mask of the "proper" woman—spiritual, passive, ethereal—, and her poetry suffered. The mask became too close to remove. Yet some of her poetry, such as the long work "Goblin Market", reveal a character far more sensuous and robust than most of what gets anthologized. And she wrote more than we've had the chance to read. Her brother screened out several poems apparently written to women when he edited her works for publication after her death.

In the case of Elizabeth Barrett Browning, anthologizers have done their best to render her "safe." Her reputation has rested almost completely on her love poems to Robert Browning. For all their freshness and force, these poems still fit the conventional conception of what women are supposed to be—specifically, existing in relation to men. Consequently they are accessible to the sensibility of male critics. What did not fit the critics' sense of what a woman could and should write, they tended not to see, or if they saw it, condemned as "unbecoming" (for a woman), and therefore "bad poetry" (for a woman). In fact, Elizabeth Barrett Browning wrote a great deal besides her love poetry, much which is overtly political and feminist—as for instance her poetic novel *Aurora Leigh* and her 1860 volume *Poems Before Congress.* Thackeray—novelist, critic, and literary editor—spoke of the political poems in the latter volume as "obviously written in a fit of insanity," and refused other work of hers as "unladylike."

In her long poem "Curse for a Nation," Elizabeth Barrett Browning redefined woman's relation to the writing of poetry, the strengths women bring to poetry and to the world. She has no intention of "writing like a man" to prove that she's a serious artist. Instead she reclaims the wholeness of perception and experience open to women. She does not deny the qualities idealized and dismissed as "feminine"—the capacity for feeling, the concern for moral value—but redirects their power:

> I heard an Angel speak last night,
>   And he said *"Write!*
> *Write a Nation's curse for me,*
> *And send it over the Western sea."*

* * * *

> "Not so," I answered once again.
>   "To curse, choose men.
> For I, a woman, have only known
> How the Heart melts, and the tears run down."

> *"Therefore,"* the voice said, *"Shalt thou write*
>   *My curse to-night.*
> *Some women weep and curse, I say*
> *(And no one marvels), night and day.*

> *"And thou shalt take their part to-night,*
>   *Weep and write.*
> *A curse from the depths of womanhood*
> *Is very salt, and bitter, and good."*

DEIRDRE LASHGARI

Notes and References

[1] In England, women were often influential patrons of the art as well; the Countess of Bedford (Sidney's sister, and a poet in her own right) is one example.

[2] Friedrich Schlegel (1772-1829); Friedrich Wilhelm Joseph von Schelling (1775-1834).

[3] "Children, kitchen, church".

[4] One of a number of literary and intellectual circles of the period.

[5] Geneviève Bianquis, *Histoire mondiale de la femme* (Paris, 1966).

[6] The Marquis de Condorcet, *Sur l'Admission des femmes au droit de cité.*

[7] Olympe de Gouges, *La déclaration des droits de la femme et de la citoyenne.* A playwright of working-class background, she had written nearly 30 plays by 1789, one of which, condemning slavery, was produced in that year at Théâtre Français. Cf. Ruth Graham, "Loaves and Liberty: Women in the French Revolution," in *Becoming Visible: Women in European History,* ed. Renate Bridenthal and Claudia Koonz (Boston: Houghton Mifflin), 1977.

[8] Mary Wollstonecraft, *A Vindication of the Rights of Woman,* (NY: Norton, 1967).

[9] Theodor Gottlieb von Hippel, *On Improving the Status of Women,* transl. and ed. by Timothy F. Sellner (Detroit: Wayne State University, 1979).

[10] Charles Fourier, *Design for Utopia: Selected Writings,* tr. Julia Franklin (NY: Schocken, 1971): "Social advances and changes of periods are brought about by virtue of the progress of women towards liberty, and the decadences of the social order are brought about by virtue of the decrease of liberty of women" (p. 77).

[11] Flora Tristan: cf. *Pérégrinations d'une paria, 1833-34,* 2 vols. (Paris, 1838); *Promenades sur Londres* (Paris, 1840); *L'Union ouvrière* (Paris, 1843); *La Tour de France, journal inédit, 1843-44* (Paris, 1973). Cf. S. Joan Moon, "Feminism and Socialism: the Utopian Synthesis of Flora Tristan," in *Socialist Women: European Socialist Feminism in the Nineteenth and Early Twentieth Centuries,* ed. Marilyn J. Boxer and Jean H. Quataert (NY: Elsevier, 1978).

[12] Including such writers as Walt Whitman (U.S. poet, 1819-1892), Matthew Arnold (British poet and critic, 1822-1888), and the Russian novelists Ivan Turgenev (1818-1883) and Feodor Dostoevsky (1821-1881).

[13] Ellen Moers, *Literary Women: The Great Writers* (Garden City, NY: Doubleday, 1977), 45-46.

[14] Barbara Alpern Engel, "From Separatism to Socialism: Women in the Russian Revolutionary Movement of the 1870s," in Boxer and Quataert, *Socialist Women.*

[15] Ian Watt, *The Rise of the Novel* (Berkeley: University of California, 1967).

[16] Male writers like Samuel Richardson (1689-1761), writing in the persona of a woman, often made use of the form as well.

[17] Cf. Abby R. Kleinbaum, "Women in the Age of Light," in *Becoming Visible,* ed. Bridenthal and Koonz.

[18]Mary Lynn McDougall, "Working-Class Women During the Industrial Revolution, 1780-1914," in *Becoming Visible,* ed. Bridenthal and Koonz.

[19]Moers, *Literary Women* (34-36).

[20]Moers, *Literary Women* (34).

[21]Cf. the history, largely negative, of the relation between women and their names in Una Stannard's *Mrs. Man* (San Francisco: Germainbooks, 1977).

[22]Barbara Welter, "The Cult of True Womanhood," in *American Quarterly,* Vol. XVIII, no. 2, pt. 1, summer 1966 (152).

[23]As Ellen Moers points out in *Literary Women* (254-5), this poetry deserves rereading; she suggests that it may have helped keep alive a tradition of "warmth of feeling" in poetry.

[24]Cf. Virgina Woolf, *A Room of One's Own* (NY: Harcourt, Brace and World, 1929).

[25]Welter, "The Cult of True Womanhood" (154, 166).

Marie-Françoise-Catherine de Beauveau, Marquise de Boufflers
France   1711–1786

Air: Sentir avec Ardeur[1]

Say what you will in two
Words and get through.
Long, frilly
Palaver is silly.

Know how to read? you *must*
Before you can write. An idiot
Will always
Talk a lot.

You need not always narrate;
  cite; date;
But listen a while and not say: "I! I!"
Want to know why?

The *me* is tyrannical;
      academical.
Early, late
Boredom's cognate mate
    in step at his side
And I with a *me,* I fear,
        yet again!

Say what you will in two
Words and get through!
Long, frilly
Palaver is silly.

Translated from the French by Ezra Pound
[1]Tune: "Strong Feelings"; compare titles in Chinese section; imitations of things Chinese were fashionable in the period.

Anna Maria Lenngren
Sweden   1755–1817

The Portraits

Upon an old estate from ancient sires descended
A widowed countess dwelt; the years her face had
   scored,
Infirm she was, drank tea of elder-flowers blended,
On twinges of her legs for weather signs depended,
And oftentimes the dame was to distraction bored.
One day—for reasons unexplored,—
When with her maid she sat where soared
The lofty hall, with gilt and paneled leather splendid,
While, each in its appointed place,
Hung portraits of her high-born race,—
She in her lofty mind bethought:
"If condescendingly I brought
Myself to speak with this dull person,
Perhaps the change would give my gout a small
   diversion;
Though surely such a stupid flounder
Would comprehend the smallest fraction,
Yet my own lungs would have some action
and this poor simpleton would be quite lost in wonder
On hearing tell of my extraction."

"Susanna," she began at length, "this hall you sweep,
Sweep it each day throughout the year,
You see what likenesses are here;
But gape, half silly, half asleep,
At them, nor guess what folk you keep from cobwebs
   clear,
Listen! . . . He on the right, sire of my grandsire dear,
Is the much travelled President,
Who knew of every fly the Greek or Latin name;
To the Academy he gave, when home he came,
A lob-worm[1] from the Orient. . . .
Well, next beyond him—in the corner by mischance—

---

[1]lob-worm, or lugworm: any of several large marine annelids that have a row of tufted gills along each side of the back, burrow in sandy beaches between tide marks in America and Europe, and are used for bait.

Is my dear only son, the Ensign[2] late-lamented,
Pattern in posture and the dance,
Whom all our hopes were fixed upon,—
Seven new pigtails he invented.
A window-draught he failed to shun,
And a catarrh set in; his glorious course was run.
A marble monument to him shall be erected. . . .
Yon lady, to my ma, the Countess, near connected,
Was in her day esteemed a beauty of much note,
And—if indeed it's true and not a fabrication—
Helped Queen Christine[3] at coronation
To hook her under-petticoat . . .
She with the mantle, much admired,
Is my great-aunt—a lovely face! . . .
That old man in the robe attired,
A worthy uncle of our race,
Once played at chess against the Czar of Russia's
    Grace. . . .
Yon portrait to the left you see,
That is my sainted spouse, the Colonel.
Who had ability and talent nigh supernal
In partridge-shooting, if not he? . . .
But now look well at yonder dame there
Within the pretty oval frame there,
Who on her swelling breast is wearing a bouquet—
Look hither—not at that one, nay!—
'Tis plain to see what pride within her glance reposes,
And mark how nobly curved her nose is!
King Frederick[4] to yon fair, one night, his court would
    pay,
But she was virtue's self and ever humbly froze his
Fond passion, daring to oppose his
Attention, till abashed: 'Ma chère,' he had to say,
You have a parlous offish way.'
Many still live to tell of that affair so naughty.—
Well, don't you recognize her, eh?
Am I not known at once by yonder forehead haughty?"
"But," cried Susanna, "God preserve us!"—
Dropping her shears and needle-case,—
"Can that be meant to be your Grace!!!"

---

[2]Ensign: (formerly) infantry or naval officer of the lowest commissioned rank.
[3]Queen Christina of Sweden (1626–1689, reigned 1632–1654).
[4]King Frederick III of Denmark and Norway (1609–1670, reigned 1648–1670).

"Be meant to be? . . . What! . . . Leave my service!
Minx, out of doors with you and your unfinished lace!—
The shame! But still it happens rightly
When one essays to talk with such a beast politely."
The Countess had at once a fresh attack of gout;
No moral to this tale has further been found out.

Translated from the Swedish by C. W. Stork

Charlotte Smith
England   1749–1806

Thirty-Eight

In early youth's unclouded scene,
The brilliant morning of eighteen,
With health and sprightly joy elate
    We gazed on life's enchanting spring,
    Nor thought how quickly time would bring
The mournful period—Thirty-eight.

Then the starch maid, or matron sage,
Already of that sober age,
We view'd with mingled scorn and hate;
    In whole sharp words, or sharper face,
    With thoughtless mirth we loved to trace
The sad effects of —Thirty-eight.

Till saddening, sickening at the view,
We learn'd to dread what Time might do;
And then preferr'd a prayer to Fate
    To end our days ere that arrived;
    When (power and pleasure long survived)
We met neglect and —Thirty-eight.

But Time, in spite of wishes flies,
And Fate our simple prayer denies,
And bids us Death's own hour await:
    The auburn locks are mix'd with grey,
    The transient roses fade away,
But Reason comes at—Thirty-eight.

Her voice the anguish contradicts
That dying vanity inflicts;
Her hand new pleasures can create,
   For us she opens to the view
   Prospects less bright—but far more true,
And bids us smile at—Thirty-eight.

No more shall *Scandal's* breath destroy
The social converse we enjoy
With bard or critic tete a tete;—
   O'er Youth's bright blooms her blights shall pour,
   But spare the improving friendly hour
That Science gives to—Thirty-eight.

Stripp'd of their gaudy hues by Truth,
We view the glitt'ring toys of youth,
And blush to think how poor the bait
   For which to public scenes we ran
   And scorn'd of sober Sense the plan
Which gives content at—Thirty-eight.

Tho' Time's inexorable sway
Has torn the myrtle bands away,
For other wreaths 'tis not too late,
   The amaranth's purple glow survives,
   And still Minerva's olive lives
On the calm brow of—Thirty-eight.

With eye more steady we engage
To contemplate approaching age,
And life more justly estimate;
   With firmer souls, and stronger powers,
   With reason, faith, and friendship ours,
   We'll not regret the stealing hours
That lead from Thirty—even to Forty-eight.

Elizabeth Barrett Browning
England   1806–1861

from Aurora Leigh

ll. 832–854

                                    Books, books, books!
I had found the secret of a garret-room
Piled high with cases in my father's name,
Piled high, packed large,—where, creeping in and out
Among the giant fossils of my past,
Like some small nimble mouse between the ribs
Of a mastodon, I nibbled here and there
At this or that box, pulling through the gap,
In heats of terror, haste, victorious joy,
The first book first. And how I felt it beat
Under my pillow, in the morning's dark,
An hour before the sun would let me read!
My books! At last because the time was ripe,
I chanced upon the poets.
                                    As the earth
Plunges in fury, when the internal fires
Have reached and pricked her heart, and, throwing flat
The marts and temples, the triumphal gates
And towers of observation, clears herself
To elemental freedom—thus, my soul,
At poetry's divine first finger-touch,
Let go conventions and sprang up surprised,
Convicted of the great eternities
Before two worlds.

A Curse for a Nation
Prologue

I heard an angel speak last night,
            And he said, "Write!
Write a Nation's curse for me,
And send it over the Western Sea."

I faltered, taking up the word:
            "Not so, my lord!

If curses must be, choose another
To send thy curse against my brother.

"For I am bound by gratitude,
        By love and blood,
To brothers of mine across the sea,
Who stretch out kindly hands to me."

"Therefore," the voice said, "shalt thou write
        My curse tonight.
From the summits of love a curse is driven,
As lightning is from the tops of heaven."

"Not so," I answered. "Evermore
        My heart is sore
For my own land's sins; for little feet
Of children bleeding along the street;

"For parked-up honors that gainsay
        The right of way;
For almsgiving through a door that is
Not open enough for two friends to kiss;

"For love of freedom which abates
        Beyond the Straits;
For patriot virtue starved to vice on
Self-praise, self-interest, and suspicion;

"For an oligarchic parliament,
        And bribes well-meant.
What curse to another land assign,
When heavy-souled for the sins of mine?"

"Therefore," the voice said, "shalt thou write
        My curse tonight,
Because thou hast strength to see and hate
A foul thing done *within* thy gate."

"Not so," I answered once again.
        "To curse, choose men.
For I, a woman, have only known
How the heart melts and the tears run down."

"Therefore," the voice said, "shalt thou write

My curse tonight.
Some women weep and curse, I say
(And no one marvels), night and day.

"And thou shalt take their part tonight,
　　　Weep and write.
A curse from the depths of womanhood
Is very salt, and bitter, and good."

So thus I wrote, and mourned indeed,
　　　What all may read.
And thus, as was enjoined on me,
I send it over the Western Sea.

The Curse

1

Because ye have broken your own chain
　　　With the strain
Of brave men climbing a Nation's height,
Yet thence bear down with brand and thong
On souls of others—for this wrong
　　　This is the curse. Write.[1]

Because yourselves are standing straight
　　　In the state
Of Freedom's foremost acolyte,
Yet keep calm footing all the time
On writhing bond slaves—for this crime
　　　This is the curse. Write.

Because ye prosper in God's name,
　　　With a claim
To honor in the old world's sight,
Yet do the fiend's work perfectly
In strangling martyrs—for this lie
　　　This is the curse. Write.

---

[1]The repetition of the injunction "Write" is found also in the Qoran, understood to have been written down by the Prophet Mohammad as dictated to him by the voice of God.

2

Ye shall watch while kings conspire
Round the people's smoldering fire,
    And, warm for your part,
Shall never dare—O shame!—
To utter the thought into flame
    Which burns at your heart.
        This is the curse. Write.

Ye shall watch while nations strive
With the bloodhounds, die or survive,
    Drop faint from their jaws,
Or throttle them backward to death;
And only under your breath
    Shall favor the cause.
        This is the curse. Write.

Ye shall watch while strong men draw
The nets of feudal law
    To strangle the weak;
And, counting the sin for a sin,
Your soul shall be sadder within
    Than the word ye shall speak.
        This is the curse. Write.

When good men are praying erect
That Christ may avenge his elect
    And deliver the earth,
The prayer in your ears, said low,
Shall sound like the tramp of a foe
    That's driving you forth.
        This is the curse. Write.

When wise men give you their praise,
They shall pause in the heat of the phrase,
    As if carried too far.
When ye boast your own charters kept true,
Ye shall blush; for the thing which ye do
    Derides what ye are.
        This is the curse. Write.

When fools cast taunts at your gate,
Your scorn ye shall somewhat abate

As ye look o'er the wall;
For your conscience, tradition, and name
Explode with a deadlier blame
    Than the worst of them all.
        This is the curse. Write.

Go, wherever ill deeds shall be done,
Go plant your flag in the sun
    Beside the ill-doers!
And recoil from clenching the curse
Of God's witnessing Universe
    With a curse of yours.
        This is the curse. Write.

Christina Rossetti
England   1830–1894

A Soul

She stands as pale as Parian statues stand;
Like Cleopatra when she turned at bay,
And felt her strength above the Roman sway,
And felt the aspic writhing in her hand.
Her face is steadfast toward the shadowy land,
For dim beyond it looms the land of day:
Her feet are steadfast, all the arduous way
That foot-track doth not waver on the sand.
She stands there like a beacon through the night,
A pale clear beacon where the storm-drift is—
She stands alone, a wonder deathly-white:
She stands there patient nerved with inner might,
Indomitable in her feebleness,
Her face and will athirst against the light.

Marceline Desbordes-Valmore
France   1786–1859

The Roses of Saadi

This morning I wanted to bring you roses
but gathered so many into my knotted sash
that the knot gave way. The roses scattered
blown on the wind, all of them, over the sea.

The flow of the waters caught them
and carried them. They will never return.
The waves turned crimson like flame.

Tonight their fragrance fills my gown.
Of the gift I brought for you, this is all that remains.

Translated from the French by Deirdre Lashgari

Annette von Droste-Hülshoff
Germany   1797–1848

On the Tower

I stand high in the belfry tower,
Where starlings scream and swirl in air;
As though I were a maenad,[1] Storm,
You run your fingers through my hair.
O spirit free, entrancing youth,
Here at the very railing, I
Would wrestle, hip to hip, against
Your hold; become alive—or die.

Below, along the sandy beach,
I see the whitecaps leap in play
Like frisky hounds tumbling the surf,
Darting in hissing, sparkling spray.
Oh, I would join them in their game,

[1]In ancient Greece a woman participating in the frenzied rites of Dionysus, god of wine, orgiastic sensuality, and creative nature.

Pursuing walrus, sportive prey,
Leading the romping pack through glades
Of coral, hunting dolphins gay.

Far off I see a pennant stream,
Bold as an admiral's banner;
I watch the masts bob in the sea,
From safe in my high-towered manor.
Oh, I would rule that tossing ship
And hold helm firm and guide her true,
Skim lightly over foaming reefs
As brushing wings of seagulls do.

If I could hunt the open fields,
Or march to war, a soldier tall,
If heaven listened to my plea,
Made me a man, even though small!
Instead, I sit here—delicate,
Polite, precise, well-mannered child.
Dreams shake my loosened hair—the wind
Lone listener to my spirit wild.

Translated from the German by James Edward Tobin

Ricarda Huch
Germany   *1864–1947*

Young Girl

Swirling spring
Blossoming tree
The flames of youth leap up around her
Untouched, her flowing skirts sweep by
the leaves left by the years
decaying at her feet

Fearless glance
Stormy stride
into the midst of the forest of danger
Clash of weapons

Beckoning song
Festive crowd with streaming hair

Brave in battle
Lovely in dance
Unconcerned with fate or reward
Fortune keep you!
What crown will be yours one day
O Amazon—

Translated from the German by Janine Canan and Deirdre Lashgari

Anna de Noailles
France   1876–1933

Poem on azure

The summer day suffocates, smothers, pants
Under the relentless sky of white porcelain.
Everything burns, consumed in a saffron veil,
Dreaming of some pungent, invisible stream . . .
Breath, bursts of song, murmurs, stop.
Between the trees, crowded by green peaks,
The sky is white like a street in Tunis.
The fragrance of carnations, balsam, lilies,
Encloses the garden in a floating bower.
The day glows like a thousand-winged chariot!
The sweet, quivering, plaintive heat
Thirsts like a furrow, like a flower's throat,
Like a child running in a Spanish garden.
O scorching dryness, kindling the fields!
The air is empty, life has withdrawn
To the coolness of woods, vineyards, hay,
Where the moist air frolics near the spring . . .
—But I, O dryness, O my yellow Numidia,
Huntress, archer, warrior of summer,
I want to touch your cheek, your swelling heart,
Your whiteness like the fine temple of Egina,
Like the white flight of Chinese swans,
Like dozing Buddhas with golden hands,
Like the immense heat of the squares at Luxor,

Like the seas of Marmara, luminous and warm,
Like the markets of Turkey where fever prowls,
Where the need to drink is such harsh desire
That a watermelon makes one sob with pleasure!
Like Tehran, its domes swollen and poised,
Like Mosul, expiring in fragrant kisses,
Where, with silver shield raised against the sky,
One would strike out at the overwhelming azure!
—But what matters, heat, your harsh cruel strength?
You are life, passionate, avid, sensual!
You who suddenly make grating and sulfurous
The soft languid edge of Western roads,
You who shine on canvas awnings
Like a sovereign morning star,
You who burst open like a fruit of Blida
The timid shutters of white verandas,
Who make a dull pond, or some idle boat
More languorous than the shores of Como,
Who make the heart, finally, shining and distant,
Drunk with leisure, death, and sensuality,
Bitter languors, fire, phosphoric secrets,
Like a white cemetery exposed by the Bosphorus . . .

Translated from the French by Betty L. Schwimmer

Hélène Swarth
Holland   1859–1941

Candles

Boy, bring me candles on a silver salver,
Strew pale roses on the fresh red fruit,
Banish the sun with a purple veil,
And tip the flagon down to the goblet.

Now to your lips set the slender flute,
O blond-haired one, and play for the nightingale,
With pure rejoicing fill the marble hall—
Or with soft complaint; a rain of sound.

The red wine flows hot as fire of the sun;

Take, sweet lad, a draught for your reward,
And let me fondle your curly blond locks

While I drift in the Land of Dreams and gaze
At the red of the candles, glowing ripe and smooth,
Full of still longing for a scarlet mouth.

Ecstasy

I saw a pale tree, the leafless boughs—but two—
Upraised to heaven, yet when I came close
I perceived it was a man who, uplifting his arms, prayed
And awaited an answer—somberly rolled the thunder
Like organ-rumblings; silkily, sheet upon sheet
Fell the soft lullaby of spring showers.
Then the sun shone. He stood in uninterrupted silence,
In the unbroken pride of one who measures himself
    with God.

His feet implanted firmly in the earth, his white locks,
Swarmed about by birds, snowed under with blossoms,
Irradiate the sun, light up the spring wind.
From a distant hamlet comes the festive sound of bells,
A boy leaps, whispering gaily, to tempt a maiden to love,
And triumphantly the laughter of a child resounds.

Translated from the Dutch by Jonathan Crewe

Henriette Roland-Holst
Holland   1869–1952

I Looked for a Sounding-Board

I looked for a sounding-board and I found none.
The hearts that I called out to, remained stone.
I no longer look, with calling I have done,
And what I sing now is for myself alone.

Concerning the Awakening of My Soul

The full days come striding with measured
steps, like tall white ladies
in fables of enchantment; flowers they hold
in their hands, and light surrounds their heads,
  golden-haired.
The days lie open like declared
secrets between friends who long
wanted to speak but were silent—so long—
until trust was full grown and each revealed her soul.

Days like flowers, wide-open nights
between; as in moon-blanched gardens
and amidst this plenty I move
with radiant eyes in the ascendant of life. Now I stand,
it seems to me, like the topmost in a row of dunes
and gaze far and wide: it is the long-awaited.

Small Paths

Small paths go straggling over the heath
and come to an end at the hovels of the poor;
nothing else takes the least pity on
the desolation of those who suffer there.

Out on the heath the thin sheep stray
bleating, in search of a new place to eat,
with better pasture, and a brimming stream;
dogs and herdsmen are worn out, and sleep.

Inside the hovels the people settle down
like sheep that no longer know where to stray;
their thoughts travel out over the heath
but find no escape, and come back again.

The paths and hovels dissolve into gray;
beyond this heath, another appears:
people reach the end of their joyless living-grief,
others continue, but things stay as they were.

The heath loses itself in the sea, the sea
loses itself in the air—and in the wider
circles of human wretchedness and grief,
in the dull distress of our pitiful sphere.

Translated from the Dutch by Jonathan Crewe

Maria Konopnicka
Poland   1842–1910

A Vision

Spring comes: the flowers learn their coloured shapes.
I look at them, but back at me there gapes
      Emptiness, white and endless.

And Summer comes to where the gold crops stand;
But I still see, as plain as my own hand,
      Emptiness, white and endless.

And death will come to dim my human sight.
My eyes, inside the tomb, will watch with fright
      Emptiness, white and endless.

A midnight, from my coffin, I shall go
Thoughtfully toward the distant fields that show
      Emptiness, white and endless.

Translated from the Polish by Jerzy Peterkiewicz and Burns Singer

Rosalia de Castro
Spain   1837–1885

plants don't talk, people say
or fountains, or birds
or the wave's sound
the star's shine
they say that; but it's not certain

they always talk to me
when I pass; saying
there goes the crazy one
dreaming eternal springtime
in life and in the grass
but soon, soon
white hair will appear
frost on the grass
there is white in my hair
frost on the grass
but I dream on
incurable sleepwalker
of life
of souls
though life ends
and fields burn
fountains stars flowers
don't complain of my dreaming
without it
how shall I praise you?
without it
how shall I live?

Translated from the Spanish by Doris Earnshaw

Charlotte Mew
England   1870–1928

Smile, Death

Smile, Death, see I smile as I come to you
    Straight from the road and the moor that I leave
      behind,
Nothing on earth to me was like this wind-blown space,
Nothing was like the road, but at the end there was a
    vision
        or a face
      And the eyes were not always kind.

    Smile, Death, as you fasten the blades to my feet for
    me,

On, on let us skate past the sleeping willows dusted with
   snow;
Fast, fast down the frozen stream, with the moor and the
   road
            and the vision behind,
      (Show me your face, why the eyes are kind!)
And we will not speak of life or believe in it or
   remember it
            as we go.

The Trees Are Down

> *—and he cried with a loud voice:*
> *Hurt not the earth, neither the sea,*
> *nor the trees—*
>
> *—from the BOOK OF REVELATION*

They are cutting down the great plane-trees at the end
   of the gardens.
For days there has been the grate of the saw, the swish of
   the branches as they fall,
The crash of the trunks, the rustle of trodden leaves,
With the "Whoops" and the "Whoas," the loud common
   talk, the loud common laughs of the men, above it all.

I remember one evening of a long past Spring
Turning in at a gate, getting out of a cart, and finding a
   large dead rat in the mud of the drive.
I remember thinking: alive or dead, a rat was a
   god-forsaken thing,
But at least, in May, that even a rat should be alive.

The week's work is as good as done. There is just one
   bough
            On the roped bole, in the fine grey rain,
               Green and high
               And lonely against the sky.
                  (Down now!—)
               And but for that,
               If an old dead rat
Did once, for a moment, unmake the Spring, I might
   never have
            thought of him again.

It is not for a moment the Spring is unmade to-day;
These were great trees, it was in them from root to stem:
When the men with the "Whoops" and the "Whoas"
   have carted the whole of the whispering loveliness
   away
Half the Spring, for me, will have gone with them.

It is going now, and my heart has been struck with the
   hearts of the planes;
Half my life it has beat with these, in the sun, in the
   rains,
      In the March wind, the May breeze,
In the great gales that come over to them across the
   roofs from the great seas.

      There was only a quiet rain when they were
         dying;
      They must have heard the sparrows flying,
And the small creeping creatures in the earth where
   they were lying—
      But I, all day, heard an angel crying:
      "Hurt not the trees."

Zinaida Gippius
Russia   *1869-1945*

She

She is shameless, despicable, vile
grey as dust, earth ashen
I am dying from this closeness
our inseparable closeness

She is coarse and cold—
a viper with jagged scales
searing, scarring
wounding me harshly

Yet I long for her fangs,
sharp sting—not this dullness

flaccid and vacant
inaccessible, deaf

Coils unremitting
caress me, smother me
And this dead thing, this dark thing
this frightful thing—is my soul

Translated from the Russian by Dianne Levitin

Europe: *1914 and After*

It might very well be—as Frank Kermode writes—"that certain good aspects of modernism[1] are to be seen as a triumph for the sex."[2] Women poets thrived under modernism, as the large space devoted here to poetry by women in this period suggests. Moreover, the movement has produced a considerable number of great women poets, Anna Akhmatova, Else Lasker-Schüler, Gabriela Mistral, and others. Something about modernism suited women—maybe the permutation of values effected by the modernist avant garde. Against pre-war emphasis on rational control and empirical fact—untenable after the absurd massacre of an entire generation of men in the trenches of World War I—the new literary school proposed to explore dream, myth, the unconscious and the qualities traditionally considered "feminine": psychological insight, intuition, feeling, and instinct. These qualities took on an exemplary value, emerged as a kind of cultural ideal; a remedy, as T. S. Eiot shows in *The Waste Land,* against the atrophy of feeling and the self-induced sterility of modern life.

It does not follow that modernist poetry by women is purely emotional and devoid of intellectual content. But the validation by the avant garde of "feminine qualities" must have been a tremendous encouragement. One imagines that the confirmation of women as a group allowed individuals to speak from a sense of strength, rather than from a defensive position of weakness and revolt—each one expressing her vision in her voice.

The importance for literary women of this reversal of values was tremendous. Virginia Woolf reminds us in *A Room of One's Own* of how difficult it must have been for a woman to take herself seriously as a writer in pre-war times. "What genius, what integrity it must have required in the face of all that criticism, in the midst of that purely patriarchal society, to hold fast to the thing as they saw it without shirking."[3] The difficulty of holding on to one's vision, of mustering the necessary confidence to speak and write with conviction, was maybe the greatest problem women have had to face. Even today, what women say and write is often automatically brushed off as trivial or silly. *To the Lighthouse* ends on a note of triumph mixed with feelings of exhaustion: "Yes, (Lily Briscoe) thought, laying down her brush in extreme fatigue, I have had my vision."[4]

However, women were not mere passive beneficiaries of a change in cultural values. The emergence of women on the public scene as writers, doctors, scientists in large numbers was the result of a long political struggle and feminist activism that began in the 1840s. Women fought arduously, using both legal and illegal means, for the right to vote, for access to education, and for the right to work in the field of their choice. Secondary education on a par with men became available in England and Germany in the 1870s, after more than a decade of struggle. University education became possible even later: not until 1900 did German universities admit women, and in England it was not until 1921 that women were awarded university degrees. Women were not allowed to vote in most Western countries until after the War: in 1918 in Sweden, in 1920 in the U.S., in 1928 in England, and in 1945 (*sic*) in France.[5] Many reasons, demographic, historical, and economic, contributed to the slow but real emergence of women on the public scene. Among these were increased industrialization, a higher standard of living, and the modernization of domestic work, as well as unionization and other means of collective political pressure.

Yet the two most important factors contributing to women's emancipation may very well have been World War I and the Russian Revolution. The former changed the social landscape as profoundly as the formation of a new mountain range. After the war, in Russia, in France, in Germany, with 10 million dead and 20 million wounded or crippled, the common lot of women was forced celibacy and widowhood. Women had to join the labor force in order to survive. They were also needed, during the war, to replace the men who were drafted. In Russia, where women in the nineteenth century had made up 2 per cent of the labor force, the figure had risen to 47 per cent in 1917.[6] In spite of obvious hardships women worked effectively in a wide range of occupations. Consequently after the war it had become much more difficult to say "Women can't think, women can't work, women can't write."

The Russian revolutionary movement, from the first stirrings of the Populists in the 1860s through the revolution in 1917, was a source of inspiration for feminists and socialists all over Europe and probably elsewhere as well. From the outset "the vision of a better world included women as comrades, fighters for a common cause."[7] Women participated actively in the political struggle from its earliest phases, running illegal printing presses, working in factories and organizing unions; even planning assassination attempts. One woman, Sofia Perovskaia, was hanged for participating in the assassination of Tsar Alexander II. The various programs of the Russian revolutionaries always included blueprints for the emancipation of women. Both men and women, including Lenin, Trotsky, and Alexandra Kollontai,[8] addressed themselves to the "woman question." In pre-industrial Russia of the 1870s, communal workshops were set up at the initiative of individuals in response to the need for working and living space for single women. Later, immediately after the revolution, a great effort was made to improve the lot of women, especially in the field of education. The Family Code of 1918 "demanded full equality in the family, control of earnings and inheritance. A wife could retain her own name, establish her own residence and have her own passports. Conjugal rights and community property no longer existed. Divorce could be obtained easily and alimony was abolished."[9]

Unfortunately, most of the reforms were later retracted. The official attitude towards women in the USSR since the 1920s has reverted to a conservative family-oriented position. Lack of funds, lack of experience, trying to do too much at once, were some of the reasons for the failure of the drive for equality. The two years of civil war that followed the revolution plunged the entire country into a state in which women suffered excessively.

> The economic difficulties were tremendous in a country that was barely beginning to industrialize; famines, factories closing, women were the last hired and the first fired. . . .

> Some communal agencies did develop, but as unavoidable crisis-measures: instead of communal restaurants—soup-kitchens; instead of especially designed dormitories—requisitioned homes where workers slept on the floor; instead of model nurseries—emergency shelters where many died.[10]

Thus the first attempt to realize an immediate and thoroughgoing liberation of women failed. But the ideas and the records of these experiments survived and inspired reformers in various places in the world: model communities in Israel were set up on this pattern, European socialist governments adapted some of these notions into their new liberal labor laws, and most recently we have seen them surface in the programs of radical feminists of the 1960s and 1970s.

These revolutionary ideas, despite their failures in realization, had a powerful effect on the intellectual European community of the time. Russian feminist theories provided intellectual ferment to discussions in cafés and literary circles all around Europe. From the Boulevard Montparnasse in Paris to Berlin, Stockholm, St. Petersburg, Zürich the new ideas were hotly debated and applied. The European intelligentsia was always on the move between capitals and ideas, restless and eager for new experience. It is difficult to imagine the exaltation they felt:

> One felt the world was making a turnabout; the future lay ahead like virgin soil, one need only sow . . . The young poets and artists, who had already rejected the roles of the past, carried within themselves the inspiring image of a new humanity, higher and more finely organized and conscious of its destiny.[11]

It was all intensely stimulating. In the cafés and literary coteries women participated in hours-long discussions as comrades and equals. There they had access to the intellectual elite and there they developed and refined their ideas on politics, literature and life in general. The excitement spread to the remotest corners of Europe. New ideals of womanhood emerged.

As well as opening to them the role of comrade and fellow socialist, the new ideology exalted women as love goddesses, femmes fatales, possessors of a vital energy and natural creativity. This put an end to pre-war repression of female sexuality, at least in some circles, but the one-sidedness of this idealized stereotype was no easier to live up to than the Victorian role of angel and virgin. A number of poets, including Anna Akhmatova, Marina Tsvetaeva and Edith Södergran have treated the theme of desire from the perspective of the woman as subject. Not surprisingly, they return again and again to the complexities of female sensuality. There is in the poetry of Edith Södergran a climate of weighty erotic dream accompanied by feelings of fine delicacy, a dream that is easily shattered:

> My hand is not at home in yours
> your hand is lust
> my hand is longing

The psychic organism is finely tuned and full of ambiguities; the poet is torn in opposite directions: towards a flamboyant promis-

cuity that, in the next instant, shrinks from the crudity and coldness of the man's embrace into withdrawal.

Anna Akhmatova was called "a nun and a whore" by one of her
male contemporaries. Yet her poetry speaks of resignation, of the
distances in love, of the danger of losing separateness. The "grey-
eyed king", embodying her longing for love, at once physical encounter and meeting of kindred souls, is buried in the end. Edith
Södergran died young, "longing for a country that is not, for all
that exists I'm weary of desiring." Akhmatova outlived her role as
love goddess to become the grand lady of Russian poetry, a moral
authority.

As the century wore on, the roles and themes available to women
poets grew broader. By World War II, their work was increasingly
shaped by the political realities they lived. There are numerous
references to the atrocities of the war. We think of Wisława Szymborska's "Starvation Camp at Jasło" and Nelly Sachs' "Chorus of
the Rescued," an elegy for the dead, of the poems of Gertrud
Kolmar, Ingeborg Bachmann, and Urszula Kozioł. The peculiar
inhumanity and dreariness of modern life looms large in other
poems, for instance in those of Sonja Åkesson. Yet the themes and
concerns of the women poets writing in Europe in the twentieth
century cannot be summed up in a few lines, for these poets have
responded to all aspects of life, and life, fortunately, will always
resist our efforts to categorize.

JOANNA BANKIER

Notes and References

[1] Modernism as a literary movement extends roughly from World War I
through the 1950's, with its strongest influence in the 1920's. Literary movements analogous to European modernism were taking place
elsewhere in the world in the early decades of this century—in China,
Japan, Iran, the Arab world, Latin America—each of which deserves
to be studied in depth. In Anglo-Saxon poetry, one of the most
important works of modernism is T. S. Eliot's long poem *The Waste
Land,* published in 1921.

[2] Frank Kermode, "Yes, Santa, There Is a Virginia," *The New York Review of
Books,* 20 (December 21, 1978), 32.

[3] Virginia Woolf, *A Room of One's Own* (New York: Harcourt, Brace, 1957).

[4] Virginia Woolf, *To the Lighthouse* (New York: Harcourt, Brace, 1955),
p. 310.

[5]Bernice Glatzer Rosenthal, "Love on the Tractor: Women in the Russian Revolution and After," in *Becoming Visible: Women in European History,* Renate Bridenthal and Claudia Koonz, eds. (Boston: Houghton Mifflin, 1977).

[6]Ibid.

[7]Barbara Engel, "Women as Revolutionaries: The Case of the Russian Populists," in *Becoming Visible,* Bridenthal and Koonz, eds.

[8]Vladimir Ilyich Lenin (1870–1924), Leon Trotsky (1879–1940), Aleksandra Mikhailovna Kollontai (1872–1952) Russian revolutionaries.

[9]Rosenthal, "Love on the Tractor."

[10]Ibid.

[11]Hagar Olsson, *Edith Södergran* (Stockholm: Bonniers, 1955), p. 35.

Anna Akhmatova
Soviet Union   *1889–1966*

July 1914

I

All month a smell of burning, of dry peat
smoldering in the bogs.
Even the birds have stopped singing,
the aspen does not tremble.

The god of wrath glares in the sky,
the fields have been parched since Easter.
A one-legged pilgrim stood in the yard
with his mouth full of prophecies:

"Beware of terrible times . . . the earth
opening for a crowd of corpses.
Expect famine, earthquakes, plagues,
and heavens darkened by eclipses.

"But our land will not be divided
by the enemy at his pleasure:
the Mother-of-God will spread
a white shroud over these great sorrows."

"Everything is Plundered . . ."

Everything is plundered, betrayed, sold,
Death's great black wing scrapes the air,
Misery gnaws to the bone.
Why then do we not despair?

By day, from the surrounding woods,
cherries blow summer into town;
at night the deep transparent skies
glitter with new galaxies.

And the miraculous comes so close
to the ruined, dirty houses—
something not known to anyone at all,
but wild in our breast for centuries.

Translated from the Russian by Stanley Kunitz

There is in human closeness a sacred boundary
which cannot be crossed by falling in love or by passion,
though lips merge in the awful silence
and the heart is torn to shreds with love.

Friendship has no power here, nor years
of sublime and fiery happiness
when the soul is free and a stranger
to the lingering torment of sensuality.

Those who rush toward it are mindless, and those
who reach it—are stricken with anguish.
Now you know why my heart
does not beat under your hand.

Translated from the Russian by Dianne Levitin

Marina Tsvetaeva
Soviet Union   *1892–1941*

An Attempt at Jealousy

How is it with another woman?
Easier I bet.
One oar stroke! Did the memory
Of me (an island floating

In the sky not the sea) grow dim
Quickly like a coastline?
O souls, you will be sister and
Brother, not lovers!

How is it with a *normal* woman,
Rid of the divine?
Now that you've dethroned your queen
And given up your throne

How is it? Do you keep busy?
Getting smaller? How
Do you get up? How are you able,
Poor man, to pay the cost

For her eternal boorishness?

"Enough of your hysterics,
I'm moving out!" How is it with
A woman who's just like

Any other, my chosen one?
Do you like her cooking?
When you're sick of it, don't whine!
How is it with a statue,

You who walked on Sinai[1]?
How is it with a stranger,
A mortal? Tell me, do you love her?
And you're not ashamed

As the scourge of Zeus lashes your brow?
How is it? How's your health?
Still singing? Tell me, what do you do
About the wounds, poor fellow,

Of your stinking conscience? How is it
With a commodity?
Expensive, eh? Plaster of Paris
Isn't as good as marble

Of Carrara[2]? (God was hewn
From it but he's smashed
To dust!) How is it with one
Of a hundred thousand,

You who have known Lilith[3]? Are
You satisfied? Magicless?
How is it with a woman of earth,
Using five senses

Only? Well cross your heart, are you
Happy? No? In an endless pit
How is it, my love? Worse than for me
With another man?

Translated from the Russian by Robert Perelman and Aleksandar Petrov

[1]The mountain in Israel where, according to Scripture, Moses received the Ten Commandments from God.
[2]In Italy, a source of high-quality marble used for statuary.
[3]In some apocryphal texts, Adam's first companion, who, because she refused to subordinate herself, was supplanted by Eve and turned into a demon.

Natalya Gorbanevskaya
Soviet Union   *1936*

Love, love! What nonsense it is,
what birdbrained idiocy.
When it is already too late
to spare me or to pity me,
then keep silent. Yes, keep silent,
do not inflame my cheeks
with that song finches learn
by heart to sing.

That song, in which the poet,
at random, traducing the theme,
cries out, then imitates
the clamour of birds,
sighs, squeaks, whispers,
moves his lips, breaks into
the obscure speech of fish—
and finally, a subterranean rumble.

Love from every quarter,
at best, simply food for verse,
for the finch's foolish song,
for the crowing of cockerels.
So keep silent. Stop talking.
Stroke my cheek with your hand.
How hot these fingers are,
How low are the ceilings.

Translated from the Russian by Daniel Weissbort

Novella Matveyeva
Soviet Union   *1934*

The Eggplants Have Pins and Needles

The eggplants have pins and needles.
Long dreams have plagued their sleep.

By the redbrick garden wall
Cucumbers droop like whips.
The poppylamps blow out in the wind.
Petals flock the air and settle
Like colored reflections.
The sun, like sea-drowned amber, peers
Through a dense silt of cloud.
But nettles go on being nettles
And roosters go on being roosters.
Listen! A stubborn beating of wings!
One bird, well-advanced in years,
Feeling the winter coming on,
Plucks up his courage and lets forth,
But has clean forgotten the song,
The words, and the rasping sound
Sticks in his gullet.
The rooster stiffens,
Clenches his pale yellow foot.
Fatigue and rheumatic pain overwhelm him,
As winter wags its blanched finger.
His plumage flutters somberly,
Like a fire behind bars.
His comb glows like elderberry.
His feathers gleam,
Rheumatically mossed,
And the rooster's faint shadow
Smells distinctly of the cold.

Translated from the Russian by Daniel Weissbort

Bella Akhmadulina
Soviet Union   1937

Fifteen Boys, or Perhaps Even More

Fifteen boys, or perhaps even more,
or perhaps even fewer than fifteen,
said to me
in frightened voices:
"Let's go to the movies or the Museum of Fine Arts."
I answered them more or less as follows:

"I'm busy."
Fifteen boys presented me with snowdrops.
Fifteen boys said to me
in broken voices:
"I'll never stop loving you."
I answered them more or less as follows:
"We'll see."

Fifteen boys are now living a quiet life.
They have done their heavy stint
of snowdrops, despair, letters.
They love girls—
some more beautiful than I,
others less beautiful.
Fifteen boys with false bravado and sometimes
    gloatingly
greet me when we meet,
greet in me when we meet
their deliverance, their normal sleep and meals.

You will come in vain, last boy.
I shall put your snowdrops in a glass
and silvery bubbles
will overgrow their stocky stems.
But you'll see, you too will stop loving me,
and mastering yourself you'll address me arrogantly
as though you had mastered me,
and I shall walk on down the street, down the street . . .

Translated from the Russian by Daniel Weissbort

Wisława Szymborska
Poland   1923

The Women of Rubens[1]

Female giants, fauna of women
naked like the rolling of barrels.
They nest in trampled-down beds

[1]Peter Paul Rubens, Flemish painter, 1577–1640.

sleep with mouths open for crowing.
Their eyes have escaped into depth
and penetrate to the centre of glands
from which yeast seeps into their blood.

Daughters of the Baroque[2]:
Dough rises in mixing bowls,
baths emit steam, wines slowly redden,
piglets of cloud trot across the sky,
trumpets neigh an alert of the senses.

Oh you creatures pumpkined to excess
doubled by the stripping of shifts
trebled by the violence of posture
you succulent dishes of love!

Your slim sisters had got up earlier
long before dawn brightened the picture.
They made their progress, in single file,
to the unpainted side of the canvas.

Exiles of style, with all ribs showing,
with birdlike feet and hands like claws.
Trying to flap their angular shoulder-blades.

The thirteenth century gave them a golden backcloth,
the twentieth—a silver screen;
the seventeenth had nothing to spare
for flat-chested women.

For even the skies are convex:
convex the angels and convex god—
a bewhiskered Phoebus[3] on a sweaty mount
heading straight
into the alcove of bubbling flesh.

Translated from the Polish by Celina Wieniewska

[2]Art style c. 1550–1700.
[3]Another name for Apollo, Greek and Roman god of the sun.

Starvation Camp Near Jasło[1]

Write it down. Write it. In ordinary ink,
on ordinary paper: no food was given them,
they all died of hunger. All? How many?
This meadow is so big. How many blades of grass
for each? Write: I don't know.
History's skeletons are recorded in round figures.
A thousand and one becomes just a thousand.
The odd one might never have existed.
An imagined foetus, an empty cradle,
a primer opened for no one,
air that smiles, shouts and keeps growing,
steps into the garden for emptiness to run down,
nobody's place in a line.

We are in that meadow where it became flesh.
It remains silent like a false witness.
Sunlit. Green. There is a wood nearby—
bark to suck for a drop of moisture
the daily ration of a view
before one goes blind. High up a bird
that moved its shadow of succulent wings
across their mouths. Jaws opened
and snapped shut, tooth struck hard on tooth.
In the night sky a lunar sickle reaped
imaginary loaves.
Hands flew in from blackened icons
holding empty cups.
On the spit of barbed wire
a man turned.
They sang, their mouths full of earth.
A jolly song about war that marches straight into one's
    heart.
Write: about the stillness here.
Yes.

Translated from the Polish by Jan Darowski
[1]concentration camp in southern Poland.

Urszula Kozioł
Poland   1935

Alarum[1]

Grief
o grief
grief for ever

Give me the right to sorrow. Let other women
stand guard their hearths, let them be brightened by the
     light of their homes
but to me leave my tear
I shall keep safe the lament for the never-lamented.

Let maidens with armfuls of flowers go bowing to
     propitious
winds. A wedding retinue of time, let them go steeply
     and in crowds
and lift the harvest overhead in lofty greeting.

While it is for me to say farewell. For many of the brave
     did perish,
not all of them full-grown, but always
in thirst for light. And from them
their light escaped before the sun went down.

An Antigone[2] did not come to bury her unburied
     brothers.
One of her, turned into smoke
or perhaps into a shadow on a stone—
another, no more than her own gesture or readiness, all
     overtaken by smoke,
shadow. So the bracket of her hands remains open
and the unaccomplished design of the act hovers.
          And thus to weep for her too, and—
great is the number of the unknown. The undivided
tears are left to be apportioned.

---

[1]archaic form of "alarm"; warning of danger.
[2]The daughter of Oedipus; accompanied her father after he had put out his eyes
and gone into exile and stayed with him until he died. After her two brothers had
killed each other in battle, and Creon, the new King of Thebes, forbade burial,
Antigone alone defied the tyrant.

Someone must be a drainpipe of tears for the
    unlamented.
For there is never enough regret, never enough
    memory.
The women of old knew it.
Mournfully dragging their hair on the ground or
    wrenching their fingers they raised alarum
and knocking their rattles performed their duty.

And yet in death—till now— there is nothing,
in death till now there is nothing but grief.

Translated from the Polish by Czesław Miłosz

Ana Blandiana
Romania   1942

The Couple

Some people see only you
Others see only me;
We are so perfectly superimposed
No one could see both at the same time.
No one dares dwell on the edge
From which we both could be seen.
You see only the moon,
I see only the sun;
You long for the sun,
I long for the moon.
We sit back to back,
Our bones knit long ago.
Blood carries whispers, murmurs
From one heart to the other.
What are you like?
I raise my arm
And stretch it way back.
I discover your sweet collar bone
And, raising my fingers, would touch
Your holy lips.
Then, suddenly, they turn and crush
My mouth till it bleeds.

What are we like?
Have we four arms to defend ourselves?
But I can hit only the enemy before me
And you only the enemy before you.
We have four feet to run,
But you can run only in your direction
I only in the opposite one.
Each step is a struggle for life and death.
Are we equal?
Shall we die together, or will one carry
For a time
The corpse of the other stuck to him
Infecting him slowly, too slowly, with death?
Or perhaps we won't even die completely
And will carry in eternity
The sweet burden of the other
Being atrophied eternity,
As a hump
As a wen . . .
Oh, only we know the longing
Of not being able to look in each other's eyes
And thus to understand everything.
We sit back to back
Grown like two branches;
If one breaks off
Sacrificing itself for a single look
He'll see only the back from which he broke,
Bleeding, chilling,
Of the other.

Translated from the Romanian by the poet, with William M. Murray

Nina Cassian
Romania   1924

Lady of Miracles

Since you walked out on me
I'm getting lovelier by the hour.
I glow like a corpse in the dark.
No one sees how round and sharp

my eyes have grown,
how my carcass looks like a glass urn,
how I hold up things in the rags of my hands,
they way I can stand though crippled by lust.
No, there's just your cruelty circling
my head like a bright stinking halo.

The Blood

Yes, I remember that pain precisely,
My ambushed soul
jerked like a beheaded chicken.
Blood poured on everything,
the street, the restaurant table.
It soaked your stunned hands.
My hair went wild.
It crawled around the glasses like a monster
strangling them, finally stood up
whirling and slicing at the air.
Then the head, axed off
fell at your feet.
Yes, I remember precisely—I smiled revoltingly,
screwed up my face to look absolutely me
and that I screamed just once,
but only later, when everyone had left
the lights were out and the blood
had been wiped off the table.

Translated from the Romanian by Laura Schiff

Vesna Krmpotic
Yugoslavia   *1932*

A December Forest

The cities of dream wander under the bark of a
    December forest
in which we wander like two trunks of love
carrying in ourselves a sleeping animal
that in dream gnaws on hazelnuts gathered last summer.

Yes, like a winter animal into its hole
love too has retreated deep into the body.

It is cold, cold around us,
over our path the bats are already sailing
and our fruit gravitates toward the earth,
our fruit, indigent before its flowering.

Translated from the Croatian by Vasa D. Mihailovich

Vesna Parun
Yugoslavia   1922

A Return to the Tree of Time

You who ask where I find the courage
to sing like a sun above love again
once I had locked it in a chest of black song
and laid it into a bird's lap.

Listen: I always return to myself
and a discovery waits for me in the bark of each tree
that I cut with the knife of memory.

But if the tree has died
and has nearly become coal,
I will plunge my hands deeply into the soil
and will dig it out as a coal.

If I return in ten years
I will dig it out as a stone.
But if I return in a hundred or more years
I will dig even deeper, and will find nothing.

For, even a stone does not remain a stone.
For, even a stone also migrates somewhere.
Do not ask about its journey
but let me sing and return
to the root of my song, the deepest to me.

Translated from the Croatian by Vasa D. Mihailovich and Ronald Morgan

Desanka Maksimovic
Yugoslavia   1898

For All Mary Magdalenes

I seek mercy
for the women stoned[1]
and their accomplice—the darkness of the night,
for the scent of clover and the branches
on which they fell intoxicated
like quails and woodcocks,
for their scorned lives,
for their love torments
unrelieved by compassion.
I seek mercy
for the moonlight and for the rubies
of their skin,
for the moonlight's dusk,
for the showers of their undone hair,
for the handful of silvery branches,
for their loves naked
and damned—
for all Mary Magdalenes.[2]

Translated from the Croatian by Vasa D. Mihailovich

[1]adulterous women were traditionally stoned to death.
[2]Mary Magdalene, follower of Jesus and type of the sinful and repentant woman.

Judit Tóth
Hungary   1936

To the Newborn

Like a round loaf, that's how small you were.
I rolled you on the board with my palm,
I kneaded you, patted you,
greased you smooth, floured you,
I shaped your roly body.
You slept in the palm of my hands.
You'd hardly dawned, your slight bones

were still soft under your skin, yet
how vehemently your vulnerable life
pulsed in your tiny torso, your folded limbs
closed about you like thick petals,
beneath, you slept like the still of a rose.

* * * *

What kind of well is the newborn's dreams?
Where do the minute dreamers descend?
Do they summon up their seas?
Among familiar algae, again
they hide, they swim back
to timelessness' cave,
to this grotto's constant quivering dark,
the blood-red fern's nest,
down, under the blood, under destiny,

And their awakening. The breath's
labored stirring,
until finally the will blasts
into terror's bantam blaring.

To what despair ·
do they wake from their indifferent seas?
This wild crying, this endless
gasping, a mnemne still of their fish-life,
yet with what a voice
is their vernal despair blessed.
They sob, they clamor, they praise,
hardly alive, they meet with their throats
the assaults of reality, the million
afflictions and pleasures of matter.
And they grab what they clamored for,
they grasp what every being grasps,
theirs the air, the earth, the milk,
the death, the lullaby, the glory.

* * * *

Wrapped in a shawl you lay in your basket,
you slept, you grew plump in your dreams.
You didn't know that I took you in my arms.
I scanned your face for my lover;
the image of his face wandered across yours,
drifting like a moon in a windy sky.

* * *

What a loveliness to hold.
What a loveliness to lift.
Light as a plume, round as the sun.
My joys that drowns out everything.
The victory of intertwining limbs
against time.
He rounded in the oven of hope,
detached at the gates of expectancy.
Yet he still floats in the boundless
past, and is here too
in the still of this shawl,
in the still of this rose
he dreams his bright dreams.

Dead Embryos

They sit in a glass egg,
the begun and abandoned flowering,
their bodies poised in a stiff shell,
millimeter ghosts.
They too slept in star wells,
dark vessels soaked up their dreams.

Oval-shaped pillows cradled
the creation, the beginning,
their microscopic sprout-solitude.
The glass-spun bony structure,
small wild-apple skulls,
hearts, arms, kidneys
could still begin their budding.

But they don't receive anything.
The air doesn't reach their lungs;
no spoon reaches their lips.
What kind of mourning does
pre-natal death deserve?

They were scraped also of decay,
naked buds, paper-thin cartilages.
Here the start and the continuum
eternally estranged.
They didn't demand their deaths,

didn't beg for anything,
didn't want flesh, bones, minerals;
they returned to nothingness' well.
The useless night peels off them,
the heavens, time—

They bow their heads to their chest,
knees tucked in, curled up,
they age in a glass egg
flung on the sands of a sunless eternity.

Translated from the Hungarian by Laura Schiff

Else Lasker-Schüler
Germany   1876–1945

My People

The rock grows brittle
From which I spring,
To which my canticles I sing . . .
Down I rush from the track
And inwardly only ripple
Far off, alone over wailing stone
Toward the sea.

Have flowed so much away
From the wine ferment
Of my blood.
Yet endlessly, yet even now that echo
In me,
When eastward, awesomely,
The brittle rock of bone,
My people,
Cries out to God.

Translated from the German by Michael Hamburger

Nelly Sachs
Germany   *1891–1969*

Chorus of the Rescued

We, the rescued,
From whose hollow bones death had begun to whittle
  his flutes,
And on whose sinews he had already stroked his bow—
Our bodies continue to lament
With their mutilated music.
We, the rescued,
The nooses wound for our necks still dangle
before us in the blue air—
Hourglasses still fill with our dripping blood.
We, the rescued,
The worms of fear still feed on us.
Our constellation is buried in dust.
We, the rescued,
Beg you:
Show us your sun, but gradually.
Lead us from star to star, step by step.
Be gentle when you teach us to live again.
Lest the song of a bird,
Or a pail being filled at the well,
Let our badly sealed pain burst forth again
and carry us away—
We beg you:
Do not show us an angry dog, not yet—
It could be, it could be
That we will dissolve into dust—
Dissolve into dust before your eyes.
For what binds our fabric together?
We whose breath vacated us,
Whose soul fled to Him out of that midnight
Long before our bodies were rescued
Into the ark of the moment.
We, the rescued,
We press your hand
We look into your eye—
But all that binds us together now is leave-taking,
The leave-taking in the dust
Binds us together with you.

Translated from the German by Ruth and Matthew Mead

Gertrud Kolmar
Germany   *1899*

Out of the Darkness

Out of the darkness I come, a woman.
I am with child and have forgotten, whose;
Once I did know it.
But now there remains no man for me . . .
All went down behind me like rills of water
Drunk by the earth.
I move on and on.
For I want to reach the mountains before day, and the
   stars are already fading.

Out of darkness I come.
Through gloomy streets I walked lonely,
When light that came gushing forth tore the gentle
   blackness with its talons,
The leopard the hind,
And a door pushed wide open spewed ugly shrieking,
   wild yelling, bestial roars.
Drunkards rolled on the ground . . .
On my way I shook it all from the hem of my dress.

And I ambled over the deserted marketplace.
Leaves floated in puddles that mirrored the moon.
Lean, hungry dogs sniffed at refuse on the stones.
Trodden fruit rotted,
And an old man in rags still tortured his poor stringed
   instrument
And sang with a thin, discordantly plaintive voice
Unheard.
And these fruits had once ripened in sunshine and dew
Still dreaming of the fragrance and joy of the loving
   blossom,
But the whining beggar
Had long forgotten that and knew no more now than his
   hunger and thirst.

In front of the mighty man's palace I stopped,
And when I trod the lowest step
The flesh-red porphyry burst with a crack under my
   sole.—

I turned about
And looked up to the uncurtained window, the late
    candle of the thinking man,
Who pondered and pondered and never found an
    answer to his question
And to the little shaded lamp of the sick man who had
    not yet learnt
How he was to die.
Under the arch of the bridge
Two repulsive skeletons were quarreling over gold.
I raised my poverty as a gray shield to my face
And walked by unendangered.
Far away the river is conversing with its banks.

Now I stagger up the stony recalcitrant path.
Scree, thorn bushes wound my blind, groping hands:
A cave awaits me
That in its deepest crevice harbours the green raven
    without a name.
There I shall enter,
Under the shelter of the great overshadowing wing I
    shall crouch down and rest.
Fading away shall listen to the dumb growing words of
    my child
And sleep, my brow inclined to the East,
Until sunrise.

Translated from the German by Michael Hamburger

Marie Luise Kaschnitz
Germany   *1901*

Humility

Ambushed myself discovered
The counterfeit blossoms
I circulate
And the forged documents
With which I travel
And the false witness
I bear before

Morning crows
And the loaded dice
With which I play
With whom
With me

Thieves' lingo deciphered
Lately
In the year of the calm sun
Blood pressure going down
And knew
It's time for humility.

Resurrection

Sometimes we get up
Get up as for a resurrection
In broad daylight
With our living hair
With our breathing skin.
Only the usual things are around us.
No mirage of palm trees
With grazing lions
And gentle wolves.

The alarm clocks don't cease to tick
Their phosphorescent hands are not extinguished.

And yet weightlessly
And yet invulnerably
Ordered into mysterious order
Admitted early into a house of light.

Translated from the German by Michael Hamburger

Christine Lavant
Germany   1915

Buy Us a little Grain

Buy us a little grain of reality!
At last we could eat coarse bread
instead of iced angels.

I don't want to go to bed hungry again
I don't want to go on drowning the angels in salt
as a punishment for my rebellious guts.

Bring in a double-sized jug of brandy
we must get really drunk at last
and say you to each other from mouth to mouth
not stagger about forever on holy water.

I don't want to go to bed again thirsty
nor ever again with vinegar will I accustom
my cursing throat to prayer.

Do Not Ask

Do not ask what rips the night
for that night is only mine,
mine the peacock's mighty scream
and, deep down inside, the tongue
with the message that's for me.
If by tomorrow the sun,
quite exhausted, almost twined
with the purgatory bud,
wants to rest, it's driven out—
for that bud is only mine
on the back of my own stone
and reserved for my next night.

Translated from the German by Michael Hamburger

Friederike Mayröcker
Germany   *1924*

Patron of Flawless Serpent Beauty

Patron of flawless serpent beauty
exalted keeper of untamable seas
cultivator of the constant fields

you comb the green pelt of the towering forest
wisps of grass thaw around your brow

the long-christened in winter: the crystal icicles
your fist collects in the basins of village ponds
and the silver-eyed warm flocks of birds
nest in your pale arteries

Mighty you are and I fear you greatly
away you gallop on my saddled desires

Translated from the German by Michael Hamburger

Sarah Kirsch
East Germany   *1935*

Dandelions for Chains

Dandelions meet me wherever I am they overrun Germany's railway embankments dusty corners fields seize
even well-trimmed gardens through hedges leaves like
fine saws new flowers every day have the wind to carry
them over rivers walled boundaries stick my fingers
together when I try to fend them off

a tough companion first of all a gay flower plaything
wreath that makes you aware of your head disappoint-
ment when its flowers won't open indoors

then Ettersberg covered with dandelions crazy joy
yellow spots shooting up from prison-camp foundations

gas warning line the steps to the crematorium flowers
for chains flowers for children beautiful yellow color of
summer

extends across the seventeenth parallel where head-
sized jungle flowers bloom

Translated from the German by Michael Hamburger

Ingeborg Bachmann
Austria   *1926–1973*

The Respite

A harder time is coming.
The end of the respite allowed us
appears on the skyline.
Soon you must tie your shoelace
and drive back the dogs to the marshland farms.
For the fishes' entrails
have grown cold in the wind.
Poorly the light of the lupines burns.
Your gaze gropes in the fog:
the end of the respite allowed us
appears on the skyline.

Over there your loved one sinks in the sand,
it rises towards her blown hair,
it cuts short her speaking,
it commands her to be silent,
it finds that she is mortal
and willing to part
after every embrace.

Do not look round.
Tie your shoelace.
Drive back the dogs.
Throw the fishes into the sea.
Put out the lupins!

A harder time is coming.

Translated from the German by Michael Hamburger

from **Songs in Flight**

> *Dura legge d'Amor! ma, ben che obliqua,*
> *Servar convensi; pero ch'ella aggiunge*
> *Di cielo in terra, universale, antiqua.*[1]

IV

Instructed in love
by ten thousand books,
taught by the passing on
of hardly varying gestures
and silly oaths—

but not initiated
into love till here—
when the lava rushed down
and its breath met us
at the foot of the mountain,
when at last the exhausted crater
surrendered the key
of those locked-up bodies—

we stepped into enchanted rooms
and lit up the darkness
with fingertips.

V

Within, your eyes are windows
on land where I stand in clearness.

Within, your breast is a sea
that drags me to the bottom.

Within, your hips are a jetty
for my ships returning home
from too great voyages.
Happiness makes a silver cable
to which I lie fixed.

Within, your mouth is a downy nest

---

[1]*Dura legge d'Amor!* . . . : from Petrarch *I Trionfi*, "Trionfo d'Amore", Terzina, 148–150; "Love's stern law we must obey, however unjust, for, ancient and universal, it unites the earth and the sky."

for my unfledged tongue.
Within, your flesh is melon-light,
endlessly sweet and relishable.
Within, your veins are calm
and filled right up with gold
that I wash with my tears
and will one day be weighed against me.

You receive titles, your arms embrace goods,
that were first on you bestowed.

Within, your feet are never on the move
but already arrived in my velvet lands.
Within, your bones are clear flutes
from which I can conjure notes
to enthrall even death . . .

Translated from the German by Daniel Huws

Judith Herzberg
Holland   contemporary

Vocation

And when they asked her what she wanted to be
she said 'Invalid' and saw herself,
legs motionless in brownish plaids,
pushed by devoted husband and pale sons;
not even a stamp to paste herself,
not a letter to write, no trip to take.
Then she would be really free at last,
look as sad as she pleased, take her
turn before others in stores, be up
in front at parades, no pretty clothes,
and every night sobbing softly
she would say, 'Not on account of myself
but all that trouble for you.'
And both boys would always
stay with her, devote
their lives to her, and nothing
would ever happen to her,
never, never would she wear out.

On the Death of Sylvia Plath

We stand naked behind the line.
Whoever is up front tries to find cover,
who stands in the back presses toward the front.

They're bidding for us.
Those who are afraid have most to fear—
nobody knows why one is being chosen.

I have heard the bad news,
myself having miraculously escaped death,
I now mourn my sister.

Mene tekel[1] is a creature,
an ant, a crab, that creeps with little
black claws from the cinders onto the hot tracks.

Consolation for those who are roofless never comes
in the shape of houses
but from the mouths of drifters.

For the astonished child that still
was born, space will not turn
inside out.

It will have to seek refuge
with wolves, if there still exist
motherly wolves.

Translated from the Dutch by Manfred Wolf

[1]*mene mene tekel upharsin:* numbered, numbered, weighed and divided (Aramaic);
in the Bible, the writing on the wall, interpreted by Daniel to mean that God had
weighed the Babylonian king and his kingdom, found them wanting, and would
destroy them.

Tove Ditlevsen
Denmark   1918–1976

Self Portrait 4

There lives in
my childhood street
an old woman
who remembers me
when I was young.
I was wild
she says
the whole house shook
when I took the stairs
in a jump from the fourth floor.

That picture of me
is disturbing
and pushes itself
in front of my own
as when photos
are superimposed
one over the other.

I fear
the place I have
in the memory of others.
They remind me of things
I myself have forgot.

They have stolen
my face
before it was
used up
they set it often
outside their own.

I do not remember
my childhood
old woman
the grown ups were
all alike and
without age.

She has a knowledge
of me she doesn't disclose
a secret I never
have told.

It fills her and
keeps death away
she lies and intends
to outlive me.
I certainly never took
the stairs in long leaps
I was a quiet child
I loathe her.

Translated from the Danish by Ann Freeman

Eeva-Liisa Manner
Finland   1921

The Lunar Games

The moon is eaten and renewed
and hoists slow sails,
glides, borrowing the light and the wind,
pours its strength, drags the seas;
the earth surrenders like a woman and gives birth to
    many.
The plants grow, and the nails and the hair,
the dogs call on the hills, the dead in their graves,
and many are murdered with different weapons,
with words and dripping knives.
They are eaten like the moon,
they are not renewed anymore,
but, in the moonlight,
        one dies lightly and stands up,
takes a boat, if the moon is a ship,
takes to witchcraft, if a drum is the moon,

for the shapes of the moon are rather variable,
she is a windy moon and the voices and the moon of the
    drums

she is the seed and the eye and the Moon-That-
  Diminishes,
the counting memory of space.

Translated from the Finnish by Jaakko A. Ahokas

Edith Södergran
Sweden   *1892–1923*

We Women

We women, we are so near the brown earth.
We ask the cuckoo what he expects from the spring,
we throw our arms around the cold pines,
we search in the sunset for signs and advice.
I loved a man once, he didn't believe in anything . . .
He came one cold day with empty eyes,
he went one heavy day with forgetfulness on his brow.
If my baby doesn't live, it's his . . .

Translated from the Swedish by Samuel Charters

Violet Twilights

Violet twilights I carry with me from my
                                    primeval times,
naked virgins playing with galloping centaurs . . .
Yellow sunshine days with bright glances,
only sunbeams pay proper homage to a
                    tender-hearted woman's body . . .
The man has not arrived, has never been, will
                                    never be . . .
The man is a false mirror thrown against the
                    cliffs in wrath by the sun's daughter,
the man is a lie, incomprehensible to white
                                    children,
the man is a rotten fruit rejected by proud lips.

Beautiful sisters, come high up to the strongest
                                    rocks

we are all fighting women, heroines,

> horsewomen,

eyes of innocence, brows of heaven, rose larvae,
heavy breakers and soaring birds,
we are the least expected and the darkest red,
tigerspots, taut strings, fearless stars.

Translated from the Swedish by Stina Katchadourian

Pain

Happiness doesn't have any songs, happiness doesn't
   have any thoughts, happiness doesn't have anything.
Break your happiness into pieces, for happiness is evil.
Happiness comes slowly with the morning's buzzing in
   sleeping thickets,
happiness slips away in light cloud pictures over deep
   blue depths,
happiness is the field that sleeps in midday's embers
or the sea's endless width under the bath of vertical sun
   beams,
happiness is powerless, she sleeps and breathes, and
   doesn't know about anything . . .
Do you know pain? She is strong and large with
   secretly clenched fists.
Do you know pain? She is hopefully smiling with eyes
   red from crying.
Pain gives us everything we need—
she gives us the keys to the kingdom of death,
she pushes us in through the gate while we're still
   hesitating.
Pain baptizes the children and watches over them with
   the mother
and hammers out all the golden wedding rings.
Pain reigns supreme over everyone, she smooths the
   thinker's forehead
she fastens the jewels around the neck of the woman
   who is desired,
she stands at the door when the man comes from his
   loved one . . .
What more does pain still give her loved ones?
I don't know any more.

She gives pearls and flowers, she gives songs and
   dreams,
she gives us a thousand empty kisses,
she gives us the only kiss that's real.
She gives us our strange souls and our peculiar
   thoughts,
she gives us all of life's highest winnings:
love, solitude, and the face of death.

Translated from the Swedish by Samuel Charters

Karin Boye
Sweden   1900–1941

A Sword

A sword
flexible, supple and strong
a dancing sword
proudly obeying the stern laws
the hard rhythms of the steel.
A sword
I wanted to be —soul and body.

I hate
this wretched willow soul of mine,
patiently enduring, plaited or twisted
by other hands.
I hate you
my lazy, dreamy soul.
You shall die.
Help me, my hate, sister of my longing.
Help me be
a sword,
a dancing sword of tempered steel.

Translated from the Swedish by Joanna Bankier

Sonja Åkesson
Sweden   1926–1977

Evening Walk

In Hässelby,[1]
on the Earth,
some pilot's wife
taking her evening walk
wonders why she's crying

the sky is high
at dusk
a distant sorrow
and the people castaways

a beetle lands
a dog is on his way
a suburban bus, dark now,
dismal light in a row
of windows

she thinks of Spinoza[2]
poetry is in all things, she whines, but
the shoe feels lonely in the gravel

turn back home?
she no longer wants
to sit there
proper
among the rest of the belongings

sewing sessions and evening courses
in psychology
she thinks of Freud
O you dog on the dunes, she whines
foreign ports?
but the earth is small

---

[1] A commuter suburb outside of Stockholm in Sweden.
[2] Baruch Spinoza, seventeenth century philosopher.

The sky is more transparent now, higher,
soon it will burst, soundless
and a fondling darkness will envelop her

A dazzling city, suburbia or Jerusalem,
a mirage in the bleak light.

Ears

Listen—help me!
I'm desperate.

Listen!

It's of course impossible
don't you think I know
it's impossible.

But still—listen you!

I'm asking for help.

Don't you hear!

What can have gone wrong?

I'm asking for help

and you just walk around
in your scarves and leatherjackets
and nyloncoats and briefcases
and your baskets and boots
and umbrellas and gloves
and tiepins and anklewarmers
and dogs and cats
and glasses and skins
and mouths and breasts
and even ears (it seems)

as if you just didn't hear.

I'm asking for help.

Aren't we living in a democratic society?
Haven't you read the Bible for instance?

Still you must hear,

Of course you can hear.

Help!

It's a cry.

You've heard it before.
It's spelled H   E   L   P —
you learned that in school
didn't you?

It's so strange to think
that you just walk around
and do nothing.

Is it because it's impossible?

If only I could understand
what all the coats and briefcases
and jackets and tablecloths
and baskets and umbrellas
and all dogs and cats
and all breasts and tiepins
and all skins and spellingrules
and all mouths and ears are for

when it's impossible anyway.

My god, what are ears for?

Translated from the Swedish by Joanna Bankier

Eleni Vakalo
Greece   1921

But there was
                    once
                         a time
                              when the bones, great
                                        skeletons
of birds and beasts glowed throughout their entire
     length spread out to the points of the wings
stable and suspended
like spacious chariots rising high over the fighting of
     invasions
And the age was in pain
Whirling of ash and dust
The salt dry
Jointed heaps sinking their compact weight
Slowly into the clay

I can recall it,
                    Suspended, the great birds
crossing their bodies at the time
Sorties of deer passed by travelling at great speed
The burials
                    —how many—
                              trees and dark animals
and as they chased them fledglings abandoned at their
     root
The whole air shook itself
Hours like shaken leaves
Smelling like leaves
And underneath were locked with it into the earth
The nests and souls of numerous small animals
With its plucked head and its small piping voice
Coming quick from the throat
Crossing—how fast—the zones of time
It gradually fought me,
Bored nests throughout my body for its fellows
And I became a dwelling for wild birds
In the midst of a desolation

The lovely bird shall dwell there now
Whilst the rodent in the foundations
Lies curled in a tangle of respiration

Translated from the Greek by John Stathatos

Katerina Anghelaki-Rooke
Greece   1939

The Body is the Victory
and the Defeat of Dreams

The body is the Victory of dreams
when shameless as water
it rises from slumber
marks and scars still asleep
these many signs
its dark olive groves
enamored
cool in the palm.

The body is the Defeat of dreams
as it lies long and empty
(if you shout inside you hear the echo)
with its anemic hair
lovelorn of time
groaning, wounded
hating its motion
its primitive black
fades steadily
waking it's yoked to the briefcase
hanging from it suffering
for hours in the dust.

The body is the Victory of dreams
when it puts one foot in front of the other
and gains the solid space.
A place.
A heavy thud.

Death,
when the body gains its place
through death
in the public square
like a wolf with a burning muzzle
it howls "I want"
            "I can't stand it"
            "I threaten—I overthrow"
            "my baby's hungry."

The body gives birth to its justice
and defends it.
The body makes the flower
spits out the pip-death
tumbles down, flies
motionless whirls around the cesspool
(motion of the world)
in dream the body is triumphant
or is found naked in the streets
enduring;
it loses its teeth
it trembles erotically
its earth bursts like a watermelon
and it's finished.

Translated from the Greek by Philip Ram

Margherita Guidacci
Italy   1921

At Night

At night the wallpaper shakes
itself loose from the walls,
rustles like a forest,
extends creepers before all the doors.

The halls become swift streams
where flocks of light-footed
wild-scented animals
shortcut through murmuring waters.

my heart through the horsetail's lance,
that heart which now holds
a name formed of mint and amber.
How much laughter I feel
climbing upward through my body.
How brilliantly my eyes shine
—eyes that mourned through 7,000 tears—!
Life tastes me as poem
and kisses taste to me like apples.
The mountain looks after the pines,
and through the rocks the sea dances.
Love dances in my heart.
He loves me. He waits for me.
I'm no longer the sad, mad girl
who cried when she heard laughter,
now I'm the sweet child
and no longer the bitter woman.

Translated from the Spanish by Philip Levine

Maria Beneyto
Spain   *1925*

Nocturne in the Women's Prison

They are dreaming of children. Torrential
rivers of blood pass,
drowning their unborn daughters.
(Every year murders another of their sons.)

They are dreaming of razors,
of poison, of a well-aimed shot;
a lake of extravagant tenderness,
a howl of silence in the shadows.

Asleep, they live, dreaming
of the man with the wounded throat,
of the man whose mouth is muddy with sin,
of the man who reaches the height of oblivion.

Caged fire. Fever.

Like wild beasts they sigh in the dark,
wild beasts of love beneath a night
free of the recurring dream of oasis.

No, there are no more angel's feathers.
Not even the faded down of a warm bird,
smashing itself in rebellion, blindly,
in mad, useless flight.

But when spring embraces
the barren wire of the rosebushes
a monstrous bird screams,
clinging, windless, to the bars . . .

And in this night full of flowers,
some of the women are singing with distant voices
(the voices of hidden children), recovered
on the friendly road to death.

Some are rocked by the whinny,
prophetic and grotesque,
of idiocy,
their eyes bright as a snakes.

Others team with exhaustion
in flames prefiguring ashes,
already consuming themselves, dreaming still,
still loving, and ageing by centuries . . .

Translated from the Spanish by Catherine Rodriguez-Nieto

Joyce Mansour
France   1928

Yesterday evening I saw your corpse
You were moist and naked in my arms
I saw your skull
I saw your bones thrust by the sea of morning
Up the white sand and under a hesitant sun
The crabs fought for your flesh

Nothing remained of your dimpled breasts
Yet I preferred you so
My flower

Translated from the French by Albert Herzing

North Express

Cobra is the night image of a chinese water-print
Cobra ignited by moonlight
Unfurls as does the sea
On beaches black with mountain ash
And oblique corridors Eyes behind goggles
Asphalt hells
The nettlegrown quarrels of the cultural owl
Subside
Cobra swallows Cobra as desire
Desire
Far from the shallow sex of habit
Far from the empty port of mechanical rape
Through the blazing hiccups of volcanic mirth
Into the foxglove The very heart of panic
Rides Pierre Alechinsky and his left-handed mirror
     Qui vive?
     Cobra

Translated from the French by the author

Lucienne Desnoues
France   1921

First Things

We come to uncrate the newness of this world,
First fruits of the season, the crates of flowers,
Orchard morning, burst and lying open,
Markets, raise your colors. Dawn is ours.
Dawn in the cities, gorged with leaves; we come
To loose the bonds of the watercress. The men

Get braced to take it—eavoe[1]!—across their backs,
Strong men, the givers of blood, they give it again.

These are not the men who hate the sun,
The ones that talk about the sick dawn;
These are men who stumble under salads
And eat the red meat and guzzle the wine.
Oh Spring of the day, the consecrated hours,
Now the whole universe agrees:
We still have time to live the day through,
To crack the hard bread, to chew the greens.

We ask for three meals, and only hope
For a little subtlety. It's a simple wish,
To find the gardens in the depths of pleasure,
The marrow of April deep in the first dish.
We want a sense of the south, resplendent and singing,
Growth like a proud green garland, thick skins
Of sharpened artichokes carved like acanthus,
Garlic, pepper polished in the winds.

Saint-Germain-des-Près,[2] so far from the fields,
Here's redemption for all the tobacco nights,
Here, set in the breast of clattery Paris,
Beats the simple proper heart of Provence.
Ah, the homage of the young fields,
Virgin asparagus barely out of the ground,
Flower of the virgin season; these radishes
Still lying in the cradle, pink and round.

My stevedore heart, grab hold, grab hold of life.
Lettuce, oh lettuce, all you poor green dummies,
Who can talk of a wasted dawn, daylight?
How I love to touch your lovely tummies!
In both my hands I hold Pomona's[3] breasts,
Innocence pushing the wicker corset apart,
Strength in a kilo, tenderness in a ton,
Hold on hard, hold on, my stevedore heart.

Translated from the French by Miller Williams

[1]Evoe—in ancient Greece, the wordless cry of the Maeneds, female worshippers
of the god Dionysos; suggests also "Heave ho!"
[2]A neighborhood on the Left Bank in Paris.
[3]In Roman mythology, the goddess of fruits and of fruit culture.

Eilean ni Chuilleanain
Ireland   1942

Swineherd

'When all this is over,' said the swineherd,
'I mean to retire, where
Nobody will have heard about my special skills
And conversation is mainly about the weather.

I intend to learn how to make coffee, at least as well
As the Portuguese lay-sister in the kitchen
And polish the brass fenders every day.
I want to lie awake at night
Listening to cream crawling to the top of the jug
And the water lying soft in the cistern.

I want to see an orchard where the trees grow in straight
  lines
And the yellow fox finds shelter between the navy-
  blue trunks,
Where it gets dark early in summer
And the apple-blossom is allowed to wither on the
  bough.'

Wash

Wash man out of the earth, shear off
The human shell.
Twenty feet down there's close cold earth
So clean.

Wash the man out of the woman:
The strange sweat from her skin, the ashes from her
  hair.
Stretch her to dry under the sun
The blue marks on her breast will fade.

Woman and world not yet
Clean as the cat
Leaping to the windowsill with a fish in her teeth;
Her flat curious eyes reflect the squalid room,
She begins to wash the water from the fish.

Helen Adam
Great Britain: Scotland   1909

I Love My Love

"In the dark of the moon the hair rules"

—ROBERT DUNCAN

There was a man who married a maid. She laughed as
    he led her home.
The living fleece of her long bright hair she combed
    with a golden comb.
He led her home through his barley fields where the
    saffron poppies grew.
She combed, and whispered, "I love my love." Her voice
    like a plaintive coo.
Ha! Ha!
Her voice like a plaintive coo.

He lived alone with his chosen bride, at first their life
    was sweet,
Sweet was the touch of her playful hair binding his
    hands and feet.
When first she murmured adoring words her words did
    not appall.
"I love my love with a capital A. To my love I give my
    All.
Ah, Ha!
To my love I give my All."

She circled him with the secret web she wove as her
    strong hair grew.
Like a golden spider she wove and sang, "My love is
    tender and true."
She combed her hair with a golden comb and shackled
    him to a tree.
She shackled him close to the Tree of Life. "My love I'll
    never set free.
No, No.
My love I'll never set free."

Whenever he broke her golden bonds he was held with
    bonds of gold.

"Oh! cannot a man escape from love, from Love's hot
   smothering hold?"
He roared with fury. He broke her bonds. He ran in the
   light of the sun.
Her soft hair rippled and trapped his feet, as fast as his
   feet could run.
Ha! Ha!
As fast as his feet could run.

He dug a grave, and he dug it wide. He strangled her in
   her sleep.
He strangled his love with a strand of hair, and then he
   buried her deep.
He buried her deep when the sun was hid by a purple
   thunder cloud.
Her helpless hair sprawled over the corpse in a pale
   resplendent shroud.
Ha! Ha!
A pale resplendent shroud.

Morning and night of thunder rain, and then it came to
   pass
That the hair sprang up through the earth of the grave,
   and it grew like golden grass.
It grew and glittered along her grave alive in the light of
   the sun.
Every hair had a plaintive voice, the voice of his lovely
   one.

"I love my love with a capital T. My love is Tender and
   True.
I'll love my love in the barley fields when the thunder
   cloud is blue.
My body crumbles beneath the ground but the hairs of
   my head will grow.
I'll love my love with the hairs of my head. I'll never,
   never let go.
Ha! Ha!
I'll never, never let go."

The hair sang soft, and the hair sang high, singing of
   loves that drown,

Till he took his scythe by the light of the moon, and he
   scythed that singing hair down.
Every hair laughed a lilting laugh, and shrilled as his
   scythe swept through.
"I love my love with a capital T. My love is Tender and
   True.
Ha! Ha!
Tender, Tender, and True."

All through the night he wept and prayed, but before
   the first bird woke
Around the house in the barley fields blew the hair like
   billowing smoke.
Her hair blew over the barley fields where the slothful
   poppies gape.
All day long its voices cooed, "My love can never escape,
No, No!
My love can never escape."

Be still, be still, you devilish hair. Glide back to the grave
   and sleep.
Glide back to the grave and wrap her bones down
   where I buried her deep.
I am the man who escaped from love, though love was
   my fate and doom.
Can no man ever escape from love who breaks from a
   woman's womb?"

Over his house, when the sun stood high, her hair was a
   dazzling storm,
Rolling, lashing o'er walls and roof, heavy, and soft,
   and warm.
It thumped on the roof, it hissed and glowed over
   every window pane.
The smell of the hair was in the house. It smelled like a
   lion's mane,
Ha! Ha!
It smelled like a lion's mane.

Three times round the bed of their love, and his heart
   lurched with despair.
In through the keyhole, elvish bright, came creeping a
   single hair.

Softly, softly, it stroked his lips, on his eyelids traced a
    sign.
"I love my love with a capital Z. I mark him Zero and
    mine.
Ha! Ha!
I mark him Zero and mine."

The hair rushed in. He struggled and tore, but
    whenever he tore a tress,
"I love my love with a capital Z," sang the hair of the
    sorceress.
It swarmed upon him, it swaddled him fast, it muffled
    his every groan.
Like a golden monster it seized his flesh, and then it
    sought the bone,
Ha! Ha!
And then it sought the bone.

It smothered his flesh and sought the bones. Until his
    bones were bare
There was no sound but the joyful hiss of the sweet
    unsatiable hair.
"I love my love," it laughed as it ran back to the grave, its
    home.
Then the living fleece of her long bright hair, she
    combed with a golden comb.

Brenda Chamberlain
Great Britain: Wales   1912

Lament

My man is a bone ringed with weed.
Thus it was on my bridal night:
That the sea, risen to a green wall
At our window, quenching love's new delight,
Stood curved between me and the midnight call
Of him who said I was so fair
He could drown for joy in the salt of my hair.
We sail, he said,

Like the placid dead
Who have long forgotten the marriage-bed.

On my bridal night
Brine stung the window.
Alas, on every night since then
These eyes have rained
For him who made my heart sing
At the lifting of the latch;
For him who will not come again
Weary from the sea.

The wave tore his bright flesh in her greed:
My man is a bone ringed with weed.

Ruth Pitter
England   1897

The Lost Tribe

How long, how long must I regret?
I never found my people yet;
I go about, but cannot find
The blood-relations of the mind.

Through my little sphere I range,
And though I wither do not change;
Must not change a jot, lest they
Should not know me on my way.

Sometimes I think when I am dead
They will come about my bed,
For my people well do know
When to come and when to go.

I know not why I am alone,
Nor where my wandering tribe is gone,
But be they few, or be they far,
Would I were where my people are!

Africa

AFRICAN WOMEN HAVE GIVEN MORE to the poetry of their cultures than this selection can show. The poetry of Africa's oral cultures, and many literate cultures as well, is unrepresented. Some societies of Africa have a long history of literacy—ancient Egypt (from 4000 B.C.); Ethiopia (the old language of Ge'ez [from the fourth century] and Amharic [fourteenth century]); North Africa (Old Berber, in ancient Carthaginian script; and Arabic); the early city-states of the East African coast and the empires of West Africa (where Arabic has been a principal language since the eleventh century, and Swahili and Hausa have long been written in an adapted Arabic script). But these cultures mainly reserved writing for non-literary uses; or if poetry was written, it was usually anonymous. (The obelisk inscriptions of the Egyptian queen Hatshepsut are an exception.) The poetic traditions of Africa's major societies, including many of the ancient kingdoms, have been primarily oral and collective, not the work of an educated elite but an integral part of the fabric of daily life.

Although specialized aspects of the oral tradition are often entrusted to professionals—skilled historians or keepers of the highest religious ritual—the greater part of the culture of the tribe involves the participation of all its members. Women take part in dance, music, and songs for religious and agricultural festivals and celebrations of birth, death, and marriage, as well as the everyday songs that accompany all aspects of work and play. And through their responsibility for educating the young, women play an important part in preserving and transmitting culture. Folktales and riddles are direct vehicles for ethical teaching. More indirectly, poetry expresses the shared attitudes and beliefs of the community—through songs for grinding grain, songs for entertaining children, and songs the children themselves sing for their mothers going off to the day's work.

Responsibilities within the family and the community are rather clearly defined along sexual lines throughout traditional Africa, although specific conditions differ from tribe to tribe. Work connected with the home, food preparation (including carrying water and collecting firewood), and caring for children is usually the job of the women, with girl-children trained in these skills and expected to bear a significant share of the work from an early age. Beyond this basic similarity, nomadic and agricultural groups differ in the status and range of work allotted to women. Among the tribes of the savannah grasslands, which stretch across Africa below the Sahara and down the Eastern corridor, the economy centers on camel or cattle raising, which is high-prestige work and is restricted to men and boys. In agricultural areas such as West Africa, women are more essential to the economy, and have significant influence and independence beyond the home. Since in these areas the prevalence of the tsetse fly makes it impossible to use cattle in the fields, human labor is crucial and is highly valued. Although men usually have official control of land use and do such work as clearing, the actual farming from planting to harvest is done mainly by women. Whatever profits a woman makes—from surplus crops, or craft work, or trade—is regarded as hers, to do with as she chooses. In practice, most of what she earns goes toward the support and education of her children, for which she, not their father, is responsible.

African women have had almost as great an impact in trade as in farming. In Nigeria, trade is largely in the hands of the market women; and since they have the help of co-wives to care for home and children, they are often able to spend weeks or months at a time away from home as they travel from village to village. Almost every woman is involved in trade to some degree, if only in the selling of home crafts in the market. It would be virtually unthinkable for a woman to be without some skill or craft, to be entirely dependent economically on her husband.

As elsewhere in traditional societies, the basic unit of relationship is the extended kinship group. Marriage constitutes a social contract between two kinship groups, with the marriage payment serving as economic compensation to the bride's family for the loss of the value of her labor. A man generally has more than one wife—the number of wives being both a measure and means of his wealth, since the success of the harvest depends on the women and children working in the fields.

Where tribes have rulers, they are generally though not always men. In a number of tribes, such as the Mende and Wolof, a woman may become chief. In other cases, there is a female organization parallel to the male ruling structure. Among the Akan, for instance, the Queen Mother bears responsibility for the actions of the chief, and has her own entourage of elders and spokesmen. Every ranking male official is monitored by a woman of the palace. Women also control taxation. There is a long tradition of women as fighters—the corps of several thousand women warriors in the kingdom of Dahomey in the 1700s; the highly organized revolt of Ibo women against the British in 1923; the strong participation of women in liberation struggles today. A tight network of village women's associations lay behind the success of the Ibo uprising; and these associations continue to be an important instrument of women's day-to-day influence within the tribes.

The traditional fabric of African life has been disrupted to varying degrees by European colonial and neocolonial domination. Missionaries undermined local social and political structures through a rigid opposition to polygamy, and taught attitudes destructive of African integrity and profitable to European interests. The urbanized cash economy imposed by European powers resulted in the further breakdown of the extended family, which was often rooted in village agriculture. The situation in South Africa is simply the most extreme form of a widespread pattern. White South Africa—especially Afrikaaner society, which dates from 1658—rests on contempt for non-whites and exploitation of their labor. African men are crowded into labor compounds to work the mines and factories, while their families—women, children, the old—are restricted to small reservations of worthless land called Bantustans. The consequences for family life, and for individual and group identity, have been severe. Although West Africa has not suffered the extremes of *apartheid,* a similar splitting of families occurred initially as men had to move to the cities for work, leaving wives and children behind. Later, when the women followed, they found their former independence and influence greatly limited. Cut off from the agricultural base that had been their power, they lacked the Western education required for positions in the urban labor market. Moreover, wage-work for an unrelated male employer was considered improper. As happened in Europe with urbanization and industrialization, those women whose husbands could afford to support them were increasingly expected to stay home.

Under colonial administrations there was a need for Africans in minor civil service positions; so missionary schools began fairly early to provide education for boys. For girls, formal education has been rare. One reason has been male bias in Islamic and European-shaped governments. There are barriers also in the structure of traditional society. The family is dependent on the young girl's labor at home and in the fields. Also, school generally involves travel away from home, in any case expenditures for books and supplies; and such investment is considered wasted on girls, who will leave their kinship group after marriage to join that of their husband. When girls do receive some schooling, it is often weighted toward cooking and sewing; and few jobs are available afterwards except village teaching. In some countries such as Guinea, Kenya, and Tanzania, enlightened leaders or socialist philosophy have created a different situation, with more nearly equal access to education and jobs.

Schooling once received has brought its own problems. In many parts of Africa, even where the culture is itself basically egalitarian, education in European schools has meant the creation of a new elite, cut off from its roots in the traditional community. Those rewarded with the privilege of serving colonial or neocolonial interests often suffered what Frantz Fanon describes as the most destructive aspect of European influence—the internalizing of the values of the oppressor, identifying with the European and hating what is African.

In the 1930s a group of African students in Paris, including Léopold Senghor and Aimé Césaire, recognized this danger and began to put forward the cultural philosophy of Négritude. Their journal *Étudiant Noir* emphasized the importance for Africans of reaffirming their Black identity and the values of their African culture and traditional heritage, within the context of contemporary international realities. (Significantly, women were important to this movement as symbols, not as poets in their own right.) This and subsequent literary movements, in conjunction with the struggle throughout Africa for political independence and social transformation, have shaped the poetry of the past half century.

With the disruption of the old systems as a result of colonialism and neocolonialism, and the needs of the modern independent state to transcend tribal divisions while drawing on tribal strengths, the principal task of modern writers has been to identify and synthesize what is valuable in both the traditional past and the present. Dominant themes in the literature are alienation, redefinition of identity as Africans, the struggle for liberation, and the effort to create new meaning from the old under the disrupting impact of the new.

One the first questions facing the African poet is the choice of language in which to write. Many, especially of the older generation, have had and would like to continue some literary contact with Europe or the United States. Even in Africa itself, European languages give access to a wider reading public than most native languages, but also a different and more elite public. In any case, in former colonial territories until very recently the language of the poet's literary education was almost certain to be European. Many poets have nevertheless chosen to write in African languages; and until their works are translated, readers limited to Western languages are unlikely to come across them.

In this collection, only two women wrote out of a long African literary tradition—Hatshepsut, in Ancient Egyptian, and Mwana Kupona Msham, in Swahili. In West Africa in the early nineteenth century, Nana daughter of Osman dan Fodio was writing in Hausa, another African language with a long written tradition. Poetry in both Hausa and Swahili is traditionally moral and didactic, very difficult to translate into modern poetic idiom. Mwana Kupona's long "Poem to Her Daughter" was so highly considered in her own culture that it was memorized and recited for years; but it is not easily accessible to a person not rooted in that deeply religious society. A similar difficulty arises with the poetry of the Tuareg, a Berber tribe of the Sahara, where there is a long written poetic tradition in the sole keeping of the women; but the symbols and metaphors are so enmeshed in the details of nomadic life that the substance and spirit of the poetry are virtually impossible to translate. The oral poetry of the Berber singer Mririda is closer to us, perhaps because of her dual urban/rural experience.

Most poets in this collection write in English. The exceptions are the three from former Portuguese territories—Noémia da Sousa from Mozambique, and Manuela Margarido and Alda do Espírito Santo from São Tomé—and the white Afrikaans-speaking poet Ingrid Jonker. Not surprisingly, it is Jonker in whom the voice of alienation appears most strongly—in her poem "I Drift in the Wind," with its bitter and despairing repudiation of the racism of her people, "who have rotted away from me." It is Black Africa with whom she feels allied, yet even in language she is separate.

The determination to be free is a strong recurring theme, especially in the work of the Portuguese-speaking poets—Margarido, de Espirito Santo, da Sousa, and in the Algerian poets Anna Greki and Leila Djabali, writing of prison and torture under the French. Several of the poems are written for family members, in affirmation of an identity rooted in the traditional past but affected by the disruptions of the present. In Marjorie Macgoye's "For Miriam," the grandmother tries to make known to her young grandchildren the self she has been and is, through all the bewildering transformations around her. Dorothy Obi in "Winds of Africa" evokes as male persona an image and voice of family to call him back to a world he has moved away from.

While Lindiwe Mabuza speaks with the idiom and consciousness of urban Black South Africa, Stella Ngatho in "Footpath" and Minji Karibo in "Superstition" speak out of the song and ritual of an older tribal reality. Ama Ata Aidoo in "Cornfields in Accra" moves toward a synthesis, using the rhythms and collective ritual refrains of the tribal tradition to create among the rubble of urban poverty a new rooting of the people in the soil from which they came.

DEIRDRE LASHGARI

Further Readings

Information in this essay comes from the following sources:

Babalola, Adegoye, "Ijala: The Traditional Poetry of Yoruba Hunters," in *Introduction to African Literature,* Ulli Beier, ed. (Evanston, IL: Northwestern University Press, 1970).

King, Bruce, and Kolawole Ogungbesan, *A Celebration of Black and African Writing* (Oxford University Press, 1975).

Knappert, Jan, "Swahili Poetry," in *Introduction to African Literature,* Beier, ed.

Meyers, Odette, personal discussions, 1980.

Owuor, Henry, "Luo Songs," in *Introduction to African Literature,* Beier, ed.

Paden, John N., and Edward W. Soja, *The African Experience,* Vol. II, "History" and Vol. IIIb, "African Languages and Literatures" (Evanston, IL: Northwestern University Press, 1970).

Scharfe, Don, and Yahaya Aliyu, "Hausa Poetry," in *Introduction to African Literature,* Beier, ed.

Stacey, Tom, *Africa from the Sahara to the Zambesi,* (Verona, Italy: Mondadori, 1972).

Taiwo, Oladele, *An Introduction to West African Literature* (London: Trinity Press, 1967).

Van Allen, Judith, "African Women, 'Modernization,' and National Liberation," in *Women of the World,* Lynne B. Iglitzin and Ruth Ross, eds. (Santa Barbara, CA: Clio Books, 1976).

Wheeler, Elizabeth Hunting, "Sub-Saharan Africa," in *Women in the Modern World,* Raphael Patai, ed. (New York: Free Press, 1967).

Hatshepsut[1]

Egypt   *ruled 1503–1482* B.C.

from the Obelisk Inscriptions

Now my heart turns to and fro,
In thinking what will the people say,
They who shall see my monument in after years,
And shall speak of what I have done.
Beware of saying, "I know not, I know not:
Why has this been done?
To fashion a monument of gold throughout,
Like something that just happened."
I swear, as I am loved of Re,[2]
As Amun, my father, favors me,
As my nostrils are refreshed with life and dominion,
As I wear the white crown,[3]
As I appear with the red crown,[4]
As the Two Lords have joined their portions for me,
As I rule this land like the son of Isis,[5]
As I am mighty like the son of Nut,[6]
As Re rests in the evening bark,
As he prevails in the morning bark,[7]
As he joins his two mothers in the god's ship,
As sky endures, as his creation lasts,
As I shall be eternal like an undying star,
As I shall rest in life like Atum—[8]
So as regards these two great obelisks,
Wrought with electrum[9] by my majesty for my father
    Amun,
In order that my name may endure in this temple,

---

[1]Widow of Thutmose II, Hatshepsut ruled as regent for two years, then had herself crowned king, legitimizing her rule by claiming the god Amun Re as her father. She was one of five women in Egyptian history crowned as king; in the inscriptions she speaks of herself as both male and female, "son" and "daughter."

[2]Re: Amun Re, the sun god

[3]white crown: refers to Upper Egypt

[4]red crown: Lower Egypt

[5]Isis: mother of Horus, chief god

[6]Nut: grandmother of Horus

[7]morning bark/evening bark: boat in which the king sails through the sky accompanying the sun god Amun Re

[8]Atum: the old creator god (senior deity from an earlier period)

[9]electrum: light yellow alloy of gold

For eternity and everlastingness,
They are each of one block of hard granite,
Without seam, without joining together! . . .
Not shall he who hears it say,
"It is a boast," what I have said;
Rather say, "How like her it is,
She is devoted to her father!"
Lo, the god knows me well,
Amun, Lord of Thrones-of-the-Two-Lands;[10]
He made me rule Black Land[11] and Red Land[12] as
   reward,
No one rebels against me in all lands.
All foreign lands are my subjects,
He placed my border at the limits of heaven,
What Aten[13] encircles labors for me.
He gave it to him who came from him,
Knowing I would rule it for him.
I am his daughter in very truth,
Who serves him, who knows what he ordains.
My reward from my father is life-stability-rule,
On the Horus[14] throne of all the living, eternally like Re.

Translated from the Egyptian by Miriam Lichtheim

[10]Thrones-of-the-Two-Lands: Upper and Lower Egypt
[11]Black Land: the Nile Valley
[12]Red Land: the desert
[13]Aten: the sun disk itself
[14]the Horus throne: the king is identified with the chief god, Horus

Mwana Kupona Msham
East Africa: Swahili   *c.1810–1860*

from Poem to Her Daughter

Daughter, take this amulet
tie it with cord and caring
I'll make you a chain of coral and pearl
to glow on your neck. I'll dress you nobly.
A gold clasp too—fine, without flaw
to keep with you always.

When you bathe, sprinkle perfume, and weave your
   hair in braids
String jasmine for the counterpane.
Wear your clothes like a bride,
for your feet anklets, bracelets for your arms . . .
Don't forget rosewater,
don't forget henna for the palms of your hands . . .

Translated from the Swahili by J. W. Allen; adapted by Deirdre Lashgari.

Mririda n'Ait Attik
Morocco: Berber   *fl. 1940–1945*

Azouou

Azouou! Evening Breeze! What a perfect name!
But why are you so mean?
I won't leave your door
Till it opens,
Or I die waiting.

I see your eyes in the sparking flint.
Your lips against your teeth
Draw me to them.
The peaches of Assermoh have the roundness
Of your breasts,
Your skin has the softness
Of a ring dove's down.
The small blue tattoo between your eyes,
The tattoo on your chin,
The tattoos on your ankles. . . .
And the hidden tattoos—
Will I never see those, Azouou?
Let your hair down over your shoulders.
I will bury my face there
Like a partridge under its wing.

Why do you turn me away?
What do you want?
What gift will please you?

Your voice cuts through my heart
With a sharp edge!
When you walk away
Your hips move within mine. . . .

Azouou! Evening Breeze! What holds you back?
Lend me your red lips,
And your moist lips will still be yours.
Lend me your body,
And your satisfied body will be yours still,

And our two hearts will be together.

Mririda

They nicknamed me Mririda.
Mririda, nimble tree-frog of the meadow.
I don't have her gold eyes,
I don't have her white throat
Or green tunic.
But what I have, like Mririda,
Is my *zezarit,* my call
That carries up to the sheepfolds—
The whole valley
And the other side of the mountain
Speak of it. . . .
My call, which brings astonishment and envy.

They named me Mririda
Because the first time I walked in the fields
I gently took a tree-frog,
Afraid and trembling in my hands,
And pressed her white throat
To my lips of a child,
And then of a girl.

And so I was given the *baraka,*
The magic that gives them their song
Which fills the summer nights,
A song clear as glass,
Sharp as the sound of an anvil
In the vibrating air before rain. . . .

Because of this gift
They call me Mririda,
And he who will come for me
Will feel my heart beat in his hand
As I have felt the racing hearts of frogs
Beneath my fingertips.

In the nights bathed in moonlight
He will call me, *Mririda, Mririda,*
Sweet nickname that I love,
And for him I will release my piercing call,
Shrill and drawn-out,
Bringing wonder from men
And jealousy from women,
Nothing like it ever heard in this valley.

Translated from the Berber into French by René Euloge; English version by
Daniel Halpern and Paula Paley

Anna Gréki
Algeria   *1931–1967*

Before Your Waking
—*for Ahmad Inal*

Before your waking I only knew
How to limit my sight to my eyes' boundary
My eyes could not see past what they remembered

I slept in beds the shape of my bones
And in the barrenness I named sleep,
Night's waters and day's eroded one shore

The earth around me quivered like mercury
And if by chance I dreamed of the sun
Its light was torn from me; I was condemned

My suitcase was stuffed with its worldwide tours; but
My life had a little window on the courtyard
You could say that I lodged inside my brain

And nothing anyone said made sense
I called a stubborn desert wisdom
And had no desires except to lament them

The bodies I touched deserted my hands
My movements were plotted by puppet strings
That I called Passion, that I called Reason

Old age was gaining time on me
I'd even forgotten what you say to a child
Who wakes, frightened, and won't let go of your hand;
If I lived at all, it was just out of habit.

Yet even somewhere at the core of this deathly
Solitude—even then—I knew you would come
I knew I was travelling toward my youth

Youth was a mandate, pronounced by your heart's
Rhythm—The future was launched in your arms
I heard it approach without knowing your step

It speaks with the strength and warmth of your courage
And that shame, to say what others keep silent
For foolishness, often, or want of faith

Now I walk hand-in-hand with the earth; and he
Who holds me today will in the end
Love me in another's body

Translated from the French by Anita Barrows

The future is for tomorrow
The future is soon

Beyond the walls closed like clenched fists
Through the bars encircling the sun
Our thoughts are vertical and our hopes
The future coiled in the heart climbs towards the sky
Like upraised arms in a sign of farewell

Arms upright, rooted in the light
In a sign of an appeal to love
To return to my life
I press you against my breast my sister
Builder of liberty and tenderness
And I say to you await tomorrow
For we know

The future is soon
The future is for tomorrow.

Translated from the French by Mildred P. Mortimer

Leila Djabali
Algeria   1933

For My Torturer, Lieutenant D——

You slapped me—
        no one had ever slapped me—
electric shock
and then your fist
and your filthy language
I bled too much to be able to blush
All night long
a locomotive in my belly
rainbows before my eyes
It was as if I were eating my mouth
drowning my eyes
I had hands all over me
and felt like smiling.

Then one morning a different soldier came
You were as alike as two drops of blood.
Your wife, lieutenant—
Did she stir the sugar in your coffee?
Did your mother dare to tell you you looked well?
Did you run your fingers through your kids' hair?

Translated from the French by Anita Barrows

Manuela Margarido
São Tomé   1926

You Who Occupy Our Land

Do not lose sight
of the skipping children:
The black khaki garbed snake
struts before the hut door.
The bread fruit trees they cut down
to leave us hungry.
The roads they watch
for fleeing cacao.
Tragedy we already know:
the flaming hut
firing up the palm-thatched roof,
the smoke smell
mixing into the smell of
guando fruit and death.
We know ourselves,
sorters of tea from hampers
bark-strippers of the cashew trees.
But you, faintly off-color
masks of men
barely empty ghosts of men
you who occupy our land?

Translated from the Portuguese by Allan Francovich

Alda do Espírito Santo
São Tomé   1926

Where are the Men Seized in this Wind of Madness?

Blood falling in drops to the earth
men dying in the forest
and blood falling, falling . . .
on those cast into the sea. . . .
Fernão Dias for ever in the story
of Ilha Verde, red with blood,

of men struck down
in the vast arena of the quay.
Alas the quay, the blood, the men,
the fetters, the lash of beatings
resound, resound, resound
dropping in the silence of prostrated lives
of cries, and howls of pain
for men who are men no more,
in the hands of nameless butchers.
Ze Mulato, in the story of the quay
shooting men in the silence
of bodies falling.
Alas Ze Mulato, Ze Mulato,
The victims cry for vengeance
The sea, the sea of Fernão Dias
devouring human lives
is bloody red.
—We are arisen—
Our eyes are turned to you.
Our lives entombed
in fields of death,
men of the Fifth of February
men fallen in the furnace of death
imploring pity
screaming for life,
dead without air, without water
they all arise
from the common grave
and upright in the chorus of justice
cry for vengeance. . . .
    The fallen bodies in the forest,
the homes, the homes of men
destroyed in the gulf
of ravening fire,
lives incinerated,
raise the unaccustomed chorus of justice
crying for vengeance.
And all you hangmen
all you torturers
sitting in the dock:
—What have you done with my people? . . .
—What do you answer?
—Where is my people? . . .
And I answer in silence

of voices raised
demanding justice. . . .
One by one, through all the line . . .
For you, tormentors,
forgiveness has no name.
Justice shall be heard.
And the blood of lives fallen
in the forests of death,
innocent blood
drenching the earth
in a silence of terrors
shall make the earth fruitful,
crying for justice.
It is the flame of humanity
singing of hope
in a world without bonds
where liberty
is the fatherland of men. . . .

Translated from the Portuguese by Alan Ryder

Noémia da Sousa
Mozambique   1927

Appeal

Who has strangled the tired voice
of my forest sister?
On a sudden, her call to action
was lost in the endless flow of night and day.
No more it reaches me every morning,
wearied with long journeying,
mile after mile drowned
in the everlasting cry: Macala!

No, it comes no more, still damp with dew,
leashed with children and submission. . . .
One child on her back, another in her womb
—always, always, always!
And a face all compassed in a gentle look,
whenever I recall that look I feel

my flesh and blood swell tremulous,
throbbing to revelations and affinities. . . .
—But who has stopped her immeasurable look
from feeding my deep hunger after comradeship
that my poor table never will serve to satisfy?

Io mamane, who can have shot the noble voice
of my forest sister?
What mean and brutal rhino-whip
has lashed until it killed her?

—In my garden the syringa blooms.
But with an evil omen in its purple flower,
in its intense inhuman scent;
and the wrap of tenderness spread by the sun
over the light mat of petals
has waited since summer for my sister's child
to rest himself upon it. . . .
In vain, in vain,
a chirico sings and sings perched among the garden
    reeds,
for the little boy of my missing sister,.
the victim of the forest's vaporous dawns.
Ah, I know, I know: at the last there was a glitter
of farewell in those gentle eyes,
and her voice came like a murmur hoarse,
tragic and despairing. . . .

O Africa, my motherland, answer me:
What was done to my forest sister,
that she comes no more to the city with her eternal little
    ones
(one on her back, one in her womb),
with her eternal charcoal-vendor's cry?
O Africa, my motherland,
you at least will not forsake my heroic sister,
she shall live in the proud memorial of your arms!

Translated from the Portuguese by Alan Ryder

Dorothy S. Obi
Nigeria   contemporary

Winds of Africa

Winds that drift over the desert,
Dance over the Niger,
Steal perfume from the flowering trees
And from the pretty girls,
Pause for an instant with my mother
Where she sits in the doorway of our house
Her hands between her knees,
Brush against my body and whisper in my ear of Africa.
"I bring you a rendezvous—remember, remember . . .
I shall be waiting for you in the village.
I am Udeaja; they will tell you I have died,
But I am waiting in the place of our childhood,
Uduchukwu has a girl child;
Ughajua has married, she called you as guest to the
    feast . . .
Now I am going, but the guests will be waiting for you.
My brother, they killed a goat in your father's
    compound;
Your sister is cooking the soup in your mother's pot . . .
They are talking of you at home,
They are speaking of you at home."

Minji Karibo
Nigeria   contemporary

Superstition

I know
    that when a grumbling old woman
Is the first thing I meet in the morning
    I must rush back to bed
    And cover my head.
That wandering sheep on a sultry afternoon
Are really men come from their dark graves
    To walk in light
    In mortal sight.

That when my left hand or eyelid twitches
Or when an owl hoots from a nearby tree
    I should need pluck
    It means bad luck.
That drink spilled goes to ancestral spirits,
That witches dance in clumps of bananas;
That crumbs must be left in pots and plates
    Until the morn
    For babes unborn.
That it's wrong to stand in doorways at dusk
For the ghosts must pass—they have right of way!
That when a hidden root trips me over
    Fault's not in my foot.
    It's an evil root.
That if I sleep with feet towards the door
    I'll not long be fit
    I know it—Yes I know it!

Stella Ngatho
Kenya   1953

Footpath

Path-let . . . leaving home, leading out,
Return my mother to me.
The sun is sinking and darkness coming,
Hens and cocks are already inside and babies drowsing,
Return my mother to me.
We do not have fire-wood and I have not seen the
    lantern,
There is no more food and the water has run out,
Path-let I pray you, return my mother to me.
Path of the hillocks, path of the small stones,
Path of slipperiness, path of the mud,
Return my mother to me.
Path of the papyrus, path of the rivers,
Path of the small forests, path of the reeds,
Return my mother to me.
Path that winds, path of the short-cut,
Over-trodden path, newly-made path,
Return my mother to me.

Path, I implore you, return my mother to me.
Path of the crossways, path that branches off,
Path of the stinging shrubs, path of the bridge,
Return my mother to me.
Path of the open, path of the valley,
Path of the steep climb, path of the downward slope,
Return my mother to me.
Children are drowsing about to sleep,
Darkness is coming and there is no fire-wood,
And I have not found the lantern:
Return my mother to me.

Lindiwe Mabuza
Lesotho   *contemporary*

Summer 1970
—*a thought to Barbara Masekela*

I heard this morning
dawn's trumpet stampede
deluge the air with spears
of Hughie's 'lovely lonely' blues.
We grew without comprehension
at the quicksands of America's time
groping for solutions
to the teary smiles
on Africa's face.

I read this morning
poems written with the color
of South Africa's bloodshot sky.
How they leapt with the wind
on the narrow prisons of pine!

We move to rooms
drenched in whey
calabashed at our fathers' fathers' birth—
along the place of dance.
Now we dance on other fields
menstruating seeds from a book
that smolders on grounds

the same that followed
with the flood
of early summer promises.

We are the transplant from the womb
whose contractions
cure the wrinkles
of the stock exchange.
Noon
we move like gold fish
in murky waters
of a glass jar—

On the faces
you cannot catch the rats
that meander
inside bewildered ends;
we mark-time
between choiceless choices
in this marble maze of human progress.

These are "they"
citizens on the run.
Today they know what I know:

How the echoing
so—
lo
falls
on
nerves pulled
like autumn
strings across
an empty gourd.

Ingrid Jonker
South Africa   1933–1965

When You Laugh

Your laughter is like a burst pomegranate
Laugh again
so I can hear how pomegranates laugh

Don't Sleep

Don't sleep, look!
Behind the curtains the day is beginning to dance
with a peacock's feather in its cap.

Translated from the Afrikaans by Elizabeth Jones

I Drift in the Wind
for Anna

Free I have my own self-reliance
from graves and from deceptive friends
the hearth I have cherished glares now at me
my parents have broken themselves off from my death
the worms stir against my mother, my father
clenches his hand that brushes loose against the sky
free I believe my old friend has forsaken me
free I believe you have toppled the mountains in me
free my landscape reeks of bitter sun and blood

What will become of me
the cornerstones of my heart establish nothing
my landscape is hardened in me
brooding embittered but open
My nation
follow the lonely fingers
people, clothe yourselves in warmheartedness
veiled in by the sun of the future

My black Africa
follow my lonely fingers
follow my absent image

lonely as an owl
and the forsaken fingers of the world
alone like my sister
My people have rotted away from me
what will become of the rotten nation
a hand cannot pray alone

The sun will cover us
the sun in our eyes for ever covered
with black crows

Translated from the Afrikaans by Jack Cope

Marjorie Oludhe Macgoye
Kenya   contemporary

For Miriam

Children, why do you fear, why turn away?
Do you not know these knobbed, harsh hands are those
that turned and pulled your brothers from the womb?
These red eyes saw you first. These swollen feet
trampled to fetch water for your father's comfort.
This failing memory was quick to count
shillings to school him with. He'll tell you how.
It is still I.

Why do you doubt? Fingers are hard and stiff?
Hard, yes, to lift pots from the fire, to hoe
the heat-cracked furrow, husk the grain, split pods,
smack children hard, but shapely, straight, complete,
supple and loving. Laughter? When did they change?
I don't remember. True, the cup shakes, the needle
evades the thread. Joints creak. Yet I caress you.
It is still I.

Dress yourself child. See how I cover myself
carefully, unless now and then fever shakes me
and I forget the time and place. Yet truly
first cloth was a puzzle to me, we were ashamed
at new-fangled ways. We knew our modest duties,

walked blithely then, lithe, dutiful, expectant,
laughed at the stranger. You laugh and I laugh too.
It is still I.

We hid from vaccinators by the river—
laugh, you can see me doing that, typical me,
with a baby crying loudly among the reeds,
the medical people furious, road and market
growing till soon we could not hide. No fear now
so long as you keep your blood to yourself and pray
separate bed and bedding. Now they cannot unmake
   me.
It is still I.

We cried for sorrow, stood rebuked, so turned
away to Jesus, changed and were made anew.
The pipe is broken and the beads dispersed,
the children schooled, the scriptures learned by heart.
I know new obligations, faces, buryings,
yet self of self in saviour still the same,
still hard, lithe, laughing. He returns myself.
It is still I.

This baby-face is pale, but see the features
line by line echo mine. This one will go to
school, that one also, one dig, one live in town.
You do not need to tell me. Have I not grown,
mounted steep stairs, seen whirling pictures speak,
eaten politely, begging whatever tools
they left out from my place. Old, no-one's fool,
It is still I.

Africa of your ancestry has not changed,
Is age unrecognized? The tissues are the same,
the blood, guarded and grounded, feeds new life.
The artery-paths have hardened into highways,
tacit exchange crystallized into cash,
the morning sunward spit dried on our lips,
migration stilled, yet Mother Africa laughs,
It is still I.

Things that were open when we thought them good
are now discreetly covered, breasts by clothing,
blood-feud by boundary-mark, weapon by holster,

paternity by collusion. Things that were covered
those times we thought them bad now lie wide open,
unwanted babies, unpaid cattle, ways
of tying up the womb. Though witchcraft walks
It is still I.

Can you recall a time *Misawa*[1] was
as strange as *Jambo*[2]? Then we fed on pulse,
millet and milk, saw our dreams come alive.
Don't talk to me of change, even of freedom:
I have seen changes and I am content,
was saved, am free. If tongue and temper wander,
flesh stiffen and decay, why do you fear?
It is still I.

[1]Misawa: a greeting used in the Luo tribal community.
[2]Jambo: a common Swahili greeting introduced more recently.

Ama Ata Aidoo
Ghana　1942

Cornfields in Accra[1]

They told us
Our mothers told us
They told us.

They told us
Our fathers told us
They told us.

They told us
Red clay
Will shine,
Shine silica,
Shine gold
Red clay will shine

It will shine

[1]The capital of Ghana.

Where you polish
How-when-where
You polish.

They told us
Our mother told us
They told us.

And so
We planted our corn:
Not whole seeds from
Last year's harvest
No,
For we are men without barns
Women without fallows.

Some said,
Referring to the corn-seeds,
"They come from Russia"
Others that the bags were marked
"Nigeria."
But we have refused to listen
Or hearing,
Have not cared.

For
When Yaa looked over her courtyard and saw Akosua's
daughter passing by with her trayful of red clay that
shone and gleamed, did she not beg a mould?
And did she wait until she knew which pit had yielded
   the clay?

They told us
Our mothers told us
They told us.

And we thought
As we fixed the pipe—
They said it will carry
50,000 cc. of water every day—
We thought
As we fixed the pipe,
"The first day it rains
We shall plant
The corn."

Plot One
Was Nikoi's
It was at the backyard
Where once stood the fitter's
shop:
There,
Among skeleton cars,
Greased and petrolled earth,
Bits of tyres, really
All types of scrap-metal.

The rest
Hmm, brother,
Was less, not more
Dignified.
Mine was by a mango tree,
A hillock of rubbish dump
A deserted vacant-lot,
With unmentionable contents of diverse chamber-pots.

Yet
Even now
When that moon has not fully died
Which rose on our planting,
Let us sing of
Dark green wavy corn.

My brother,
My sister,
Take the refrain,
Swell the chorus,

They told us
Our mothers told us
They told us.

Finally,
When we have harvested, gleaned and
Threshed our corn,
Or roasted it aromatic,
That is,
After office hours
On Saturdays and throughout the whole of Sunday,
We shall sit firmly on our bottoms
And plant our feet on the earth,

Then
We shall ask to see
Him
Who says
We
Shall not survive among these turbines.

Who
Says
We shall not survive among the turbines?

Latin America

IN LATIN AMERICA, poetry is usually thought of in terms of the Hispanic tradition that begins with Spanish and Portuguese explorations and colonialization. However, there is another, earlier tradition that predates and later parallels that tradition. Native poetry, oral and written, was created by the many different Indian tribes of Central and South America, from prehistoric times up through history and into the present. Unfortunately, much of the earliest was not recorded, and much that was recorded was destroyed by the invading Spanish conquistadors[1] or the missionaries that followed, who wanted to root out everything that was heathen.

Much has been written about the impact of this dual culture on Latin American men. However, as far as I can determine, no one has yet tackled a history of Latin American women in the two cultures. The subject is vast, the records (until this century) are scanty, and those that exist are preserved in widely separated locales. But until we know more about the lives of women in all walks, we can only begin to address the problems and successes of women who wanted to create poetry. The problems are also complicated when we generalize about Latin American poetry because so many different countries and cultures are involved, and few scholars or critics can hope to speak with equal authority of all of them—countries with cultures as diverse as the heavily Indian Andean nations and the Europeanized southern nations, Indian cultures from the Guaraní of Paraguay to Auracanians of Chile. For these reasons, any statements about the situation of Latin American women poets must be tentative.

Clearly, in the early Indian cultures with their tight class structures and dependence on physical labor, the women who could have had access to the education and leisure necessary for the composition of poetry would tend to be women of the upper classes or concubines of men of the upper classes on the one hand, and shamans or priestesses on the other.

In addition to the Native tradition, there is a second tradition, the colonial one, which starts for women poets in the seventeenth century with the great Sor Juana Ines de la Cruz (Juana de Asbaje, 1651–1695), who lived in Mexico, and who wrote in dozens of verse forms, poems as good as any in her time, including a lively one scolding men for criticizing women. Precocious enough to read at three, Sor Juana was a woman of Renaissance accomplishments, and she chose the only life that accorded with those accomplishments, a life serving the church. Her poetry demonstrates virtually every form common in her time, and most of the techniques and ornaments. Unfortunately, her absorption in books and poetry was increasingly seen as dangerous by the church, and, after several warnings, she finally gave up reading and writing and devoted herself wholly to the self-denial and self-castigation of the religious life. The problems of Sor Juana, a woman of brilliance, talent, power, and courage, exemplify the problems of women poets in the seventeenth and eighteenth centuries. If Sor Juana was forced to give up poetry, how could women cast in traditional roles, or less endowed with vitality and courage, or lacking access to the riches of education be expected to become poets?

It was almost 200 years after Sor Juana before substantial numbers of women were writing and publishing their work. In 1875, an anthology appeared that included 50 women poets, but it was made up of conventional and undistinguished work. However, out of all the women writing poetry in Latin America in the nineteenth century, one has retained a place in literary history: Gertrudis Gómez de Avellaneda (1814–1873), who is considered one of the important figures of Spanish romanticism. When she was 22, her family moved from Cuba to Spain, and it was in Spain that she wrote her poems, novels, plays, and translations. Treating her life as a model for other women, she wrote voluminously presenting women as both strong characters and as victims. She was interested in the work of other women writers, especially the French writers Madame de Staël and George Sand, and in the unconventional lives they led. She criticized the sexist ideas and customs of her time. In her era, only Avellaneda among Latin American women writers was able to become a part of the masculine literary scene.

The early twentieth century saw the emergence of four women writers who stand out from all the other women writing then— Delmira Augustini (1886–1914), Alfonsina Storni (1892–1938), Gabriela Mistral (1889–1957), and Juana de Ibarbourou (1897–1979). Delmira Augustini wrote skilfully crafted poems that combined the erotic and the intellectual. Even though her work barely reflects the literary movements that were exciting writers of her time, her poems do occasionally break free of their naive romanticism:

> Blue pupil of my park
> is the sensitive mirror
> of a clear lake, so clear
> so clear that sometimes I believe
> that on its crystalline page
> my thought is imprinted.
> Flower of air, flower of water,
> lake's soul is a swan
> with two human pupils . . .

> Water I give him in my hands
> and he seems to drink fire;
> and I appear to offer him
> all the glass of my body . . .

No other contemporary woman poet approaches Alfonsina Storni's bitterness and outspoken feminism in certain poems (perhaps Rosario Castellanos of the following generation comes close). At its best, her verse is fresh, spontaneous, direct, and painful. Her language is conversational, informal, terse. In a poem entitled "Loneliness," she says: "I could shout/my pain/till my body breaks in two. . . ." Her alienation and isolation are expressed in poems like "The Clamor" in which the speaker, stoned by her fellow townsmen for having been loving, ends bloody but defiant. Her poems show the new tendencies to depict the human isolation in cities and the effect of their ugliness on the human heart: "The sky, even grayer/than the city,/descends over me,/takes over my life-/stops up my arteries,/turns off my voice. . . ." Finally, disillusioned with love, cynical about men and society, she committed suicide by walking into the sea rather than face her final illness alone. In spite of the current interest in women's poetry, no full-length collection of her poetry has yet appeared in translation.

Chilean Gabriela Mistral was the winner of the 1945 Nobel Prize for Literature and is the only Latin American woman poet who has ever won it. Her work is the best known in this country, but, even so, the body of her work still remains to be translated. Mistral took the conventional themes of motherhood, love of children, and nature, and made of them something fresh, subtle, ardent, and

somber. Her language, which is colloquial and simple, helped free
Latin American poetry from the hold of *modernismo*, with its vagueness, symbolism, intellectuality. Her poems are spare, crisp, and
painful:

Old Woman

She is one hundred and twenty years old, one twenty,
and she's more wrinkled than Earth.
She wears so many wrinkles that she wears
nothing but tucks and tucks like the poor mat.

So many wrinkles are made by the wind on the dune,
and it's the wind that powders her with dust and creases her;
so many wrinkles she shows that we look only
at her poor eternal carp scales. . . .

Her religious poems are direct, passionate, and never doctrinaire:

Interrogations

How, Lord, do the suicides remain sleeping?
A curdling in the mouth, the two breasts emptied,
the moons of the eyes white and swollen,
the hands set toward an invisible anchor?

Disappointed in an early love, Mistral never married. Instead,
she became a teacher, and thus was free to write. Because her
pedagogical ideas were acclaimed, she was invited to speak all over
Chile and in other countries. Expressing her motherliness and her
love of children both in her teaching and in her poems, Gabriela
Mistral was the most accepted and celebrated of Latin American
women poets.

Uruguay's Juana de Ibarbourou was named "Juana de America"
in 1929 by her country's government because of the popularity of
her poetry and the purity of her song. Her first editor called her
"Hebraic" and spoke of her "contagious pantheism" and "fragrant
sensuality." Her poems were most frequently on properly "feminine" subjects: nature and love. Her most distinctive qualities never
reach a full originality, but, instead, her spontaneity and freshness
were muted by the veil of *modernismo*. To a contemporary reader,
her love poems seem tame,

I grew
For you
Cut me . . .

> I flowed
> For you
> Drink me . . .

but for the reader of her time, such verse was frank and direct for a woman. Unluckily, her virtues as a poet have not been sufficient to give her a place in literary history.

Today there are many more women poets writing, women poets born in this century. However, women today also face constraints that control what they say, how they say it, and even prevent them from writing at all. Patriarchal societies, bolstered by the Catholic Church, prevent women from pursuing non-traditional roles and make it difficult for them to support themselves in jobs that will allow them the independence and the "rooms of their own" that they require. Even when they are rich, public and family pressure may militate against the concentration and single-mindedness necessary for literary achievement. Social class, in most countries, remains an important obstacle too—free public education is either unavailable or, where available, not possible for a poor girl who must work to help her family. Another factor at work is the deliberate aloofness of Indian groups, which, while preserving their own culture, may prevent a woman poet writing in an Indian language from having an audience.

Generally speaking, there is no organized feminist movement in Latin America, although there are feminists (largely among women of the upper classes). Many women say that the economic, social, and political crises of their countries are so great that they must take precedence and that the problems women have are secondary and must wait. Political repression also shapes, controls, and limits the writing of women. In many cases, this has meant a retreat into poetry that may be skillfully written but that is oblique, symbolist or surrealist, otherworldly—distant from the tattered, dirty, and agonizing reality that is Latin America today. Still, there are striking exceptions. Many of the poets in this section voice an anguished outcry against the suffering of the poor, the plight of children, the torture of dissidents, and the limitations imposed on women's lives.

MARY CROW

Juana de Asbaje
Mexico   1651–1695

Stay, shade of my shy treasure! Oh, remain,
Thou image of the charmer I love best—
Fair dream, for which I die with joyful breast,
Illusion sweet, for which I live in pain!

Thy winning graces all my heart enchain;
It follows as the steel the magnet's test;
But wherefore gain my love and make me blest
If thou must mock me, fading soon again?

Yet canst thou never boast, with fullest pride,
Triumphant o'er me is thy tyranny;
For though thou from the close embrace dost glide
That held thy visionary form to me,
No matter! In my arms thou wilt not bide,
But fancy builds a prison still for thee!

Translated from the Spanish by Alice Stone Blackwell

Green enravishment of human life,
smiling frenzy of demented hope,
inextricable dream of them that wake
and, as a dream, of riches destitute.

Spirit of the world, robust old age,
imagination of decrepit vigour,
longing for the happy ones' to-day
and for the unhappy ones' to-morrow.

Let those who, with green glasses spectacled,
see all things sicklied o'er with their desire,
questing for thy light pursue thy shadow:

But I, more mindful of my destiny,
imprison my two eyes in my two hands
and see no other thing than it I touch.

Translated from the Spanish by Samuel Beckett and Octavio Paz

Gertrudis Gómez de Avellaneda
Cuba   1814–1873

On Leaving Cuba, Her Native Land

Pearl of the sea! Star of the West!
Beautiful Cuba! On your bright sky
descends the veil of night,
heavy as the pain that mantles my brow.

I am to leave! . . . The crew, in haste
to tear me from my native land,
raises the sails, and your warm breeze
awakens, ready for its vigil.

Farewell, dear homeland, my beloved Eden!
Wherever fate in its fury may drive me,
your sweet name shall soothe my ear!

Farewell! . . . The sails rustle and swell . . .
the anchor lifts . . . and trembling, the ship
cuts through the waves and flies in silence!

Translated from the Spanish by Catherine Rodriguez-Nieto

Delmira Augustini
Uruguay   1886–1914

Vision

Maybe all I saw was the mirror
of my desires, an illusory
frame around it all . . .
Or it's simply a miracle: did I really
see you the other night, watching me sleep?
Loneliness and terror had made my bedroom
huge; you appeared at my side
like a giant fungus, both dead and alive,
in the corners of the night,
damp with silence,
greased with solitude and darkness.

You leaned toward me, utterly
toward me—as toward the lake, the crystal cup
on the desert's tablecloth.
You leaned toward me as an invalid
leans toward the drugs that won't fail him,
toward the stone bandages of death.

You leaned toward me as a believer
toward the blessed communion wafer—
the snowflake that tastes
of stars, nourishing the lilies of man's flesh;
God's spark, a star for man.
You leaned toward me as sadness, the large willow,
leans toward silence, its deep pools.
You leaned toward me like pride's tower,
its marble quarried by the monster sadness,
leaning toward its own shadow, its great sister.
You leaned toward me as if my body
in this dark page of a bed
was where your destiny began.
You leaned toward me as toward a window looking out
upon whatever follows death.

And you leaned even more!

My vision was a snake
aimed through eyelashes of brambles
toward your body, oh reverent swan.
And my lust was a snake
gliding through dark canyons
toward your body, oh statue of lilies.
You leaned farther and farther, and so far,
you leaned so far,
that my sexual flowers grew to twice their size
and my star has been larger since then.
Your whole life was imprinted on mine.

Anxious, uncertain, I waited
for the rustling wings that signal a magnificent embrace,
a miraculous and passionate embrace,
an embrace of four arms; flight!
The enchanted arms can be
four roots of a new race.

Anxious, uncertain, I waited
for the rustling wings that signal a magnificent
    embrace . . .
                                    And when

I opened my eyes—like a soul—to you:
I saw you'd fallen back, you were wrapped
in some huge fold of darkness!

Translated from the Spanish by Marti Moody

Juana de Ibarbourou
Uruguay   1897-1979

Life-Hook

If I die, don't take me to the cemetery.
My grave is opening
right at the surface of the earth, near the laughing
clatter of some birdhouse,
near a fountain and its gossip.

Right at the surface, love. Almost above ground
where the sun can heat my bones, and my eyes
can climb the stems of plants to watch
the sunset, its fierce red lamp.

Right at the surface. So the passage
will be short. I already see
my body fighting to get back above the soil,
to feel the wind again.

I know my hands may never calm down.
The ghosts around me will be dim, juiceless, but my
    hands
will scratch like moles.

Sprout seeds for me. I want them growing
in the yellow chalk of my bones.
I'll climb the roots like a grey staircase, and watch you
from the purple lilies.

Translated from the Spanish by Marti Moody

Amanda Berenguer
Uruguay   contemporary

Housework

I brush the spider webs from the dismantled sky
with the same everyday utensil,
I brush the obedient dust
off the regular objects, I brush
the dust, I brush the astral
dust, the usual cosmic depression
everdead caress
covering the earth's furniture.
I dust doors and windows, clean their
panes to see more clearly,
I sweep the floor covered with trash,
crumpled leaves, ashes,
crumbs, footprints,
gleaming bones,
I sweep the earth, farther and farther down
and I'm slowly making a pit
to fit the circumstances.

Translated from the Spanish by Priscilla Joslin

Alfonsina Storni
Argentina   1892–1938

Ancestral Weight

You said: *My father didn't cry.*
You said: *My grandfather didn't cry.*
The men of my family
never cried. They were like steel.

Saying this you
shed a tear.
It fell in my mouth, more poison.
I've never drunk from a cup
so small.

Frail woman, poor woman
who understands,
I drank centuries of pain
in your tear, and my
soul just can't bear
all that weight.

They've Come

Today my mother and sisters
have come to see me.

For some time I'd been alone
with my verses, my pride; in short, nothing.

My sister, the older one, has grown up,
still slight and fair; the first dream passes
through her eyes. I've said to the little one:
Life is sweet. What's bad goes away . . .

My mother smiles, as those who know souls
are accustomed to smile.
She puts her two hands on my shoulders,
she looks at me very steadily . . .
                   I burst into tears.

We've eaten together, in the most
lived-in room of the house.
A springlike sky . . . All the windows open
so we could see it.

And as we talk, we tranquil women,
of so many old and forgotten things,
my sister, the younger one, interrupts:
The swallows are passing . . .

Translated from the Spanish by Marti Moody

Pain

This divine October afternoon I would like
to walk along the distant shore;

to have the gold sand and green waters
and pure skies see me pass . . .

to be tall, arrogant, perfect
like a Roman woman, in order to be in accord

with the great waves, and the dead rocks
and the wide beaches that gird the sea.

To let myself go with slow step and cold eyes
and silent mouth;

to see how the blue waves break themselves
against the granite and not to blink;

to see how the predatory birds eat
the small fish and not to sigh;

to think that the fragile boats could
sink in the sea and not awaken;

to see that he advances, the most beautiful man,
his throat bare and not to want to love . . .

to lose the look, absentmindedly,
to lose it and never find it again;

and body erect between sky and beach,
to feel the perennial forgetfulness of the sea.

Translated from the Spanish by Merrilee Antrim

Olga Orozco
Argentina   *contemporary*

Sphinxes inclined to be

One hand, two hands. Nothing more.
I still hurt from the hands I lack,
those that remained glued to the fantasmal boat that
  brought me

and shake the coast with drum rolls
and fistfuls of sand against nostalgic, migrant waters.
Transparent hands that make the world slip beneath my
    feet,
that come to me and go away again.
But these hands that extend my dense body
beyond any possible hearth
further than any impossible paradise,
they are not hands which open the shadows ever so
    slightly,
to remove the veils, bolting them shut once again.
I don't understand these hands.
Yes, much too near,
and yet too distant,
foreign as my own flight corraled inside another's skin,
as the insomnia of one who flees beyond reach of my
    fingers.
Sometimes I find them almost hiding myself from me
or betting in favor of another ornamented body
that conspires with night and sun.
They make me uneasy, these hands which play with
    mystery and chance.
They change my food for streams of ants,
they search for a ring in the desert,
they transform the innocent into knives,
persevering as valves in malice and error.
When I watch them they pleat and unpleat evasive fans,
a wandering vision which loses itself between feathers
    and wings of plunder,
while they follow themselves, pursue themselves,
these hands grow till they cover immensity or reduce to
    dust my hollow days.
They are as two sphinxes that weave my condemnation
into a half of crime,
and a half of mercy.
And this expression of trapped fish,
anxious birds,
impassive vulture men who assist at their own ritual!
a wicked, contagious ceremony, idolatrous plague.
One caress is enough to multiply black seeds of leprosy,
and phosphorous beams which propagate silk and
    passion,
errant threads that weave calamity and thirst.

And that incessant ember that slips from one to the
    other
as a reddened secret,
as a flame which burns far too much!
I ask myself, I tell myself
what trap from future time are these two hands plotting
yet they are the same hands.
Nothing more than two hands, strangely alike, two
    hands in their duty of being just hands,
from beginning to end.

Translated from the Spanish by Leslie Keffer

Cecilia Meireles
Brazil   1901–1964

Song

I placed my dream in a boat
and the boat into the sea;
then I ripped the sea with my hands
so that my dream would sink.

My hands are still wet
with the blue of the slashed waves,
and the color that runs from my fingers
colors the deserted sands.

The wind arrives from far away,
night bends itself with the cold;
under the water in a boat
my dream is dying away.

I'll cry as much as necessary
to make the sea grow
so that my boat will sink to the bottom
and my dream disappear.

Then everything will be perfect:

the beach smooth, the waters orderly,
my eyes dry like stones
and my two hands—broken.

Translated from the Portuguese by Eloah F. Giacomelli

Renata **Pallottini**
Brazil   *contemporary*

Message

Tell your son, my son,
what we endured:
there were taped confessions
and pictures full face.
Tell how we shrunk
like beaten beasts;
that nobody had the courage,
that we breathed in shame,
eyes fleeing other eyes,
hands cold and sweating.
And tell how for ten years past
we have had
little hope:
we ask someone to bear witness
and we cannot take it any longer.
Maybe your son, my son,
will live in an open world,
but it is basic
you tell him calmly
and in minutest detail
the story of those daggers
stuck in our afternoons.
Yet if for this reason
you give up having sons
as some of us have
leave inscriptions as I do
signs on tree bark,
letters on elusive paper,
so this puny flare,
lightning, will o' the wisp,

will not go dark.
Pure memory of those days
in which we were free sons
of happier parents.
Tell whoever you can, my son.
What in you were words
in them shall be roots.

Translated from the Portuguese by Monique and Carlos Altschul

Gabriela Mistral
Chile   1889–1957

Bread
—for Teresa and Enrique Diez-Canedo

They have left bread on the table,
half-burnt, half-white, with its crown
broken open in large crumbs.

It seems new to me
like something never seen,
yet I have eaten nothing else.

Prodding its soft center like a sleepwalker,
my sense of touch and smell are forgotten.

It has the odor of my mother giving milk,
the odor of three valleys I have walked—
Aconcaqua, Patzcuaro, Elqui—
and the odor of my insides when I sing.

There are no other odors in the room,
and so I was summoned,
there is no one else in the house
but this bread, broken, on a plate—
it knows me with its body
and I know it with mine.

Eaten in all climates,
a hundred brothers, this bread

is the bread of Coquimbo and Oaxaca,
of Santa Ana and Santiago.

As a child I knew its shapes—
sun, halo, fish, its heat of pigeon feathers,
my hand its friend . . .

I have forgotten it since then,
until we meet this day,
I with an old woman's body,
and it with the body of a child.

Dead friends, with whom in other valleys
I have eaten bread,
smell the misted odor of bread
mown in August
milled in September in Castilla.

Different, it is still the same
we ate in lands where you now rest.
I open its crust and give you its heat;
I turn it and release its breath.

My hand overflows with it,
its glance is in my hand;
in sorrow I cry out
for such long forgetfulness
and my face ages or is reborn
in this discovery.

How empty the house is,
may we who have met again
be united
at this table without meat or fruit
we two in this human silence
until the time we shall be one
and our day over . . .

Translated from the Spanish by Allan Francovich and Kathleen Weaver

Teresa de Jesús
Chile   contemporary

All of a Sudden

What is it with these people-swallowing streets
all of a sudden?
They've become cannibal streets
all of a sudden
these straight, commonplace streets
groomed every hour
with the blue cream of an everyday smog.
All of a sudden
the streets at either hand are goons of death,
long ways direct to jail cells.
No one knows if he knows his destination
is his destiny.
All of a sudden
only the street knows
how many guards wait at the corner,
how many policemen in disguise
watch for the one who leaves his house.
All of a sudden
they've become accomplices in crime.
All of a sudden
they've become spies and assassins.
All of a sudden
they eat people with shoes
with i.d. cards
with a snapshot of the sweetheart,
it all disappears down the throat
of this new executioner.
All of a sudden
these same streets, strolling with
mothers with babies,
sweet
pregnant women—
are knitting treacherous webs
and posting an agent at each corner.
All of a sudden
these urbane streets,
everyday-like,
start howling
and from the fog

the throats of wolves come out.
All of a sudden
a sly perfect coup
and they swallow the boy,
the girl,
for 15 days,
       for a month,
             for ever

Translated from the Spanish by Maria A. Proser, Arlene Scully, and James Scully

'They go by, go by, love, the days and the hours'

They go by, go by, love, the days and the hours
the blue sky turns
cement and sand
and again it's blue
open as a hyacinth.
And you?
How is your
sky in the deep cell?
Is memory shadow-like
or can you still
bathe
your look
in a bit of sky?

I am gathering skies
like a madwoman—
jealously I watch over them
for you, poor love,
I string, string, string
chip of sky
blues, oranges,
             grays and purples
into a necklace I'm threading
for when
the guards doze off
and I see you I
take your silent hands
and kiss your eyes, old
from pain and from cold

Translated from the Spanish by Maria A. Proser, Arlene Scully, and James Scully

Magda Portal
Peru   contemporary

W o m a n

Woman with broad, rough hands
with flourishes of varicose veins
before dawn your day breaks
your tiredness has no end

woman   always pregnant   resigned
setting lives alight   haphazardly
                    off-handedly
no bread under your arm
                        following no path

compliments were not made for you
or luxury cinemas
your garden is the earth
unpaved roads
streets with no walks
full of stinking pools
where children play, fight
and kick balls made of dirty rags

and sometimes it gets dark early—
not even the Sun will stay on
to shine down the public light
                    your neighborhood doesn't have

and sometimes you dream   of a clean house
      hot food   with no hurry
           a good chair
to sit down in   and just rest
and not have to rise   exhausted
to wait on others.

And never hear the sharp insistent cries
                        of husband and sons
cursing
        snarling
                barking commands.

NO—no one need know
you think sometimes
that sometimes a strange light burns
in your dark, watchful eyes
as they look far off   gauging distances
                              beyond the walls
to where the air   would be yours alone
deep expanding chestfuls of air
        and the sea perhaps   some way
            and the sea so very far

Translated from Spanish by Irene Vegas-Garcia and Kathleen Weaver

Blanca Varela
Peru   contemporary

The Captain

We are tied to Mars' tail. The previous days
have been beautiful, but now we sweat like Africans.
It is a strange battle.
The first to fall is me, but I continue.
It's been a long time since I've made love, the last
nights have been terrible. I could touch my breath, take
    it
by the wings like an insect and throw it overboard.

We captains are chaste and roar like the sea, red and
solitary we disdain the earth's submission.
Even in the tropics, yes, even in the tropics, when
the island emerges like a pale teat, the tearful camellias,
the barbarous perfume of the home.
We captains are sleepless by nature.

The first dead shine on the bridge, their bare
chests are intact. They have never been more solid
or smiling. Down gilds their still tense muscles
and their flesh, that can do nothing, can move us.
This lasting death is the booty of the battle, the memory
during the loneliness of the next voyage. We are
    comforted.

Our recently sowed hate is our ideal. With death within
reach of our lips, we grow dizzily like a legend
for those who are not here.

The waves moan, we sail over a forest of sadness. The
night indefensible for the world. We, standing,
invade the darkness, we break the final accord with
a terrible war march.
Our swords cross the firmament like lightning bolts, our
eyes travel like suns, our hair grows violently
and our lawless smiles multiply.
A hand snatches the trophy from the shadow, the
pulsating and blue gut: glory.

Victors' dawn surprises us. Were we dreaming?

The hero's urine has dried, the wilted anger
throws off a bitter fruit that stains the morning.
Livid, warm, effeminate, the warriors contemplate
the new day astounded.

The captain is sleepless by nature and yet he dreams.
His breath turns against him like a thirsty gadfly. The
battle always waits for him beyond the horizon. And in
the waiting under the bronze of his skin, the muscles
    hang
flacid like those of a girl sick with malaria, while
his armies couple in the damp holds.

Only the sea sings this legend.

Translated from the Spanish by Lynne Alvarez

Magdalena de Rodríguez
Nicaragua   contemporary

June 10

The city of Esteli
woke up taken by the kids.
"A free country or death" sang all the roosters.

"Country or death" and a great trembling
reverberated through the ruins and the rubble
that twice the barbarism had left.
There are parties in the ruins and parties in the souls.
They have arrived and with them the voice of patriotism
strengthened and enlarged
and it runs down the roads. It climbs the trees
and enters the houses and the rubble flowers
and also the jasmine and rose bushes flower.
Everything sings. The machine guns sing,
the FAL rifles, wise soothsayers.
The aged sing, the adults, the children.
It rains and amid the puddles the frog sings.
In the streets barricades flower
that tireless hands have raised.
Fierce party in the streets. The evening falls.

Translated from the Spanish by Nina Serrano

Rosario Castellanos
Mexico   1925

Useless Day

Nocturnal water, primaeval silences,
the first forms of life, struggle,
a crushed scale, blood and horror
have flown through me.
A net in the depths, I return,
rising to the surface
without a single fish.

Translated from the Spanish by Maureen Ahern

Foreign Woman

I come from far away. I have forgotten my country.
I no longer understand the words
they use there for money or implements.
I have attained the mineral silence of a statue.

For sloth and contempt and something
that I cannot make out have defended me
from this language, from this heavy
jewel-studded velvet, with which the people
among whom I live cover their rags.

This land, like the other land of my childhood,
still bears on its face
the brand of fire, injustice and crime,
its scars of slavery.
Alas, as a girl I slept to the hoarse cooing
of a black dove: a conquered race.
I hid beneath the sheets
because a great beast
was crouching in the shadows, ravenous and yet
hard and patient as a stone.
Compared with it, what is the sea or disaster
or love's thunderbolt
or annihilating happiness?
What I mean is then
that I had to grow up quickly
(before terror devoured me)
and go away and put a firm hand
on the rudder and steer my life.

Too early
I spat in those places
that the common people consecrate for worship.
And among the crowd I was like a dog
that offends with its scabs and copulations,
and its sudden barking in the middle
of the rite, and the important ceremony.

And yet. Youth
—although serious—was not quite mortal.
I recovered, I got well. With a skilful pulse
I learnt to assess success, renown,
honour and riches.
I had what the mediocre envy, what the
triumphant dispute, and only one attains.
I had it, and it was like eating spray,
like stroking the back of the wind.

Supreme pride is supreme
renunciation. I did not want

to be the dead star
that absorbs borrowed light to revive itself.
Nameless, without memories,
naked as a ghost I turn
in a narrow domestic orbit.

But even so I ferment
in the dull imagination of others.

My presence has brought
to this sleepy inland city
a salty breath of adventure.

When they look at me, men remember
that fate is the great hurricane
that splits boughs and fells firm trees,
and confirms in its dominion—
over human poverty—
the pitiless cosmic law.
The women smell me from afar, and dream
like beasts of burden when they sniff
the brutal gust of the storm.

Before the elder, however,
I perform a passive role
as the caller-up of legends.

And when at midnight
I open the windows wide, it is so that
the sleepless man, the man who is brooding on death,
and the man who is suffering on the bed of his remorse,
and the youth too
(beneath whose head the pillow burns)
may question the dark through me.

Enough. I have concealed more than I have said.

The upland sun burnt my hand,
and on the finger that is called here the heart-finger
I wear a gold ring with an incised seal.

The ring that serves
to identify corpses.

Translated from the Spanish by J. M. Cohen

Lucha Corpi
Mexico   1945

Dark Romance

A flavor of vanilla drifts
on the Sunday air.

Melancholy of an orange,
clinging still,
brilliant, seductive
past the promise of its blooming.

Guadalupe was bathing in the river
that Sunday, late,

a promise of milk in her breasts,
vanilla scent in her hair
cinnamon flavor in her eyes,
cocoa-flower between her legs

and in her mouth a daze
of sugarcane.

He came upon her there
surrounded by water
in a flood of evening light.

And on the instant cut the flower
wrung blood from the milk

dashed vanilla on the silence
of the river bank
drained the burning liquid
of her lips

and then he was gone,
leaving behind him a trail of shadow
drooping at the water's edge.

Her mother found her there, and at the sight
took a handful of salt from her pouch
to throw over her shoulder.

A few days later, her father
accepted the gift of a fine mare.

And Guadalupe . . . Guadalupe hung her life
from the orange tree in the garden,
and stayed there quietly,
her eyes open to the river.

An orange clings to the branch
the promise lost of its blooming.

Ancestral longing
seizes the mind.

A scent of vanilla drifts
on the evening air.

Translated from the Spanish by Catherine Rodriguez-Nieto

Nancy Morejón
Cuba   1944

The Reason for Poetry

At this time I find the bed very arid
The sheets do not conform to my body
I write:
> "and later on
> Japanese architecture
> screamed
> concise and trim, reformist

> and later on
> a strident sparrow
> bursting with roses
> oblique eyes"
I am alone
inside a shapeless bladder
listening to the last words of the professor:
> "Is that clear?
> good . . . we'll continue in the next
>   class . . ."

I find that the night is ever more night
Each minute is the time that consumes
Records each daily event:
The literature class, guard duty, the clock
The conference, movies, the harvest
The exhibit, Fidel's hands
Albums, the corny ballads
This anxious revolution
I discover all this
And more
Now, I am alone
here

The entire room becomes sadness and bereavement
If I jumped up and ran, no one would know it
And I strike a blow at my books
And I hurriedly get some paper
And I believe that the bird will come tonight
To envelop me in its flame
And I strike a blow at my books
Because the night brings me the greatest loneliness

Please hear me I am alone

Translated from the Spanish by Anita Whitney

North America

Cultural Influences: Euro-American

When Emily Dickinson complained in the 1860s "They shut me up in Prose/ As when a little Girl/ They put me in the Closet—/ Because they liked me 'still,' "[1] she was describing a constraint shared by women writers across America. For until the twentieth century, American women were expected to behave with modesty, sweetness, delicacy, helpfulness, and cheeriness, traits that do not contribute to poetic assertion.[2] Most were quite literally shut up in prose, their lives shaped by such commonplace tasks as baking, butter making, sweeping, laundering, and mending. Even Dickinson, whose household included a full-time servant, excused her tardy correspondence to friends by explaining, "If it wasn't for broad daylight, and cooking stoves, and roosters, I'm afraid you would have occasion to smile at my letters often."[3] And it wasn't only that women were shut into prosaic daily living. When they did have the inclination and the time to write, they were subtly limited to prose as a literary genre. It was understood that an educated woman might need to support herself by writing novels; many female novelists, such as E.D.E.N. Southworth and Caroline Lee Hentz, enjoyed prolific and financially successful careers.[4] But although such women writers often outsold male fictionalists, they did not view themselves as serious artists; rather, they saw themselves as professionals with a living to make. Further, women novelists in nineteenth-century America were derided by male literary figures—Hawthorne, for instance, worrying about the unprecedented sales of women's fiction, referred to feminine writers as a "damned mob of scribbling women."[5]

True, many women also published poetry: the moralistic "graveyard" verse popularized in the nineteenth century by such poets as Lydia Sigourney filled pages of the gift books considered safe reading for elderly aunts and adolscent boys and girls. But although such melancholy subjects as infant death (a common event in nineteenth-century women's lives) were considered suitable for women to treat in pious, imitative verse, poetry, as a serious art form was not an acceptable genre for women writers until the twentieth century. Nineteenth-century magazines of the intellectual aristocracy, whose editors were establishing the canon of American literature, included few poems by women.[6] As Sandra M. Gilbert and Susan Gubar have argued, verse writing in England and America has historically been defined as an almost sacred vocation, performed only by a highly educated male elite.[7]

Small wonder, then, that Colonial American women produced little poetry. Although girls and boys in early America received a similar elementary education, women lucky enough to become well informed tended to hide their knowledge, fearing they would appear immodest, impure, or even dangerous. John Winthrop voiced Puritan suspicion of intellectual women when he described a young colonial lady "who was fallen into a sad infirmity, the loss of her understanding, and reason, which had been growing upon her divers years, by occasion of her giving herself wholly to reading and writing."[8] Similarly, Thomas Parker publicly condemned his sister: "Your printing of a Book beyond the Custom of your Sex, doth rankly smell."[9] In order to allay such anxieties about feminine literary accomplishment, Anne Bradstreet's brother-in-law and publisher John Woodbridge assured readers that *The Tenth Muse Lately Sprung Up in America* was written by a woman known "for her gracious demeanor, her eminent parts, her pious conversation, her courteous disposition, her exact diligence in her place, and discreet mannaging of her family occasions." Perhaps most important, he added reassuringly that the poet had not neglected her womanly duties, that she wrote only during her spare time, in hours "curtailed from her sleep and other refreshments."[10] Even though Bradstreet had been educated in the Elizabethan tradition, which valued educated and artistic women, it was not her wide reading that Woodbridge commended but rather the "feminine" virtues of self-abnegnation, which for seventeenth-century readers comprised necessary moral qualification for a woman poet.

By the nineteenth century American definitions of femininity had become more specific. Elaborate and flowery theories rested on the premise that although Eve as the first woman had brought sin into the world, Christianity had elevated Eve's daughters to spiritual heights pratically impossible for men to reach. This paradoxical image of woman as both devil and angel governed many nineteenth-century American values and customs. As angels, women were expected to be fragile creatures, blushing at the slightest "indelicacy," weeping to express any emotion, whether joy or sorrow, and fainting under stronger stress. This angelic frailty was in fact often caused by very real poor health: American food was drowned in grease, medical and dental practices were poor, houses were badly ventilated, exercise was thought unladylike, and childbirth was hazardous. Moreover, women's clothes undoubtedly contributed to female delicacy, for corsets were tightly laced and skirts covered long, voluminous, heavy petticoats. Considered naturally quiet, sober, meek, and pious, women were expected to attend all religious services, devote spare moments to charity, and perhaps participate in "Culture," which was considered women's special province. But paradoxically, because women were so impressionable (as Eve had been), women themselves had to be protected from such cultural dangers as reading novels that might encourage strong emotions, or singing secular lyrics that might arouse earthly passions. Appropriate female singing was to sound like "angel whisperings."[11]

But even as early as the eighteenth century, some of the smaller religious groups had more liberal ideas about women. In fact, it is from the tenets and practices of the eighteenth-century Quakers and Shakers that the feminist movement in America was gradually to emerge. The Shakers, who drew heavily on the doctrines of the Quakers, held that God possessed a dual personality, both male and female; under the English-born Mother Ann Lee, the Shakers established communities based not only on celibacy but also on the common holding of property. The Quakers were particularly liberal because they believed that "the inner light was available to women as well as to men, and that therefore women as well as men could preach and pray in meeting."[12] Quakers also provided comparable education for both women and men and were instrumental in the political and social agitation that eventually led to better education for women.

Educational opportunities for women did in fact change significantly over the course of the nineteenth century, causing enormous shifts in the overall American view of female intellectual potential. As the century progressed, women's education shifted away from the mainly private training that emphasized feminine "accomplishments" necessary for success on the marriage market. As early as 1837, Mary Lyon's Mount Holyoke Seminary (which Emily Dickinson attended) trained many girls to go beyond what Lyon called the "genteel nothingness" of most women's lives;[13] graduates of Mount Holyoke often began teaching careers abroad and in the American West. The first public high school for girls had opened in Worcester, Massachusetts, in 1824, and the number of such high schools grew rapidly in succeeding decades. Gradually, public high schools even became coeducational. By the 1830s colleges for women began appearing, although their quality did not parallel that of reputable men's colleges. Then in 1855 Elmira Female College opened in Elmira, New York, with a curriculum modeled on that of Yale. Vassar opened in 1865, Smith and Wellesley in 1875, and Bryn Mawr in 1880. Coeducation gradually invaded male colleges: Oberlin admitted women in 1837 (although female graduates in 1841 were not allowed to read their commencement essays in public), followed by Antioch in 1853, and various state universities including Iowa, Wisconsin, Kansas, Indiana, Minnesota, Michigan, and California. The first "Ivy League" school to allow women to enroll was Cornell, in 1870. Harvard in the 1870s reluctantly permitted women to attend classes, and since many Cambridge residents insisted on a Harvard education for their daughters, the Harvard Annex was formed in 1879, and renamed Radcliffe College in 1894. Columbia's "annex" opened in 1889 under the name Barnard College.

None of these changes happened easily. Conservatives raged that too much education would weaken women's already frail constitutions, causing sterility, and that higher education would make women unattractive to men, causing the birth rate to drop. Moralists quivered with fear at the thought of bringing young men and women together in college; as Dr. E. H. Clarke warned in 1873, "Identical education of the two sexes is a crime before God and humanity."[14] However, Clarke's argument was effectively refuted by the Collegiate Alumnae's report of 1885, which concluded that regular college work did not adversely affect women's health, although college women did marry less frequently than noncollege women and had fewer—although healthier—children.[15] Curricula of the new colleges were also subjects of heated debate: some insisted that girls should have the same traditional courses as boys; others argued that, since all were expected to marry and have families, training should help young women assume family responsibilities. Nevertheless, by 1870 21 per cent of all college students were women, and by 1920, the percentage had risen to 47.

Other factors besides educational improvements contributed to the enormous changes American women experienced between 1800 and 1900. As doctors began urging that women needed better exercise and less-constricting clothes, ice skating, croquet, and by the end of the century, bicycling became popular sports for women. By the first decade of the twentieth century, women's clothes no longer included tight laces, petticoats, or bustles; the

"New Woman," personified by Charles Dana Gibson's "Gibson Girl," wore simple blouses and skirts and even played tennis. The "New Woman" also had job opportunities unheard of in the early nineteenth century. Albeit slowly, the medical and legal professions opened to women, and with the advent of typewriters, sewing machines, and other mechanized conveniences women had more jobs to choose from and more and more women chose to work outside the home. In 1840 the prominent British-born feminist Harriet Martineau had contended that only seven occupations in the United States were open to women—teaching, needlework, keeping boarders, setting type, working as servants, or laboring in bookbinding and cotton factories. But by the 1890 census only nine out of 369 occupations did not include women (although the fields that many women entered remained low-paying).[16]

Improved opportunities also resulted from sustained efforts by women reformers. All along, American society had praised such charitable feminine activities as carrying a basket of groceries to a poor family or sitting at the bedside of a sick friend. But during the nineteenth century, these individual attempts to alleviate misery became collective. The Salvation Army and Jane Adams' Hull House provided aid to city slum dwellers, the Young Women's Christian Association found proper housing for girls coming to the city, and the New England Club of Boston aided hospitals and immigrants. In 1874 The Women's Christian Temperance Union began a vigorous and influential crusade not only for the elimination of liquor but also for more rights for women, especially the right to vote. The Abolitionist movement of the 1840s and 1850s also had strong feminist connections, counting among its leaders Lucretia Mott, Susan B. Anthony, and Sarah and Angelina Grimke, who were later to become central figures in the feminist movement. However, their effectiveness in the Abolitonist movement was compromised by discrimination against women: in particular, increasing hostility to their speaking in public. Incensed at this inequality of treatment within a movement which proposed to abolish inequality, women called a convention at Seneca Falls in 1848 that marked the beginning of the modern feminist movement. At Seneca Falls 32 men and 68 women signed a "Declaration" specifically listing the wrongs suffered by women and demanding changes, including the right to vote. By 1914 most activist women had united around suffrage as the central common concern. Finally, on August 18, 1920, the Nineteenth Amendment became law, giving American women the right to vote.

Even before American women could vote, however, they had begun to move into the literary mainstream. In 1912 Harriet

Monroe founded *Poetry: A Magazine of Verse,* which "discovered" more good poets than any other magazine published in English and which has shaped twentieth-century American poetry. Monroe published Pound, Yeats, H.D., Vachel Lindsay, William Carlos Williams, D. H. Lawrence, Robert Frost, Marianne Moore, Carl Sandburg, Wallace Stevens, T. S. Eliot, and Amy Lowell, who also promoted the "new" twentieth-century poetry, and who, like Monroe, sponsored several other poets, including D. H. Lawrence. In Europe after World War I the American Gertrude Stein influenced not only Ernest Hemingway but an entire generation of writers. In 1952 Marianne Moore's *Collected Poems* received the National Book Award, the Pulitzer Prize, and the Bollingen Award; in 1960 H. D. was the first woman to receive the Award of Merit Medal for Poetry given by the American Academy of Arts and Letters.

Literary women did not, however, experience an uninterrupted, steady widening of opportunities. The 1950s were characterized by both covert and overt antifeminism, at least partly based on the popularity of pseudo-Freudian theories that women could attain emotional stability only through domesticity and motherhood. When Parisian designer Christian Dior introduced the "new look" in 1947, American women abandoned the narrow skirts and suits of the 1940s and began wearing long, full skirts held out by crinoline petticoats, tight corsets that cinched in waists and emphasized breasts, and high-heeled shoes that made walking difficult. Popular literature glorified housework and motherhood, and the consensus held that women could not manage both work and family. In Sylvia Plath's novel *The Bell Jar,* young Esther Greenwood sees her life branching before her like a green fig tree:

> From the tip of every branch, like a fat purple fig, a wonderful future beckoned and winked. One fig was a husband and a happy home and children, and another fig was a famous poet and another fig was a brilliant professor, and another fig was Ee Gee, the amazing editor, and another fig was Constantin and Socrates and Attila and a pack of other lovers with queer names and offbeat professions, and another fig was an Olympic lady crew champion, and beyond and above these figs were many more figs I couldn't quite make out.
>
> I saw myself sitting in the crotch of this fig tree, starving to death, just because I couldn't make up my mind which of the figs I would choose. I wanted each and every one of them, but choosing one meant losing all the rest. . . .[17]

But although in the 1950s women felt they had to choose only one "fig," they did nevertheless have a variety of choices, unlike their nineteenth-century foremothers.

By the 1960s and 1970s, these choices were no longer mutually exclusive; acceptable female roles had expanded so that the woman poet experienced unprecedented encouragement. Women's studies as an academic subject became incorporated into college and university curricula; in 1972 three scholarly journals devoted to women's studies appeared. And by the late 1970s, both mainstream literary magazines and new woman-edited and published journals included poems by women. It began to seem that women could—as Emily Dickinson had written a century before—"dwell in Possibility—/ A fairer House than Prose."[18]

WENDY BARKER

Notes and References

[1]*The Poems of Emily Dickinson,* Thomas H. Johnson, ed. (Cambridge, Mass.: The Belknap Press of Harvard University Press, 1951), II, p. 613.

[2]Sandra M. Gilbert and Susan Gubar, "Introduction: Gender, Creativity, and the Woman Poet," in *Shakespeare's Sisters: Feminist Essays on Women Poets,* (Bloomington and London: Indiana University Press, 1979). Gilbert and Gubar argue that "the self-effacing withdrawal society has traditionally fostered in women" has contributed to women's difficulties in writing and publishing poetry, since poetry involves the utterance of a strong and assertive 'I.' "

[3]*The Letters of Emily Dickinson,* Thomas H. Johnson, ed. (Cambridge, Mass.: The Belknap Press of Harvard University Press, 1958), I. p. 264.

[4]See Nina Baym, *Woman's Fiction: A Guide to Novels by and about Women in America, 1820–1870* (Ithaca and London: Cornell University Press, 1978) for a thorough discussion of nineteenth-century American female novelists, their lives, and their works.

[5]See Hawthorne's letter of January 1855 to his publisher, William D. Ticknor, in Caroline Ticknor, ed., *Hawthorne and His Publisher,* p. 141.

[6]See Emily Stipes Watts, *The Poetry of American Women from 1632 to 1945* (Austin, Texas: University of Texas Press, 1977) for an extensive study of American women poets. Watts argues that although female poets were often "at the outer edge of prosodic experimentation and innovation," the poems that were anthologized and therefore preserved fell within the confines of male-defined "female poetry," that is, poetry exhibiting modesty, nonassertiveness, and a dependence on "the affections."

[7]See Gilbert and Gubar, "Introduction," in *Shakespeare's Sisters.*

[8]Quoted in Cora Kaplan, ed., *Salt and Bitter and Good: Three Centuries of English and American Women Poets* (New York and London: Paddington Press, Ltd., 1975), p. 14.

[9]Wendy Martin, "Anne Bradstreet's Poetry: A Study of Subversive Piety," in Gilbert and Gubar, eds., *Shakespeare's Sisters*, p. 26.

[10]Ibid., p. 27.

[11]Robert E. Riegel, *American Women: A Story of Social Change* (Rutherford, Madison, and Teaneck, NJ: Fairleigh Dickinson University Press, 1975), p. 59.

[12]Ibid., p. 28.

[13]Quoted in Richard B. Sewall, *The Life of Emily Dickinson* (New York: Farrar, Straus and Giroux, 1974), II, p. 366.

[14]Riegel, p. 76.

[15]Ibid., p. 77.

[16]Lois W. Banner, *Women in Modern America: A Brief History* (New York: Harcourt Brace Jovanovich, 1974), p. 6.

[17](New York: Bantam Books, 1971), pp. 62–63.

[18]*Poems*, II, 657.

Cultural Influences: Afro-American[1]

Afro-American women have been creating poetry ever since they were brought to America some 400 years ago. The existence of numerous songs and folktales treating subjects of work, courtship, and love, as well as the equally large body of spirituals, testifies to the rich oral tradition collectively created by slave women and men. This tradition clearly ran counter to the accepted norms of European poetry, for it utilized pervasive African stylistic motifs such as "call and response" that were unfamiliar to European ears. It was not until the early part of the twentieth century that spirituals and blues began to be considered as art.

In addition to this oral tradition, there is a written tradition in Afro-American poetry reaching back into the eighteenth century. The tension between the unacknowledged art of the Black culture and contemporary Euro-American aesthetic norms has critically influenced the development of this poetry. As early as 1765, a precocious slave girl named Phillis Wheatley was well-known throughout the American colonies and the mother country for her

---

[1] For further reading, see Dexter Fisher, ed. *The Third Woman*: Minority Women Writers of the United States. (Boston: Houghton Mifflin, 1980; Sharon Harley and Rosalyn Terborg-Penn, eds. *The Afro-American Woman: Struggles and Images* (Port Washington, NY: Kennikat Press, 1978); Gloria Hull and Patricia Scott and Barbara Smith, eds. *And Some of Us Were Brave* (Old Westbury, NY: Feminist Press, 1981); Gerda Lerner, ed. *Black Women in White America: A Documentary History*, (NY: Random House, 1973).

poetry about death in the neo-classical style of Alexander Pope. Her story is, in heightened form, that of all Afro-American writers, for she would not have written at all but for the approval and support of her white masters. It was her ability to imitate European poets rather than the expression of her cultural sensibility that brought prestige. Her poetry reflects little of her identity either as Black or a woman, except that in a few of her poems she attempted to justify slavery on the grounds that through it Africans were introduced to Christianity. Yet, as Alice Walker points out, Phillis preserved for her descendants the "notion of song" in the only manner she could.

Phillis Wheatley died poor and malnourished in 1784. Her verse was published again in 1838 by the abolitionists in order to prove that Black slaves could write poetry. By that time, the institution of slavery was being challenged by an interracial abolitionist movement. This movement, in addition to arousing public opinion against slavery, also became the arena for the first intense participation of American women in national politics and profoundly affected the status of American women in general. Because the men in the movement were denying women the right to speak in public, women created their own organizations, or women's auxiliaries, out of which the first feminist organizations developed.

Aspects of slavery were seen not only as dramatic instances of the immorality of slavery but also specifically as women's issues: the practice of forcing Black women to bear children in order to increase the master's slaveholding was felt as an extreme instance of the commodity status of women in society as a whole. It is not surprising, then, that Black women activists such as Sojourner Truth were central in the nineteenth century both to the abolitionist and the women's rights movements.

However, by the 1890's the unified women's rights movement had split over the issue of racism, and Black women had already begun to establish their own institutions to fight against such assaults on Blacks as a whole as segregation and lynching. The question of women's rights, increasingly seen as an integral part of the Black struggle for emancipation, had won the support of Black male leaders such as Frederick Douglass, who acknowledged that the prevailing definition of woman was a result of societal norms rather than natural law.

The first significant Afro-American literature emerged within the context of the Black struggle for equality, a fact that was to become extremely important for the development of that literature in the twentieth century. The poet was seen as having a responsibility to her racial community, as well as to her own sensibility; the discussion of the condition of women was seen as an integral aspect of Black thought and expression rather than as separate from it.

Frances Harper, the most important of nineteenth-century Afro-American women writers, protested the society's treatment of Black women within the larger context of slavery and racism. She wrote more as a speaker for her race and sex than she did as an individual. Because she measured her poetry by its effectiveness as protest, she tended to write highly meolodramatic verse directed toward a popular audience However, because her reading audience was necessarily White, she only occasionally used specific Afro-American folk forms, as in the selection in this anthology.

When Blacks won emancipation in the 1860s and attempted to become a part of the American nation, they began increasingly to adopt the nineteenth-century White American definition of womanhood. By the period which is known as the Harlem Renaissance (1917–1929) many Blacks felt pressured to demonstrate that Black women were as good as White women—that is, that they would be middle-class ladies were it not for racism. Only if such an ideal was supported, many felt, would the race be respected.

While Afro-American poetry of the nineteenth century had been primarily concerned with gaining the rights of citizenship for Blacks, the poets of the Harlem Renaissance asked: "What does being both Black and an American mean?" and "What does such a combination mean for the Black poet?" This question was then and continues to be a complex one, since Blacks came from Africa rather than Europe, since as slaves they were forcibly separated from their culture, and since they continue to be oppressed economically and culturally in America. Most White Americans in the 1920s saw "Art" not even as American but as European, a tradition to which the Black poet had questionable access. Yet, because many Black ideologues saw art as a means of proving the worth of the race, the emphasis on racial pride in the period was often expressed in creating an Afro-American art that would match the "quality" of a basically elitist European tradition. The most celebrated Black poet of the period, Countee Cullen, imitated the English Romantic poet John Keats and wished to be seen as "poet," not "Black poet." On the other hand, Langston Hughes, the major poet of the period from our present perspective, was not particularly appreciated at that time because he used Afro-American folk forms and harshly criticized contemporary society. In fact, Hughes was to be a major force in the development of a specifically Afro-American poetic tradition, folk and working-class oriented in both form and content.

The poetry written by Black women that was published during

this time must be seen in this context. Although the Harlem Renaissance was a time of enormous Afro-American poetic activity, only a few Black women were known as poets. In contrast to the nineteenth century, these women were not an integral part of the literary movement; they worked individually and wrote fairly conventional verse. Although they sometimes wrote specifically as women, it was primarily to idealize the Black woman, whose image was under attack in the general society. It might be said that the genuine poetry of the Black woman of this time appeared not in literature but in the lyrics of blues singers like Bessie Smith. Female blues singers were extremely popular and wrote their own song lyrics about the Black woman's autonomy and vulnerability, her sexuality and her spirituality. Perhaps because the blues were seen as "race music" directed to a Black audience, Black women were better able to express themselves both as individuals and as part of a racial group in that art form.

The devastating political and economic impact of the Depression changed the tone of Afro-American writing. In the 1930s and 1940s Afro-American writers such as Richard Wright increasingly presented the Black person as a proletarian doubly oppressed by race as well as by poverty and urban life. As northern ghettos grew larger, the alienating effects of segregation on the personality of Blacks became a major theme. Two Afro-American women, Margaret Walker and Gwendolyn Brooks, were the major poets of the 1940s and 1950s. As different as these poets were, they both emphasized the qualities of everyday life in their poetry rather than the sophisticated world presented in the 1920s, and they both presented the impact of racism on the way Black women are viewed in America.

While Margaret Walker tends toward broad historical strokes, Gwendolyn Brooks is a poet of intense concentration. It is interesting that the poem for which Brooks received the Pulitzer Prize, *Annie Allen,* was in Chaucerian rime royal. Her importance for the development of subsequent poetry, however, lies in her effective use of both Afro-American and European forms.

Gwendolyn Brooks wrote much of her poetry during the 1940s and 1950s when Blacks were striving to achieve integration into the American social structure. By the 1960s, the Civil Rights movement gave way to the Black Power movement. Brooks' later work, published in the late 1960s and early 1970s, reflects that shift. The dominant literary movement of that period, Cultural Nationalism, focused on the development of Black selfhood and nationhood. There was a renewed interest in African and Afro-American history and culture. Poets saw themselves as revolutionaries in the service of their people. The writing of women like Nikki Giovanni, Sonia Sanchez, and Carolyn Rodgers reflects this movement.

In the last decade, these poets and others such as June Jordan, Alice Walker, Audre Lorde, and Ntozake Shange have increasingly focused on themselves as women as well as Blacks. The contemporary feminism of the 1970s, which had many of its roots in the Civil Rights movement as the nineteenth century struggle for women's rights sprang from the abolitionist movement, raised critical issues about the nature of sexism in this country. Black women poets have struggled to redefine their relationship with Black men, a relationship that has been continually distorted by the social and economic effects of racism. They insist that their search for self must take place within the context of a transformation of the entire society.

With the shared goal of such radical social transformation, Afro-American women poets today have forged alliances with other Third World and White women in an intense literary activism. These poets are insisting on the critical importance of race and class in the struggle for women's rights. Since the wealth of poetry being published by Black women today is in part a result of the impetus of the women's movement, the visibility and continuing development of this poetry will be influenced by the extent to which the women's movement as a whole responds to this larger political imperative. For the history of Afro-American poetry suggests that unless the issues of race, class, and gender are dealt with together, the Black woman's voice will not be fully heard.

BARBARA CHRISTIAN

Cultural Influences: Asian/Pacific American

The poetry of Asian/Pacific American women is only recently beginning to appear in small magazines and special anthologies throughout the United States. Until the 1970s, no book of poetry by a single Asian/Pacific American woman was published and no body of literature by this group existed. A few poets were published in national magazines as early as 1945, but their works were too scattered and too few to constitute a tradition in any sense. On the whole the finely crafted poems by these accomplished poets have gone unnoticed by the literary world.

In the 1970s there was something of a poetic renaissance, with the publication of books of poetry by Mei-Mei Berssenbrugge, Fay

Chiang, Jessica Tarahata Hagedorn, Geraldine Kudaka, Janice Mirikitani, Barbara Noda, Nellie Wong, and Mitsuye Yamada. This emergence of Asian American women poets was largely an outgrowth of the combined forces of the civil rights movement and the women's movement, which provided an impetus as well as an audience of their works. In addition, the grassroots poetry of the 1960s brought freer forms of poetic language as well as some understanding of pluralism in American poetry.

Asian American women, along with other groups of women in the United States, began to see that they had been experiencing the reality of their lives through the language habits and cultural assumptions of the dominant society. Through their new awareness, they discovered a need for a new language that reflected the condition of their lives as women and as Asians. As a result, they have begun to produce poetry exploring the culture that is uniquely theirs. In their present impatience, many of them have wondered why it took over a hundred years after the arrival of their first ancestors for their writing to be acknowledged. Why have they not had the advantage of their "very own literature" to cut their teeth on?

We might remember that Emily Dickinson was born two hundred years after the arrival of her ancestors from England, and only recently is the full measure of her greatness being appreciated. She wrote in a form unheard of in nineteenth-century New England, and was uncompromising about her subject matter and her form. Her voice was often characterized by critics as that of an eccentric woman or a petulant child. However much Emily Dickinson suffered under such sexist attitudes, she did not have the additional handicap of color and race. Asian women have suffered not only from sexism but also from an institutionalized racism which has confronted their people since they arrived in the United States.

The first Asians to enter this country were a small band of Chinese men who landed in California in 1847. These immigrants were tolerated at first as a dependable supply of common laborers to work in the mines, on the railroads and ranches, and in the laundries and kitchens. A few women came independently or as wives of the workers. Soon a series of laws was passed, aimed specifically at the Chinese people—starting with the Foreign Miners' License Law passed in California in 1850, the Immigrant Head Tax in 1855, and the Chinese Exclusion Act of 1882, which created untold hardships for these early Chinese pioneers. Nellie Wong in her poem "It's in the Blood" writes how her mother had to come to this country as her father's sister because the Exclusion Act was designed to keep wives out (only blood relatives were permitted to enter), presumably to keep the Chinese from propagating in this country.

The next group of Asians to arrive were Japanese men in 1872, who were met with the same attitudes that prevailed against the Chinese. Like the Chinese, the Japanese men came primarily to work in the labor force. Because of the practice of "marriage by photograph" (*shashin kekkon*, long distance marriage contracts made by families in Japan on behalf of their daughters through exchange of photographs), Japanese women were able to join their husbands and establish families much sooner than the Chinese. After 1920, however, passports ceased being issued to "picture brides" in response to criticism of the system as "barbaric."

The Japanese, no different from the European immigrants with their visions of a new life in a new land, continued to come and work to make homes for themselves built on their dreams. Attempts to frustrate these dreams continued. In response to popular feeling against Asians, the Anti-Alien Initiative Measure of 1920 was passed, which prohibited the owning of land by Japanese or the leasing of farms to them; and in 1924, the Oriental Exclusion Act was enacted to stop the continuing flow of Japanese immigrants and deny them the right to become naturalized citizens. To replace the supply of labor lost by this law, Pilipinos were brought in to work the farm lands.

The early Asian women did not come with their men as settlers. They usually came because they were told they "must follow their husbands," and found, instead of the riches they were led to expect in this "land of plenty," their husbands laboring amidst a trail of shattered dreams. There was hardly any time for these women to adjust to the alien culture or learn the language of the new land, for they became simply another hired hand on the farm. Full mastery of the English language would come later with the second, third and fourth generations of Asian Americans.

The pattern of discrimination is a familiar one for most immigrants, but for the Asians new hurdles were added each time an old one was overcome. The most devastating blow to the Asian/Pacific American community came when 110,000 Japanese on the West Coast—70,000 of them second generation American citizens—were incarcerated in concentration camps during World War II. By this time, the Japanese had established thriving communities up and down the West Coast, but they found that this was no protection against being suddenly singled out as objects of suspicion and legal persecution. The question of the constitutional rights of this nation's citizens during wartime still has not been resolved.

After World War II, several laws favorable to Asians were passed due to the exigencies of the war and the post-war period. The Exclusion Act was repealed in 1943 in deference to the Chinese, who were the "friendly Asians" at the time. In August 1945 the war ended, and American soldiers in the troops occupying Japan demanded the right to return with their Japanese brides; the Amended War Brides' Act of 1947 was passed to permit these wives of servicemen to enter the country. This law also allowed Chinese wives, long excluded, to enter the country to join their husbands. Finally in 1952 the Walter-McCarran Immigration and Naturalization Act was passed, which permitted Asians the right of citizenship.

The long history of oppression against Asian immigrants has led to an avoidance of "foreign" looking and sounding habits among many second and third generation Asian Americans. For them, the principal concern has been assimilation; and the small body of literature in prose and poetry written by early Asian American writers has seemed irrelevant to their values and experience. Only recently has a strong movement for cultural self-affirmation arisen among Asian/Pacific Americans, which has led to a new appreciation of the early literary pioneers and a forging of new and powerful literary forms appropriate to the present struggle.

The Asian/Pacific American women poets writing today are two, three, and four generations removed from their ancestral ties. With a desire to directly confront themselves and to speak out specifically about the condition of their lives as women and as Asians, Asian/Pacific American women are writing poetry which permits a close look at the self. As tone, subject, and language stretch to permit an uncensored expression of experience, we are hearing strong poetry from increasing numbers of women of color, including working-class women and lesbians, who until now have been doubly silenced. They are constantly redefining themselves in their work in opposition to the multi-stereotyping they face, not only as women and as Asians, but also specifically as Chinese, Japanese, Koreans, Pilipinas, Samoans, Vietnamese.

The struggle to be oneself is not an easy one for Asian/Pacific American women. Merle Woo, a Korean-Chinese American woman writer, articulates an additonal problem facing them today:

> To fight the sexism within Asian culture is not to deny that culture. It is to assume that all of those forces which oppress and deny us freedom of choice are not natural and eternal, and that is all. To interpret this struggle as man-hating or Asian culture-hating is a distortion of the truth and a manipulative measure to keep Asian women silent.[11]

The poets in this section represent a few of the voices among Asian/Pacific American women poets today who are not keeping silent, who are speaking out with clarity and strength in affirmation of their identity as individuals and as a cultural community.

MITSUYE YAMADA

Suggested Readings

Aquino, Belinda. "The History of Pilipino Women in Hawaii." *Bridge: An Asian American Perspective.*

Hirata, Lucie Cheng. "Chinese Immigrant Women in 19th Century California." In *Women in America: A History.* Carol R. Berkin and Mary B. Norton, eds. Boston: Houghton Mifflin, 1979.

Ichioka, Yuji. "American Nadeshiko: Japanese Immigrant Women in the U.S. 1900–1924." *Pacific Historical Review,* May 1980. Available from PHR, University of California, Berkeley, CA 94720.

Jung, Betty. "Chinese Immigrant Women." In *Asian Women.* Asian Women's Journal. Berkeley: University of California, 1971. Available from Asian American Studies Centers, UCLA, Los Angeles, CA 90024.

Anzaldúa, Gloria, and Cherrie Moraga, eds. *This Bridge Called My Back: Writings by Radical Women of Color.* Watertown, Massachusetts: Persephone Press, 1981. This book has an excellent bibliography of Asian Pacific women's literature, works by and about them.

Cultural Influences: Chicana

The poems by Chicanas (American women of Mexican heritage) presented in this anthology cover a broad range of themes: Ana Castillo's evocation of back-breaking field work in "Napa, California," Teresa Palma Acosta's tribute to women's work in "My Mother Patched Quilts," Lorna Dee Cervantes' indictment of racism ("Poem for the Young White Man") and affirmation of herself as writer ("The Woman in My Notebook"), Alma Villanueva's evocation of childhood and a special way of seeing ("I was always").

The Chicana, through her writing, explores her own selfhood as a woman of color and her own interpretation of the Chicano experience.

Chicano literature itself must be understood in dynamic relationship to a specific historical experience. Since 1848, that historical experience has been one of economic oppression and social inequality. The vast majority of Chicanos in the United States belong to the working class. The absence of upward social mobility, exacerbated by the racism of linguistic discrimination, has resulted in severly limited access to education and literacy. The exclusion of Chicanos as a social group from middle-class forms of literary production requiring printing presses, distribution systems, and educated readers with enough time and money to make up a market has had profound repercussions for Chicano literary expression, which has been largely popular in form and oral in transmission.[1] The Chicano Movement that gained momentum in the mid-1960s is not the beginning but rather the continuation of a long tradition of militance and resistance. Political activity on various fronts has been accompanied by a corresponding flurry of artistic activity, which tends toward the strengthening of popular modes of expression. This led to a creative renovation of language, especially in its popular and bilingual strains, and to the cultivation of "rascuachismo," a rough, funky quality opposed to the refined or finished quality of bourgeois or "high" art. At the same time, the lack of access to the mainstream literary establishment has been countered by the creation of a Chicano communications network, in the form of community newspapers featuring the work of local, grass-roots poets and later in the growth of Chicano literary magazines and publishing houses.[2]

In recent years, more Chicano poets are being educated in the universities, where "learning to write" means learning to write a certain way. The resulting influence on language and form has created a style more easily assimilated into American literature, though the content may still reflect Chicano experience. Admission to the literary mainstream manifests itself in the form of prestigious prizes and publishers and open doors to certain magazines. The underlying assumptions of mainstream anthologies ultimately determine the selection of poets: the Chicanas represented will be those who write in English and whose poetry is closest in style and form to "American" poetry and the accepted norms of "good" poetry. Other modes exist within Chicana poetry that by definition fall outside the sphere of mainstream validation, for example the work of grass-roots poets working within oral and popular traditions, those writing in Spanish or in a heavily bilingual mode, such as Emy López or Evangelina Vigil, or those with an explicit political, feminist and/or lesbian perspective, such as Jo Carrillo, Cherrie Moraga and Gloria Anzaldúa.

Chicanas within the women's movement have found points of contact based on gender and shared problems of sexism, but also important differences based on race, culture and class. A recent book, *This Bridge Called My Back* edited by Moraga and Anzaldúa,[3] documents the rage and frustration of women of color after years of trying to reconcile these differences. Although the analysis of racism within the white women's movement is bitter (poetically captured in Carrillo's "And When You Leave, Take Your Pictures with You"), the book initiates some very positive and long-neglected connections among women of color. Within the Chicano movement, where the Chicana feels more at home on the grounds of class, race, and culture, problems of gender have sparked dissension. Given the cultural nationalist thrust of the movement with its tendency to see culture as a static essence, women's questioning of traditional notions of family, home, and sex roles has often been viewed as cultural betrayal. Chicanas have resisted the assertion that the primary goal of the movement is to combat oppression, pointing out the interlocking nature of different oppressive systems. In the last analysis, it is impossible to separate race from class from sex oppression. The dilemma that confronts Chicanas is how to develop their full potential as women and fight sexism within their culture while retaining the racial and cultural identity that defines them as Chicanas. Their willingness to challenge certain components of culture—the traditional family structure and the role of the church, for example—does not indicate a rejection of their cultural identity but rather a concept of culture as dynamic and malleable, changing as historical and social experience changes.

While many Chicano writers have recognized the important role of literature in combating negative stereotypes and generating new self-images, these same writers often continue to propagate the traditional images of women in their work. The Chicana writer, especially in poetry, has realized that it is up to her to chart the geography of her self and her experience. In this task, she shares certain concerns and problems with white women writers, but faces additional ones because of her race, her culture and her class. Her main problem is access to literacy in an often indifferent and monolingual school system; when she does learn to read and write, she does so in English and often suffers the loss of her native tongue. Once she has learned to read and write she must overcome the pressure of the "tracking" mechanism in the educational system, which teaches her that she cannot become a writer. And once she has convinced herself that she indeed has something important to say, she must somehow find leisure time for writing, in the midst of a battle for economic survival more acute for those of her class. White women writers may be invisible and inaudible in the white male literary mainstream; Chicana writers have yet to gain just representation in either the white feminist or the Chicano literary worlds. One limited solution within the Chicano literary circuit has been special issues of Chicano magazines dedicated to "La Mujer" ("The Woman"). While these issues demonstrate the wealth of artistic and literary activity among Chicanas, they do not solve the problem of the meager proportion of women published in the regular issues of these magazines. Only an aggressive editorial policy can redress this inequity, and this is usually brought about when Chicanas themselves open up admission to the power structures incarnated in editorial boards. A more effective solution has been Chicana publishing ventures put together by women themselves, who know that they will have to create the conditions that make their writing and publishing possible.

Validating their affinities with their male Chicano counterparts and white women writers alike, but with a clear consciousness of their differences, Chicana writers are engaged in developing their authentic voice. They are determined not to "make it" by becoming less "different," either formally or ideologically. They are determined to break stereotypes in their writing, both for themselves and for others. They are committed to the exploration of their selves as women, to the abolition of self-hatred—shared by all women but exaggerated in them as women of color—and to the celebration of their own creative power: "I/ woman give birth:/ and this time to/ myself" (Alma Villanueva). They are exploring the self within their cultural history: challenging or affirming certain cultural values; documenting the past in their present as a colonized people with a tradition of resistance; capturing the racial tension inherent in their social environment; writing about the importance of work in their lives, their own and that of their ancestors; allowing themselves an identity as writers; feeling their way through their relation to men, their relation to other women, a precious gift. The strong ties among females is a recurrent theme in Chicana poetry, appearing often in the examination of the family. In these poetic genealogies we are struck by the prominence of mothers and grandmothers. "My Mother Patched Quilts" is a moving testimonial to the mother's weaving covers from their life's experience, the bonding point of diversity, as well as a celebration of working-class women's culture.

In the search for their own voice, Chicana writers are also developing their own language, often in conscious opposition to dominant culture. Many write all in Spanish or bilingually. Others mourn the loss of their mother tongue, feeling that in practice they have been denied both languages. Moraga speaks of her need for a "language to clarify my resistance to the literate." This search for a new tongue leads at time to the fear of incomprehensibility, a fear Moraga expresses ("her voice in the distance/ unintelligible illiterate/ These are the monster's words"), at other times to the affirmation of continuity and change, as in Cervantes: "I come from a long line of eloquent illiterates."[4]

YVONNE YARBRO-BEJARANO

Notes and References

[1]Joseph Sommers, "From the Critical Premise to the Product: Critical Modes and Their Applications to a Chicano Literary Text," *New Scholar,* 6 (1977), pp. 51–52, 61.

[2]Tomás Ybarra-Frausto, "The Chicano Movement and the Emergence of a Chicano Poetic Consciousness," *New Scholar,* 6 (1977), pp. 81–109.

[3]Watertown, MA: Persephone Press, 1981.

[4]For further reading, see Gloria Anzaldúa and Cherrie Moraga, eds., *This Bridge Called My Back: Writings by Radical Women of Color* (Watertown, MA: Persephone Press, 1981); Adelaide de Castillo, ed., *Mexican Women in the United States: Struggles Past and Present* (Los Angeles-UCLA Chicano Studies, 1980); Dexter Fisher, ed., *The Third Woman-Minority Women Writers of the United States* (Boston: Houghton Mifflin, 1980); and Margarita B. Melville, ed., *Twice a Minority-Mexican American Women* (St. Louis: C. V. Mosby Co., 1980).

Euro-American

Anne Hébert
Canada: French 1916

The Wooden Chamber

Honeyed by time
the shining walls
golden ceiling
flowery knots
    whimsical wooden hearts

Closed chamber
light-colored coffer where my childhood unrolls
as a necklace unstrung.

I sleep on leaves grown tame
the scent of pine is a blind old maid-servant
the song of the water strikes my temple
a small blue broken vein
the whole river goes past the memory.

I am walking
in a secret wardrobe.
The snow, scarcely a handful,
blooms under a globe of glass
like a bridal crown.
Two frail pains stretch out
and draw back their claws.

I will sew my dress with this lost thread.
I have blue slippers
and a child's eyes
that are not my own.

I must live here
in this polished space.
I have provisions for the night
provided I do not tire
of the even song of the river
provided the trembling maid-servant
does not drop her burden of scents

all of a sudden
irretrievably.

There's neither lock nor key here
I am enclosed by old wood,
I love a little green candlestick.

The midday sun burns on the silvery tiles
the world is flaming like a forge
the anguish gives me shade
I am naked and all black under a bitter tree.

Translated from the French by Birgit Swenson

Marya Fiamengo
Canada: English   *contemporary*

In Praise of Old Women

Yes, Tadeusz Rozewicz,[1] I too
prefer old women.
They bend over graves
with flowers,
they wash the limbs of the dead,
they count the beads of their rosaries,
they commit no murders
they give advice
or tell fortunes,
they endure.

In Poland, in Russia,
in Asia, in the Balkans,
I see them shawled, kerchiefed,
bent-backed, work-wrinkled.

But Tadeusz,
have you been to America?

[1]Tadeusz Rozewicz, contemporary Polish poet, well-known for his non-metaphorical, unadorned style. Deeply influenced by his experiences during World War II, he has said he writes in order to recover the use of words "after the end of the world."

Where we have no old women.
No Stara Babas,[2]
no haggard Madonnas.

Everyone, Tadeusz, is young in America.
Especially the women
with coifed blue hair
which gleams like the steel
of jets in the daytime sky.
Smooth-skinned at sixty,
second debuts at fifty
renascent
they never grow old in America.

And we have in America
literate, sexually liberated women
who wouldn't touch a corpse
who confuse lechery with love,
not out of viciousness
but boringly
out of confusion, neurosis, identity crises.

Tadeusz,
I go to the cemetery
with my mother
one of us stoically old,
the other aging,
and I tell you, Tadeusz,
I will grow old in America.
I will have no second debut.
I will raise my son on old battles,
Kossovo,[3] Neretva,[4] Thermopylae,[5]

[2]Stara Babas (Polish): old women
[3]Kossovo, or Kosovo: two historically important battles were fought at Kosovo Polje (Field of the Blackbirds) located in present Yugoslavia. The first, in 1389, ended with the encirclement of the crumbling Byzantine Empire by Turkish armies; the second, in 1448, halted the last major Christian crusader offensive to free the Balkans from Ottoman rule.
[4]Neretva: a river in Yugoslavia; during World War II the crossing of the Neretva by partisan forces avoided encirclement by superior German forces.
[5]Thermopylae: a narrow pass on the east coast of central Greece; in 480 B.C., during the second Persian invasion of Greece, a small Greek force held it for 3 days against a large Persian army before being overwhelmed. This battle became celebrated in history and literature as an example of heroic resistance against great odds.

Stalingrad[6] and Britain[7]
and I will wrinkle adamantly in America.

I will put salt in the soup
and I will offer bread and wine
to my friends,
and I will stubbornly praise old women
until their thin taut skins
glow like Ikons[8] ascending on escalators
like Buddhas[9] descending in subways,
and I will liberate all women
to be old in America
because the highest manifestation of
Hagia Sophia[10]
is old and a woman.

[6]Stalingrad: the Battle of Stalingrad (summer 1942–Feb. 1943) was a major turning point in World War II; the unsuccessful German assault on Stalingrad marked the limit of the German advance in the East and the beginning of a successful Soviet counter-offensive.

[7]Britain: the Battle of Britain: a massive series of raids directed against Britain by the German Air Force between June 1940 and April 1941. Successful resistance by the British Royal Air Force forstalled a planned invasion of Britain.

[8]*Ikons,* or *icons:* sacred images venerated in churches and homes of Eastern Christianity, depicting Christ, the Virgin Mary, a saint, or some other religious subject in the conventional manner of Byzantine art.

[9]Buddha: Gautama Buddha (c. 483 BC): Indian philosopher who founded Buddhism; also, any representation of the Buddha.

[10] Hagia Sophia (Greek): "Holy Wisdom".

Margaret Atwood
Canada: English   1939

At first I was given centuries
to wait in caves, in leather
tents, knowing you would never come back

Then it speeded up: only
several years between
the day you jangled off
into the mountains, and the day (it was
spring again) I rose from the embroidery
frame at the messenger's entrance.

That happened twice, or was it
more; and there was once, not so
long ago, you failed,
and came back in a wheelchair
with a moustache and a sunburn
and were insufferable.

Time before last though, I remember
I had a good eight months between
running alongside the train, skirts hitched, handing
you violets in at the window
and opening the letter; I watched
your snapshot fade for twenty years.

And last time (I drove to the airport
still dressed in my factory
overalls, the wrench
I had forgotten sticking out of the back
pocket; there you were,
zippered and helmeted, it was zero
hour, you said Be
Brave) it was at least three weeks before
I got the telegram and could start regretting.

But recently, the bad evenings
there are only seconds
between the warning on the radio and the
explosion; my hands
don't reach you

and on quieter nights
you jump up from
your chair without even touching your dinner
and I can scarcely kiss you goodbye
before you run out into the street and they shoot

Anne Bradstreet
Colonial America   1612–1672

Before the Birth of One of Her Children

All things within this fading world hath end,
Adversity doth still our joys attend;
No ties so strong, no friends so dear and sweet
But with death's parting blow is sure to meet.
The sentence past is most irrevocable,
A common thing, yet oh, inevitable.
How soon, my Dear, death may my steps attend,
How soon't may be thy lot to lose thy friend,
We both are ignorant, yet love bids me
These farewell lines to recommend to thee,
That when that knot's untied that made us one,
I may seem thine, who in effect am none.
And if I see not half my days that's due,
What nature would, God grant to yours and you;
The many faults that well you know I have
Let be interred in my oblivious grave;
If any worth or virtue were in me,
Let that live freshly in thy memory
And when thou feel'st no grief, as I no harms,
Yet love thy dead, who long lay in thine arms.
And when thy loss shall be repaid with gains
Look to my little babes, my dear remains.
And if thou love thyself, or loved'st me,
These O protect from step-dame's injury.
And if chance to thine eyes shall bring this verse,
With some sad sighs honour my absent hearse;
And kiss this paper for thy love's dear sake,
Who with salt tears this last farewell did take.

from "Contemplations"

31

The Mariner that on smooth waves doth glide,
Sings merrily, and steers his barque with ease,
As if he had command of wind and tide,
And now become great Master of the seas;
But suddenly a storm spoiles all the sport,

And makes him long for a more quiet port,
Which 'gainst all adverse winds may serve for fort.

32

So he that saileth in this world of pleasure,
Feeding on sweets, that never bit of th' sowre,
That's full of friends, of honour and of treasure,
Fond fool, he takes this earth ev'n for heav'ns bower.
But sad affliction comes and makes him see
Here's neither honour, wealth, nor safety;
Only above is found all with security.

33

O Time the fatal wrack of mortal things,
That draws oblivion's curtains over kings,
Their sumptuous monuments, men know them not,
Their names without a Record are forgot,
Their parts, their ports, their pomp's all laid in th' dust
Nor wit nor gold, nor buildings scape time's rust;
But he whose name is grav'd in the white stone
Shall last and shine when all of these are gone.

Emily Dickinson
United States   1830–1886

508

I'm ceded—I've stopped being Theirs—
The name They dropped upon my face
With water, in the country church
Is finished using, now,
And They can put it with my Dolls,
My childhood, and the string of spools,
I've finished threading—too—

Baptized, before, without the choice,
But this time, consciously, of Grace—
Unto supremest name—
Called to my Full—The Crescent dropped—
Existence's whole Arc, filled up,
With one small Diadem.

My second Rank—too small the first—
Crowned—Crowing—on my Father's breast—
A half unconscious Queen—
But this time—Adequate—Erect,
With Will to choose, or to reject,
And I choose, just a Crown—

754

My life had stood—a Loaded Gun—
In corners—till a Day
The Owner passed—identified—
And carried Me away—

And now We roam in Sovereign Woods—
And now We hunt the Doe—
And every time I speak for Him—
The Mountains straight reply—

And do I smile, such cordial light
Upon the Valley glow—
It is as a Vesuvian[1] face
Had let its pleasure through—

And when at Night—our good Day done—
I guard My Master's Head—
'Tis better than the Eider-Duck's
Deep Pillow—to have shared—

To foe of His—I'm deadly foe—
None stir the second time—
On whom I lay a Yellow Eye—
Or an emphatic Thumb—

Though I than He—may longer live
He longer must—than I—
For I have but the power to kill
Without—the power to die—

---

[1]Mount Vesuvius, a volcano near Naples, Italy.

410

The first Day's Night had come—
And grateful that a thing
So terrible—had been endured—
I told my Soul to sing—

She said her Strings were snapt—
Her Bow—to Atoms blown—
And so to mend her—gave me work
Until another Morn—

And then—a Day as huge
As Yesterdays in pairs,
Unrolled its horror in my face—
Until it blocked my eyes—

My Brain—begun to laugh—
I mumbled—like a fool—
And tho' 'tis years ago—that Day—
My Brain keeps giggling—still.

And Something's odd—within—
That person that I was—
And this One—do not feel the same—
Could it be Madness—this?

605

The Spider holds a Silver Ball
In unperceived Hands—
And dancing softly to Himself
His Yarn of Pearl—unwinds—

He plies from Nought to Nought—
In unsubstantial Trade—
Supplants our Tapestries with His—
In half the period—

An Hour to rear supreme
His Continents of Light—
Then dangle from the Housewife's Broom—
His Boundaries—forgot—

H. D. (Hilda Doolittle)
United States   *1886–1961*

The Mysteries Remain

The mysteries remain,
I keep the same
cycle of seed-time
and of sun and rain;
Demeter[1] in the grass,
I multiply,
renew and bless
Iacchus[2] in the vine;
I hold the law,
I keep the mysteries true,
the first of these
to name the living, dead;
I am red wine and bread.

I KEEP THE LAW,
I HOLD THE MYSTERIES TRUE,
I AM THE VINE,
THE BRANCHES, YOU
AND YOU.

[1]Demeter (called Ceres by the Romans): one of the great divinities of the Greeks; goddess of earth's fruits, especially of the corn; her powers were celebrated in the Eleusinian Mysteries, mystical cults involving secret initiation.
[2]Iacchus: in the Eleusinian Mysteries, regarded as the son of Zeus and Demeter; later identified with Bacchus (Dionysus), god of wine.

Marianne Moore
United States   *1887–1972*

The Mind is an Enchanting Thing

is an enchanted thing
          like the glaze on a
katydid-wing

subdivided by sun
till the nettings are legion.
Like Gieseking[1] playing Scarlatti[2];

like the apteryx[3]-awl
as a beak, or the
kiwi's[4] rain-shawl
of haired feathers, the mind
feeling its way as though blind,
walks along with its eyes on the ground.

It has memory's ear
that can hear without
having to hear.
Like the gyroscope's fall,
truly unequivocal.
Because trued by regnant certainty,

it is a power of
strong enchantment. It
is like the dove-
neck animated by
sun; it is memory's eye;
it's conscientious inconsistency.

It tears off the veil; tears
the temptation, the
mist the heart wears,
from its eyes,—if the heart
has a face; it takes apart
dejection. It's fire in the dove-neck's
iridescence, in the
inconsistencies
of Scarlatti.
Unconfusion submits
its confusion to proof; it's
not a Herod's[5] oath that cannot change.

---

[1]Walter Gieseking (1895–1956), well-known classical pianist.
[2]Domenico Scarlatti (1685–1757), Italian baroque composer.
[3]Kiwi bird.
[4]A flightless bird of New Zealand.
[5]Herod, ruler of Judea under Rome at the time of Christ.

Edna St. Vincent Millay
United States   1892–1950

Conscientious Objector

I shall die, but that is all that I shall do for Death.
I hear him leading his horse out of the stall; I hear the
    clatter on the barn-floor.
He is in haste; he has business in Cuba, business in the
    Balkans, many calls to make this morning.
But I will not hold the bridle while he cinches the girth.
And he may mount by himself: I will not give him a leg
    up.

Though he flick my shoulders with his whip, I will not
    tell him which way the fox ran.
With his hoof on my breast, I will not tell him where the
    black boy hides in the swamp.
I shall die, but that is all that I shall do for Death; I am
    not on his pay-roll.

I will not tell him the whereabouts of my friends nor of
    my enemies either.
Though he promise me much, I will not map him the
    route to any man's door.
Am I a spy in the land of the living, that I should deliver
    men to Death?
Brother, the password and the plans of our city are safe
    with me; never through me
Shall you be overcome.

Kadia Molodowsky
United States: Yiddish   1894

Song of the Sabbath

I quarreled with kings till the Sabbath,
I fought with the six kings
of the six days of the week.

Sunday they took away my sleep.
Monday they scattered my salt.

And on the third day, my God,
they threw out my bread: whips flashed
across my face. The fourth day
they caught my dove, my flying dove,
and slaughtered it.
It was like that till Friday morning.
This is my whole week,
the dove's flight dying.

At nightfall Friday
I lit four candles,
and the queen of the Sabbath came to me.
Her face lit up the whole world,
and made it all a Sabbath.
My scattered salt
shone in its little bowl,
and my dove, my flying dove,
clapped its wings together,
and licked its throat.
The Sabbath queen[1] blessed my candles,
and they burned with a pure, clean flame.
The light put out the days of the week
and my quarreling with the six kings.

The greenness of the mountains
is the greenness of the Sabbath.
The silver of the lake
is the silver of the Sabbath.
The singing of the wind
is the singing of the Sabbath.

And my heart's song
is an eternal Sabbath.

Translated from the Yiddish by Jean Valentine

[1]The Sabbath (Saturday), the day of rest ordained by God in the Jewish tradition,
is often spoken of as a queen.

God of Mercy

O God of Mercy
For the time being
Choose another people.
We are tired of death, tired of corpses,

We have no more prayers.
For the time being
Choose another people.
We have run out of blood
For victims,
Our houses have been turned into desert,
The earth lacks space for tombstones,
There are no more lamentations
Nor songs of woe
In the ancient texts.

God of Mercy
Sanctify another land
Another Sinai.
We have covered every field and stone
With ashes and holiness.
With our crones
With our young
With our infants
We have paid for each letter in your Commandments.

God of Mercy
Lift up your fiery brow,
Look on the peoples of the world,
Let them have the prophecies and Holy Days
Who mumble your words in every tongue.
Teach them the Deeds
And the ways of temptation.

God of Mercy
To us give rough clothing
Of shepherds who tend sheep
Of blacksmiths at the hammer
Of washerwomen, cattle slaughterers
And lower still.
And O God of Mercy
Grant us one more blessing—
Take back the gift of our separateness.

Translated from the Yiddish by Irving Howe

Louise **Bogan**

United States   *1897–1970*

Roman Fountain

Up from the bronze, I saw
Water without a flaw
Rush to its rest in air,
Reach to its rest, and fall.

Bronze of the blackest shade,
An element man-made,
Shaping upright the bare
Clear gouts of water in air.

O, as with arm and hammer,
Still it is good to strive
To beat out the image whole,
To echo the shout and stammer
When full-gushed waters, alive
Strike on the fountain's bowl
After the air of summer.

Muriel **Rukeyser**

United States   *1913–1980*

The Question

Mother and listener she is, but she does not listen.
I look at her profile as I ask, the sweet blue-grey of eye
going obdurate to my youth as I ask the first grown
    sexual
question. She cannot reply.
And from then on even past her death, I cannot fully
have language with my mother, not as daughter
and mother through all the maze and silences
of all the turnings.
Until my own child grows and asks, and until
I discover what appalled my mother long before,
    discover

who never delivered her, until their double weakness
   and
strength in myself
rouse and deliver me from that refusal.
I threw myself down on the pine-needle evening.
Although that old ancient poem never did come to me,
not from you, mother,
although in answer you did only panic, you did only
   grieve,
and I went silent alone, my cheek to the red pine-needle
earth, and although it has taken me all these years
and sunsets to come to you, past the dying, I know,
I come with my word alive.

Denise Levertov
United States   1923

Woman Alone

When she cannot be sure
which of two lovers it was with whom she felt
this or that moment of pleasure, of something fiery
streaking from head to heels, the way the white
flame of a cascade streaks a mountainside
seen from a car across a valley, the car
changing gear, skirting a precipice,
climbing . . .
When she can sit or walk for hours after a movie
talking earnestly and with bursts of laughter
with friends, without worrying
that it's late, dinner at midnight, her time
spent without counting the change . . .
When half her bed is covered with books
and no one is kept awake by the reading light
and she disconnects the phone, to sleep till noon . . .
Then
selfpity dries up, a joy
untainted by guilt lifts her.
She has fears, but not about loneliness;
fears about how to deal with the aging
of her body—how to deal

with photographs and the mirror. She feels
so much younger and more beautiful
than she looks
At her happiest
—or even in the midst of
some less than joyful hour, sweating
patiently through a heatwave in the city
or hearing the sparrows at daybreak, dully gray,
toneless, the sound of fatigue—
a kind of sober euphoria makes her believe
in her future as an old woman, a wanderer,
seamed and brown,
little luxuries in the middle of life all gone,
watching cities and rivers, people and mountains,
without being watched; not grim nor sad,
an old winedrinking woman, who knows
the old roads, grass-grown, and laughs to herself . . .
She knows it can't be:
that's Mrs. Doasyouwouldbedoneby from THE WATER
  BABIES,[1]
no one can walk the world any more,
a world of fumes and decibels.
But she thinks maybe
she could get to be tough and wise, some way,
anyway. Now at least
she is past the time of mourning,
now she can say without shame or deceit,
O blessed Solitude.

[1]Popular late nineteenth century English novel for children by Charles Kingsley.

Anne Sexton
United States   *1928–1974*

Her Kind

I have gone out, a possessed witch,
haunting the black air, braver at night;
dreaming evil, I have done my hitch
over the plain houses, light by light:
lonely thing, twelve-fingered, out of mind.

A woman like that is not a woman, quite.
I have been her kind.

I have found the warm caves in the woods,
filled them with skillets, carvings, shelves,
closets, silks, innumerable goods;
fixed the suppers for the worms and the elves:
whining, rearranging the disaligned.
A woman like that is misunderstood.
I have been her kind.

I have ridden in your cart, driver,
waved my nude arms at villages going by,
learning the last bright routes, survivor
where your flames still bite my thigh
and my ribs crack where your wheels wind.
A woman like that is not ashamed to die.
I have been her kind.

Adrienne Rich
United States   1929

Translations

You show me the poems of some woman
my age, or younger
translated from your language

Certain words occur: *enemy, oven, sorrow*
enough to let me know
she's a woman of my time

obsessed

with Love, our subject:
we've trained it like ivy to our walls
baked it like bread in our ovens
worn it like lead on our ankles
watched it through binoculars as if
it were a helicopter
bringing food to our famine

or the satellite
of a hostile power

I begin to see that woman
doing things: stirring rice
ironing a skirt
typing a manuscript till dawn

trying to make a call
from a phonebooth

The phone rings unanswered
in a man's bedroom
she hears him telling someone else
Never mind. She'll get tired.
hears him telling her story to her sister
who becomes her enemy
and will in her own time
light her own way to sorrow

ignorant of the fact this way of grief
is shared, unnecessary
and political

Sylvia Plath
United States   1932–1963

The Moon and the Yew Tree

This is the light of the mind, cold and planetary.
The trees of the mind are black. The light is blue.
The grasses unload their griefs on my feet as if I were
    God,
Prickling my ankles and murmuring of their humility.
Fumey, spiritous mists inhabit this place
Separated from my house by a row of headstones.
I simply cannot see where there is to get to.

The moon is no door. It is a face in its own right,
White as a knuckle and terribly upset.
It drags the sea after it like a dark crime; it is quiet

With the O-gape of complete despair. I live here.
Twice on Sunday, the bells startle the sky—
Eight great tongues affirming the Resurrection.
At the end, they soberly bong out their names.

The yew tree points up. It has a Gothic shape.
The eyes lift after it and find the moon.
The moon is my mother. She is not sweet like Mary.
Her blue garments unloose small bats and owls.
How I would like to believe in tenderness—
The face of the effigy, gentled by candles,
Bending, on me in particular, its mild eyes.

I have fallen a long way. Clouds are flowering
Blue and mystical over the face of the stars.
Inside the church, the saints will be all blue,
Floating on their delicate feet over the cold pews,
Their hands and faces stiff with holiness.
The moon sees nothing of this. She is bald and wild.
And the message of the yew tree is blackness—blackness
     and silence.

Mushrooms

Overnight, very
Whitely, discreetly,
Very quietly

Our toes, our noses
Take hold on the loam,
Acquire the air.

Nobody sees us,
Stops us, betrays us;
The small grains make room.

Soft fists insist on
Heaving the needles,
The leafy bedding,

Even the paving.
Our hammers, our rams,
Earless and eyeless,

Perfectly voiceless,
Widen the crannies,
Shoulder through holes. We

Diet on water,
On crumbs of shadow,
Bland-mannered, asking

Little or nothing.
So many of us!
So many of us!

We are shelves, we are
Tables, we are meek,
We are edible,

Nudgers and shovers
In spite of ourselves
Our kind multiplies:

We shall by morning
Inherit the earth.
Our foot's in the door.

Marge Piercy
United States   1936

The Total Influence or Outcome of
the Matter: THE SUN

Androgynous child whose hair curls into flowers,
naked you ride a horse without saddle or bridle
easy between your thighs from the walled garden
    outward.
Coarse sunflowers of desire whose seeds birds crack
    open
nod upon your journey, child of the morning whose sun
can only be born from us who strain bleeding to give
    birth.
Grow into your horse, let there be
no more riders or ridden.

Child, where are you heading with arms spread wide
as a shore, have I been there, have I seen that land
    shining
like sun spangles on clean water rippling?
I do not know your dances, I cannot translate your
    tongue
to words I use, your pleasures are strange to me
as the rites of bees: yet you are the yellow flower
of a melon vine growing out of my belly
though it climbs up where I cannot see in the strong
    light.

My eyes cannot decipher those shapes of children or
    burning clouds
who are not what we are: they go barefoot like savages,
they have computers as household pets; they are seven
    sexes
and only one sex; they do not own or lease or control.
They are of one body and of tribes. They are private as
    shamans[1]
learning each her own magic at the teats of stones and
    trees.
They are all technicians and peasants.
They do not forget their birthright of self
or their mane of animal pride
dancing in and out through the gates of the body
    standing wide.

A bear lumbering, I waddle into the fields of their work
    games.
We are stunted slaves mumbling over the tales
of dragons our masters tell us, but we will be free.
Our children will be free of us uncomprehending
as we of those shufflers in caves who scraped for fire
and banded together at last to hunt the saber-toothed
    tiger,
the tusked mastodon, the giant cave bear,
predators that had penned them up cowering so long.

---

[1]Among tribal peoples, a magician, medium and healer. The shaman derives
power from invisible forces or spirits that are thought to pervade the visible world;
some shamans have been women and male shamans often assumed female dress
and identity.

The sun is rising, feel it: the air smells fresh.
I cannot look in the sun's face, its brightness blinds me,
but from my own shadow becoming distinct
I know that now at last
it is beginning to grow light.

Judy Grahn
United States   *1940*

from The Common Woman
4. Carol, in the park, chewing on straws

> She has taken a woman lover
> whatever shall we do
> she has taken a woman lover
> how lucky it wasn't you.

And all the day through she smiles and lies
and grits her teeth and pretends to be shy,
or weak, or busy. Then she goes home
and pounds her own nails, makes her own
bets, and fixes her own car, with her friend.
She goes as far
as women can go without protection
from men.
On weekends, she dreams of becoming a tree;
a tree that dreams it is ground up
and sent to the paper factory, where it
lies helpless in sheets, until it dreams
of becoming a paper airplane, and rises
on its own current; where it turns into a
bird, a great coasting bird that dreams of becoming
more free, even, than that—a feather, finally, or
a piece of air with lightning in it.

> She has taken a woman lover
> whatever can we say.

She walks around all day
quietly, but underneath it
she's electric;
angry energy inside a passive form.
The common woman is as common
as a thunderstorm.

Susan Griffin
United States   *1943*

Song My

(Oh God, she said.)

It began a beautiful day by the sun up
And we sat in our grove of trees of smiles
Of morning eggs and toast and jam
and long talks, and baby babble
Becky sitting in her chair
spreading goo in her hair.

(Oh God, she said, look at the baby)

saying "hi" "ho" "ha" hi hi, goggydoggymamadada HI
and the light was coming through the window
through the handprints on the glass
making shadow patterns, and the cold day
was orange outside and they were muddling
in their underwear, getting dressed,
putting diapers on the baby,
slipping sandals on her feet.

(Oh God, she said, look at the baby)
He has blood all over, she cried)

Then the postman came,
And she went out on the steps
and got her magazine. They stood
by the stairs and looked, the baby
tugging at her skirt saying
mamamamama upupup mememe
and they looked at the pictures of Song My.

(Oh God, she said, look at the baby
He has blood all over, she cried,
Look at that woman's face, my God,
She knows she's going to get it.)

Going to get it, they knew
they were going to get it,

and it was a beautiful day,
the day that began in the fields
with the golden grain against the blue sky
the babies singing as if there were not
soldiers in the air.

Linda Gregg
United States   *contemporary*

Lilith[1]

I

The light is on my body also.
Even now when I am alone in the woods.
That is something they never tell you.
And I have always been alone.
Even when men found me and used me,
it never lasted. I knew lust
can be satisfied and I would be
returned to myself before long.
Would see everything as it was.
Dark trees, bright lights.
Speech only was lost.

II

I line up five stones on the ground.
I count them. I laugh
even though I am alone.
Remembering how the men never knew
how reasonable I am. Every day
I walk to the edge of the world
and look at the ocean.
And then return to my home.
It goes on like this.
They are afraid of the pain
they have given me. I made a dam

---

[1]According to some Apocryphel Hebrew texts, Lilith was created at the same time
as Adam. As she refused to subordinate herself to him, she was supplanted by Eve.
In later writings she appears as a legendary evil demon, satanic seducer of men.

in the creek today and then took
the stones away. I make a fire
to keep warm when it is necessary.
How can they think I am crazy?

III

A woman comes to my door and asks for bread.
It is winter. I look at her face
and recognize myself. I say: Lady, you hurt me
with your pain. She sings: Are you afraid
when the branches scrape the window panes?
Are you? Never has there been more agreement
between anyone. Go away, I say. Go away.
And slam the door. I fall down crying
for anything but woman to ease my suffering.
Death would be more kind. I open the door.
She is standing there with tears on her face,
just like before. Unsure whether to start again.

IV

Statuary used to fill the gardens of rich
and powerful men. At the end in Paris
they were of women. That is all gone now.
The wars came. Lists of dead were horrible.
I walk through the fields of rotting bodies
at evening to get a bucket of water
to carry back to the house on my head.
Gradually there will be gardens again.
First for food and then also for flowers.

Afro-American

Phillis Wheatley
West Africa/United States   *c. 1753–1784*

from To the Right Honourable William, Earl of Dartmouth, His Majesty's Principal Secretary of State for North America, &C.

No more, *America*, in mournful strain
Of wrongs, and grievance unredress'd complain,
No longer shalt thou dread the iron chain,
Which wanton *Tyranny* with lawless hand
Had made, and with it meant t' enslave the land.

Should you, my lord, while you peruse my song,
Wonder from whence my love of *Freedom* sprung,
Whence flow these wishes for the common good,
By feeling hearts alone best understood,
I, young in life, by seeming cruel fate
Was snatch'd from *Afric's* fancy'd happy seat:
What pangs excruciating must molest,
What sorrows labour in my parent's breast?
Steel'd was that soul and by no misery mov'd
That from a father seiz'd his babe belov'd:
Such, such my case. And can I then but pray
Others may never feel tyrannic sway?

Frances Harper
United States   *1825–1911*

Deliverance

And if any man should ask me
If I would sell my vote,
I'd tell him I was not the one
To change and turn my coat. . . .

But when John Thomas Reder brought
His wife some flour and meat,

And told her he had sold his vote,
For something good to eat,

You ought to see Aunt Kitty raise,
And heard her blaze away;
She gave the meat and flour a toss,
And said they should not stay. . . .

You'd laughed to seen Lucinda Grange
Upon her husband's track
When he sold his vote for rations
She made him take 'em back.

Day after day did Milly Green
Just follow after Joe,
And told him if he voted wrong
To take his rags and go.

I think that Curnel Johnson said
His side had won the day,
Had not we women radicals
Just got right in the way. . . .

Alice Dunbar Nelson
United States   1875–1935

I Sit and Sew

I sit and sew—a useless task it seems,
My hands grown tired, my head weighed down with
    dreams—
The panoply of war, the material tread of men,
Grim-faced, stern-eyed, gazing beyond the ken
Of lesser souls, whose eyes have not seen Death,
Nor learned to hold their lives but as a breath—
But—I must sit and sew.

I sit and sew—my heart aches with desire—
That pageant terrible, that fiercely pouring fire
On wasted fields, and writhing grotesque things
Once men. My soul in pity flings

Appealing cries, yearning only to go
There in that holocaust of hell, those fields of woe—
But—I must sit and sew.

The little useless seam, the idle patch;
Why dream I here beneath my homely thatch,
When there they lie in sodden mud and rain,
Pitifully calling me, the quick ones and the slain!
You need me, Christ! It is no roseate dream
That beckons me—this pretty futile seam,
It stifles me—God, must I sit and sew?

Margaret Walker
United States   *1915*

Childhood

When I was a child I knew red miners
dressed raggedly and wearing carbide lamps.
I saw them come down red hills to their camps
dyed with red dust from old Ishkooda mines.
Night after night I met them on the roads,
or on the streets in town I caught their glance;
the swing of dinner buckets in their hands,
and grumbling undermining all their words.

I also lived in low cotton country
where moonlight hovered over ripe haystacks,
or stumps of trees, and croppers' rotting shacks
with famine, terror, flood, and plague near by;
where sentiment and hatred still held sway
and only bitter land was washed away.

Alice Walker
United States   1944

Women

They were women then
My mamma's generation
Husky of voice—Stout of
Step
With fists as well as
Hands
How they battered down
Doors
And ironed
Starched white
Shirts
How they led
Armies
Headragged Generals
Across mined
Fields
Booby-trapped
Ditches
To discover books
Desks
A place for us
How they knew what we
Must know
Without knowing a page
Of it
Themselves.

June Jordan
United States   1936

Unemployment/Monologue

You can call me Herbie Jr. or Ashamah
Kazaam. It don't matter much. The thing
is you don' wan' my name you
wanna mug shot

young
black
male
who scares you chickenshit just
standin' on the street just lookin'
at you pass me by.
But I ain' doin' nothin' an'
you
know it an'
if you call me "Herbie" I don' mind
or "Junior"/that's all right
or "Ashamah Kazaam"/that's cool.
I say it don't really matter much
and then again/see
I may call you sweetmeat
I may call you tightass I might
one night I might break the windas
of the house you live in/I
might get tight and take your
wallet outasight/I might
hide out in the park to chase
you in the dark/etcetera/it
don' matter/I
may stay in school or quit
and I say
it
don' matter much
you
wanna mug shot
and the way I feel about it/well
so what?

you got it!

Gwendolyn Brooks
United States   1915

When You Have Forgotten Sunday: The Love Story

That the war would be over before they got to you;
—And when you have forgotten the bright bedclothes
  on a

Wednesday and a Saturday,
And most especially when you have forgotten Sunday—
When you have forgotten Sunday halves in bed,
Or me sitting on the front-room radiator in the limping
    afternoon
Looking off down the long street
To nowhere,
Hugged by my plain old wrapper of no-expectation
And nothing-I-have-to-do and I'm-happy-why?
And if-Monday-never-had-to-come-
When you have forgotten that, I say,
And how you swore, if somebody beeped the bell,
And how my heart played hopscotch if the telephone
    rang;
And how we finally went in to Sunday dinner,
That is to say, went across the front-room floor to the
    ink-spotted table in the southwest corner
To Sunday dinner, which was always chicken and
    noodles
Or chicken and rice
And salad and rye bread and tea
And chocolate chip cookies—
I say, when you have forgotten that,
When you have forgotten my little presentiment
And how we finally undressed and whipped out the
    light and
flowed into bed,
And lay loose-limbed for a moment in the week-end
Bright bedclothes,
Then gently folded into each other—
When you have, I say, forgotten all that,
Then you may tell,
Then I may believe
You have forgotten me well.

Sonia Sanchez
United States   1935

Present

this woman vomiten her
    hunger over the world
this melancholy woman forgotten
before memory came
    this yellow movement bursten forth like
Coltrane's[1] melodies all mouth
      buttocks moven like palm trees,
this honeycoatedalabamianwoman
raining rhythms of blue/blk/smiles
this yellow woman carryen beneath her breasts
    pleasures without tongues
    this woman whose body weaves
    desert patterns,
this woman, wet with wanderen,
reviven the beauty of forests and winds
is tellen u secrets
gather up yo odors and listen
as she sings the mold from memory

          there is no place

for a soft/blk/woman
there is no smile green enough or
summertime words warm enough to allow my growth
and in my head
i see my history
standen like a shy child
and i chant lullabies
as i ride my past on horseback
tasten the thirst of yesterday tribes
hearen the ancient/blk/woman
me singen hay – hay

    hay – hay – hay – ya – ya – ya
    hay – hay – hay
    hay – hay – ya – ya – ya

[1]John Coltrane (1926–1967): jazz tenor saxophonist.

          like a slow scent
beneath the sun

          and i dance my
creation and my grandmother's gatheren
from my bones like great wooden birds
spread their wings
while their long/legged/laughter
stretches the night.

          and i taste the

seasons of my birth. mangoes. papayas
drink my woman/coconut/milks
stalk the ancient grandfathers
sippen on proud afternoons
walk with a song round my waist
tremble like a new/born/child troubled
with new breaths
          and my singen
becomes the only sound of a
blue/blk/magical/woman. walken.
womb ripe. walken. loud with mornings. walken
maken pilgrimage to herself. walken.

Nikki Giovanni
United States   1943

They Clapped

they clapped when we landed
thinking africa was just an extension
of the black world
they smiled as we taxied home to be met
black to black face not understanding africans lack
color prejudice
they rushed to declare
cigarettes, money, allegiance to the mother land

not knowing despite having read fanon[1] and davenport[2]
hearing all of j.h. clarke's[3] lectures, supporting
nkrumah[4] in ghana and nigeria in the war that there was
    once
a tribe called afro-americans that populated the whole
of africa
they stopped running when they learned the packages
on the women's heads were heavy and that babies didn't
cry and disease is uncomfortable and that villages are
    fun
only because you knew the feel of good leather on good
pavement
they cried when they saw mercedes benz were as
    common
in lagos[5] as volkswagens are in berlin
they shook their heads when they understood there was
    no
difference between the french and the english and the
    americans
and the afro-americans or the tribe next door or the
    country
across the border
they were exasperated when they heard sly and the
    family stone[6]
in francophone[7] africa and they finally smiled when
little boys
who spoke no western tongue said "james brown"[8] with
    reverence
they brought out their cameras and bought out africa's
    drums

---

[1]Frantz Fanon (1925–61): French-educated writer, influential in the Algerian struggle for independence, author of the *The Wretched of the Earth;* calls for an anti-colonial revolution and advocates pride in the nonwhite heritage of colonized peoples.

[2]Benjamin Davenport: black writer whose work *Blood Will Tell* was originally published in 1902 as part of the Black Heritage Library.

[3]John Henrik Clarke (1915): writer, editor (*Harlem Quarterly*), and historian, whose books include *Marcus Garvey and the Vision of Africa.*

[4]Kwame Nkrumah (1909–1972): first president of modern Ghana.

[5]Capital of Nigeria:

[6]Sly and the Family Stone: a mainly black rock group popular in the late 60s and early 70s with both black and white audiences.

[7]French-speaking; connected with France by culture and colonial history.

[8]James Brown (1928): called "the King of Soul"; a rhythm-and-blues vocalist widely admired among blacks in the 50s and 60s, virtually unknown to white audiences until the late 60s.

when they finally realized they are strangers all over
and love is only and always about the lover not the
   beloved
they marveled at the beauty of the people and the
   richness
of the land knowing they could never possess either

they clapped when they took off
for home despite the dead
dream they saw a free future

Audre Lorde
United States   1934

Between Ourselves

Once when I walked into a room
my eyes would seek out the one or two black faces
for contact or reassurance or a sign
I was not alone
now walking into rooms full of black faces
that would destroy me for any difference
where shall my eyes look?
Once it was easy to know
who were my people.

If we were stripped of all pretense
to our strength
and our flesh was cut away
the sun would bleach all our bones
as white
as the face of my black mother
was bleached white by gold
or Orishala[1]
and how
does that measure me?

I do not believe

---

[1]Orishala: another name for Obatala, Yoruba god of creation. The worshippers
of Obatala must wear white cothes and eat white food.

our wants have made all our lies
holy.

Under the sun on the shores of Elmina[2]
a black man sold the woman who carried
my grandmother in her belly
he was paid with bright yellow coins
that shone in the evening sun
and in the faces of her sons and daughters.
When I see that brother behind my eyes
his irises are bloodless and without colour
his tongue clicks like yellow coins
tossed up on this shore
where we share the same corner
of an alien and corrupted heaven
and whenever I try to eat
the words
of easy blackness as salvation
I taste the colour
of my grandmother's first betrayal.

I do not believe
our wants
have made our lies
holy.

[2]Elmina: seaport town in south Ghana, founded by Portuguese traders, developed as a major gold-trading center.

Ntozake Shange
United States   1948

somebody almost walked off wid alla my stuff
not my poems or a dance i gave up in the street
but somebody almost walked off wid alla my stuff
like a kleptomaniac workin hard & forgettin while
    stealin
this is mine/ this aint yr stuff/
now why dont you put me back & let me hang out in my
    own self
somebody almost walked off wid alla my stuff

& didnt care enuf to send a note home saying
i was late for my solo conversation
or two sizes too small for my own tacky skirts
what can anybody do wit somethin of no value on
a open market/ did you getta dime for my things/
hey man/ where are you goin wid alla my stuff/
this is a woman's trip & i need my stuff/
to ohh & ahh abt/ daddy/ i gotta mainline number
from my own shit/ now wontchu put me back/ & let
me play this duet/ wit this silver ring in my nose/
honest to god/ somebody almost run off wit alla my
    stuff/
& i didnt bring anythin but the kick & sway of it
the perfect ass for my man & none of it is theirs
this is mine/ ntozake 'her own thing'/ that's my name/
now give me my stuff/ i see ya hidin my laugh/ & how i
sit wif my legs open sometimes/ to give my crotch
some sunlight/ & there goes my love my toes my chewed
up finger nails/ niggah/ wif the curlers in yr hair/
mr. louisiana hot link/ i want my stuff back/
my rhythms & my voice/ open my mouth/ & let me talk
    ya
outta/ throwin my shit in the sewar/ this is some delicate
leg & whimsical kiss/ i gotta have to give to my choice/
without you runnin off wit alla my shit/
now you cant have me less i give me away/ & i waz
doin all that/ til ya run off on a good thing/
who is this you left me wit/ some simple bitch
widda bad attitude/ i wants my things/
i want my arm wit the hot iron scar/ & my leg wit the
flea bite/ i want my calloused feet & quik language back
in my mouth/ fried plantains/ pineapple pear juice/
sun-ra[1] & joseph & jules/ i want my own things/ how i
    livcd them/
& give me my memories/ how i waz when i waz there/
you cant have them or do nothin wit them/
stealin my shit from me/ dont make it yrs/ makes it
    stolen/
somebody almost run off wit all my stuff/ & i waz
    standin
there/ lookin at myself/ the whole time
& it waznt a spirit took my stuff/ waz a man whose

---

[1]Contemporary jazz bandleader.

ego walked round like Rodan's shadow/waz a man
   faster
n my innocence/ waz a lover/ a niggah/ i made too much
room for/ almost run off wit alla my stuff/
& i didnt know i'd give it up so quik/ & the one running
   wit it/
dont know he got it/ & i'm shoutin this is mine/ & he
   dont
know he got it/ my stuff is the anonymous ripped off
   treasure
of the year/ did you know somebody almost got away
   with me/
me in a plastic bag under their arm/me
danglin on a string of personal carelessness/ i'm
   spattered wit
mud & city rain/ & no i didnt get a chance to take a
   douche/
hey man/ this is not your prerogative/ i gotta have me in
   my
pocket/ to get round like a good woman shd/ & make the
   poem
in the pot or the chicken in the dance/ what i got to do/
i gotta have my stuff to do it to/
why dont ya find yr own things/ & leave this package
of me for my destiny/ what ya got to get from me/
i'll give it to ya/ yeh/ i'll give it to ya/
round 5:00 in the winter/ when the sky is blue-red/
& Dew City is gettin pressed/ if it's really my stuff/
ya gotta give it to me/ if ya really want it/ i'm
the only one/ can handle it

Asian/Pacific American

Laureen Mar
United States   1953

**My Mother, Who Came from China,
Where She Never Saw Snow**

In the huge, rectangular room, the ceiling
a machinery of pipes and fluorescent lights,
ten rows of women hunch over machines,

their knees pressing against pedals
and hands pushing the shiny fabric thick as tongues
through metal and thread.
My mother bends her head to one of these machines.
Her hair is coarse and wiry, black as burnt scrub.
She wears glasses to shield her intense eyes.
A cone of orange thread spins. Around her,
talk flutters harshly in Toisan wah.[1]
Chemical stings. She pushes cloth
through a pounding needle, under, around, and out,
breaks thread with a snap against fingerbone, tooth.
Sleeve after sleeve, sleeve.
It is easy. The same piece.
For eight or nine hours, sixteen bundles maybe,
250 sleeves to ski coats, all the same.
It is easy, only once she's run the needle
through her hand. She earns money
by each piece, on a good day,
thirty dollars. Twenty-four years.
It is frightening how fast she works.
She and the women who were taught sewing
terms in English as Second Language.
Dull thunder passes through their fingers.

[1]Toisan wah: *wah* means language; Toisan is a region of Canton province.

Nellie Wong
United States   *1934*

How a Girl Got Her Chinese Name

On the first day of school the teacher asked me:
What do your parents call you at home?

I answered: Nellie.

Nellie? Nellie?
The teacher stressed the l's, whinnying like a horse.
No such name in Chinese for a name like Nellie.
We shall call you *Nah Lei*
which means *Where* or *Which Place.*

The teacher brushed my new name,
black on beige paper.
I practiced writing *Nah Lei*
holding the brush straight, dipping
the ink over and over.

After school I ran home.
Papa, Mama, the teacher says my name is *Nah Lei*.
I did not look my parents in the eye.

Nah Lei? Where? Which Place?
No, that will not do, my parents answered.
We shall give you a Chinese name,
we shall call you *Lai Oy*.

So back to shcool I ran,
announcing to my teacher and friends
that my name was no longer *Nah Lei,*
not *Where,* not *Which Place,*
but *Lai Oy, Beautiful Love,*
my own Chinese name.
I giggled as I thought:
Lai Oy could also mean *lost pocket*
depending on the heart
of a conversation.

But now in Chinese school
I was *Lai Oy,* to pull out of my pocket
every day, after American school,
even Saturday mornings,
from Nellie, from *Where,* from *Which Place*
to *Lai Oy,* to *Beautiful Love.*

Between these names
I never knew I would ever get lost.

Jessica Hagedorn
United States   *1949*

Listen

I am a thief
    your guardian angel
      who watches you

        watch out

This is the music of thieves
    dancing in the night

      chasing away murderers
        who haunt bedrooms
          and threaten my love

      watch out

I am a thief who smiles
    and invents words
      to sing with animals

I wear the hat of a thief
    and my wings are invisible

I am your guardian angel
    your most secret lie

I conjure up whistles and tears
    for your children

      trust me

I twist lyrics into melodies
    as gifts for my friends

      remember my smell
      in the streets
        of your cities

      and listen
      always listen
        to the silent air

Mitsuye Yamada
United States 1923

from **Camp Notes**
On the Bus

Who goes?
Not the leaders of the people
combed out and left
with the FBI.
Our father
stayed behind
triple locks.
What was the charge?
Possible espionage or
impossible espionage.
I forgot which . . .

Only those who remained
free in prisons
stayed behind.

The rest of us went to
Camp Harmony
where the first baby
was christened

Melody.

from **Camp Notes**
In the Outhouse

Our collective wastebin
where the air sticks
in my craw
burns my eyes
I have this place to hide
the excreta and
the blood which
do not flush down
nor seep away.

They pile up
fill the earth.

I am drowning.

Jonny Kyoko Sullivan

United States   *contemporary*

SAGIMUSUME: The White Heron Maiden

I am fixed in waiting
by these silks that bind me
and shorten my footsteps.

One suitor's laughter
breaks out harshly
flushing swallows from the trees
as we walk among the blossomings
of Mount Yoshino.

If the other places
his hand, tentatively,
on the small of my back,
I shudder
as if brushed by a web.

My mother scolds me,
tells me my heart is as uncontrollable
as the silk she works
into narrow pleats
for my skirts.

She says love is an umbrella
of oiled paper, spinning
round and round.
Finding it is as difficult
as collecting salt
from the salt-makers' fires
on Suma Beach.
She tells me I will suffer

for those admiring eyes
I do not answer.

But she does not know
the patience of my bones,
waiting,
for the hands like water
to unfasten me
and send these skirts
unravelling at my feet.

Janice Mirikitani
United States   contemporary

Sing with Your Body
—for my daughter, Tianne Tsukiko

We love with great difficulty
spinning in one place
afraid to create
                    spaces
                        new rhythm

the beat of a child
dangled by her own inner ear
takes Aretha with her

                        upstairs, somewhere
go quickly, Tsukiko,

                        into your circled dance
go quickly

                        before your steps are
                        halted by who you are not

go quickly

                        to learn the mixed
                        sounds of your tongue,

go quickly

                  to who you are

                  before

                            your mother swallows
                            what she has lost

Mei-Mei Berssenbrugge

United States   1947

Spring Street Bar

And last night a man came in
to tell her of stars and clouds moving fast
though the day itself had been dark and thick
when she tried to write to George, at first
without paper, which worked fine from Mercer Street
where bits of cloth and poisonous gas held letter
shapes well, but in the sheer air over his house
words ascended instead of entering the chimney
clearly marked by smoke. He was baking bread
with the yellow dog napping beside him
Each word rose on an updraft the hawk used, too
then dissolved among ghosts of indians and fish
when the poisons were flushed down by snow

She knew about ghosts and also the hawk
they had watched rise without moving at the edge
of the plain, until it was gone. Then she asked
could he still see it, to hear *yes* and watch
his blue eyes scan space. The trail to the ruin
had seemed to crumble under her feet. Handholds
pocked with braille instead of rain had warned her
So she took some paper and began as she used to
when there had been a sky, to write about the sky

Diana Chang
United States   contemporary

Cannibalism

When I put myself out on a saucer
  in the sun
    or moonlight
       of the back stoop
cats
in
the form of
images
come feeding

Chicana

Teresa Palma Acosta
United States   contemporary

My Mother Pieced Quilts

they were just meant as covers
in winter
as weapons
against pounding january winds

but it was just that every morning I awoke to these
october ripened canvases
passed my hand across their cloth faces
and began to wonder how you pieced
all these together
these strips of gentle communion cotton and flannel
  nightgowns
wedding organdies
dime store velvets

how you shaped patterns square and oblong and round
positioned
balanced

then cemented them
with your thread
a steel needle
a thimble

how the thread darted in and out
galloping along the frayed edges, tucking them in
as you did us at night
oh how you stretched and turned and re-arranged
your michigan spring faded curtain pieces
my father's santa fe work shirt
the summer denims, the tweeds of fall

in the evening you sat at your canvas
—our cracked linoleum floor the drawing board
me lounging on your arm
and you staking out the plan:
whether to put the lilac purple of easter against the red
    plaid of winter-going
into-spring
whether to mix a yellow with blue and white and paint
    the
corpus christi noon when my father held your hand
whether to shape a five-point star from the
somber black silk you wore to grandmother's funeral

you were the river current
carrying the roaring notes
forming them into pictures of a little boy reclining
a swallow flying
you were the caravan master at the reins
driving your threaded needle artillery across the mosaic
    cloth bridges
delivering yourself in separate testimonies.

oh mother you plunged me sobbing and laughing
into our past
into the river crossing at five
into the spinach fields
into the plainview cotton rows
into tuberculosis wards
into braids and muslin dresses
sewn hard and taut to withstand the thrashings of
    twenty-five years

stretched out they lay
armed/ready/shouting/celebrating

knotted with love
the quilts sing on

Ana Castillo
United States 1953

Napa, California
Dedicado al Sr. Chávez, Sept. 1975

We pick
       the bittersweet grapes
       at harvest
       one
           by
               one
       with leather worn hands
As they pick
       at our dignity
       and wipe our pride
       away
       like the sweat we wipe
       from our sun beaten brows
       at mid day
In fields
       so vast
       that our youth seems
       to pass before us
       and we have grown
       very
           very
               old
                    by dark . . .

(bueno pues ¿qué vamos hacer, Ambrosio?
bueno pues, ¡seguirle, compadre, seguirle!
¡Ay, Mamá!

Si pues ¿qué vamos hacer, compadre?
¡Seguirle, Ambrosio, seguirle!)[1]

We pick
        with a desire
        that only survival
        inspires
While the end
        of each day only brings
        a tired night
        that waits for the sun
        and the land
        that in turn waits
        for us . . .

[1]OK, well what we gonna do, Ambrosio?
OK, well stick with it, old pal, stick with it! [lit.: "follow him"]
Oh, mamá!
Yeah but what we gonna do, old pal?
Stick with it, Ambrosio, stick with it!

Alma Villanueva
United States   *1944*

I was always fascinated
with lights then,
with my hands
with my fingers
with my fingertips, because

if I squinted my eyes at them
lights sprayed off
burst off
and a joy burst inside me
and it felt good on my
eyes to see it, so

I squinted my eyes at
everything in this manner
and everything had joy

on it, in it. it was
my secret. only

my grandma knew. I knew
she knew by the way
she looked at things
long and slow and peaceful
and her face would shine, lights
all over, coming out of
her tiniest wrinkles;
she became a young girl.
there were things that could not
shine lights. we
avoided these. these things
had no joy
gave no joy. these things
took joy. these things
could make you old. I didn't
know it then, but

these things were death.

Lorna Dee Cervantes
United States   *1954*

Poem for the Young White Man Who Asked Me How I, an Intelligent, Well-Read Person, Could Believe in the War Between Races

In my land there are no distinctions.
The barbed wire politics of oppression
have been torn down long ago.
There are no boundaries. The only reminders
of past battles, lost or won, is the slight
rutting in the fertile fields.

In my land people write poems about love.
They dance on the rooftops, all
of their babies are fat, everyone reads
Russian short stories and weeps;
there are no colors; there is no race;

there are only hands
softly stroking thighs, only words
full of nothing but contented childlike syllables,
and the only hunger is a real hunger,
none of this complicated starving
of the soul from oppression.

I am not a revolutionary.
I don't even like political poems.
Do you think I can believe in a war between races?
I can deny it. I can forget about it
when I'm safe,
living on my own continent of harmony
and home, but I am not
there . . .

I believe in the revolution
because everywhere there is an enemy waiting,
sharp-shooting diplomats round every corner,
there are snipers in the schools . . .
(I know you don't believe this,
you think this is nothing
but faddish exaggeration, but
they are not shooting
at you!)
Their bullets are discrete and designed to kill slowly.
They are aimed at my children.
These are facts.
Let me show you my wounds: my stumbling mind, my
"excuse me" tongue, and this
nagging preoccupation
with the feeling of not being good enough.

These bullets bury deeper than logic.
Racism is not intelligence.
I can not reason these scars away.

Outside my door
there is a real enemy
who hates me.

I am a poet who yearns to dance on rooftops,
to whisper delicate lines about joy
and the blessings of human understanding.

I try. I go to my land, my tower of words and
shut the door, but the typewriter doesn't fade out
the sound of the blasting,
the screams, the muffled outrage . . .
My own days bring me slaps on the face.
Every day I am deluged with reminders
that this is not
my land.
I do not believe in a war between races

but in this country
there is war.

The Woman in My Notebook

The woman in my notebook
has escaped.

She is a prickly pear woman,
a thunder and spit
woman, a spiteful
woman.
She is armed.

She winks:
a dangerous
Harley Davidson
dried blood
grin.

She is a frightening woman
but she is the clasp
in my pointed
pocket book poor
life. She closes
and opens me.

I stop bending,
stop groveling around
in a spooked silence
when she

enters:
elegant as a ginko,
breathtaking—a tidepool
of lavender and crimson,
singing
with spikes.

She has broken the rules of poetry

and I find her now, a fine
power the color of goldenrods
in my hair, smudged across
my meek sweater, under my
breath. A fine
woman.

The woman I have always tried
to keep subdued

under lock
and ink.

Native American

MOST NATIVE AMERICAN POETS WRITING today are very much a part of the general culture of the United States, in experience, in language, and in specific literary training. They also write in the context of a cultural tradition that developed centuries before the coming of the Europeans and that transcends North American/Latin American distinctions. Specific Native American societies have differed greatly in almost every aspect of culture and social organization. Almost any generalization one could make, whether in regard to the role of women or the attitude toward song and myth, would be open to counter examples. What can be said with some accuracy is that tribal experience and values were originally transmitted orally, and the word was regarded as a spiritual link between the individual, the community, and the entire nonhuman world. With the impact of the Europeans, this oral tradition and the vision of the world it shaped were seriously disrupted. The written literature of Native peoples has in part been a history of the attempt to preserve—and create anew—a cultural tradition in the face of this disruption.

Most Native cultures share a respect for the word as embodied spirit. The forces that permeate the world may move and speak through the individual; and the poem that emerges is regarded as one's own, like the name bestowed on one in dream. It is also the poet's gift to the community, a channel through which the identity of the tribe is defined, affirmed, carried on. And magical as well as sacred, it holds power to transform the material world.

In both literate and oral Native cultures, the word has played a central part—as story and song—in the daily lives of the people. In fifteenth-century Mexico, the Aztec nobility often concluded their meals with poems sung to the accompaniment of musical instruments.[1] Among Eskimos, the communal feasting house was the focal point of village life, and song festivals were held there often lasting 14 to 16 hours. The Eskimo poet Orpingalik says, "It is as important for me to sing . . . , as it is to draw breath."[2]

When the Europeans arrived, Native peoples were confronted with an alien and incomprehensible way of being in the world. There was no way to speak to the violent presence of the invaders with any language they knew. In the early 1800s, Sequoyah, a Cherokee, concluded that lack of a written language contributed to the dangerous vulnerability of his people. He invented a syllabary and established a printing press and newspaper in a futile attempt to safeguard the lives and culture of his tribe. When whites discovered gold in the hills of Georgia the Cherokees were driven out, by presidential order, on the infamous Trail of Tears. Nor had literacy provided much protection to the Aztecs. In 1519 when the Spaniards first invaded Mexico, the Aztecs had a highly developed written literature. Most of this was lost during the Spaniards' systematic annihilation of the Aztecs as a political and cultural entity. What we know of that literature comes from the little that was preserved in manuscript, and from reconstructions, in Latin alphabet, of the great Aztec histories.

The Aztec and the Eskimo represent two instances of strong indigenous traditions about which, by historic chance, we have considerable information. Poetry was highly esteemed among the Aztecs. Officials and their families, including women, prided themselves on poetic achievement. At Texcoco, "where everything to do with fine language was particularly honoured," one of the four great councils of government was called the "Council of Music and the Sciences." It was responsible for encouraging poetry, and organized competitions at which the winners received prizes from the king. In addition to educated people among the nobility who wrote poetry, there were also professional poets officially connected with great men, whose work celebrated heroes, royal grandeur, and the transient delights of human life, with flowers and death appearing as constant motifs. Those who wanted to learn the arts of singing and music studied under these poets, or "song-crafters," in the "houses of song" (*cuicacalli*) that were attached to the palaces or supported by the districts.[3]

Since Aztec written literature was still young at the time of the Spanish conquest, poetry remained close to its oral roots. Poems were usually sung, and always accompanied by instruments— flutes, drums, and two-toned gongs. At the same time there was a sense of the high level of crafting involved, of the poem as precious artifact:

I chisel the jade, I pour gold in the crucible:
Here is my song!
I inlay the emeralds:
Here is my song.[4]

Women held considerable influence within clearly demarcated spheres of action. Royal power in Mexico seems to have originated with a woman, Ilancueitl; and fairly early women are mentioned as rulers, for instance at Tula. With the concentration of power in cities, women's influence and mobility diminished. They did retain the right to hold property and to transact business, indirectly at least, through itinerant traders. In certain professions, such as that of priestess, midwife, and healer, women had considerable independence. Another special group of women were the *auianime*, courtesans who accompanied the young warriors, and held an important place with them in religious ceremonies.[5] Women were also highly respected in their role as mothers:

> A woman who died in childbirth was upon the same footing as a warrior who died in battle or as a sacrifice. . . . It was said that . . . the sun took her with him because of her courage.[6]

Polygamy existed, especially among the upper classes, with no discrimination against secondary wives or their children. Women took part in the great poetic dramas, and some were themselves known as poets—among them the ""Lady of Tula," favorite concubine of the ruler Nezaualipilli,[7] and Macuilxochitl, daughter of Tlacaelel, who was counsellor to the first great ruler of the Aztecs, Itzcoatl.[8]

In many ways, Eskimo life as described in the 1920s by the Danish Eskimo explorer Knud Rasmussen was very different from that of the Aztecs. Aztec society was highly stratified; the wealth of the nobility, which gave them the leisure to devote to education and the arts, rested on the labor of large numbers of peasants. Eskimos on the other hand were hunters and markedly egalitarian; everyone shared in the harsh struggle for daily survival. And since the culture was oral, not literate, the creation of poetry was not limited to a trained elite; the breath of song was potential in every member of the community—women, men, even the children.

What the two cultures share is a strong sense of the immanence of spirit and the interrelatedness of all aspects of the created world. The Eskimo like the Aztec sees poetry as song, to be shared with the community through performance, with perhaps more sense of mystical inspiration, the inbreathing of spirit, in the process of creation. Eskimo poetry is also highly crafted. The oral poet labors long and with great care, often in solitude, to shape the words into a finished creation.[9]

Eskimos see the solid "thingness" of the poem, and the care that goes into its shaping, as akin to the objects and actions of daily life. The poet Kilimé says:

> Let me cleave words,
> sharp little words,
> like the fire-wood
> that I split with my axe.[10]

"Words (like snow, or bones, or reindeer skin) are part of the material environment." Perceived as both powerful and malleable, "they are carved at a distance from the self, thus preserving what the self would otherwise lose."[11]

The crafting is in the hands of the poet. But the initial inspiration is seen as awesome, mysterious. Kilimé says, "We do not know how songs arrive with our breath, in the form of words and music and not as ordinary speech."[12] Song often bursts forth under the influence of powerful emotion. When a meteor hurtled toward Uvavnuk from the night sky, permeating her with its light, a song poured out that henceforth evoked her powers as shaman. Orpingalik says:

> A person is moved like an ice-floe which drifts with the current. His thoughts are driven by a flowing force when he feels joy, when he feels fear, when he feels sorrow. Thoughts can surge in on him, causing him to gasp for breath, and making his heart beat faster. Something like a softening of the weather will keep him thawed. And then it will happen that we, who always think of ourselves as small, will feel even smaller. And we will hesitate before using words. But it will happen that the words that we need will come of themselves—
>
> When the words that we need shoot up of themselves—we have a new song.[13]

Anerca means both "breath" and "poetry"; and a song is regarded as belonging to the singer specifically. It is also communal and collective, both in performance and celebration, and in the attachment the village has to the songs made by its members. People delight in song competitions, which take place in the *qagshe* or feasting house. Performance involves a highly skilled integration of words, dance, drumming, and chorus; and people use every possible moment for practicing and perfecting. "One very rarely sees men or women at their work without their humming a song."[14]

Social roles among the Eskimos are fairly strictly defined: women sew and cook; men hunt. Consequently, women are ordinarily dependent upon men for survival. As Qernertoq describes, the life of a woman without husband or sons or brothers is harsh, without hope:

> Now I'm like a beast
> caught in the snare
> of my hut.
> Ijaja-ijaja.
>
> Long will be my journey
> on the earth.
> It seems as if
> I'll never get beyond
> the foot-prints that I make
>
>   * * * *
>
> A worthless amulet
> is all my property:
> while the northern light
> dances its sparkling steps
> in the sky.
>   —*from "The Widow's Song"*[15]

Women as well as men were poets. And women could become shamans—the seers, makers of magic, spiritual guides. The two realms come together. Shamans were often powerful poets; and all poets were to some extent workers of magic in their capturing and transforming of the world through words. In a song celebrating the bringing of food to a starving village, Tutlik (an Iglulik Eskimo woman) is both hallucinating with hunger and working magic to make the very earth participate in the ecstatic joy of the singer:

> Joy has distorted
> everything in sight:
> the leather boats lift themselves
> away from their ropes,
> the straps follow them,
> the earth itself
> floats freely in the air!
> Aj-ja-japapé.
>   —*from "Dancing Song"*[16]

As Orpingalik says:

> No one can become a poet who has not complete faith in the
> power of words. . . . The singer's faith in the power of words
> should be so enormous that he should be capable of *believing*
> that a piece of dry wood could bleed, could shed warm, red
> blood—wood, the driest thing there is.[17]

Within the United States the place of women varied from tribe to
tribe. At one extreme, among the Kwakiutl of the Northwest
women are regarded as one more object to possess. Two meta-
phorical expressions for marriage in the Kwakiutl language are "to
make war on the princess" and "to try to get a slave."[18] Among the
Navajos, on the other hand, each pole of the traditional hogan
carries the name of a female deity; literally, the support of the
home depends on the female. Perhaps the best known example of
women's role in tribal government comes from the Iroquois Great
Law of Peace:

> The lineal descent of the people of the Five Nations shall run in
> the female line. Women shall be considered the progenitors of
> the nation. They shall own the land and the soil. Men and
> women shall follow the status of their mothers. You are what
> your mother is; the ways in which you see the world and all
> things in it are through your mother's eyes. What you learn
> from the father comes later and is of a different sort. The
> chain of culture is the chain of women linking the past with the
> future.

> As litany in every calling together of the Longhouse Iroquois
> people, these words are said in order to recall the original
> instructions given to humans at the time of our creation:

> "We turn our attention now to the senior women, the Clan
> Mothers. Each nation assigns them certain duties. For the
> People of the Longhouse, the Clan Mothers and their sisters
> select the chiefs and remove them from office when they fail
> the people. The Clan Mothers are the custodians of the land,
> and always think of the unborn generations. They represent
> life and the earth. Clan Mothers! You gave us life—continue
> now to place our feet on the right path."[19]

Women's influence diminished as the fabric of tribal organization was weakened progressively during the nineteenth century.
First through treaties made and broken by white settlers, then

increasingly through laws and presidential decrees,[20] tribes were driven from the lands that had provided traditional livelihood and crucial spiritual symbolism. The Cherokees, an agricultural people, were driven first into the desolate red hills of Georgia, then into the dry plains of the midwest. Plains tribes were confined to an increasingly small area below the Arkansas River, which made it impossible to feed their people by hunting the buffalo; those who survived were pressured to take up farming on individual plots, a way of life wholly incompatible with those tribes' traditional social structure and sacred vision.[21]

Religious practices viewed as dangerous by whites were outlawed, such as the Sun Dance, central to the spiritual and cultural identity of the Sioux tribes, and the new Ghost Dance religion to which many Plains Indians had turned in hope of restoring the buffalo and the way of life they had made possible.[22] This hope was completely destroyed with the massacre of Indians at Wounded Knee in 1890. Resistance was no longer possible. "By 1910 the government estimated that 210 thousand Indians were left of the 10 to 15 million people who were natives of America when Europe first made contact with the New World at the end of the fifteenth century."[23]

Physical and material attacks on traditional life were closely connected with increasingly difficult cultural survival. By the end of the century Indian children were forcibly removed from their tribes to white-run boarding schools where they were punished for speaking their native languages,[24] with the result that the younger generation was often cut off from its tribal roots. Some male Native American writers of the nineteenth century, feeling understandably that assimilation to white society represented the only possibility of survival, wrote of the Native experience from a distance, as if through white eyes. Others, now educated in English but deeply concerned for the preservation of Native culture, began to put the myths, songs, and history of their people into writing. Among the first narratives by women are Sarah Winnemucca Hopkins' *Life Among the Piutes*, written in 1883, and *Old Indian Legends* (1901) by Zitkala-Sa, a Dakota Sioux woman. In her preface, Zitkala-Sa writes, "I have tried to transplant the native spirit of these tales—root and all—into the English language since America in the last few centuries has acquired a second tongue."[25]

Contemporary Native writers are for the most part born into the English language, certainly educated in it. They often hold graduate degrees in creative writing from the same schools and writing workshops as Anglo writers. They frequently find themselves pulled between their identity as "poet," writing out of the universal human experience, and their affirmation of their identity as Native American—or more specifically, as Hopi or Ojibwe or Laguna Pueblo. Most of the contemporary poets included here are teaching in colleges and universities; several have received prestigious national literary prizes and recognition. Yet most are determined not simply to disappear into the Euro-American mainstream, but rather to redefine that mainstream to include a wider perspective in which their distinct voices can be heard.

This is difficult when gaining a general audience means being published in mainstream journals. Nonwhite poets face unspoken pressure to censor their work, to shift style and tone down meaning lest the poem be dismissed as "unpoetic" by Euro-American standards. Before the creation of strong Third World journals and anthologies, when poets spoke out singly, the pressure was severe. There were strict criteria for "good poetry"; a Native poet speaking in any other voice would be heard, if at all, only by ethnographers.

Tekahionwake (E. Pauline Johnson) (1869–1913) wrote at a time when it seemed necessary to distort and deny one's voice. To be taken seriously as a poet she had to adopt a language and voice which were not natively hers—the English language, and the cumbersome apparel of Tennysonian symmetry and sentiment. As the poem "The Cattle Thief" shows, she was keenly aware of the danger implicit in the fact that while Indians were forced to be bilingual, white culture was not. Whites cannot understand the "language of the Cree," and can see the Indian only through stereotypes that are literally deadly. Tekahionwake turns this distorted perspective inside out, and uses it to speak against the attempted destruction of Native society. Despite the fact that the voice she was forced to borrow is alien to her own, and difficult for us now, she stands as a powerful example of the protest and reaffirmation which inspire Native women today.[26]

Deirdre Lashgari

Notes and References

[1]Jacques Soustelle, *Daily Life of the Aztecs on the Eve of the Spanish Conquest* (Menlo Park, Ca: Stanford Univ. Press, 1961), 158. After meals the well-to-do class "loved . . . to hear poems recited or sung to the accompaniment of flutes, drums and two-toned gongs *(teponaztli)*. The guests themselves danced to the sound of these instruments, after the feast."

[2]Tom Lowenstein, *Eskimo Poets of Canada and Greenland*, ed. and tr. from

material originally collected by Knud Rasmussen (Pittsburgh: Univ. of Pittsburgh Press, 1973), xvii, pp. 102, 105, 146.

[3]Soustelle, *Daily Life*, 236 (quoting from Ixtlilxochitl, *Relaciones*, in Torquemada, vol. I, 146–147).

[4]Ibid., 236 (quoting from Garibay, *Historia de la literatura nahuatl*, p. 66). Translated by Jacques Soustelle.

[5]Ibid., 183–184.

[6]Ibid., pp. 190–191.

[7]Ibid., pp. 240.

[8]Macuilxochitl was born around 1435 in Tenochtitlan, which was an important commercial center. As the daughter of a noble during the Aztec golden age, she was probably well-educated, and was certainly highly trained in the craft of poetry. She seems to have taken an interest in the political activities of her father; the poem excerpted here celebrates a victory of Axayacatzin, whom her father counselled in battle. Cf. Leon-Portilla, *Trece poetas del mundo azteca* (Thirteen poets of the Aztec World) (Mexico, D.F.: Universidad Nacional Autonoma de Mexico, Instituto de Investigaciones Historicas, 1967).

[9]Lowenstein, *Eskimo Poets*, pp. 121, 146 (notes from Rasmussen's *Report of the Fifth Thule Expedition*).

[10]Ibid., p. xxi, excerpt from "The Abduction."

[11]Ibid., p. xxii.

[12]Ibid., p. xix.

[13]Ibid., p. xxiii.

[14]Ibid., p. 146.

[15]Ibid., p. 19–20.

[16]Ibid., p. 29.

[17]Ibid., p. 128.

[18]Margot Astrov, "Introduction" to *American Indian Prose and Poetry*, ed. Margot Astrov (Toronto: Longmans, 1962), p. 6.

[19]Shirley Hill Witt, "The Brave-Hearted Women," *Civil Rights Digest*, 8, No. 4 (Summer 1976), 39. See also Valerie Shirer Mathes, "A New Look at the Role of Women in Indian Society," American Indian Quarterly, 2, No. 2 (Summer 1975), 121–130, and John and Donna Terrell, *Indian Women of the Western Morning: Their Life in Early America* (New York: Dial Press, 1974), p. 27.

[20]For example, "the Indian Removal Act of 1830, under the direction of the Bureau of Indian Affairs (BIA) established in 1824, ordered the eviction of almost all Indians east of the Mississippi into the lands of the West. . . . Reservations were established in 1851, replacing the policy of removal, and in 1879 the first off-reservation school for Indians opened. . . ." See Dexter Fisher's introduction to the Native American section of her valuable anthology *The Third Woman: Minority Woman Writers of the United States* (Boston: Houghton Mifflin, 1979).

[21]Dee Brown, *Bury My Heart at Wounded Knee: An Indian History of the American West* (New York: Harper and Row, 1971).

[22]For a complete analysis of the religion and its outcome, see James

Mooney, *The Ghost Dance Religion and the Sioux Outbreak of 1890* (Chicago: Univ. of Chicago Press, 1965; originally published as Part 2 of the Fourteenth Annual Report of the Bureau of Ethnology to the Secretary of the Smithsonian Institution, 1892–1893).

[23]Fisher, *The Third Woman.*

[24]A friend has told me how her grandmother, later a medicine woman and council elder of the Ojibwe Turtle Clan, twice as a child ran away from BIA boarding school several hundred miles back to her family.

[25]Zitkala-Sa, *Old Indian Legends* (Boston: Ginn, 1901). At the time of Columbus's first contact with the New World, Native Americans spoke over four hundred different languages, which derived from at least seven language families, each as complex as Indo-European. With few exceptions, the language of American Indian literature is English because this is the first written language that Indians learned.

[26]I am indebted to Dexter Fisher, Robin Lakoff, and Wendy Rose for their valuable suggestions in response to an earlier version of this essay.

Tekahionwake (E. Pauline Johnson)

Canada: Mohawk 1869–1913

The Cattle Thief

They were coming across the prairie, they were gallop-
ing hard and fast;
For the eyes of those desperate riders had sighted their
man at last—
Sighted him off to Eastward, where the Cree encamp-
ment lay,
Where the cotton woods fringed the river, miles and
miles away.
Mistake him? Never! Mistake him? the famous Eagle
Chief!
That terror to all the settlers, that desperate Cattle
Thief—
That monstrous, fearless Indian, who lorded it over the
plain,
Who thieved and raided, and scouted, who rode like a
hurricane!
But they've tracked him across the prairie; they've fol-
lowed him hard and fast;
For those desperate English settlers have sighted their
man at last.

Up they wheeled to the tepees, all their British blood
aflame,
Bent on bullets and bloodshed, bent on bringing down
their game;
But they searched in vain for the Cattle Thief: that lion
had left his lair,
And they cursed like a troop of demons—for the
women alone were there.
"The sneaking Indian coward," they hissed; "he hides
while yet he can;
He'll come in the night for cattle, but he's scared to face
a *man*."
"Never!" and up from the cotton woods rang the voice
of Eagle Chief;
And right out into the open stepped, unarmed, the
Cattle Thief.
Was that the game they had coveted? Scarce fifty years
had rolled

Over that fleshless, hungry frame, starved to the bone
and old;
Over that wrinkled, tawny skin, unfed by the warmth of
blood.
Over those hungry, hollow eyes that glared for the sight
of food.
He turned, like a hunted lion: "I know not fear," said
he;
And the words outleapt from his shrunken lips in the
language of the Cree.
"I'll fight you, white-skins, one by one, till I kill you *all*,"
he said;
But the threat was scarcely uttered, ere a dozen balls of
lead
Whizzed through the air about him like a shower of
metal rain,
And the gaunt old Indian Cattle Thief dropped dead on
the open plain.
And that band of cursing settlers gave one triumphant
yell,
And rushed like a pack of demons on the body that
writhed and fell.
"Cut the fiend up into inches, throw his carcass on the
plain;
Let the wolves eat the cursed Indian, he'd have treated
us the same."
A dozen hands responded, a dozen knives gleamed
high,
But the first stroke was arrested by a woman's strange,
wild cry.
And out into the open, with a courage past belief,
She dashed, and spread her blanket o'er the corpse of
the Cattle Thief;
And the words outleapt from her shrunken lips in the
language of the Cree,
"If you mean to touch that body, you must cut your way
through *me*."
And that band of cursing settlers dropped backward
one by one,
For they knew that an Indian woman roused, was a
woman to let alone.
And then she raved in a frenzy that they scarcely
understood,

Raved of the wrongs she had suffered since her earliest
babyhood:
"Stand back, stand back, you white-skins, touch that
dead man to your shame;
You have stolen my father's spirit, but his body I only
claim.
You have killed him, but you shall not dare to touch him
now he's dead.
You have cursed, and called him a Cattle Thief, though
you robbed him first of bread—
Robbed him and robbed my people—look there, at that
shrunken face,
Starved with a hollow hunger, we owe to you and your
race.
What have you left to us of land, what have you left of
game,
What have you brought but evil, and curses since you
came?
How have you paid us for our game? how paid us for
our land?
By a *book*, to save our souls from the sins *you* brought in
your other hand.
Go back with your new religion, we never have
understood
Your robbing an Indian's *body*, and mocking his *soul* with
food.
Go back with your new religion, and find—if find you
can—
The *honest* man you have ever made from out a *starving*
man
You say your cattle are not ours, your meat is not our
meat;
When *you* pay for the land you live in, *we'll* pay for the
meat we eat.
Give back our land and our country, give back our herds
of game;
Give back the furs and the forests that were ours before
you came;
Give back the peace and the plenty. Then come with
your new belief,
And blame, if you dare, the hunger that *drove* him to be
a thief."

Macuilxochitl

Aztec   1435–late 15th cent.

Battle Song

I lift my songs
I, Macuilxochitl
to please the Giver of Life.
Let the dance begin!

Will my songs
be borne to his house
where he dwells in mystery?
Or do thy flowers bloom
here only?
Let the dance begin!

The hero of Matlatzinco
is the best of your people, Lord Itzcoatl:
Axayácatzin, you conquered
the city of Tlacotépec!
There your flowers whirled,
your butterflies.
With this you gave gladness.
The hero of Matlatzinco
is in Toluca, in Tlacotépec.

Slowly he makes offering,
gives flowers and feathers
to the Giver of Life,
places the eagle shields
on the arms of his men,
there on the plains,
there where war is burning,
Like our songs,
like our flowers,
even so, warrior of the shaven head,
you also give pleasure
to the Giver of Life.

The eagle flowers
are in your hands,

Lord Axayácatl.
With divine flowers,
with the flowers of war
he is covered,
he grows drunk with them,
he who is at our side.

The flowers of war
are opening above us
in Ehacatépec, in México,
he grows drunk with them,
he who is at our side.[1]

Translated from the Nahuatl by Miguel León-Portilla; English version by Catherine Rodriguez-Nieto.

[1]Excerpted from a much longer poem

Maria Sabina
Mexico: Mazatec   *1894*

Shaman[1]

I am the woman of the principal fountain
I am the woman of the fountain of the sea
I am a river woman
the woman of the flowing water

I am a woman of clarity
a woman of the day
because I am a woman who lightnings
a woman who thunders
a woman who shouts
a woman who whistles

hummingbird woman, it says
woman who has sprouted wings, it says
thus do I descend primordial
thus do I descend significant

[1]Among tribal peoples, a magician, medium and healer. Shamans derive their power from invisible forces or spirits that are thought to pervade the visible world; many shamans have been women.

I descend with tenderness
I descend with dew.[2]

Translated from the Spanish by Henry Munn

[2]Excerpted from a long oral poem composed in a state of trance.

Kibkarjuk

Canada: Caribou Eskimo   fl. c. 1920

Song of the Rejected Woman

Inland,
far inland go my thoughts,
my mournful thoughts.
To never leave the woman's bench
is too much to endure:
I want to wander inland,
far inland.
  Ija-je-ja.

My thoughts return
to hunting:
animals, delightful food!
To never leave the woman's bench
is too much to endure:
I want to wander inland,
far inland.
  Ija-je-ja.

I hunted like the men:
I carried weapons,
shot a reindeer bull,
a reindeer cow and calf,
yes, slew them with my arrows,
with my arrows,
one evening toward winter,
as the sky-dusk fell
far inland.
  Ija-je-ja.

This is what I think about,
this is what I struggle with,
while inland, under falling snow,
the earth turns white,
far inland.
      Ija-je-ja.

Translated by Tom Lowenstein from material originally collected and published
in Danish by Knud Rasmussen

Akjartoq
Canada: Caribou Eskimo   *fl. c. 1920*

An Old Woman's Song

Alas, I draw breath heavily,
my lungs breathe heavily,
as I call for my song.

When the news arrived
of far-off friends,
starving for winter game,
I wanted to sing:
to invoke the words from above,
the music from above.
Hajaja!

I forget the fire in my chest,
and the wheeze of the lungs
while I sing,
and I remember the old times
when I was strong.

These were times
when no-one rivalled me
at flensing seal;
when all alone, I boned and cut
the lean flesh
of three great reindeer-bulls
for drying!

Look: delicious slices
spread out on the mountain-stones,
while the sun rides up the sky
in the cool morning,
in the cool morning!

Translated by Tom Lowenstein from material originally collected and published
in Danish by Knud Rasmussen.

Uvavnuk
Canada: Iglulik Eskimo   fl. c. 1920

A Woman Shaman's Song

The great sea stirs me.
The great sea sets me adrift.
It sways me like the weed
on a river stone.

The sky's height stirs me.
The strong wind blows through my mind.
It carries me with it,
so I shake with joy.

Translated by Tom Lowenstein from material originally collected and published
in Danish by Knud Rasmussen

Jane Green
Canada: Ojibwe (Chippewa)   c. 1940

Songs of Divorce

I guess you love me now.
I guess you admire me now.
You threw me away like something that tasted bad.
You treat me as if I were a rotten fish.

I thought you were good at first.

I thought you were like silver and I find you are like
    lead.
You see me high up.
I walk through the sun.
I am like the sunlight myself.

Translated from the Ojibwe by Frances Densmore

Roberta Hill
United States   *1947*

Leap in the Dark

> *The experience of truth is indispensable for*
> *the experience of beauty and the sense of*
> *beauty is guided by a leap in the dark.*
>
> —ARTHUR KOESTLER

I

Stoplights edged the licorice street with ribbon,
neon embroidering wet sidewalks. She turned

into the driveway and leaped in the dark. A blackbird
perched on the bouncing twig of a maple, heard

her whisper, "Stranger, lover, the lost days arc over.
While I walk from car to door, something inward opens

like four o'clocks in rain. Earth, cold from autumn,
pulls me; I can't breathe the same

with dirt for marrow and mist for skin
blurring my vision, my vision's separate self.

I stand drunk in this glitter, under the sky's grey shelter.
The city maple, not half so bitter, hurls itself

in two directions, until both tips darken and disappear,
as I darken my reflection in the smoking mirror

of my home. How faint the sound of dry leaves,

like the clattering keys of another morning, another
   world."

II

She looked out the window at some inward greying
   door.
The maple held her glance, made ground fog from her
   cigarette.

Beyond uneven stairs, children screamed,
gunned each other down. Then she sealed her nimble
   dreams

with water from a murky bay. "For him I map
this galaxy of dust that turns without an answer.

When it rains, I remember his face in the corridor
of a past apartment and trace the anguish around his
   mouth,

his wrinkled forehead, unguarded eyes, the foreign
   fruit
of an intricate sadness. With the grace that remains,

I catch a glint around a door I cannot enter.
The clock echoes in dishtowels; I search love's center

and bang pans against the rubble of my day, the lucid
grandeur of wet ground, the strangeness of a fatal sun

that makes us mark on the margin of our loss,
trust in the gossamer of touch, trust in the late-plowed
   field."

III

When the sun opened clouds and walked into her
   mongrel soul,
she chopped celery into rocky remnants of the sea,

and heard fat sing up bread, a better dying.
The magnet in each seed of the green pepper kept her
   flying,

floating toward memories that throb like clustered stars:
the dark water laughter of ducks, a tangle of November
 oaks,

toward sudden music on a wheel of brilliant dust
where like a moon she must leap back and forth

from emptiness. "I remember the moon shimmering
loss and discovery along a water edge, and skirting

a slice of carrot, I welcome eternity in that eye of
 autumn.
Rare and real, I dance while vegetables sing in pairs.

I hug my death, my chorus of years, and search
and stretch and leap, for I will be apprentice to the
 blood

in spite of the mood of a world
that keeps rusting, rusting the wild throats of birds."

IV

In lamplight she saw the smoke of another's dream:
her daughter walk woods where snow weighs down the
 pine,

her son cry on a bridge that ends in deep-rooted dark,
her man, stalled on a lonely road, realize his torque

was alcohol and hatred. "Hungry for silence, I listen
to wind, the sound of water running down mountain,

my own raw breath. Between the sounds, a seaborn god
plays his reed in the caverns of my being.

I wear his amethyst, let go my dreams: millers,
 lacewings,
and junebugs scatter, widen and batter the dark,

brightening this loud dust with the fever of their eyes.
Oh crazy itch that grabs us beyond loss

and lets us forgive, so that we can answer birds and deer,
lightning and rain, shadow and hurricane.

Truth waits in the creek, cutting the winter brown hills:
it sings of its needles of ice, sings because of the scars."

Leslie Marmon Silko
United States   1948

Where Mountain Lion Lay Down with Deer
February 1973

I climb the black rock mountain
    stepping from day to day

                    silently.
I smell the wind for my ancestors
      pale blue leaves
        crushed wild mountain smell.
Returning
    up the gray stone cliff
    where I descended

              a thousand years ago.
Returning to faded black stone
where mountain lion lay down with deer.
It is better to stay up here
           watching wind's reflection
              in tall yellow flowers.
The old ones who remember me are gone
           the old songs are all forgotten
and the story of my birth.
How I danced in snow-frost moonlight
         distant stars to the end of Earth,
How I swam away
         in freezing mountain water
      narrow mossy canyon tumbling down
           out of the mountain
          out of deep canyon stone
              down
           the memory
           spilling out
         into the world.

Wendy Rose
United States   1948

I Expected My Skin and My Blood to Ripen

> *"When the blizzard subsided four days later*
> *(after the massacre), a burial party was sent*
> *to Wounded Knee. A long trench was dug.*
> *Many of the bodies were stripped by whites*
> *who went out in order to get the ghost shirts*
> *and other accoutrements the Indians*
> *wore . . . the frozen bodies were thrown into*
> *the trench stiff and naked . . . only a handful*
> *of items remain in private hands . . . exposure*
> *to snow has stiffened the leggings and moc-*
> *casins, and all the objects show the effects of*
> *age and long use . . . " There follows: moc-*
> *casins at $140, hide scraper at $350,*
> *buckskin shirt at $1200, woman's leggings at*
> *$275, bone breastplate at $1000.*
>
> —*Plains Indian Art: Sales Catalog, 1977*

I expected my skin and my blood
to ripen
not be ripped from my bones;
like green fruit I am peeled
tasted, discarded; my seeds are stepped on
and crushed
as if there were no future. Now
there has been
no past.   My own body gave up the beads
my own arms handed the babies away
to be strung on bayonets, to be counted
one by one like rosary stones and then
to be tossed to each side of life
as if the pain of their borning
had never been.
My feet were frozen to the leather,
pried apart, left behind—bits of flesh
on the moccasins, bits of papery deerhide
on the bones. My back was stripped
of its cover, its quilling intact; was torn,
was taken away, was restored.

My leggings were taken like in a rape
and shriveled to the size of stick figures
like they had never felt
the push of my strong woman's body
walking in the hills.
It was my own baby whose cradleboard I held,
would've put her in my mouth
like a snake
if I could, would've turned her
into a bush or old rock
if there'd been enough magic
to work such changes. Not enough magic
even to stop the bullets.
Not enough magic
to stop the scientists.
Not enough magic
to stop the collectors.

Marnie Walsh
United States   contemporary

Thomas Iron-Eyes
Born circa 1840.
Died 1919, Rosebud Agency, S.D.

I

I woke before the day, when the night bird
Knocked three times upon my door
To warn the Other Sleep was coming.
By candlelight I painted the two broad stripes
Of white across my forehead, the three scarlet spots
Upon my cheek. I greased well my braids
With sour fat from the cooking pot, then tied them
With a bit of bright string saved for the occasion.
From the trunk I took the dress of ceremony,
The breechclout and the elkskin shirt,
The smoke of their breaths strong in my nose;
Smoke not of this time, this life or place,
But of my youth, of the many lodges I dwelt within;
The pony raids, the counting coup;

The smell of grass when it first was green,
And the smell of coming snows, when food was plentiful
Within the camp, and ice crept over the rivers.
Carefully I put on the dress, then the leggings with
　scalps,
As thin now and as colorless as the hair
Of sickly animals, sinew-tied along the seams;
And on my feet the red-beaded moccasins
Worn by none but the bravest of warriors.
I lie here, waiting, my dry bones and ancient skin
Holding my old heart.
The daystar finds me ready for my journey.

II

Another time, another life, another place,
My people would have wrapped me in deerskin,
Sewed me in the finest of furs;
Then borne me in honor to the cottonwood bier,
Laying at my right hand the sacred pipe,
And at my left the arrows and bow, the lance
I long ago bound with thongs and hung
With the feathers from the eagles breast.
Below the scaffold of the dead
My pony of the speckled skin and fierce heart
Would be led, and with a blow of the stone ax
Upon his skull, lie down to wait my need.
I would know that far above
In the sacred hoop of the sky
Long-sighted hawks, hanging on silent wings,
Marked my passage.

III

When the Life-Giver hid from the night,
The dark wind would speak to my spirit
And I would arise, taking up my weapons.
Mounting my horse I would follow
The great path over the earth,
The road leading to the Old Grandfathers
Beyond the stars.
I would see the glow of their cooking fires
Bright as arrow tips across the northern sky;
Waiting for me, old friends dance and feast
And play the games of gambling.

Behind me drums would beat, and willow whistles cry
Like the doves of spring who nested
In the berry bushes near the river by my village.
I would pause to hear my sons in council
Speaking of my deeds in war, my strength and wisdom,
Praising me; knowing my women in their sorrow
Were tearing their clothing, their faces bloodied
And smeared with ashes.

IV

But I am Thomas. I am here,
Where no grass grows, no clear rivers run;
Where dirt and despair abound,
Where heat and rain alike rust out
The souls of my people, the roofs of tin;
Where hunger sits in the dooryards,
Where disease, like a serpent, slips from house to house.
I am Thomas, waiting for the wagon
To bring the government box of pine;
Waiting for the journey to the burying ground
Below sandy buttes where rattlesnakes
Stink in burrows, and the white man's wooden trinities
Stand in crooked rows.
There I shall be put beneath the earth.
There shall my spirit be sealed within
The planks of the coffin.
There I shall not hear the dark wind's cry
To come and ride the starry road
Across the holy circle of the sky.

Dolly Bird
United States   1950

Can I Say

And it's hard to see the mountains
when you're sitting in the subway
It's hard I said to feel the wind
When you're waiting in some welfare office
but I'm not a case, I'm not a number

I can do quillwork
Mister, I can ride with no
saddle and hey, listen
my brother with his own carved
arrows can stalk a deer.
Why? are you checking boxes
when I am trying to talk   no
I do not have outside income
but there is a tall
cottonwood I know and sometimes
I go to see the leaves and this
morning I heard a meadowlark
     when is the end . . . to die is not the end
     when is the end . . . to die is not the end.
he said, I made my ears like a fox stand
to hear and I never even go in
a bank so I got no account
There is an old man I heard
saying, "make moccasins . . ."
no he does not give me money, he
said to the people
"make moccasins for your children, it
is time to go" and I guess we are going
on the plains south where you are always facing
many winters wise. I want someday to bring
when the sun makes white sparks on
the creek like dancing fires, I
want to bring some *kinnikinnik* to him
he remembers the red willow smoke and a
buckskin bag and why do your eyes
say I tell lies?
I never been insane, I
never been in jail, I do not drink, I am not
an addict. I have no car, I do
not have syphilis or cavities, I did
have TB, I did drop out, and I
did get fired, I did not commit mail fraud, I
did not overthrow the government (lately)
with your pencil flying, mister,
can I say there is a good red road
and a sacred hoop of our people
which was broken but I would like
to help mend so the old man would
be happy. My brother

428 Women Poets of the World

brought fresh meat to him
but the old man says there is not
much time before he will feed the wolves
I want him to know that the
rivers run free—I do not have
a pen to sign here—the forests grow
tall, the plains—I was just in my mind
thinking mister during this investigation—
of the plains where the dirt is living
and wild horses disappear behind a hill,
I wanted to see the old man at dawn stand
on the living plains with his
horse near, see him raise his
arms to the sun, hear him say
"Thank you father"

                                                    . . . again

Paula Gunn Allen
United States   1939

Catching One Clear Thought Alive

Second-hand platitudes like antique watches
engraved with unreadable scrolled initials of another
    time, tick,
carry you from present to another place
in abstraction tempo, unmetronomed, untimed, not
yesterday, not this second, not of anyone's doing, but
counted, like implicit truths, left-overs from last night's
    faith.

You carry the seconds (hard) in your pocket
rolling time around in your hand like spare change:
listening to the click of days, of hours, of walks,
unattached, down morning streets.
And this is how you spend it, waiting for hope (bearded
and gold-chained like grandfather) to come to you, to
roll your mornings in flavored papers from the past, to
    give
taste to someone else's meanings, someone's words,
unspeakable in this place, this ungraspable time.

And hungry like Coyote in a gopherless land
(gone crazy in no time) you stalk time and incidence
as though they were a herd of grazing sheep you are
　circling,
watching for the one that is too small, too
weak, too separate to be kept safe in the fostering circle,
the living matrix of what is known; you watch
for the one too slow to stop your leap, your
teeth in time.

Anna Lee Walters
United States　1946

I Have Bowed Before the Sun

My name is "I am living."
My home is all directions and is everlasting.
Instructed and carried to you by the wind,
I have felt the feathers in pale clouds and bowed before
　the Sun
who watches me from a blanket of faded blue.
In a gentle whirlwind I was shaken,
made to see on earth in many ways.
And when in awe my mouth fell open,
I tasted a fine red clay.
Its flavor has remained after uncounted days.
This gave me cause to drink from a crystal stream
that only I have seen.
So I listened to all its flowing wisdom
and learned from it a Song—
This song the wind and I
have since sung together.
Unknowing, I was encircled by its water and cleansed.
Naked and damp, I was embraced and dried
by the warmth of your presence.
Dressed forever in the scent of dry cedar,
I am purified and free.
And I will not allow you to ignore me.
I have brought to you a gift.
It is all I have but it is yours.
You may reach out and enfold it.

It is only the strength in the caress of a gentle breeze,
But it will carry you to meet the eagle in the sky.
My name is "I am living." I am here.
My name is "I am living." I am here.

A Note on Names

China and Japan: The family name preceeds the given name, in both modern and traditional usage: e.g., in *Yosano Aikiko*, *Yosano* is the family name, *Aikiko* the given name. In Japanese where *no* occurs in a name, it corresponds to "of" followed by a place name: e.g., "Ono who lives in Komachi." *Shikibu* means "Lady"; we have used *Shikibu* or *Lady*, depending on the form in which the particular poet's name has most commonly appeared in this country.

India: Some poets are known by both given and diminutive forms of their names: e.g., Vidya (Vijjika); Mahadevi (Mahadeviyakka). Again, we use the form most common in sources published in English.

Arab World and Iran: For names in Arabic, we have used traditional transliteration, but without diacritical marks. Iranian names are transcribed rather than transliterated, so as to indicate actual pronunciation in Farsi, which differs from Arabic. (An exception occurs when the names of Iranian or Farsi-speaking Indian poets are Arabic in form; then we have made concessions to customary Arabic transliteration: e.g., Qorratu'l-Ayn and Zibu'n-Nisa (Makhfi). Poets known primarily by the name they took as writers (e.g., Makhfi, "The Hidden") are listed by that name. Until the modern period (around 50 years ago, when birth certificates and family names began to be required by central governments), most people were known by given name, followed by father's or mother's given name and/or the place with which they were associated (e.g., Aisha bint Ahmad al-Qurtubiyya, or "Aisha daughter of Ahmad of Cordoba").

Israel: Rachel and Zelda are alphabetized under their given names, since this is how they are known and published as poets.

Medieval Europe: Here too, the poets were usually known by their given names, with frequent addition of the place with which they were associated (e.g., Gandersheim, Pisan). With Bertha Jacobs we begin to find increasing use of the modern family-name form. Compiuta Donzella is a poet known only by her epithet "Accomplished Lady."

Spanish: In the case of compound family names, the first part of the compound is the name by which the person is known (e.g., Gertrudis *Gomez* de Avellaneda).

Index of Authors

*Asterisks indicate authors of introductory essays;
italicized numbers indicate mention of author in introductions or notes.

Åkesson, Sonja, *217*, 251–253
Abu Khalid, Fawziyya, 107–108
Adam, Helen, 266–269
Adnan, Etel, 102–105
Aidoo, Ama Ata, *276*, 295–298
Aisha bint Ahmad al-Qurtubiyya, 97
Akazome Emon, 39
Akhmadulina, Bella, 223–224
Akhmatova, Anna, *1*, *213*, *216–217*, 219–220
Akjartoq, 417–418
Allen, Paula Gunn, 428–429
Ambapali, 53
Amiri, Akhtar, 85–87
Andresen, Sophia de Mello Breyner, 258–259
Anghelaki-Rooke, Katerina, 255–256
Anonymous (Chinese), 28
Atimantiyar, 54
Atwood, Margaret, 350–351
Augustini, Delmira, *300–301*, 305–307
Auvaiyar, 54–55

Bachmann, Ingeborg, *217*, 242–244
*Bankier, Joanna, 1–8, 119–127, 136–141, 213–218
*Barker, Wendy, 327–334
Barrett, Elizabeth. *see* Browning, Elizabeth Barrett
Beatrice de Die, *149*, 156–157
Beauveau, Marie-Françoise-

Catherine de (Marquise de Boufflers), 192
Behn, Aphra, *167–168*, 179–180
Beneyto, Maria, 261–262
Berenguer, Amanda, 308
*Bergmann, Emilie, 163–170
Berssenbrugge, Mei-Mei, *338*, 392
Bird, Dolly, 426–428
Blandiana, Ana, 228–229
Blaustein, Rachel. *see* Rachel
Bogan, Louise, 361
Boye, Karin, 250
Bradstreet, Anne, *188*, *328*, *334*, 352–353
Brooks, Gwendolyn, *337*, 377–378
Browning, Elizabeth Barrett, *188–189*, 197–201

Carenza, *149*, 155–156
Cassian, Nina, 229–230
Castellanos, Rosario, *301*, 321–323
Castillo, Ana, *342*, 395–396
Castro, Rosalia de, 208–209
Cervantes, Lorna Dee, *342*, *346*, 397–400
Chamberlain, Brenda, 269–270
Chang, Diana, 393
Chaudhari, Kirti, 60
Chedid, Andrée, 99–100
*Christian, Barbara, 334–338
Christine de Pisan, *149*, *150*, 160–161

*Chung, Ling, 9–14
Coignard, Gabrielle de, 176
Colonna, Vittoria, *165*, *166*, 172
Compiuta Donzella, 157–158
*Connelly, Bridget, 88–92
Corinna, *136*, *137*, 143
Corpi, Lucha, 324–325
*Crow, Mary, 299–303

Das, Kamala, 61–62
Deborah, *2*, *121*, 128–129
Desbordes-Valmore, Marceline, 202
Desnoues, Lucienne, 263–264
*D'Evelyn, Thomas, 136–141
Dickinson, Emily, *1*, *4*, *6*, *327*, *329*, *333*, *334*, *339*, 353–355
Ditlevsen, Tove, 246–247
Djabali, Leila, *275*, 283
Doolittle, Hilda. *see* H.D.
Droste-Hülshoff, Annette von, 202–203

*Earnshaw, Doris, 146–150
Eifuku, Empress, 40
Enheduanna, *111–112*, 114–117
Erinna, *137*, 144–145
Espírito Santo, Alda do, *275*, 284–286
E'tesami, Parvin, *69*, 77

Farrokhzad, Forugh, 7, *69*, *70*, 77–84
Fiamengo, Marya, 348–350
Finch, Anne, Countess of Winchelsea, 181–182, *187*
Fuertes, Gloria, 259–261

Giovanni, Nikki, *338*, 380–382
Gippius, Zinaida, 211–212
Goldberg, Leah, 129–130
Gómez de Avellaneda, Gertrudis, *300*, 305
Gorbanevskaya, Natalya, 222
Grahn, Judy, 369
Green, Jane, *2*, 418–419
Gregg, Linda, 371–372
Greiffenberg, Catharina Regina von, 176–177

Gréki, Anna, *275*, 281–283
Griffin, Susan, 370–371
Guidacci, Margherita, 256–257
Guillet, Pernette de, *167*, 174

Hafsa bint al-Hajj, 99
Hagedorn, Jessica, *339*, 388
Harper, Frances, *336*, 373–374
Hatshepsut, *271*, *275*, 277–278
H.D. (Hilda Doolittle), *332*, 356
Hébert, Anne, 347–348
Herzberg, Judith, 244–245
Hildegard von Bingén, *148*, 153–154
Hill, Roberta, 419–422
Hind bint Utba, 94–95
Hind bint Uthatha, 95–96
Horikawa, Lady, 40
Hroswitha von Gandersheim, *148*, 153
Huang O, 21–23
Huch, Ricarda, 203–204

Ibarbourou, Juana de, *300*, *302*, *303*, 307
Ise, Lady, *30*, 37–38
Ise Tayu, 40
Iselda, 155–156
Ishigaki Rin, 42
Izumi Shikibu, 38–39

Jacobs, Bertha (Suster Bertken), 161–162
Jesus, Terésa de, 316–317
Johnson, E. Pauline, *see* Tekahionwake
Jonker, Ingrid, *275*, 292–293
Jordan, June, *338*, 376–377
Juana de Asbaje (Sor Juana Inés de la Cruz), *167*, *170*, *300*, 304

Kaccipettu Nannakaiyar, 54
Karibo, Minji, *276*, 288–289
Kasa, Lady, 36
Kaschnitz, Marie Luise, 238–239
Kassia, *148*, 152–153
Kawai Chigetsu-Ni, 41
al-Khansa (Tumadir), *88–89*, *91*, 93
Kibkarjuk, 416–417

Kii, Lady, 35–36
*Kilmer, Anne Draffkorn, 111–113
Kirsch, Sarah, 241–242
Kolmar, Gertrud, *217*, 237–238
Konopnicka, Maria, 208
Koziol, Ursula, *217*, 227–228
Krmpotic, Vesna, 230–231
Kubatum, *111*, 118
Kupona, Mwana. *see* Msham, Mwana Kupona

Labé, Louise, *166*, *167*, *170*, 175
Labriola, Gina, 257–258
Lalleswari (Lal Ded, or Lalla), *49*, 58
*Lashgari, Deirdre, 1–8, 66–72, 183–191, 271–276, 401–410
Lasker-Schüler, Else, *127*, *213*, 235
Lavant, Christine, 240
Lee, Mary, Lady Chudleigh, 180–181
Lenngren, Anna Maria, 193–195
Levertov, Denise, 362–363
Liadain, *150*, 151
Li Ch'ing-chao, *10*, *11*, *13*, 20
Lorde, Audre, *338*, 382–383

Mabuza, Lindiwe, *276*, 290–291
Macgoye, Marjorie Oludhe, *275*, 293–295
Macuilxochitl, *403*, *408*, 414–415
Mahadeviyakka, 57
Mahsati, *67*, 73–74
Makhfi (Zibu'n-Nisa), 59–60
Maksimovic, Desanka, 232
al-Mala'ika, Nazik, 7, 101–102
Manner, Eeva-Liisa, 247–248
Mansour, Joyce, 262–263
Mar, Laureen, 385–386
Margarido, Manuela, *275*, 284
Marie de France, *149*, 158–159
Maryam bint Abi Ya'qub al-Ansari, 99
Matveyeva, Novella, 222–223
Mayröcker, Friederike, 241
Mechthild von Magdeburg, *148*, 154–155

Mehri (Mihru'n-Nisa of Herat), *67*, 68, 75
Meireles, Cecilia, 312–313
Mew, Charlotte, 209–211
Millay, Edna St. Vincent, 358
Mira Bai, *49*, 58–59
Mirikitani, Janice, *339*, 391–392
Mistral, Gabriela (Lucila Godoy y Alcayaga), *213*, *300*, 301, *302*, 314–315
Molodowsky, Kadia, *126*, 358–359
Moore, Marianne, *332*, 356–357
Morejón, Nancy, 325–326
Mririda n'Ait Attik, 2, *275*, 279–281
Msham, Mwana Kupona, *275*, 278–279
Murasaki Shikibu, *3*, *30*, 38
n'Ait Attik, Mririda. *see* Mririda n'Ait Attik

Nelson, Alice Dunbar, 374–375
Ngatho, Stella, *276*, 289–290
ni Chuilleanain, Eilean, 265
Noailles, Anna de, 204–205

Obi, Dorothy S., *276*, 288
Ono no Komachi, *30*, *31–34*, 36–37
Orozco, Olga, 310–312
Otomo no Sakanoe, 30

Padeshah Khatun, 74
Pallottini, Renata, 313–314
Palma Acosta, Teresa, *342*, *345–346*, 393–395
Pan Chao, *11*, 15
Parun, Vesna, 231
Petróczi, Kata Szidónia, 177–178
Philips, Katherine, *167*, *168*, 178–179
Piercy, Marge, 367–369
Ping Hsin (Hsieh Wan-ying), 26
Pitter, Ruth, 270
Plath, Sylvia, *332*, 365–367
Portal, Magda, 318–319
Praxilla, *136*, *137*, 144
Pritam, Amrita, 62–65

Qorratu'l-Ayn (Umm-i Salma), 75–76

Rabi'a al-Adawiyya, *90*, *91*, *92*, 97
Rabi'a of Balkh, *66*, *67*, *68–69*, *71*, 73
Rabi'a bint Isma'il of Syria, 96
Rachel (Blaustein), 130
Ravikovitch, Dahlia, 134–135
Rich, Adrienne, 364–365
Rodriguez, Magdalena de, 320–321
Roland-Holst, Henriette, 206–208
Rose, Wendy, 423–424
Rossetti, Christina, *188*, 201
Rukeyser, Muriel, 361–362

Sabina, Maria, 415–416
Sachs, Nelly, *127*, *217*, 236
Saffarzadeh, Tahereh, 84–85
Safiya bint Musafir, 94
Sanchez, Sonia, *338*, 379–380
*Sandahl, Stella, 49–52
Sappho, epigraph, xxi, *1*, *3*, *31–34*, *136*, *137*, *138*, *139*, 142–143
Sa'udi, Mona, 109–110
Senesh, Hannah, 126, 131
Sexton, Anne, 363–364
Shange, Ntozake, *338*, 383–385
Shiraishi Kazuko, *31*, 43–45
Shneurson, Zelda. *see* Zelda
Śilabhattarika, 56
Silko, Leslie Marmon, 422
Smith, Charlotte, *187*, 195–196
Södergran, Edith, *4*, *216*, *217*, *218*, 248–250
Sousa, Noémia da, *275*, 286–287
Stampa, Gaspara, 173–174
Storni, Alfonsina, *300*, *301*, 308–310
Sullivan, Jonny Kyoko, 390–391
Sun Yün-fêng, 24
Swarth, Hélène, 205–206
*Swigart, Rob, 29–34

Szymborska, Wisława, *217*, 224–226

Tan Ying, 27
T'ang Wan, 21
Tekahionwake (E. Pauline Johnson), *408*, 411–413
Teresa, Saint, of Ávila, *168*, *169*, *170*, 171
Tomioka, Taeko, 45–48
Tóth, Judith, 232–235
Ts'ai Yen, *11*, 15–18
Tsvetaeva, Marina, *216*, 220–221
Tuqan, Fadwa, 100–101
Tzu Yeh, 18–19

Ukihashi, 41
Uvavnuk, *404*, 418

Vakalo, Eleni, 254–255
Varela, Blanca, 319–320
Vidya (Vijjika), 55–56
Villanueva, Alma, *342*, *345*, 396–397

Walker, Alice, *335*, *338*, 376
Walker, Margaret, *337*, 375
Wallada, *90*, *91*, *92*, 98
Walsh, Marnie, 424–426
Walters, Anna Lee, 429–430
Wang Wei, 23
Wheatley, Phillis, *334*, *335*, 373
Wong, Nellie, *339*, 386–387
Wu Tsao, 24–26

*Yamada, Mitsuye, 338–342
Yamada, Mitsuye, *339*, 389–390
*Yarbro-Bejarano, Yvonne, 342–346
Yosano Aikiko, *7*, *31*, 41–42
Yü Hsüan-chi, 13, 19

Zelda, 131–133
Zerbe, Evelyn Arcad, 106–107
Zibu'n-Nisa. *see* Makhfi

Index of Translators

Ahern, Maureen, 321
Ahokas, Jaakko, 247–248
Allen, J. W., 278–279
Altschul, Carlos, 313–314
Altschul, Monique, 313–314
Alvarez, Lynn, 319–320
Antrim, Merrilee, 309–310
Arthur, Marylin, 144–145
Atsumi Ikuko, 35–42
Ayusawa Takako, 42

Banani, Amin, 77–81
Bankier, Joanna, 160–161,
   250–253
Barnard, Mary (epigraph), xxi
Barrows, Anita, 281–283
Basham, A. L., 53
Beckett, Samuel, 304
Blackwell, Alice Stone, 304
Bloch, Chana, 134–135
Bogin, Meg, 157
Boullata, Kamal, 101–102,
   107–110
Bownas, Geoffrey, 35

Canan, Janine, 203–204
Charters, Samuel, 248–250
Chung, Ling, 15–19, 21–27
Cohen, J. M., 321–323
Connelly, Bridget, 93–96, 155–156
Cope, Jack, 292–293
Crewe, Jonathan, 161–162,
   205–208

Darowski, Jan, 225–226
Densmore, Frances, 418–419
Diehl, Patrick, 152–154

Earnshaw, Doris, 155–157,
   208–209

Euloge, René, 279–281

Francovich, Allan, 284, 314–315
Freeman, Ann, 246–247

Ghossein, Mirène, 99–100
Giacomelli, Eloah F., 312–313
Gorowara, Krishna, 62–65
Grierson, George, 58
Guest, Harry, 46–48
Guest, Lynn, 46–48

Halpern, Daniel, 279–281
Hamburger, Michael, 235, 237–242
Hart, George, 55
Hay, Peter, 131
Hazo, Samuel, 99–100
Herzing, Albert, 263
Hoffman, Hannah, 133
Hossaini, Hatem, 100–101
Howe, Irving, 360
Hsu, Kai-yu, 26, 28
Hughes, Glenn, 41
Huws, Daniel, 243–244

Ingalls, Daniel, 55
Iwasaki, Yozan T., 41

Jacobsen, Thorkild, 118
Jones, Elizabeth, 292
Joslin, Priscilla, 308

Kahn, Sholom J., 130
Kajima Shozo, 46–48
Katchadourian, Stina, 248–249
Keene, Donald, 37–38
Keffer, Leslie, 310–312
Kessler, Jascha, 77–81

Kilmer, Anne Draffkorn, 114–117
Kolb, Elene Margot, 97, 99
Kunitz, Stanley, 219

La Palma, Marina, 256–257
Lashgari, Deirdre, 73–77, 82–85, 94–96, 98, 202
Lattimore, Richard, 142–144
León-Portilla, Miguel, 414–415
Levine, Philip, 259–261
Levitin, Alexis, 258–259
Levitin, Dianne, 211–212, 220
Lichtheim, Miriam, 277–278
Longfellow, Henry Wadsworth, 171
Lowenstein, Tom, 416–417
Lucchi, Lorna de', 174

Mahamadi, Fereshte, 85–87
Masson, J. Moussaieff, 56
Mather, Richard, 15
Mead, Matthew, 236
Mead, Ruth, 236
Menzies, Lucy, 154–155
Merwin, W. S., 56
Mihailovich, Vasa D., 230–232
Miłosz, Czesław, 227–228
Mitchell, Stephen, 129–130
Monroe, James, 98
Moody, Marti, 305–309
Morgan, Ronald, 231
Mortimer, Mildred P., 282–283
Munn, Henry, 415
Murray, William M., 228–229

Nathan, Leonard, 60
Nilsson, Usha, 58–59

O'Connor, Frank, 151
Oliver, Raymond, 174–176
O'Shaughnessy, Arthur, 158–159

Paley, Paula, 279–281
Pauk, Edgar, 257–258
Paz, Octavio, 304
Perelman, Robert, 220–221
Peterkiewicz, Jerzy, 208
Petrov, Aleksandar, 220–221
Pound, Ezra, 192

Priest, Harold M., 173
Proser, Maria A., 316–317

Ram, Philip, 255–256
Ramanujan, A. K., 54–55, 57
Rasmussen, Knud, 416–417
Rexroth, Kenneth, 15–19, 21–27, 35–42
Rodriguez-Nieto, Catherine, 261–262, 305, 324–325, 414–415
Ryder, Alan, 284–287

Sato Hiroaki, 45–48
Schiff, Laura, 177–178, 229–230, 232–235
Schoolfield, George C., 176–177
Schwimmer, Betty L., 204–205
Scott, Michael, 99
Scully, Arlene, 316–317
Scully, James, 316–317
Serrano, Nina, 320–321
Singer, Burns, 208
Singh, Khushwant, 62–65
Smith, Margaret, 97
Stathatos, John, 254–255
Stork, C. W., 193–195
Stortoni, Laura, 157–158
Swenson, Birgit, 347–348
Swigart, Rob, 15, 36–37

Thwaite, Anthony, 35
Tobin, James Edward, 202–203

Valentine, Jean, 359
Vegas-Garcia, Irene, 318–319

Wagner, Marsha, 20
Walls, Jan W., 19
Weaver, Kathleen, 314–315, 318–319
Webster, Brenda, 172–173
Weissbort, Daniel, 222–224
Whalley, Paul, 59–60
Whitney, Anita, 326
Wieniewska, Celina, 224–225
Williams, Miller, 263–264
Wolf, Manfred, 244–245

Zimmerman, Father Benedict, 171

Index of Titles and First Lines

Air: Sentir avec Ardeur, 192
Alarum, 227–228
All of a Sudden, 316–317
Although they are, epigraph
Ancestral Weight, 308–309
The Annunciation, 62–65
Appeal, 286–287
As a hungry fledgling, who sees and hears, 172
As I am unhappy, 41
At first I was given centuries, 350–351
At Night, 256–257
At the Badr Trench, 94
An Attempt at Jealousy, 220–221
Aurora Leigh (excerpt), 197
Azouou, 279–280

The bare branches tremble, 19
Battle Song (excerpt), 414–415
The beauty of the Friend it was that taught me, 59
Before the Birth of One of Her Children, 352
Before Your Waking, 281–282
The Beirut—Hell Express (excerpt), 102–105
Between Ourselves, 382–383
A bird comes, 42
Birthplace, 84–85
Black and glossy as a bee and curled was my hair, 53
The Blood, 230
The Body Is the Victory and the Defeat of Dreams, 255–256

Bookmark, 171
Bread, 314–315
But there was/once/a time, 254–255
Buy Us a Little Grain, 240

Can I Say, 426–428
Candles, 205–206
Cannibalism, 393
The Captain, 319–320
Catching One Clear Thought Alive, 428–429
The Cattle Thief, 411–413
Childhood, 375
Chorus of the Rescued, 236
Cocoon, 42
Come to me from Crete to this holy temple, 142
Coming Across, 75
The Common Woman: Carol, in the park, chewing on straws, 369
Composed on the Theme "Willows by the Riverside", 19
Concerning the Awakening of My Soul, 207
Conscientious Objector, 358
Contemplations (excerpts), 352–353
Cornfields in Accra, 295–298
The Couple, 228–229
A Curse for a Nation, 197–201

Dandelions for Chains, 241–242
Dark Romance, 324–325
Dead Embryos, 234–235
A December Forest, 230–231

438

Deeply repentant of my sinful
ways, 174
Deliverance, 373–374
The Distaff, 144–145
A Ditty, 161–162
Do Not Ask, 240
Doesn't he realize, 36
Don't Sleep, 292
Drinking the Wind, 27

Ears, 252–253
Ecstasy, 206
*The Eggplants Have Pins and Nee-
dles*, 222–223
*Eighteen Verses Sung to a Tatar Reed
Whistle* (excerpt), 15–18
Elegy XXIII, 175
Elegy for her brother, Sakhr, 93
En las internas entrañas, 171
Epilogue to Sir Patient Fancy, 180
Evening Walk, 251–252
Everything is Plundered, 219

The farmer's clothes are soaked
through, 40
Fifteen Boys, or Perhaps Even More,
223–224
The first Day's Night had come,
355
First Things, 263–264
Footpath, 289–290
For All Mary Magdalenes, 232
For Miriam, 293–295
For My Torturer, Lieutenant D—, 283
For the Courtesan Ch'ing Lin, 24–25
Foreign Woman, 321–323
Fountain of tears, river of grief,
160–161
From Behind the Bars (excerpt),
100–101
Fury Against the Moslems at Uhud,
94–95
The Future and the Ancestor, 99–100
The future is for tomorrow,
282–283

Gain without gladness, 151
Girl of the lovely glance, looking
out through the window, 144

God of Mercy, 359–360
Good repute is water carried in a
sieve, 58
Grasshoppers, 41
Green enravishment of human
life, 304

Handsome friend, charming and
kind, 157
He the Beloved (excerpt), 75–76
He who stole my virginity, 56
Her Kind, 363–364
Here too the Spirit shafts,
154–155
Hiding in the/cucumber garden,
56
Hills of Salt, 134–135
His Wife, 130
Housework, 308
How a Girl Got Her Chinese Name,
386–387
How do I enter the silence of
stones as evening enters the city,
109
How long will it last?, 40
Humility, 238–239
Hunger, 173

I am a lioness, 97
I Am a Woman (excerpt), 85–87
I am now so weary with waiting,
173
I can give myself to her, 41–42
I disapprove even of eloquent/
Myrtis, 143
I dreamed I held, 36
I Drift in the Wind, 292–293
*I Expected My Skin and My Blood to
Ripen*, 423–424
I go out of darkness, 38
I had not fastened my sash over
my gown, 18–19
I Have Bowed Before the Sun,
429–430
I know the reputation, 35–36
I Looked for a Sounding-Board, 206
I Love My Love, 266–269
I praise the disk of the rising sun,
55

I set forth hopeful—cotton-blossom Lal, 58
I Sit and Sew, 374–375
I was always fascinated, 396–397
I, who cut off my sorrows, 39
I Write Poems, 259–260
If I consider, 38
If it were real, 37
I'm ceded—I've stopped being Theirs, 353–354
In Memory of My Arab Grandmother, 106–107
In my heart's depth, 39
In Praise of Old Women, 348–350
In the dusk the path, 39
In the Home of the Scholar Wu Su-chiang, 25–26
In the outhouse, 389–390
Inanna Exalted (excerpt), 114–117
Inertia, 60
An Introduction, 61–62
The Introduction, 181–182
It is night again, 18
It is the time of rain and snow, 39

Jamila, 101–102
June 10, 320–321
July, 1914, 219

Lady of Miracles, 229–230
Lament, 269–270
Leap in the Dark, 419–422
Life Story, 46–48
Life-Hook, 307
Like the honeycomb dripping honey, 154
Like the very gods in my sight is he who, 142
Like/treasure hidden in the ground, 57
Lilith, 371–372
Listen, 388
Living Together, 48
The Lost Tribe, 270
Love Flows from God, 154
Love! love! What nonsense it is, 222
Love Song to King Shu-Suen, 118
Love Which Frees, 260–261

Loveliest of what I leave behind is the sunlight, 144
The Lunar Games, 247–248

Marriage is a lovely thing, 160
Message, 313–314
The Mind is an Enchanting Thing, 356–357
The Moon and the Yew Tree, 365–366
Mother's Inheritance, 107–108
Mririda, 280–281
Mushrooms, 366–367
My life had stood—a Loaded Gun, 354
My lover capable of terrible lies, 54
My Mother Pieced Quilts, 393–395
My Mother, Who Came from China, Where She Never Saw Snow, 385–386
My People, 235
My true love makes me happy, 156–157
My wish for you, 73
The Mysteries Remain, 356

Napa, California, 395–396
Needle and Thread, 15
No moon, no chance to meet, 36–37
Nocturne in the Women's Prison, 261–262
Non que je veuille ôter la liberté, 174
North Express, 263
Not even in dreams, 37
Nowhere, not among the warriors at their festival, 54

O brothers, why do you talk, 57
O crimson blood, 153–154
O King, I know you gave me poison, 58–59
O Realm Bejeweled, 77–81
Obelisk Inscriptions (excerpt), 277–278
Observation of a Bee, 129–130
An Old Woman's Song, 417–418

On Leaving Cuba, Her Native Land, 305
On the bus, 389
On the Death of Sylvia Plath, 245
On the Road at Night There Stands the Man, 134
On the Road through Chang-Te, 24
On the Tower, 202–203
One-two-three, 131
Orgy (that is, vegetable market, at Sarno), 257–258
Out of the Darkness, 237–238

Pain, 249–250
Pain, 309–310
Paphnutius (excerpt), 153
Patron of Flawless Serpent Beauty, 241
Phallic Root, 43–45
plants don't talk, people say, 208–209
Please say something, 45
Poem for the Young White Man Who Asked Me How I, an Intelligent, Well-Read Person, Could Believe in the War Between Races, 397–399
Poem on azure, 204–205
Poem to Her Daughter (excerpt), 278–279
Poem to the tune of "Tsui hua yin", 20
Poem to the tune of "Yi chian mei", 20
The Portraits, 193–195
Prayer, 176
Present, 379–380

The Question, 361–362

The Reason for Poetry, 325–326
The Respite, 242
Resurrection, 239
A Return to the Tree of Time, 231
Roman Fountain, 351
The Roses of Saadi, 202

SAGIMUSUME: The White Heron Maiden, 390–391
Seeking a Mooring, 23
Selected Epigrams, 152

Selected Quatrains, 73–74
Self Portrait 4, 246–247
Sent from the capital to her elder daughter, 35
Shall I charge like a bull, 54
Shall I come there, or you here?, 99
Shaman, 415–416
She, 211–212
Since I've felt this pain, 37
Since "the pillow knows all", 37
Sing with Your Body, 391–392
Small Paths, 207–208
The Small Square, 258–259
Smile, Death, 209–210
Some there are who say that the fairest thing seen, 143
somebody almost walked off wid alla my stuff, 383–385
Someone Like No One Else, 82–84
Song, 312–313
Song from Chartivel, 158–159
Song from The Lucky Chance, 179–180
Song My, 370–371
Song of Deborah, 128–129
Song of the Rejected Woman, 416–417
Song of the Sabbath, 358–359
Songs in Flight (excerpt), 243–244
Songs of Divorce, 418–419
Sonnet XVIII, 175
A Soul, 201
Sovereign Queen, 74
Sphinxes inclined to be, 310–312
The Spider holds a Silver Ball, 355
Spring Street Bar, 392
The Spring Waters (excerpts), 26
Spring-Joy Praising God. Praise of the Sun, 176
The Stars (excerpts), 26
Starvation Camp Near Jasło, 225–226
Stay, shade of my shy treasure, 304
Sticheron for Matins, Wednesday of Holy Week, 152–153
Sufi Quatrains, 96
Summer 1970, 290–291
Superstition, 288–289
Swift Floods, 177–178

Swineherd, 265
A Sword, 250

The Tale of the Genji (excerpt), 38
Tambourine Song for Soldiers Going
    into Battle, 95
Tenson, 155–156
There is in human closeness a sa-
    cred boundary, 220
They Clapped, 380–382
They go by, go by, love, the days
    and the hours, 317
They've Come, 309
Thirty-Eight, 195–196
Thomas Iron-Eyes, 424–426
To a Hero Dead at al-Safra, 95–96
To his father on praising the honest life
    of the peasant, 77
To Ibn Zaidun, 98
To leave the world, 157
To love somebody, 36
To My Excellent Lucasia, on Our
    Friendship, 178–179
To the Ladies, 180–181
To the Newborn, 232–234
To the Right Honourable William,
    Earl of Dartmouth (excerpt), 373
To the tune "The Fall of a Little Wild
    Goose", 22–23
To the tune "The Phoenix Hairpin",
    21
To the tune "Red Embroidered Shoes",
    22
To the tune "Soaring Clouds", 21–22
To the white-mantled maidens,
    143
The Total Influence or Outcome of the
    Matter: THE SUN, 367–369
Translations, 364–365
The Trees Are Down, 210–211
Two Prayers, 97

Unemployment/Monologue, 376–377
Useless Day, 321

Violet Twilights, 248–249
Vision, 305–307
A Vision, 208
Vocation, 244

Wait till the darkness is deep, 98
Wake up, dear boy that holds the
    flute, 59
Wash, 265
A wave of coldness, 41
We dressed each other, 40
We Women, 248
We're OK, 260
What can you expect, 99
When the loneliness of the tomb
    went down into the marketplace,
    109
When the Orient is lit by the great
    light,172
When You Have Forgotten Sunday:
    The Love Story, 377–378
When You Laugh, 292
Where Are the Men Seized in This
    Wind of Madness? 284–286
Where Mountain Lion Lay Down with
    Deer, 422
Whether I sit or lie, 41
Why don't I write in the language
    of air? 109–110
The Wicked Neighbor, 131–133
Winds of Africa, 288
With my breath I cut my way
    through the six forests, 58
Woman, 318–319
Woman Alone, 362–363
The Woman in My Notebook,
    399–400
A Woman Shaman's Song, 418
Women, 376
The Women of Rubens, 224–225
Women Transport Corps, 28
The Wooden Chamber, 347–348

Yesterday evening I saw your
    corpse, 262–263
You are fortunate, dear friends,
    that you can tell, 55
You stand and hold the post of my
    small house, 55
You Who Occupy Our Land, 284
Young Girl, 203–204
The Young Girl and the Beach, 259